# A STAFF OFFICER'S SCRAP-BOOK

VOLUME II

Major-General Fujii
Chief of the Staff 1st Army

# A STAFF OFFICER'S SCRAP-BOOK

## DURING THE RUSSO-JAPANESE WAR

BY LIEUT.-GENERAL
SIR IAN HAMILTON, K.C.B.

WITH ILLUSTRATIONS, MAPS AND PLANS

*IN TWO VOLUMES*

VOLUME II

The Naval & Military Press Ltd

*Published by*

**The Naval & Military Press Ltd**
Unit 5 Riverside, Brambleside
Bellbrook Industrial Estate
Uckfield, East Sussex
TN22 1QQ England

Tel: +44 (0)1825 749494

www.naval-military-press.com
www.nmarchive.com

*In reprinting in facsimile from the original, any imperfections are inevitably reproduced and the quality may fall short of modern type and cartographic standards.*

# PREFACE

THE spectator who elbows his way into the playhouse on a crowded first night is mainly taken up with the struggle towards his seat, the effect of his white waistcoat, the purchase of a programme and the disposal of his hat. The curtain rises; the actors play their parts, the scene shifts, the plot thickens. The spectator now sits in the shadow, passive and detached, watching with wrapt attention the development of the drama.

And so it was with me. At first the small things seemed to matter most. But afterwards, when images of battle swept to the sound of dreadful clang and shout through the smoke-clouds of the shrapnel; when army rushed to meet army, and in the shock of their encounter strewed the country with corpses—then, I seemed for a moment to see clearly the warrior spirit of Japan as it emerged, triumphant, from the bloody tumult.

I speak of what I have seen and heard, and leave the rest to the reader. The deeper his insight the more intimate will be his sympathy with the great-hearted patriotism which animated all ranks in Kuroki's force. Mutual understanding is the only bed-rock upon which alliances, whether diplomatic or matrimonial, can find enduring foundations. Flatteries, cajoleries, exaggerations, insincerities, are the prelude to disillusionment, if not to divorce.

IAN HAMILTON.

TIDWORTH,
*February* 21, 1906.

# Preface to new edition

The Russo-Japanese War was the first time that the tactics of entrenched positions for infantry were defended with machine guns and artillery. This was the first twentieth-century war in which the technology of warfare became increasingly important, factors which came to dominate the evolution of warfare during the First World War. Hamilton wrote that cavalry was obsolete in such a conflict, regarding their role as better accomplished by mounted infantry. He became a supporter of non-traditional tactics such as night attacks and the use of aircraft. Conversely, the successful Japanese infantry assaults convinced him that superior morale would allow an attacker to overcome prepared defensive positions.

Hamilton's career in the British army is forever remembered with the disastrous Gallipoli Campaign. In March 1915, Lord Kitchener appointed Hamilton, aged 62, to the command of the Allied Mediterranean Expeditionary Force, with orders to gain control of the Dardanelles straits from the Ottoman Empire and to capture Constantinople. Whilst a senior and respected officer, perhaps more experienced in different campaigns than most, Hamilton was considered too unconventional, too intellectual and too friendly with politicians to be given a command on the Western Front. With the Gallipoli Campaign stalled, Hamilton was recalled to London on 16 October 1915, effectively ending his military career. After Adolf Hitler's rise to power, Hamilton described himself as "an admirer of the great Adolf Hitler" and dismissed 'Mein Kampf' as a "youthful excess".

# CONTENTS OF VOLUME II

| CHAP. | | PAGE |
|---|---|---|
| XIX. | REFLECTIONS BY THE WAY | 1 |
| XX. | THE BATTLE OF THE TWENTY-SIXTH OF AUGUST | 35 |
| XXI. | THE RUSSIANS RETIRE | 59 |
| XXII. | WITH THE GUARDS DIVISION | 75 |
| XXIII. | KUROKI CROSSES THE TAITSUHO | 88 |
| XXIV. | MANJUYAMA | 102 |
| XXV. | LIAOYANG | 122 |
| XXVI. | SOJOURN AT FENSHAN | 145 |
| XXVII. | THE ARMIES IN CONTACT | 171 |
| XXVIII. | OKASAKI'S DASHING ASSAULT | 187 |
| XXIX. | THE BATTLE CONTINUES | 209 |
| XXX. | OTA'S SUN-FLAG | 230 |
| XXXI. | THE ASSAULT OF THE TALL HILL | 244 |
| XXXII. | THE RUSSIANS RECROSS THE SHAHO | 257 |
| XXXIII. | THE LITTLE MAN IN GREEN | 264 |
| XXXIV. | BANQUETS AND REVELS | 277 |
| XXXV. | NAKAMURA ENCOUNTERS SANTA CLAUS | 290 |
| XXXVI. | THE DEVIL'S PLOUGHING | 306 |
| XXXVII. | NANSHAN AND TELISSU | 320 |
| XXXVIII. | FUJI VEILS HER FACE | 349 |
| | INDEX | 365 |

# ILLUSTRATIONS

| | |
|---|---:|
| Major-General Fujii, Chief of the Staff, First Army . . . *Frontispiece* | |
| A Good Comrade . . . . . . . . . *To face page* | 12 |
| Colonel Kawasaki and Lt.-General Nishijima . . . . ,, | 44 |
| Swallow's Nest Hill and the Pontoon across the Taitsuho . . ,, | 92 |
| General Kuroki and Staff on Swallow's Nest Hill during the Battle of Liaoyang . . . . . . . . ,, | 106 |
| Some Officers of the 12th Division Mountain Artillery . . ,, | 190 |
| The Commander of the Mixed Brigade on the right of the First Army, and other Officers . . . . . ,, | 132 |
| The Temple to the God of Children on Sankwaisekisan . . ,, | 210 |
| Chinese Gods in the Temple on Terayama . . . . ,, | 260 |
| A Visit to the 30th Regiment in Winter Quarters at Shotatsuko ,, | 292 |
| The Officer Commanding the 2nd Division Field Artillery in his winter abode at Hamatang . . . . . ,, | 294 |
| Sir Ian Hamilton and "Rooski," December 1904 . . . ,, | 298 |
| Japanese Field Artillery on the March in Winter . . . ,, | 302 |
| View from "Golden Hill" of the Japanese Transports sunk to block the Entrance to the Harbour at Port Arthur . ,, | 310 |
| View of Port Arthur and the Russian Warships from Golden Hill, January 1905 . . . . . . . ,, | 316 |
| The British Attaché with the 2nd Division, First Army, Captain B. Vincent, R.F.A. . . . . . . ,, | 350 |
| Some of Nogi's Infantry on their March North from Port Arthur . . . . . . . . . ,, | 356 |

## MAPS AND SKETCHES

XVII. View of the Russian Position South of Kiuchorei (Kungchanling) taken by 2nd Division, First Army, between 4 A.M. and 11-15 A.M., August 26, 1904 . *To face page* 50

XVIII. Battle of Liaoyang. First glimpse of the Plains, August 27, 1904 . . . . . . . „ 62

XIX. Russian Rear-Guard Action, August 28. View of the Position in front of the 2nd Division, First Army . . . . . . . . „ 70

XX. The Battle of Liaoyang as seen on August 30 and 31, 1904 . . . . . . . „ 86

XXI. View from Swallow's Nest Hill looking Westward towards Manjuyama. September 1, 1904 . . „ 94

XXII. Map showing the lines of advance of the First Japanese Army during the Battle of Liaoyang . „ 142

XXIII. General Map of the Battle of Liaoyang, showing Russians and Japanese . . . . . „ 170

XXIV. View of the Battlefield of the Shaho from Yentai Coal-Mine Hill . . . . . . „ 206

XXV. Sankwaisekisan (Three Great Rock Hill) captured before dawn on October 12, 1904, by the 10th Division, Fourth Army . . . . . „ 212

XXVI. Sketch of Okasaki Yama from the Position of the First Army Headquarters, October 13, 1904, captured by the 15th Brigade, 2nd Division . . „ 250

XXVII. View from the top of the Pass at Chosenrei looking towards Penchiho . . . . . . „ 244

XXVIII. View from Honda Yama, the right of the Japanese Position near Penchiho . . . . . „ 228

XXIX. View of the Taitsuho Valley near Weining from the most advanced Japanese Trenches . . . „ 236

XXX. View of the Japanese Position near Penchiho from the Russian side . . . . . . „ 242

## Maps and Sketches

| | | |
|---|---|---|
| XXXI. View of Gunki Yama (Standard Hill) from the Japanese trenches at the Taling (Pass). | To face page | 234 |
| XXXII. View of Taling from the road by which the Russians attacked at dawn, October 12 | ,, | 230 |
| XXXIII. Map showing the operations of the 2nd and Imperial Guards Divisions at the Battle of the Shaho | ,, | 254 |
| XXXIV. Map showing the action of Prince Kanin's Cavalry Brigade near Penchiho on October 12 | ,, | 238 |
| XXXV. Yentai Coal-Mine Hill—Our Winter Quarters | ,, | 290 |
| XXXVI. 203 Metre Hill near Port Arthur | ,, | 308 |
| XXXVII. View of Port Arthur Harbour from the top of 203 Metre Hill | ,, | 318 |
| XXXVIII. View of the Russian Position at Nanshan from the Walls of Kinchou | ,, | 324 |
| XXXIX. View looking North from the Russian Position at Nanshan | ,, | 326 |
| XL. Plan of the Battlefield of Telissu | ,, | 332 |
| XLI. View from the left of the Russian Position at Telissu, June 15, 1904 | ,, | 334 |
| XLII. Plan of the Battle of Heikoutai | ,, | 358 |

**The position of Maps and Sketches within the book may be slightly different to that shown in the index due to the new layout and larger page size adopted to facilitate this reprint on modern printing presses.**

## CHAPTER XIX

### REFLECTIONS BY THE WAY

LIENSHANKUAN, *August 3rd*, 1904.—The work of the First Army as an independent unit is now ended. All the anxieties of the General Staff, all the privations and endurance of the officers and men, have become so much food for history. In future we shall fight shoulder to shoulder with our friends of the Second and Fourth Armies—at present our tents are pitched by pleasant waters where the vast shadow of the Heaven-reaching Pass lends grateful coolness to the air. No soldier, surely, could wish better fortune, and yet,

"After a life spent training for the sight,"

I feel as if not even the unknown glories of to-morrow could repay me for the home-sickness of to-day. Naughty boys are tamed by being put in the corner, but is it possible that mere isolation can overcome an essence so divine as the spirit of adventure? It may be so. Assuredly my depression is not fairly chargeable to my Japanese hosts, who lose no chance of showing me kindness, and who, ever since the days of Fenghuangcheng, have left me an absolutely free hand to go wherever I like and to see whatever I may wish to see. But I must always be accompanied by an officer or a non-commissioned officer, and whenever I walk and wherever I go, or whatever I do, I am unceasingly a target for curious eyes. There is no help for it, I know, but in course of time this sense of being watched gets upon the nerves and I long with an intense longing for one of the two most secluded situations of the world—the desert of the Sahara or a hansom cab in London.

I went this afternoon for a walk with Sergeant-Major Sumino. I gathered from him that the men are burning to advance, and that there is a saying current amongst them to the effect that the way back to Japan lies through Liaoyang. Also, he tells me that two days ago the horse of a Russian officer was shot, and that in the wallets were found hollow-nosed, or dum-dum, revolver bullets. He hinted that if the officer had been caught he would have had short shrift. He had hardly finished speaking, and I was in hopes of getting him to go on, when our promenade was interrupted.

About four miles out from Lienshankuan, the road we were pursuing led us over a little saddle or *col*. Just as we reached the top, my heart stood still as I found myself face to face with a column of Russians who were marching up from the other side. It took two seconds at least to realise that I was not confronted by the formidable invaders of the Himalaya, as they periodically appear in the imaginations of our frontier officers, but by an unhappy batch of prisoners coming in from the Yushuling battlefield. There were sixty of them under a small escort. They all wore 34 or 35 on their shoulder-straps. A large proportion of these prisoners were fine-looking men who might have been drafted into the ranks of our Guards forthwith, and only four or five of them at the most had the very heavy, dull, half-finished features and expression I had noticed in the prisoners taken on the Motienling. Some were old—forty; some looked ill; all looked exhausted, with hollow, pinched cheeks and weary eyelids. It was sad indeed to see brave soldiers reduced to such an extremity.

With the party were two lieutenant-colonels, a captain and a doctor. The doctor spoke German *furchtbar schlecht*, and asked me if I was a journalist. When I said I was a British officer, he and the other officers to whom he passed the information very politely exchanged salutes with me. The senior lieutenant-colonel asked the doctor to inquire if I could induce the corporal to let them sit down and rest for ten minutes, as they were deadly tired, having marched that day all the way from Chaotao. I easily persuaded Sumino to arrange this. The doctor said the battle had been bloody and the losses terribly heavy. I daresay I could have got a good lot of interesting information out of him; but on the one hand Sumino was on pins and needles at this unauthorised conversation taking place when I was under his charge, and on the other I felt so sorry for the poor fellows that I did not like to bother them with questions. I went on, therefore, and left the dreary little party sitting on the top of the *col*. As soon as were alone, Sumino expressed to me his astonishment that officers who had been taken prisoners could accommodate themselves so easily to their lot. I said, "How can you say they do not care; they seemed to me very sad." "Ah," he replied, "but they ought to be quite desperate!"

LIENSHANKUAN, *August 4th*, 1904.—One of the Staff looked in soon after six o'clock this morning and so caught me before I was dressed. He came to announce that the Second Army had entered Haicheng last night. The Fourth Army was ready to co-operate, but as there was no opposition they have remained at Takubokujo,* from the vicinity of which the Russians have now cleared away. I expressed some surprise that Nodzu, with the Fourth Army, was not pressing up to stretch out his hand to Kuroki so as to close the dangerous gap on our left. My friend replied :

"That movement is not so easy in Manchuria as it would be at the Staff College. Owing to the efforts of our line of communications staff we ourselves have munitions and food-supplies sufficient to justify us in advancing to-morrow, *but*, do you believe that behind the Second and Fourth Armies enough stores have been collected to enable them to march vigorously forward? So as to show, I mean to say, the full quickness of the Japanese foot? We must reserve all lightning movements for essays on tactics, and meanwhile we do not quite know what to make of the unopposed entry of Oku into Haicheng. Perhaps its garrison had been withdrawn to overwhelm our Twelfth Division at Yushuling, or perhaps Kuropatkin is going to concentrate. If so, the agitating question which we have to put to ourselves is whether he will make his stand at Anshantien, at Liaoyang, or at some point still further to the north. These are, in my opinion, the three alternatives, but there are officers—and I am not sure that Marshal Kuroki does not share their opinion—who think it is still possible that the enemy may concentrate

* Chinese, Tomucheng.

in great force to our front and attack us in our present position. I wish I could believe there was any chance of this happening, for we should then be saved the cruel anxiety of groping still further into these horrible mountains. But, alas, I fear the Russians won't accept the risk. It would take Kuropatkin some time to collect sufficient troops for an attack upon us here, and Oku and Nodzu are not the men to sit inactive whilst forces are being withdrawn from their front for such a purpose. From the outpost line of Sasaki's Brigade the heights overlooking Liaoyang can plainly be distinguished, and the First, Fourth and Second Manchurian Armies are now close enough together to be able to co-operate, at least to the extent of preventing one force being overwhelmed whilst the others look on."

I said, "I admit the mountains in front of us look very forbidding, but it is ungrateful of you to call them horrible or speak of groping into them, for they suit the Japanese tactics, armament and *personnel* much better than those of the Russians, and after all, however formidable a mountain may be, it can usually be turned."

My visitor agreed, and added that the attack of July 31st could not have been carried out unless the mountains had furnished a screen behind which the flanking movement could be made.

I asked him if the Guards were at all downcast by their failure on that occasion to get in on the enemy's right. He replied, "On the contrary; the Chief Staff Officer of the Imperial Guards, in reporting the losses of the Division, added a remark to the effect that it was most fortunate that the enemy had defended themselves with vigour, as the Divisional Commander,

Lieutenant-General Hasegawa, had thus been enabled to test the quality of his troops."

KINKAHOSHI,* *August 8th*, 1904.—Have moved with Kuroki into new quarters on the western side of the Motienling. Not a bad little house, and we are all busy making a garden and transplanting wild flowers into it. This afternoon an adjutant in the Imperial Guards told me that Nogi had "as good as captured" the two hills on the Russian extreme right at Port Arthur, within 5000 yards of the harbour. There is now only one line of fortifications remaining between Port Arthur town and the Japanese. A furious battle had been raging all the night of the 7th, and up to midday to-day, when the message was sent. In my room are a box of German mixed biscuits (made up for Chinese consumption to resemble as nearly as possible the time-honoured tins used by a famous English firm), and two bottles of champagne. I am on my honour not to touch these until Port Arthur falls. So I look at them every day with the feelings of a ragged urchin who flattens his nose against the plate-glass window of a pastry-cook's shop. I now begin to have hope, and I asked my young friend when he thought I might put away the causes of my hourly temptation. He thinks about the 12th instant, which will suit me very well.

KINKAHOSHI, *August 9th*.—Walked over with an orderly to call on Vincent and the foreign officers attached to the headquarters of the Second Division at the village of Tiensuitien. Found the river in flood, and practically unfordable on foot. On the other side a coolie of the military train was engaged in washing

* Chinese, Chinchiaputsu, two miles south of Tiensuitien. See Map XXII.

a shirt. Seeing my difficulty he went up to the village and brought down a pony which he rode across and offered to me. I got on to the pony, and the coolie led me over with great difficulty, as the rushing water came up to his waist. I returned by the help of the same kind man, and when I got to my own side of the river I offered him the equivalent of five shillings. As soon as he understood that I wanted to tip him he simply roared with laughter and utterly declined to have anything to say to the base metal which, compared with his pay of $1\frac{1}{2}d.$ a day, was a considerable fortune. In vain the orderly I had brought with me explained that I was a foreigner who did not understand things, and that as I was possessed of a plethora of cash, it might, after all, be as well to humour me. He replied, that although only a coolie he wore the military uniform, and his heart also was purely that of a soldier, and so I had to let him go back across the river unrewarded, except by my heartfelt thanks.

On my return to Kinkahoshi, I found that an officer of the Guards, whose acquaintance I had made at Fenghuangcheng, had ridden over to see me. In the course of conversation he told me that amongst the masses of correspondence captured on July 31st by the Twelfth Division at Yushuling was a tabular statement dated Harbin, July 3rd, in which the strength and composition of the Japanese forces is duly set forth. Hagino has translated it into Japanese, and its perusal throws light on much that has hitherto been obscure. According to the statement, Kuroki's army is put at just double its actual strength. It is supposed to consist of six Divisions of which the strength, the names of most of the commanders, and all the regiments are given in detail. Kuroki is also credited with an independent cavalry brigade, which, on the date of publication, was supposed to be quartered at Saimachi. One of the imaginary Divisions is cantoned at Hamaton by the Yalu! The independent cavalry brigade is a magnificent Russian tribute to the impression created by the solitary squadron of the Twelfth Division! Of the imposing total of six Divisions, three were shown at Fenghuangcheng; one was at Antung, one at Kuantienchen, and one, as already stated, at Hamaton. The Second Army was placed with its four Divisions just south of Nanshan and at Dalny, whilst the Fourth Army, consisting of three Divisions, was at Takushan and Siuyen. (See Map I., vol. i.)

Imagination is a valuable qualification for an intelligence officer, provided it is kept quite clear of statistics. Once, however, fancy is permitted to play about with figures, the results are apt to be disastrous. The retreat on July 17th is now easy to understand, and if Rennenkampf has truly believed that there was a cavalry brigade at Saimachi and a Division at Hamaton he may well be excused for not having made more vigorous attempts upon our communications.

Whilst discussing the recent fighting, I mentioned to my friend the remark made to me by the young doctor of Sokako, to the effect that strong anti-Russian feeling accounted to some extent for the intense keenness of the Japanese rank and file. Much to my interest he indorsed the doctor's views in words almost identical. He said, "Our army will always eagerly go forward to do battle with whomsoever his Majesty the Emperor may designate. But this Russian war is certainly an exception, in so far that each private soldier enters into it with burning feelings of personal anger which are a legacy of all the rapacity and deception and contempt displayed by Russia towards Japan for a long time past. I do not go so far as to say that our men would fight less courageously against other nations, but I do agree with the doctor in thinking that in such a case we should not see young soldiers denying themselves river water when consumed with thirst lest perchance a colic might lose them even one single chance of firing off their bullets at the enemy."

KINKAHOSHI, *August 15th*, 1904.—Pouring with rain. Doctor Sugiura has been delegated by headquarters to tell me that on the 10th inst. the whole of the Russian fleet came out of Port Arthur in battle array and were met and completely defeated by Togo. The *Askold, Bayan, Cesarewitch* escaped to Kiaochau; the *Novik* showed a clean pair of heels and got away. The rest of the enemy's fleet fled back into Port Arthur. More than this, yesterday at daybreak Kamimura met the Vladivostock fleet north of Tsushima and sank the *Rurik*, the other two Russian ships escaping north. Headquarters are overjoyed and Sugiura says they expect that Port Arthur will fall in three or four days, and that the fleet will become the spoil of the conquerors. Moreover, a fresh army will thus be released to reinforce our line of battle at Liaoyang.

After Sugiura's departure, I had a delightful visit from a colonel commanding a line regiment, an old Fenghuangcheng acquaintance. He tells me that twenty years ago only some three or four of the year's recruits for each company in the Japanese army were able to read or write. The officers, therefore, had to set themselves to be schoolmasters of primary schools, as it was absolutely necessary that the brains of the men should be awakened and exercised in the first instance; otherwise it was useless to expect them to make good progress with their military training. "Now," he said, "every single recruit who joins can read, whilst, at the very most, there may be three or four who cannot write. The first essential to the equipment of a modern soldier is a good education. The Russian Government, in order to maintain the stability of its despotism, finds it undesirable to educate its people, forgetful of the fact that on military grounds this has become quite necessary. The fact of the matter is that conscription is only applicable to an educated, intensely patriotic nation like Japan. Otherwise it is impossible to teach the soldier all that is required of him in the very limited time. When England is educated up to our level, then she can have conscription, if she cares to do so, but at present she shows her great wisdom in enlisting only men of a natural martial inclination, and in giving them a very thorough training before they are passed into the reserves. Conscription, with its system of short colour service, and masses of rusty reserves insufficiently welded together by officers and N.C.O.s of the reserve, is capable of proving a broken reed in time of trouble especially if, as with Russia in the present case, the national feeling has not a natural warlike bias. Russia, above all nations, should have provided herself with a long-service voluntarily enlisted army, and in that case we should have encountered a very different type of fighting man in our recent battles."

These views were put forward with a sublime unconsciousness which disarmed my ruffled pride. Do they not, after all, contain more than a grain or two of truth? Conscription does not keep the uneducated man long enough with the colours to make him fully capable of meeting all the conditions under which modern battles must be fought. These conditions—the magazine rifle, smokeless powder, wide extensions, &c. &c.—make much heavier demands upon the time, willingness and intelligence of the recruit than at any period in the world's history. Simultaneously all Continental nations, owing to popular pressure, are reducing their colour service to an extent which in the old days would have seemed to constitute a militia standard. Besides being an infinitely more trustworthy support to a Government in time of internal trouble, a long-service voluntarily enlisted army ought also to be very much more effective in the field. I do not forget that in Russia the colour service is exceptionally long; still, it is not long enough, taking into consideration the protracted winters when no work is done; the slackness with which duties are carried out even in summer and, most of all, the intense initial ignorance of the raw material.

KINKAHOSHI, *August 17th*, 1904.—Still pouring. Exercise impossible. Roaring torrents in all directions. There is talk amongst the men that every one is going on to half rations. I shall then be able to sympathise with the man in my own column in South Africa who, on reading the order thanking the force for their gallantry and announcing the necessity for a further reduction in the issue of beef and biscuit, said, "Just the old story; full compliments and half rations."

At dinner to-day I had a disappointment. A dish was brought forward with much pomp, which excited my keenest hopes. It was shaped like a pyramid, and they called it "German pudding." It turned out to be mashed potatoes sweetened with sugar. To the Devil with all such puddings!

KINKAHOSHI, *August 18th*, 1904.—It has been pouring in torrents ever since the last entry, and under such conditions my official reports and this diary have become my only distractions.

I have had a good deal of conversation at odd times lately concerning the marked distinction the Japanese make between a commander and a Staff officer. To them the two classes stand as sharply contrasted as a bowler does to a batter. Our allies never confound commanders and Staff officers under the hackneyed label of "able officer." Every one knows the qualifications of the Staff officer: energy, tact, accuracy, erudition, industry, health and horsemanship; without which last two all the others may be lost just when they are most wanted. But it is not every one who knows how little, and yet how very much, the Japanese require of their commanders. They seem to insist on one quality only, a quality which bulks in their eyes so largely that items such as reputation, judgment, character and even innate love of fighting fall into quite a secondary position. "*Du calme; il a du calme*," say the French-speaking Japanese when praising a commander. "*Er ist kaltblütig*," say the speakers of German.

Some three weeks ago, discussing with me the action of the Twelfth Division at Chaotao on the 19th of July, a distinguished young Staff officer said: "Before the attack I was very nervous; terribly nervous. I could not sleep at night, and all the Staff were restless and disturbed. But Kuroki was not troubled. Oh no; he was quite tranquil!" I did

A Good Comrade

CAPTAIN SHOJIRO TANAKA OF THE HEADQUARTERS STAFF

not take this too literally, as I know the Staff in their unwavering loyalty to Kuroki are capable of making an imputation against themselves, provided at the same time they are able to do honour to their chief. Still, the remark throws a light on the Japanese standard for a general's qualifications. I have put it to Japanese officers that there is no more difficult quality to recognise than that of true imperturbability. They assent readily, and admit that until a man has been tried by fire it is not possible to say whether he will be prepared to stake 10,000 human lives with a stout heart.

It seems then that the supreme qualification for a Japanese General, as understood by his fellow countrymen, is a philosophy which enables him to be calm under any circumstances and a record which guarantees that he possesses this attribute actually, and not only in seeming. Mere knowledge of regulations, languages, military history, science, are qualities which should be embodied in a Chief of the Staff who acts for the commander, just as a shorthand writer acts for a financier. This is the theory. But in practice, brains will tell, and the power of the General Staff is becoming enormous. Kuroki's method is in ordinary times to leave as much as possible to his Staff. He stands by, cool and aloof, and lends the great prestige of his name and reputation when orders are given and arrangements are made. His true value lies in doing little beyond taking responsibility as long as things go well. In a supreme emergency, as I shall more than once have occasion to point out, he is capable of taking the greatest risks entailing the heaviest responsibility, but generally speaking he is content to let the Staff carry on without too much interference.

At this particular moment Kuroki assumes much the same attitude to his General Staff as the Mikados used to do to their Shoguns. The Japanese mind seems readily to lend itself to the system of one man supporting all the weight, pomp, and responsibility of a position, whilst another man works free and untrammelled in the shadow afforded by that latent power.

It is extraordinarily interesting to a foreigner to see the organisation in this transitional state. If the same type of Generals and the same type of General Staff officers continued to be appointed for many years to come, I have no doubt whatever that the commander would recede more and more into the background, whilst the Chief of the General Staff would step more and more to the front. But after this war some of the new type of highly educated Staff officers will be senior enough to be made commanders. It will be curious to see if they initiate a different principle, or whether the Japanese will prefer to perpetuate the present arrangement of keeping many of the moving spirits in the background.

Meanwhile, at its present stage of development, the system works well. I take it that Kuroki, with his renown, his popularity in Japan, and his perfect, philosophical calm, really does relieve the more nervous, modern General Staff of a weight of responsibility which might otherwise to some extent paralyse their plans. I do not take it that the Japanese think that education necessarily impairs the quality of calmness. What they seem to think is that calmness, like noble birth, is quite independent of cleverness, and that where the qualities can be recognised, the clever man should be made the servant of the imperturbable philosopher, especially if this latter has the good luck to have been born in the purple.

I feel, of course, that even this combination of strength and ability does not by any means complete the category of the virtues required of the head of an army in the field. There is the imaginative *flair* to which mountains offer no concealment; the eye for country which is inborn and can yet be so greatly improved by practice in war; to the quickness in seizing an opportunity; the iron character which brushes all objections aside, and the engaging personality which fascinates subordinates and half disarms even a jealous rival.

It is strange indeed how little the Japanese are influenced by the personality of a commander. Individualism is a western, not an eastern, product. I doubt very much if the average Japanese has the capacity for hero-worship of living men. So far as I can discover, there is less personal enthusiasm for their superior commanders amongst Japanese soldiers than I should have expected, admirably qualified as these commanders are to inspire the warmest affection. There is the same indifference to the divisional and brigade commanders, and even to regimental or battalion commanders. The old feudal feeling has become transformed into respect for the officers as a caste, and not to the officers as individuals. Japanese discipline seems to produce a curious quality of impersonality. I firmly believe that if Kuroki changed places with Nogi, either army would be delighted to receive the distinguished leader of the other. Perhaps I am mistaken, but at any rate I am not writing all this down without having first taken thought and trouble in forming an opinion. Comparing Japanese subalterns with those of other nations, I should say that they are more bound up in their profession and have fewer distractions than their western *confrères*. There are few virtues, however, which have not some compensating weakness to counterbalance them, and this devotion to duty is no exception to the rule.

As far as I can grasp the characters of the subordinate Japanese officers, they seem to be extremely good at carrying out orders, but are not distinguished by any exceptional self-confidence when acting on their own initiative in ordinary matters, although I am bound to add that their apparent want of moral courage in such respects often seems to be transformed into boldness when they come actually into contact with the enemy. A few are very clever, but, generally speaking, they find full scope for their interests in looking after their men and in the thorough performance of their daily work. According to our ideas, they live on very familiar terms with the rank and file. In one village not far from here, the officer commanding a battalion is quartered in the same house with eighteen of his men, and I have seen a lieutenant playing "*go*" with his own private soldiers, though I doubt if this was quite correct, even according to the Japanese standard.

On the other hand, there is no falling off in discipline such as would inevitably result in our army, and still more so in most continental armies, if such familiarity was permitted. The saluting is splendid, just as smart and as good as it was in Tokio, and the severity and sharpness of the orders and remarks which pass on duty show that the officers have in no wise been compelled, by the hardships or promiscuity of active service, to relax in the smallest degree their severe and rigid disciplinary code.

The fact that the Japanese military forces have been strictly modelled on the Prussian organisation helps to explain some of its characteristics. One of the most striking features of the Japanese, as of the Prussian, army, and a great source of its efficiency, is to be found in its indifference to the personality of its leaders, whilst retaining a full sense of respect for any qualified leader as such. This quality alone is almost sufficient to ensure their success against hostile forces commanded by mediocrities. For the Western Europeans as well as the Russians follow the individual and not the mere epaulet, and unless this individual commands their respect and admiration they will not, and cannot, put forth their full strength. On the other hand, if a Russian Skobeleff were now to appear upon the scene—brilliant, swift, daring—adored by his troops and possessing the true military imaginative instinct, then I believe the Japanese might find that there was an element in Western warfare with which they have not yet been called upon to count.

KINKAHOSHI, *August 19th*, 1904.—Still pouring. The men are being put on short rations, and the Chinese fear that if the unseasonable deluge continues their ripening crops will be rusted. After breakfast, I was handed a present from Tokio—a bottle of beer and a copy of a book in a white cover, "Bushido, the Soul of Japan," by Inazo Nitobe. Every military attaché with the First Army gets a similar gift, which comes from Army Headquarters in Tokio.

Some drafts from the Second Division are marching past the house. They are the cream of the young manhood of the north-east of Japan; physically the pick of the whole island, going to join their fellows and keep the dwindling *cadres* up to full strength.

Compare this homogeneous, complete organisation, not only complete at the start, but with all its apparatus in good order for remaining complete under all conditions—compare it with our patchwork, extemporised, motley crew of regulars, colonials, militia, volunteers, yeomanry! How have we carried through the great things we have done in the past, and how are we going to continue to do all the great things we mean to do in the future? Partly, I take it, because in each Englishman, whether town or country bred, there exists, atrophied perhaps, but still living, a sense, a sentiment, a memory, which vibrates to the stirring sound of the call to arms. Partly because of our captains and subalterns, so many of whom possess natural aptitude for leading, and who can thus carry not only their own countrymen but even alien races with them in times of difficulty and danger.

The drafts are still marching by. Poor fellows, they would be a sad sight for their mothers to-day! Here is true war shorn of its tinsel trappings. Woebegone lads, pale and hollow-cheeked, plastered from head to foot with mud, whilst the pitiless rain streams off their caps and capes in miniature cascades as they squelch through the sticky clay or ford the torrents which sweep across the road.

Has any one ever considered the extraordinary difference in the conditions under which men face death in battles on sea and on land? If the bluejacket feels a bit hot, he can take off his blue jacket. If he feels cold, he slips on a sweater. When the enemy is signalled he is ordered (under the flag of the Rising Sun) to change his underclothing lest perchance a shred of foul linen be carried into a wound. After this, he may still have time to make all snug within by a nice hot cup of tea or a tot of *saké*. Should he get wounded there is a doctor at his elbow. He has no temptation to run away. Only its own commander can put a ship to flight. There was a friend of mine who when he was a boy used to know an old pensioner who had been a sergeant at the battle of Waterloo. Over and over again the old man had to tell his blood and thunder story to the eager boy. Time after time this boy asked the veteran, "And did you not want to run away?" To which invariably the same answer was returned, "*Where* was I to run to?" This is the precise position of the sailor, with all its advantages as well as its one obvious drawback.

On the other hand, think of the soldier of an infantry battalion, half dead with the fatigue of a night march carried out in some infernal extreme of climate, wet and shivering, or exhausted with heat and thirst; scrambling up mountains carrying 50 or 60 lb. on his back and with hundreds of people shooting at him; charging the enemy, coming under fire of the second line; his captain killed, his subalterns and colour-sergeant wounded; no difficulty now in shirking; lots of opportunity to skulk—lots of temptation; but no, on he goes; in his path flows a river, its waters whipped white by the bullets; never a pause—onwards is the word—up to his armpits in the water—he reaches the further bank; he fixes his bayonet, and amidst the rip of rifles and crackling showers of shrapnel raises the loud exultant cheer and gets right home. Well, each service has special hardships no doubt. The seaman has the consolation that if the ship founders all go down together; the landsman has anyway solid mother earth under his weary feet. Food and conveniences are not everything and life on board a torpedo-boat is, I believe, not exactly a bed of roses, but still, honour, great honour, to the soldier of the line, say I, for on his head he does it, God bless him.

KINKAHOSHI, *August 21st*, 1904.—Drizzling. Persistent rumours of an early advance. I hear that at Port Arthur, Nogi has secured a footing on an important *col* between two hills which overlook Pigeon Bay on the one side and a permanent fort on the other. Also, that on the Japanese left, half of the crest of a hill has been captured, a capture which, in the Chinese war, was the immediate precursor of the fall of the citadel.

The Headquarters Staff are amused at some European appreciations of our situation, which have found their way into the Japanese newspapers. It seems that, on the map, we have already reached a spot north or north-east of Mukden. The critics have evidently not paused to figure out the enormous number of carts we should require to march from our base to the Yalu to attain such dangerous isolation. It should be remembered that a Japanese soldier must have his pound of rice per diem, for, if man does not live by bread alone, neither can he continue to exist for long on patriotism and water. We are not little tin soldiers, but must draw our rations, or die!

I have read "Bushido" and drunk the bottle of beer. I am glad I have read the book, and sorry I have finished the beer. Mr. Inazo Nitobe writes admirably, and his work has furnished me, as it must every one who reads it, with much matter for thought.

The main question which each of us must ask himself is whether a feudal code can possibly hold its own against the exigencies of modern life. I yield to no one in my admiration for the knightly virtues of the old Samurai. But the Samurai are already men of yesterday, and so, if the old Bushido lingers awhile, it is as a transient shadow falling athwart a threshold from which the guest has already taken his first irrevocable step on a far journey.

I study the Japanese from morning to night; I talk to them, walk with them, eat with them, and drink with them also, whenever there is anything worth drinking. I am watching them all the time, for I have little else to do. As a result of my patient investigations, everything about these strangers is becoming so obscure and contradictory that I can only marvel at the temerity I displayed in dashing down what purported to be an analysis of their characters before I had lived with them a month.

For instance: the modesty of the Japanese is a trait which above all others has won my profound and unstinted respect. Never has there been so much as a tinge of exultation or what, in its most vulgar form, our colonials call "blowing," about the officers, non-commissioned officers or men of the First Army. There have been many unconscious revelations of a sense of superiority to the European, but I cannot call to mind one single occasion of a sober Japanese making a consciously swaggering remark, even in the triumphant reaction immediately after a victory.

It has always been a special pleasure to recognise and do homage to so generous, high and knightly a quality, but now a corner of the veil has been uplifted, and lo, I seem to perceive a figure like that of Pride sitting throned upon the Japanese heart in great aloofness. The Japanese do not boast after a victory because they are incapable of imagining for one moment that they are not going to win. Bad men may bet on certainties, only fools would boast about them. I am not a theologian, and do not feel called upon to say whether this quality is to be ranked amongst the cardinal virtues or the deadly sins. Certainly self-reliance was considered by the Romans a virtue of the first order. *Possunt quia posse videntur.* But I am sure, nevertheless, that whatever the quality may be, it is not modesty.

Another quality for which I have been anxiously on the watch is that of gratitude—the capacity for gratitude. Here again in the midst of my heart-searching endeavours to reconcile conflicting evidences, I stumbled against that same stony figure of Pride barring the way to meek and gentle gratitude which otherwise would be so frequent and welcome a visitor to the Japanese heart. Our allies are always truly and unfeignedly thankful for small mercies. An act of consideration or politeness or generosity or hospitality they will repay, if they can, fourfold. But weightier obligations are supported by them, it seems to me, nobly perhaps, but with effort and difficulty. In writing thus I am thinking of four or five things, big things which have come under my own observation. I believe the natural instinct of the Japanese would be to acknowledge fully and eagerly any obligations they are under to the West were it not that, in the case of some men, pride throttles the intention before it can, in any way, declare itself.

My little Bushido book says nothing about either gratitude or modesty, except on one occasion when modesty is said to be an important ingredient of the quality of politeness. The Japanese are certainly very proud of their politeness, and although I doubt very much whether modesty has anything to do with it, the politeness is no doubt very real. Politeness and pugnacity can co-exist in a Japanese to an extent Europe has not witnessed since the days when French and English had a bowing match at Fontenoy as to who should have the exquisite pleasure of discharging the first volley. The man who is capable of considering his "P's" and "Q's" when hovering on the brink of eternity makes a good comrade when tiger hunting is to the fore, and I feel myself at last on safe ground when I declare that the world has not yet seen, and certainly will never see again, a race more devoted than the Japanese to all ceremonious observances. To say that a Japanese gentleman would die sooner than be impolite is inadequate. He would rather die a thousand deaths.

Life is not ordinarily a procession of great emergencies, but even the actions of every day gain some dignity from the virtue—or shall I call it the accomplishment ?—of *la politesse*. As a Briton, I may claim the melancholy satisfaction of discoursing quite impartially on the subject. Whether it is their rough natural independence of habit or the want of that discipline which is entailed by military service, or merely because their Governments have shirked paying the extra twopence for the schooling of their youngsters, the fact remains that, from the standpoints of continental Europe or of Asia, both Americans and British are hopeless barbarians in all that concerns etiquette.

This is rather a pity, seeing that, although superficial politeness may be no more than a useful social lubricant, it becomes a positive quality of no mean value when it is of the class which can be warranted to wear well under stress of constant discomfort and hardship. Such a warranty I gladly give to all Japanese, although I must firmly refuse it to the average continental European. Japanese suavity and good manners are solid, and will stand any amount of rough usage, whereas the urbane smiles and bows of Europe are a mere veneer, good for drawing-rooms and clubs, but hardly to be depended on to stand a shower of rain or a journey in an ordinary railway train. True politeness makes an easy travelling companion; spurious politeness is much worse than no politeness once it is transplanted into uncongenial surroundings.

Thus it comes that if I have to share my tiny room with a stranger, I much prefer a Japanese officer to the citizen of any other country but my own. At times, it is true, the unfailing ceremony so much oppresses my untutored mind that I long to do or say something irretrievably vulgar and shocking. But I recognise all the time that I am wrong, and that manners mend the man even if they do not make him.

I have said that Japanese politeness is more genuine and deep-rooted than the European variety, but I have not yet made a very necessary qualification to the effect that the Japanese type, though true and permanent of its kind, is different in some respects from that of the Western world. For if there is a conflict between an engagement to an absent friend and the claims of one actually present, the code requires that the former should absolutely give way.

The most undeniable of all the virtues vaunted in

Bushido are the fortitude which welcomes death and the honour which disdains gold. I have no need to say much more about a courage to which each successive battle bears eloquent witness. It is not precisely a counterpart of Western valour. There is some philosophy and passivity about it; more conscious self-sacrifice; less Berserker joy of battle and longing to do some glorious act. All Japanese soldiers go into battle expecting and prepared to conquer and die; brave British soldiers go into battle hopeful and prepared to conquer *or* die. There is a mighty difference between the two. Japanese officers have constantly to explain to their men that they must not consider the main object of a battle is to get killed; British officers have no occasion thus to admonish their men, who, although they are aware that in all probability many will bite the dust, are each individually of the opinion that they will manage to pull through. The faces of the two races as they advance to the attack wear very different expressions. But I feel that no one who has not seen for himself will ever understand me if I try to go more deeply into these strange things.

I will only add, then, that it displays the most gross misconception of the truth to write, as some continental authorities are apparently writing, about Japanese fanaticism. As one who has some acquaintance with the ghazi, I may permit myself to be dogmatic here. In some cases, Japanese patriotism may take the form of a deep-rooted dislike to foreigners; in others it may assume the guise of an overweening contempt for everything outside their own islands. But if such feelings are fanatical, then surely John Bull himself is a ghazi of the most rabid type, which is absurd. The one and only point of superficial resemblance between the fanatic and the Japanese soldier is the positive hope often cherished by both that they may be privileged to die on the battlefield. The apparent similarity will not, however, bear close examination. The motives of the ghazi are selfish. He hopes by his act to gain access to a very material paradise where he may flirt with hosts of houris. The motives of the Japanese are as purely impersonal as it is possible for those of a human being to be. Though troubling himself little about a future life, he has a dim idea that if killed in action, his spirit will be aware of the gratitude the Emperor and the nation will bear him for having sacrificed himself on their behalf. He longs to die for his country; not in order that he himself may reap some glorious reward, but in the hope that he may be worthy of those who have preceded him, and that his example may usefully guide the unknown generations who are to follow him in the hereafter.

No Western can quite understand these extraordinary soldiers: at one moment cold, distant, reserved, suspicious stoics; at another, merry laughing children; and then again, resigned, sad, "determined-to-die" heroes. But one thing at least is quite certain: the Japanese Samurai may be philosophers, they most assuredly are not fanatics.

So much for the Japanese soldier's depreciation of life, now for his disdain for pelf.

Few even of the military coolies with the Second Division will consent to accept a tip either small or great for service rendered, and a full private would be infinitely insulted by the offer of a present, no matter whether it consisted of one silver yen or a bag of gold. I admit I never tried them with the bag of gold, but I am certain that, if I did so, over 13,000 of the 14,000 men with the Second Division would refuse the offer, some with horror and indignation, others with amusement and contempt. Scorn for money is a piece of pure Bushido, or Samurai, tradition, which has transplanted itself, apparently without too much difficulty, from feudalism into the army. But the merchants, canteen men, photographers, and other civilian camp followers, are as ready to turn a dishonest penny as their prototypes of South Africa, where the moral atmosphere was not exceptionally bracing. Also, although private soldiers are generally immaculate in their honesty, there are signs here and there amongst individuals of higher status that money is no longer the mere dross it was to their ancestors, and that they might not in all cases be too scrupulous as to how it was procured. True, anything I have noticed in this respect has been on a very petty scale, and I am convinced the main channels along which run the public moneys of the Japanese are kept scrupulously sweet and clean. The soldier seems to be endowed with a most delicate instinct which warns him that any tampering, or even want of due economy, with public funds is a sin against patriotism—against his country. The Western man is inclined to be more lax where Government is the keeper of the purse; the feeling of the Japanese is precisely the opposite. But I wonder, in view of small signs which have come to my personal notice, how long the army will be able to maintain a different and loftier standard from their brethren in civil life? Has the noble tree transplanted from feudalism truly struck its roots down into the new, rich soil, or is it destined soon to wither and die under the strange conditions, quite foreign to its original growth, which now surround it? I pray myself that it may endure for ever, but there is a tendency, an inclination, just making itself visible to a friendly observer, which will need the close attention of the Japanese nation.

If the transition from the status of Bushido to the status of industrialism had been more gentle and gradual, it would then, I believe, have been easier for a Samurai permanently to transfer some of his soldierly ideas of honour into the service of Mammon. But the plunge has been too violent and, in this year of grace 1904, the Japanese knight, shorn of his twin souls, his swords, has had his heart swept and garnished in preparation for an entirely fresh ideal of life. Only a few selected, most valued pieces of the old knightly armoury have been temporarily conserved, and it is these which have rendered the descendants of the Samurai invincible in the field. But the emblematic swords are gone never to return, and I very much fear that the spiritual attributes of Bushido will not long outlive them.

What is to take their place? Is it possible for a non-Christian nation to borrow Christian ideals?

Do we Christians offer such an example of the vivifying effects of our own ideals as to encourage a new nation to adopt them?

But if Christianity is to be rejected by the Japanese, and if Confucius is worn out, are living, burning beliefs to be replaced by a cold copybook code of morals based on such maxims as "Honesty is the best policy"? Can a great nation be evolved from so unspiritual and earthly a basis? We shall see; Japan may have as many surprises for us in the future as she has had in the past. It is not possible to imagine a more tremendous issue. Will industrial Japan succeed in grafting itself onto the gnarled stem of antique tradition, or will the modern commercial conceptions demand a fresh basis and complete emancipation?

There is no doubt a conceivable compromise whereby the old spirit would linger on as a living force in the army whilst it ceased to exist in the hearts of the civil population. In that case another danger would menace the Japanese Empire—the danger, namely, that the noble spirit of the army would become dangerously divorced from the new commercial spirit of the nation. Even in this camp—amongst troops flushed with success—burning with patriotism, there are indications to show that the military caste must hasten the process of modernising its spirit unless it is to lose touch with the mass of the people.

It has been impossible to remain blind to the ultra-radical, sometimes frankly socialistic, views of some of the civilian Japanese here who have been to America, or to ignore their freely expressed hatred of the caste of military officers. This is a sign of coming trouble, for it cannot be doubted that when the few non-military men with us furnish several examples of such a state of mind there must be many thousands in Japan who hold similar views. The change from Bushido to Chicago is too violent. The sceptical, individualistic ideas prevalent in parts of the United States act like corrosive sublimate upon the Samurai spirit of loyalty and self-sacrifice. The old bottles are still in excellent condition, but it is trying them very high to select the newest, most effervescent, of all vintages when they have to be refilled.

Here a question arises which I have fully discussed with my Japanese military comrades. Cannot something be done to meet the danger half way? If it is desirable that the Japanese should go slow in matters of education, why not select venerable places of instruction such as Oxford or Cambridge, Edinburgh, Glasgow or St. Andrews? These hoary institutions possess a spirit which is far less violently at variance with the traditions of old Japan than that, so brilliant in itself, which sparkles through the colleges of the United States of America. The former are capable of leading the Samurai student very gradually and very gently to the new inevitable ideals; the lessons of the latter may produce good results, but may also, as I have myself seen, be so badly assimilated that they destroy the equilibrium of the student. It comes to this. Do Japanese fathers and mothers care to run even the smallest risk that their sons may return to their native land out of harmony with their surroundings and with a contempt—concealed, perhaps, possibly arrogant and out-spoken—for all old-fashioned things, themselves amongst the number? Or, would they like them to preserve to a reasonable and moderate extent, their love and admiration for their ancestors and for the old days of Japan? How often an Englishman, Scotchman or Irishman may be heard to say, in answer to the question, "Why is this so?" "It has always been so," or, "It was good enough for my father; it will serve for me." Whereas, except in New England and the South, such sentiments are not very popular in the States.

Every one must recognise that there is an American spirit of Boston as well as an American spirit of Chicago, but it is the latter which catches hold of the young Japanese student, and he is apt to find it a bit too heady. As a soldier who has studied the American Civil War I yield to no one in admiration for our go-ahead cousins, from their great President downwards, but it does not necessarily follow that they are the most wholesome companions for the Japanese just at the present stage of their respective developments. I would confidently send any young relative of my own to imbibe American notions, but I would advise the Samurai's son to refrain. Anyway, what I am concerned at present to conclude, is:

(1) The precepts of Bushido have, to some extent, been successfully transplanted from the old Samurai code to the army, but have failed signally to strike root in the domain of commerce. Therefore, these precepts as accepted in the army must be adapted to the new order of things or perish. Already Bushido stirs the antagonism of some of the foreign educated men who mean to try and rule the new Japan. These intellectuals regard military officers with greater dislike than a German professor displays towards a Prussian junker. They pine for the emancipation of women; they burn to humble the caste pride of the military and naval officers, and at all costs they are bent on democratising Japanese institutions in every direction. I am not imagining these things. I am voicing the feelings of Japanese civilians who have expressed them to me on many occasions. I heartily disagree; but even if they are right in holding such views I think they are premature and unpatriotic in their desire to kill Bushido, and this desire they have conceived, I fear, from an injudicious

application of principles, good perhaps in themselves, which they have picked up in America.

(2) It would be an irretrievable loss to Japan if Bushido was clean wiped out, leaving no trace upon the national character.

(3) Therefore the Japanese should try and put a drag upon the wheel, and if they must send some of their boys abroad, they should select for the purpose a country where people still believe a good deal more than they care to confess in the greatness of their great-great-grandfathers.

To say that I have carried out the foregoing moral reconnaissance with the diffidence which springs from an acknowledged want of grip of my subject is to state my want of qualification too mildly. When I try to penetrate the Japanese mind I am baffled by contradiction on contradiction. The very man who speaks of a steam hammer borrowed from Armstrong's or a system of attack taken from Germany as if he had originated it himself, atones for all by ending humbly, "We have a lot still to learn—a lot to learn." The Japanese seem to be gifted with a much higher nervous energy than any other Asiatics. They are exceedingly curious and eagerly welcome any new thing or novel idea. On mechanical points or details they are especially inquisitive. I should say their genius was entirely prosaic and material, were it not for the inevitable contradiction: their love for poetry—art—painting—but especially poetry. And although the poetry consists in a great measure of verbal conceits or puns, there is real feeling in it too. In music the inquirer imagines he has reached one rock of certitude amidst so much that is contradictory and vague. The whole world of western music is certainly closed to the Japanese;—and yet—see a private soldier hanging in perfect rapture on the trill of a nightingale—where now is the theory that his soul is on that account dead to melody? A Japanese cares nothing, as far as I have been able to observe, for scenery in our sense of the word, but just as so much seems beyond question, you find a whole company entranced; lost in the purest artistic admiration of a waterfall. As for flowers, they are simply adored by the whole army. The language is probably more unlike English than any other, and yet, if the distance is sufficient to make the listener lose the precise words, there is a strange familiarity about the intonation.

I fear I have been writing as if Japan had everything to learn from us. We can still teach her something, no doubt, but, in the greatest quality any nation can possess, the power, namely, of imbuing its sons and daughters with the idea that the public interest comes first and the private interest comes a long way second, we have everything to learn from her. If life is to be lifted out of the dull, ordinary rut, there must be some ideal in the background which, in moments of illumination, may reveal the possibility of existence on a higher plane. Such moments may not often be vouchsafed, but those are the most ready to perceive the flash and respond to the appeal who have kept before them a sense of patriotic obligation—a love of their country with all that such love implies of gratitude for its past; hope for its future and determination to defend it. Too often, with us, is the noble word freedom degraded by being confused with the right of the individual as against the State. What is *right* compared with *duty*? Is it too much to hope that the coming generation at least may be brought up to believe that the public good must take the first place in each poor little life, which only thus can succeed in catching some ray of reflected grandeur? For a nation lives only in the hearts of the people. When it dies there, no wealth, no territory will save it. The Jew from no man's land, the New York Irishman, the French-speaking Canadian, descendant of Fraser's Highlanders, alike belong far more truly to the Jewish, Irish or Scotch nations than some of those Englishmen who are frankly selfish in their lives and cosmopolitan in their sympathies belong to England.

## CHAPTER XX

### THE BATTLE OF THE TWENTY-SIXTH OF AUGUST

KINKAHOSHI, *August 23rd*, 1904.—Immense excitement. The march against Kuropatkin's communications is about to begin. What a splendid thing to be alive, and to be here taking part in the great final trek of the Manchurian War!

The three Divisions are to keep in their respective positions. Guards on the left, Kuroki with the Second Division in the centre, and the Twelfth Division on the right. The Guards lead off and march to-night westwards down the big Liaoyang road as far as the angle where it turns again to the northwards (*see* Map XXII.). They are to take the Second Division Field Artillery with them, as our line of advance will lead us over a country impracticable for anything but infantry and mountain guns. It is rumoured that there is a good number of the enemy on the Guards' left flank, but it is said that the Fourth Army is stretching out a hand to us so as to lessen our difficulties in that direction.

The *Novik* has been sunk by two Japanese cruisers going through the Hokaido Straits.

KINKAHOSHI, *August 24th*, 1904.—I am to start at 2.30 P.M. to-morrow with Kuroki and the Headquarters Staff, taking three days' rations with me on my horse and probably sleeping *à la belle étoile* for the next few nights.

Too busy making arrangements to write any more, although the joy of an army under orders to advance affords a tempting theme.

*Under an oak tree, near* NIDOREI,* *August 25th, 1904.*—Writing by the light of "Mangatsu," the full harvest moon, my heart shares the adoration with which to-night all true Japanese regard the inconstant orb. In every direction stretches the ripening corn, which does not, even by a rustle, break the phantasmal silence, oppressive to one who knows that he is closely encircled by a vast invisible host. Sheaves of bayonets project with an ominous glitter from the ears of grain, and occasional bluish ribbons of smoke trailing up lazily towards the cloudless sky betray the ranks of the slumbering army.

*A hut near a village called* KOKAHOSHI,† *August 26th, 1904.*—I am soaked to the skin and ravenous withal, but excitement sends me a transient spurt of pluck to set to work at my scribbling. We are not going to march into Liaoyang the day after to-morrow; so much is clear, and it is equally evident I cannot attempt to write a comprehensive story of the battle until I get settled under a watertight roof. That is to say, I must content myself meanwhile with jotting down my personal adventures and observations from day to day as they arise.

At 3-30 this morning, I was awakened and told that Kuroki and his Staff had decamped, and that I was to follow. The moon hung very low over the mountains, and I could hear a few dropping shots in the far distance. After going a little way north up the

* Chinese, Altauling (*see* Map XXII.)  † Chinese, Hochiaputsu.

# THE BATTLE OF THE TWENTY-SIXTH OF AUGUST 37

Tiensuitien valley, we turned westwards and climbed about 1½ miles up a narrow nullah leading into the next big valley.

When we got on to the watershed, we were met by an adjutant who said that General Kuroki had taken up his position on a peak immediately to the south of where I stood, and that he hoped I would come up there and join him. At the very top of the mountain, which is called Gokarei* (Map XII.), was a patch of smooth turf surrounded by thick hazel scrub. On the miniature lawn were set four camp chairs in a row. I sat in great glory on the second chair from the left between General Kuroki and H.I.H. Prince Kuni. This is the first time I have ever seen a chair on a battlefield, and to find myself sitting in one makes me think of Marshal Saxe and of the good old days when they did such things in great style.

Behind us and beneath us lay the Tiensuitien valley running north and south, and to our front, looking westwards, there rose, at a distance of about four miles, a high continuous range still in the possession of the Russians. Behind this range, but hidden by it from our view, ran the Tangho, across which river Oyama has ordered Kuroki to drive the enemy. All the approaches to the position now held by the Russians were broken up into a wild jungle of peaks, ridges and ravines. It was a sort of country suitable for very young men and wild goats. Take a sheet of foolscap; crumple it up; pull it out again; multiply the scale by 50,000; then perhaps some adequate idea may be formed of the configuration of the terrain (*see* Sketch XVII. and Map XXII.).

The Second Division had carried the enemy's out-

* Chinese, Wuchialing.

post line with the bayonet by moonlight, and were now in possession of the broken ground between us and the high range to the westwards. They had even made good a small portion of the main Russian position, on their extreme right and the Russian left. But when I came upon the scene, the centre and right of the enemy were still maintaining their ground, and the Japanese were mostly on the lower slopes of the big mountains whose crests were crowned with Russian trenches.

The first time I looked at my watch it was 7 A.M. There was then a heavy musketry fight in progress, the double tic-toc of the heavier Russian rifle rather predominating. Eleven miles to our left, to the southwest, an artillery duel had begun about an hour previously between the sixty guns belonging to, or attached to, the Guards, and five Russian batteries firing from gun-pits just behind the crest lines of the ridges. The Japanese guns were in action along the line Roshisan–Tashinpou,* and the Russian guns were replying from the line Daidenshi–Kohoshi † (Map XXII.). The little snowy smoke-balls all clustered together over one spot look like a flock of innocent gulls hanging over a shoal of fish. But just as a carcase is denoted by the vultures, so too is death clearly indicated by these far-off fleecy clusters of clouds whose iron rain can be seen even at this distance raising clouds of yellow dust all round the Russian gun-pits. So much for the centre and left.

About ten miles to our right, to the north, there lay athwart the horizon a huge, black, straight-backed mountain bearing a small knob on its far, or western,

* Chinese, Langtsushan–Tashintun.
† Tatientsu–Kaofengtsu.

# THE BATTLE OF THE TWENTY-SIXTH OF AUGUST 39

extremity. The mountain is called Kosarei.* I am told that all the reconnaissances have shown that this Kosarei mountain will be a terrible hard nut to crack, rising as it does almost sheer 1600 feet above the rivers. Kuroki is not even certain whether it was practicable on its northern flank—practicable, that is to say, for an armed man to climb. Kosarei forms the left of the Russian position, and is the objective of the hot-headed Twelfth Division. Even now, at the hour I am writing, no one knows for certain what has happened there, or in whose hands the mountain has remained.

At 7.30 A.M. an orderly brought us cups of hot tea, and Kuroki gave me a cigar for which a Staff officer struck a match. I said it was a proud position for me to be sitting during a great battle by the side of the commander of a Japanese army smoking his cigars which were lit by another great man. Kuroki laughed quite light-heartedly, as if he was genuinely free from all care. I said, "Your Excellency does not anticipate very heavy losses, I hope?" He replied that his only anxiety was about the Twelfth Division, which was so far distant he could get no news of its progress. He was able to see from the shrapnel bursts that the line of battle of the Guards was where he expected it to be, and he was confident that the Second Division in front of us would more than make good what they had gained by their night attack with the bayonet.

Kuroki is truly a delightful man. Not a beribboned, overbearing, jealous General, but gentle, unassuming, sympathetic and charming. Occasionally little jokes were made at which he and his Staff laughed heartily. Nor was any small touch of politeness or etiquette

* Chinese, Hungshaling.

omitted. In short, there was not the slightest sign of strain or excitement. Only keen interest.

I am told that instructions were found on a Russian Staff officer who had been wounded and taken prisoner about a week ago, warning the Divisional Generals opposed to us that they must be specially careful about their flanks. The glimpse Kuroki thus obtained into the enemy's plans determined him to try a bold frontal attack on the centre, as he considered it a fair presumption that this part of the Russian line would be comparatively weakly held and ill prepared.

Meanwhile the musketry fire became violent in the extreme all along the lower slopes of the big mountains opposite; it clanged and echoed through the high mountains as if thousands of riveters were working for dear life on a monster battleship, and yet the Japanese did not seem to gain a yard. Far away on the left the fire of the sixty guns with the Imperial Guards was perceptibly weakening, whilst the Russian guns opposite to them were now able to divert some of their fire from the Japanese batteries to other parts of the battlefield, where evidently the infantry advance was being fiercely contested.

Kuroki is a great smoker, and consumed cigar after cigar. Eventually he lay down on his back and used the cigar-box as a pillow, putting his handkerchief over it.

When messages arrived by the hand of anxious adjutants or orderlies they were generally delivered to the senior Staff officer present, who read them first and then took them to Kuroki, but occasionally the adjutant would step forward and read the contents of his note-book in a clear loud voice so that all could hear.

## The Battle of the Twenty-sixth of August

At 7.50 A.M. we noticed that one particular Russian battery entrenched on the south side of a small hillock had been singled out for the terrible concentrated fire of the whole of the Guards' artillery, who were simply pouring shrapnel and high explosive shell upon it. Ball after ball of cottony white smoke was piled over the eight Russian field-pieces by the invisible agency of the growling, snarling Japanese guns, whilst every now and then a huge column of greenish black vapour would rise up from the edge of the gun-pits, showing where a high explosive shell had that moment alighted. All our glasses were glued to this tumultuous scene, when suddenly, amidst murmurs of interest from the General Staff, the Russians were seen to be withdrawing their guns and bringing them out again into an alternative set of gun-pits on the northern side of the hillock, from whence they soon re-opened fire, whilst the Guards' artillery kept on pounding away at the empty entrenchments to the south. The General Staff, instead of fuming as Europeans or Americans would probably have done at the success of the Russian artifice, were genuinely interested and quite pleased. They exclaimed: "*Ils luttent bien!*"*

At 8 A.M. an adjutant appeared with a despatch, saluted, and read out a message from the Commander of the Twelfth Division announcing that, at 6.30 A.M., he had carried the northern and most difficult part of the Kosarei position on the extreme Russian left, but that the enemy was still vigorously disputing his attempts to improve his advantage. This was great news, but not sufficiently definite or conclusive to make the General Staff quite happy.

* I believe "*Ils se battent bien*" is the more correct formula, but I give it as it was said.—I. H.

At 8.15 a breathless messenger arrived, saying that the enemy in front of the Second Division were beginning to fall back on Amping. The rattling and crackling of the musketry was now continuous as the noise of a blazing bonfire. I was tempted to ask leave to run on and see the infantry fight at closer quarters, but I reflected that if I were to elect to witness the exploits of companies I must forego the unique experience of being solitary spectator of such a vast battle panorama as now lay smoking and resounding at my feet.

At 8.20 a second despatch reached us from the Twelfth Division, saying that Kigoshi, who is to the Twelfth Division what Okasaki is to the Second, had, with five battalions, scaled the lofty black ridge north of Kosarei, and that the Russians were quite driven off the northern half of the mountain at the time of writing, namely, at 7.20 A.M. This news was read out aloud, and for once the Japanese permitted their assumed mask of insensibility to drop, and were as excited and frankly delighted as a lot of schoolboys. A very senior officer even went the length of calling out "Bravo!" and a few moments later he whispered to me, chuckling, "*Das war die Hauptsache!*"

As far as I could judge by the map and the lie of the ground, the ridge which had been half taken was the key to the left and centre of the enemy's position. By its occupation, the Japanese had gained a *point d'appui* for an immediate advance on Amping, which, if successful, would render untenable the whole of the country lying between the Tangho and the Lanho (Map XXII.). Either, so it seemed to me, the Russians must retake the Kosarei ridge, or else there was no secure foothold for their left and centre until they fell back west over the Tangho or north over the Taitsuho. The right of the Russians, which was engaged with the Imperial Guards, was not so immediately threatened, as they could always retire on to Liaoyang by the main Pekin road, which ran clear of the town of Amping. Nevertheless, if the Russian left and centre were forced back, the opponents of the Imperial Guards would ultimately have to follow suit. I wrote out, therefore, a cable to India, and got it censored on the spot, saying that although the Russians were still making a good fight, an important victory was practically assured. The General Staff were just despatching an orderly back to Tiensuitien, and they kindly allowed him to take my cable.

Hardly had he disappeared from view, when bad news began to come in from the front, and, not for the first time, I was sorry I had been in such a hurry.

At 8.25 a messenger arrived saying that, although one column of the enemy did appear to be falling back on Amping, another heavy column of fresh troops had appeared on the left of the Second Division, where a counter-attack was momentarily expected. Lieutenant-General Nishi, commanding the Second Division, did not feel himself well situated to resist such a movement, as he had now only one battalion in hand, and he earnestly begged therefore for reinforcements from the 29th Regiment of Kobi, which was held by Kuroki at Tiensuitien as an army reserve. Kuroki was perfectly calm. He refused the reinforcements, and I gathered that he would be enchanted if the counter-attack was delivered. For the country was so bad and broken that the only result of a successful Russian advance against the Second Division would be to involve their own centre inextricably amidst the mountains. They could not bring up artillery to improve their advantage, and meanwhile the Twelfth Division might be able to get to Amping in their rear and cut them off entirely from their line of retreat.

One minute after Nishi's alarming message, that is to say, at 8.26, an orderly arrived from the Imperial Guards saying that the situation on that wing was becoming very serious. The Guards, he reported, could make no sort of progress either by asserting their artillery superiority or by advancing their infantry. On the contrary, the enemy to their front was rapidly increasing and was threatening to envelop and force back their left brigade, under Asada, which had, it seems, crossed the upper waters of the Tangho and got somewhat isolated. Now faces grew grave, and after a very brief deliberation, orders were given to the whole of the Army Reserve to march from Tiensuitien to the assistance of the Guards. The Army Reserve consisted, as I have just written, only of the 29th Regiment of Kobi,* which had, an hour previously, come in to Tiensuitien from Antung, having marched the whole distance in forty-eight hours,† up to date the record march made by any unit of the First Army.

So long as it remained at Tiensuitien, this reserve was in rear of the centre of the Japanese line of battle, but once it was sent to the extreme left it would cease to be available for the reinforcement of centre or right.

Kuroki knew very little about the course of events

* In the Japanese Army organisation Kobi are the 2nd Reserve, *i.e.*, men who have done their three years colour service and three years in the Yobi, or 1st Reserve. They remain ten years in the Kobi.

† I find this clearly entered in my diary, but am somewhat staggered to find from the map that the distance in question is 85 miles!—I. H.

Colonel Kawasaki
COMMANDING 30TH REGIMENT, OKASAKI BRIGADE

Lt.-Gen. Nishijima
COMMANDING 2ND DIVISION 1ST ARMY

on his right, except that the Twelfth Division had taken half of the position they had been told off to attack and that they were still fighting; he had just heard that a serious attack was about to be launched against his centre, which was only three or four miles to his own immediate front, and he could plainly hear and see for himself that the Russians in this part of the field were numerous and full of fight. In giving such an order then, I think that he had come to what one of the Staff described as *une decision un peu audacieuse*. In fact it was an action demanding an uncommon amount of nerve to part with the 29th Regiment at a moment so critical.

Few Generals I have ever met would have had the hardihood to deprive themselves with this reasoned, unfaltering completeness of every single man of their reserves at a moment when the ever-increasing fury of the musketry, and the pale, breathless messengers from the firing-line all foreboded the approach of a crisis in that part of the fight which was raging under their very eyes.

There is no bottling-up-the-Old-Guard tendency about Kuroki. His method of handling his reserves is the very acme of boldness. Never will Kuroki merit the reproach which Napoleon levelled at Joseph after Talavera, when he told him the plain truth and said that a General who retreats before he has used all his reserves deserves to be shot forthwith. But Napoleon himself did not always act up to his own principles, and although he was the acknowledged master in the art of using his reserves, yet it has been plausibly contended that at Borodino he hesitated and was lost.

If, however, I admire the commander of our dashing First Army for accepting a crushing responsibility, not only without tremor but with a smile, I admire the General Staff just as much, though in quite another way, for the eager and positive loyalty with which they labour untiringly to impress all outsiders with the idea that Kuroki thinks of everything for himself whilst his assistants are merely the blind and passive instruments of his authority. What a contrast to some of us, who, without wielding one tithe of the power of the Japanese General Staff, are quite ready to encourage the inferences of our admiring friends that the General was the puppet whilst we were the true originators of any success which for once in a way the poor man may chance to have achieved. If ever I get back safe to England and people ask me, "What are the lessons of the Manchurian War?" I ought, if I have the pluck of a mouse, most certainly to reply, "To change our characters, my dear friend, so that you and I may become less jealous and egotistical, and more loyal and disinterested towards our own brother officers. This is the greatest lesson of the war."

By 8.30 A.M. the Second Division were holding on like grim death to what they had won, and that was all they could do. The right of their attack had effected a lodgment on the summit of the high mountain overlooking the Tangho, but the crest of the same mountain in front of their left and left centre was still in the hands of the enemy. Here the Russian fire had become so heavy as almost to drown the single reports of the Japanese rifles.

Later on in the day I heard that at this juncture the situation was specially critical, inasmuch as the Russian right was not only containing the Japanese left, but also threatening to roll up their centre and right.

## The Battle of the Twenty-sixth of August 47

A happier complexion was, however, soon put upon the combat by a mountain battery which, since 8 A.M., had been trying to help the right centre of the Japanese infantry from the crest of the great ridge, by firing occasionally in the direction of Amping (*see* Sketch XVII.). So far they had not done much good, as the fire of the Russian field-guns had been too much for them. Now, however, finding themselves threatened on their left flank, they withdrew a few yards so as to put the crest line between them and the opposing batteries near Tsuigo and opened fire in every direction; just, as a lieutenant-colonel put it to me, like a bundle of squibs. Then, not content with a mere defensive action, two of these pop-guns, for they are little more, proceeded to give a very striking example of the mighty power of artillery when quite unopposed by its own arm.

It was ten o'clock when the two guns were withdrawn from the main ridge, and were brought down into the bottom of the valley, where they advanced through some millet fields to within about one mile of the obstinate Russians (at "T"). There was no difficulty in following the subsequent action. From Gokarei both sides were clearly revealed by a pair of good glasses. The Russian trenches ran a short distance below the summit of the mountain, having evidently been placed there instead of on the crest line, so as to cover ground which would otherwise have been dead. From one point of view such an arrangement was good; indeed, it was necessary. From another it was weak, inasmuch as the trenches leaned forward towards the valley as if inviting a howitzer to lob a shell into them. There may seem to be some inconsistency in saying at the same time that an arrangement was necessary and that it was faulty. The explanation is of course that the military art is not so easy as a tyro might imagine it to be, and that perfect, flawless defence by field-works of a natural position is a sheer impossibility.

The Japanese had been gradually climbing the slopes and occupying knoll after knoll, but had not been able, during the past hour, to make any further progress. The heaviest fire came from the penultimate peak or knoll of mountain "T" (*see* sketch), under shelter of which about two Japanese battalions were engaging the Russian trenches at a range of 500 yards.* Covered by this infantry fire, groups of from ten to twenty men had been working up independently to closer quarters, and had gradually collected into three large, irregular-shaped, mud-coloured mobs, crouching in depressions which gave them cover from fire, within 200 yards from the trenches immediately west of "T," and from the actual summit which was ringed round with a very conspicuous excavation.

When the little groups rushed and climbed and crept upwards, they made no attempt to use their rifles, but trusted entirely to the covering fire of the battalions behind the spur. I was too far to notice this myself, but I heard it in the afternoon from an officer who had been with them. I was able, however, to see that the three big mobs were glued fast to their cover, and that the fire from the trenches was exceedingly heavy.

I suppose the Russians were too much absorbed in their desperate musketry conflict to notice the two little guns creeping up through the millet; otherwise,

---

* I heard later on in the day that the Japanese losses here, and in the assaulting columns, had amounted to some 40 officers and 600 men.

at a range of 1700 yards, they should have been able to plaster them with rifle bullets. Strange it is to think what agencies the Almighty employs to change the face of history or to humble a nation's pride. Sometimes it may be one single valiant private soldier who, by a mere cry or gesture, inspires his comrades with hope in the hour of their blackest despair; sometimes a shower of rain may cast one empire into mourning for the loss of its bravest and its best and raise another to a pinnacle of power and pride; this time, so it seemed to me, the instruments chosen were just a couple of mountain guns. It was 10.20 when the guns opened on the Russian position, catching it obliquely and dropping one high explosive shell after another bang into the trenches. The enemy did not seem to be able to stand this at all. They began to give way all along the line, and quitted their cover a dozen at a time to gain the shelter of the sky-line. Sooner or later, under such insistence from the artillery, they were almost bound to go; so at least it seemed to me. The Japanese gunners worked very methodically, beginning with the ringed work round the top of the peak, and carrying on along the trenches from south to north, dropping their high explosive shells, in the proportion of about one to every three fired, actually into the works. It was a beautiful piece of gunnery practice to witness, but I could not help thinking of the bitterness of heart of the Russian officers as their men were thus forced to give way.

So soon as the Russians had all vacated their trenches and were crouching behind the crest line, then the ground in front of the Japanese storming parties became once more dead.

Now was the time, and sure enough, at 11 A.M., the

mud-coloured blot on which my glasses were fixed, suddenly sent out the steely sparkle of hundreds of bayonets and then changed its irregular rounded form into that of a long thin winding snake-like column pressing up the spur with a sun-flag waving at its head. The mountain guns now ceased fire, and the Russians stood up on the sky-line to empty their magazines at the approaching Japanese. At this moment, the little banner detached itself, a spot of dancing life-like colour, and raced forward alone a clear distance of eighty or one hundred yards in advance of the forlorn hope. A splendid feat of arms! Every moment we looked to see it fall; but no, the Russians disappeared, the firing ceased, the flag waved on the very sharp spiked summit of the peak. Then the firing recommenced, but now only with the single reports denoting that the rifles were pointing away from the listener.

My glasses had been fixed on the right storming party, but apparently the two crowds of men I had noticed to the left had assaulted simultaneously, for looking along the crest line I could now see the Japanese everywhere in possession, and at least half a dozen of their flags planted at intervals on the highest peaks of the range. We must have our Jacks too for our next bit of fighting. The whole army becomes inspirited by seeing the advance of the beloved emblem of their country, and although on this occasion the artillery did not fire up to the very last moment, it seemed to me that, with such a conspicuous mark to denote the head of the column, they ought to have been able to do so without having much fear of damaging their own men.

The Second Division had now occupied the whole of the Russian position, and the enemy's centre was broken. Bravo the brave Second! These men of the north are the biggest, bravest and least clever men in Japan. They are the Bœotians of the Far East. They stand a head and shoulders above the ordinary Japanese to be met with on a railway platform in Tokio or in the streets of London, and in build and muscular development would be very hard to beat anywhere. Many Japanese would strongly question their pre-eminence in bravery, but I use the word here in the English and not the Celtic sense. Other Divisions may do more dashing feats, but the Second are solid, stolid and unimaginative, and although it would never occur to them, as it might, for instance, to the men of the Twelfth Division, to court danger for its own sake, yet they can meet it with supreme indifference whenever it crosses their path.

It was about this time that a friend in high places said to me: "The news which has just come in from the Twelfth Division is good, but not quite so good as we had hoped. The right brigade, under Kigoshi, which stormed the northern part of Kosarei, is still fighting desperately, and is unable to carry the southern part of the mountain. The left brigade of the Twelfth Division has advanced as far as Chipanling and Papanling, driving the enemy before it. The Second Division has now succeeded in occupying the ground held by the enemy's centre. Marshal Kuroki has still some hope, therefore, that the Twelfth and Second Divisions may yet make good before nightfall the right bank of the Tangho. The Guards are at present fighting across the upper waters of that river, and if they can only manage to give the enemy a handsome beating they may perhaps be able to reach Kohoshi before dark." (Map XXII.)

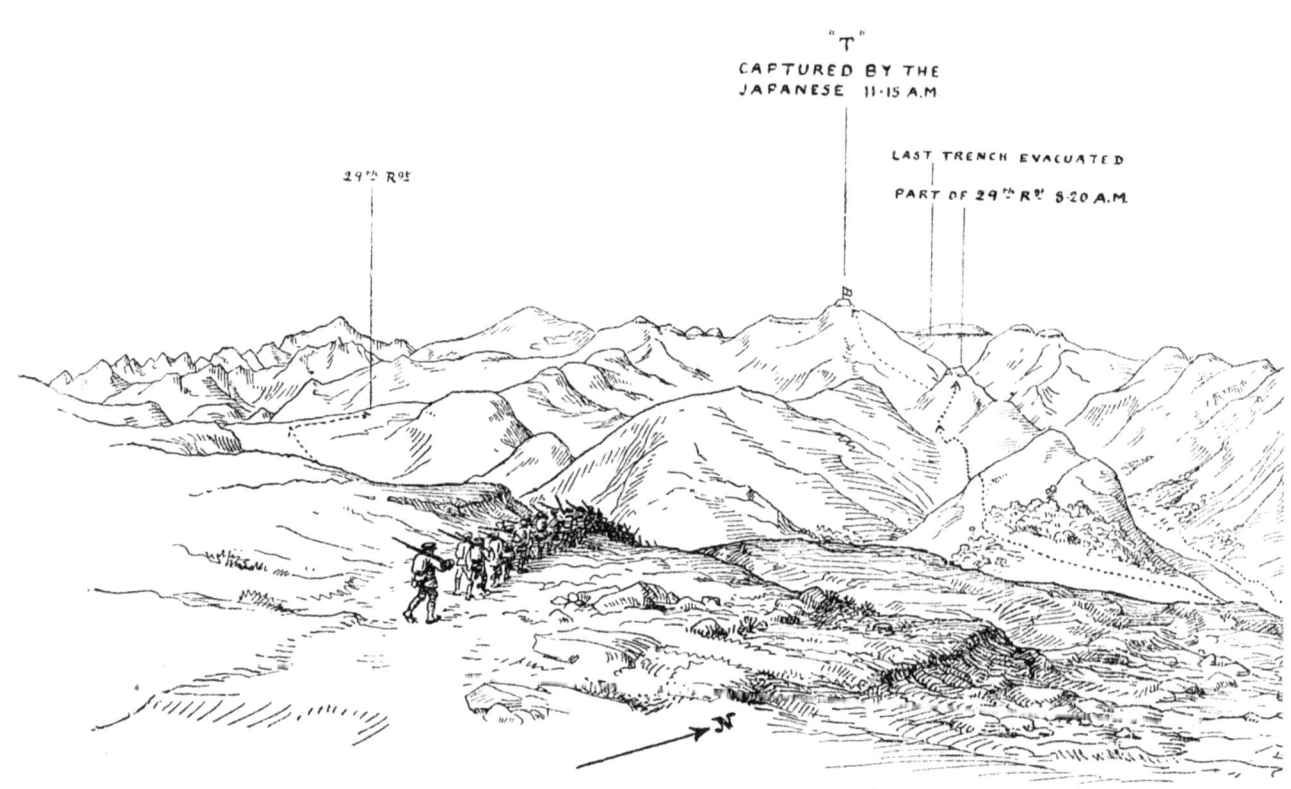

View of the Russian Position South of Kiuchorei (Kungchangling) taken

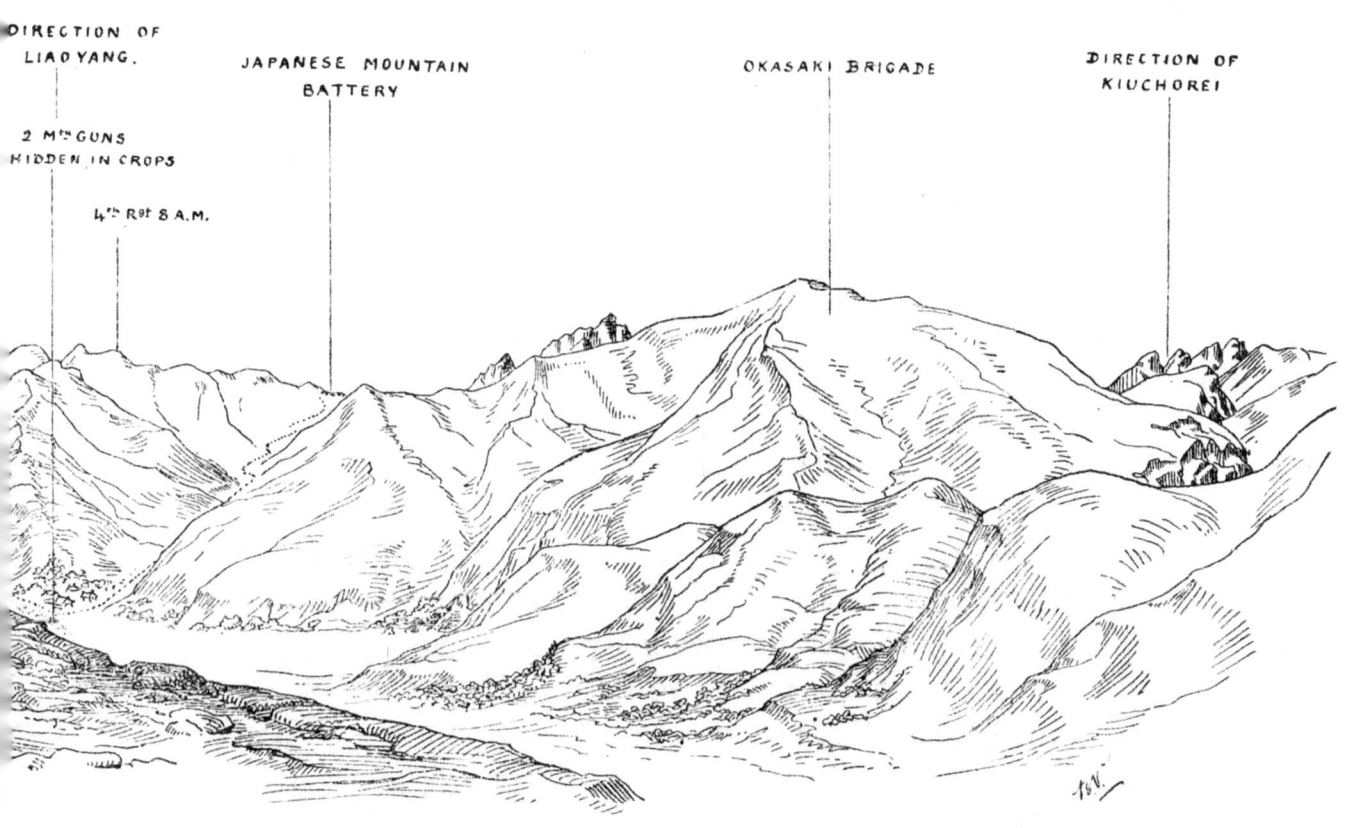

BY THE 2ND DIVISION 1ST ARMY BETWEEN 4 A.M. AND 11.15 A.M., AUGUST 26, 1904

A few minutes later, a German-speaking officer came in to report that detachments of the Fourth Army were now visible from the extreme left of the First Army. After he had delivered his message, I engaged him in conversation, and learnt that the left brigade of the Guards, having made a wide turning movement, was now marching north-east and endeavouring to outflank the Russian right, which was a mile or two south of Kohoshi. I told him the marshal commanding hoped that the Guards might occupy Kohoshi before dark, when he replied that he expected the Guards were by now too busy defending themselves to give much thought to Kohoshi. By 11 A.M. the musketry to our front had quite died away, and only the bursting of Russian shells over the summit of the ridge, which the Second Division had just captured, and the artillery duel between the Guards and the Russian right, eleven miles away to the west, showed that fighting was still going on.

At 1 P.M. an adjutant of Kuroki's came back from the front, and reported that in one hour's time a road would be cut through the mountains enabling the field artillery to get up into position on the big ridge to our front and fire on the retreating Russians.

The General Staff asked many eager questions of the adjutant, and made no secret of their opinions that the Russian retirement was being admirably well done. It seems that the whole of their line fell back simultaneously, and in so doing concentrated on Amping. Had each Russian unit acted independently the Japanese detachments already in close contact with them might have pressed on independently in pursuit. As it was, however, the Russians not only maintained their cohesion, but drew closer together

# The Battle of the Twenty-sixth of August 53

with every step they took towards Amping, during which movement they were covered by a heavy fire from twenty-four guns posted north of Chuchaputsu. The Japanese had no guns wherewith to reply, except the mountain battery whose exploits have just been narrated; and, moreover, they were still in some disorder after having delivered the assault. I do not myself think that a pursuit would have had any result beyond heavy losses to the pursuers until it could be supported by artillery. The troops had been marching, climbing, fighting, charging for over twelve hours. They had only four small mountain guns in position. The enemy had given way, it is true, but had not been put to headlong flight or apparently been demoralised to any great extent. They were concentrating on Amping under the protection of a powerful artillery. Kuroki did well to leave them alone.

From the moment it was decided that the Second Division was not to pursue, the battlefield became less interesting, for it was not possible to keep up a great deal of excitement about exchanges of shell between the Guards and the Russian right wing at a distance of over ten miles from our point of observation. A fine, chilly rain began to fall, and I got under the lee of a small but thick hazel bush, and pulled out of my haversack a weekly *Times*, dated July 1st, which has been a record delivery up to date. It contained a long letter from Tolstoi. I see he considers that aggressive nations can be appeased, or shamed, or tired out, by constantly inviting them to smite the other cheek. I doubt if the great writer fully appreciates the insatiate hunger for cheek-smiting which gnaws at the vitals of certain sections of mankind. If the Russian people possessed the docile, spiritless characters with which he would fain see them endowed, their Empire would soon be parcelled out and divided between more martial races.

At 5.30 P.M., one of the Staff came and sat under my bush, observing that an old campaigner always secures the best shelter from the storm. He told me that the chief anxiety was now about the First Brigade of the Guards under Asada, who, in endeavouring to turn the extreme right of the Russians, had got too far away from the Second Brigade under Watanabe. Asada seemed to be in some peril as there was a formidable concentration against him, and when the latest news came to hand he was reported as being only just able to hold his own, pending the arrival of the Army Reserves from Tiensuitien at 8.30 A.M.

On the other flank of the Japanese line of battle, Kigoshi's Twenty-third Brigade has done a magnificent feat of arms.

The ridge of Kosarei, which somewhat resembles a glorified Cæsar's camp at Ladysmith, rises 1600 feet above the Taitsuho—the last 150 yards of the ascent being so steep as to render any idea of an ordinary assault by daylight quite hopeless. The Japanese advanced up the northern ridge of this mountain, painfully climbing—sometimes on hands and knees. The Russian picquets, seeing that there was no firing, mistook them for a mere reconnaissance, and did not immediately give a general alarm or hurry up reserves to the threatened spot to man the trenches. On the contrary, their outposts kept steadily falling back, occasionally halting to fire or roll down rocks, and imagining apparently that the Japanese would be frightened away, or at least

# The Battle of the Twenty-sixth of August

that they would pause to reply. But Kigoshi continued his advance inexorably, silently; until, without halt or haste, he reached the northern extremity of the summit, and, wheeling southwards, marched down the narrow back of the mountain, still—as the saying is—as death. No shout was raised. Not a shot was fired. But those of the enemy who lingered were overwhelmed by the steel-crested wave. Picquets, supports and reserves were swept away one after the other before the dread onslaught, like straws before a torrent. No one on the Russian side seems clearly to have realised the terrible, imminent danger, and Kigoshi, pressing on, never gave his opponents one moment to think, or to rally, or to take up any fixed line of defence.

At last, in the grey of dawn, the Japanese reached a spot where the back of the mountain narrows into the ledge with almost precipitous sides which forms the actual pass of Kosarei. There was a battery of Russian guns on the other side of the ledge within a few yards. The guns could not be switched on to the Japanese, as they could only, owing to their position and the formation of the ground, fire eastwards in the direction from which an attack had been anticipated, and not northwards in the direction from which the sudden Kigoshi had now mysteriously appeared. But the ledge was so narrow that a few Russian riflemen, lying amongst stones on the southern side, were able to check a further advance, and once the defenders got breathing-space they seemed to be immediately able to organise a stout resistance.

Since 7.20 A.M., in fact, when the advance of Kigoshi had been arrested for the first time, not one yard had he gained! The Russians were at bay behind rocks on the south side of the rocky ledge, and the Japanese could not get beyond the cover of some rocks at fifty yards distance from the same ledge on its northern side. Kigoshi, from his last message, seemed to have little hope of forcing a passage until after dark. The battery was under fire from both sides. Neither could the Russians remove the guns or the Japanese definitely capture them.

I think General Kuroki is fairly easy in his mind. The capture of the whole of the Kosarei mountain has not been achieved, it is true, but the possession of even its northern half enables Kigoshi to threaten the communications of every Russian east of the Tangho. (*See* Map XXII.)

Sasaki's Twelfth Brigade of the Twelfth Division has captured Papanling and Chipanling without much trouble or loss.

The Second Division has stormed, and now holds, the formidable line of mountain called Kungshan, immediately overlooking Amping, which is only four or five miles distant.

The Guards' Second Brigade, under Watanabe, have been brought to a standstill opposite Daidenshi on the main Pekin road, but should by now have been joined by the Army Reserve, consisting of the 29th Kobi from Tiensuitien.

The Guards' First Brigade, under Asada, on the extreme left of the line, is causing much greater anxiety. The Russian extreme right is entrenched on the hills forming the western slopes of the valley, through which flow the upper waters of the Tangho. Asada's Brigade had marched north-west from Tashinpou with the intention of outflanking and turning these entrenchments. In executing the movement they have lost touch with the Second Brigade under Watanabe, and whilst thus isolated their attack has not only been repulsed, but they are in danger of being surrounded by reinforcements which the Russians are rushing down the main road from Liaoyang.

To sum up: The division and a half forming our centre and right centre have been definitely successful and have occupied the enemy's positions. Our extreme right is still fighting, but has already carried a point which dominates the battlefield to the east of the Tangho. Our left centre can make no impression on the enemy, and the left finds itself in a perilous situation.

Without in any way wishing to depreciate the painstaking preparations of the Japanese leaders, or the unfailing valour of their men, it may be admitted, I think, that they have owed something to Dame Fortune on this eventful day. Had Kigoshi failed to carry the northern half of the Kosarei ridge, I feel, having seen the ground and considering the bad position of affairs in front of the Guards on our left, that it might not have been possible for the centre and right centre to maintain their success. They had, according to their intention, driven a wedge into the enemy's centre. But the wedge could make no further headway beyond the positions actually carried, and if it had been threatened on both flanks by the Russians holding on to right and left of them, they would very possibly have had to fall back. But the seizure by Kigoshi of the northern half of the Kosarei ridge relieved them of all fear on their most exposed flank, and at the same time threatened the Russian communications and line of retreat. Therefore every one here feels confident and happy, even although they may be a little anxious about the Guards.

All these sanguine anticipations are based on Kigoshi's brilliant stroke on the right far more than on the victory of the Second Division which I have just seen and described. How, then, did Kigoshi come to take those almost inaccessible crags upon which his Rising Sun flag now so proudly floats? If the first Russian detachments encountered half-way down the slopes of Kosarei had made a resistance sufficiently stubborn to enable the defenders of the steeper upper section of the ridge to man their prepared lines of sangars, then (as they showed later under less favourable conditions and with half the ridge already torn from their grasp) they were capable of offering a resistance to the Japanese which they might have found it impossible to overcome. But it was fated to be otherwise, and as at the mountain of Makurayama on the 31st of July, so to-day—or rather, I may now say, yesterday, for it is past midnight—the carelessness and bad leading of an outpost have been, humanly speaking, the cause of the defeat of a great army.

It was not until 6 P.M. that I descended the steep western slopes of the Gokarei mountain, together with Kuroki and the Headquarters Staff. The rain fell in torrents as we floundered through the mud as far as this hovel. Water comes trickling through the roof, but I am indeed thrice fortunate to be one of the very, very few out of the tens of thousands of Russians and Japanese in our neighbourhood who has a roof over him at all. Alas for the poor wounded. Rain is a cruel torment to badly wounded men. Do I not still recall with a shudder the anguish of the biting cold and of the heavy raindrops falling, falling all night long, on my sun-blistered face as I lay outstretched on the veldt beneath Majuba?

## CHAPTER XXI

### THE RUSSIANS RETIRE

KOKAHOSHI, *August 27th*, 1904.—Slept soundly till 8 A.M. It was then wet and misty. Guns were firing at intervals near us, but they must have made random shooting, as it is not possible to see further than 100 yards. In the direction of the Imperial Guards the artillery fire is heavy and continuous, so I suppose there is not so much fog to westwards. All the soldiers here look pale and tired. Their knapsacks had been left behind when they started on the night of the 25th to make their night attack, and their thin khaki is soaked and clinging clammily to their limbs. Nevertheless, they manage to be cheerful whilst making their morning toilette by the banks of the muddy streamlet. Many of them are wounded, but none the less happy on that account unless they suspect that the doctor may take too serious a view of such a trifle as a bayonet wound in the eye or a bullet through the foot, and put them temporarily on the shelf. For the tenth time at least I must write down that the Japanese infantry consist of superb material. Guileless as children, brave as lions, their constant ruling thought is to do their duty by their ancestors and by the Emperor.

The fog seemed to become more dense as the morning wore on, and the Second Division, in the midst of whom I had slept, did not dare advance blindfold into the unknown. I watched many wounded being brought down the valley, and amongst them several Russians. They had all been lying in the rain and were in a pitiful state, caked with mud and blood. I also saw rows of dead Japanese being burnt. A colonel who was amongst them was honoured by having his bonfire a little apart from the others.

At midday I went in to have some food, and learnt that the Russian left had cleared during the night, leaving Kigoshi's Brigade in possession of the precipitous ledge of rock at Kosarei, and of the guns, as well as the whole of the southern half of the mountain. The Twelfth Division is now supposed to be advancing against Amping from the north, but the Guards are still in difficulties, and are unable to make good their objective.

After a *bento* of good hot rice I rode with Sergeant Watanabe to the headquarters, and, obtaining permission to see what I could, made my way, after a stiff climb, to some of the trenches captured yesterday. Here I found a battalion of Japanese infantry peering out into the opaque mist-curtain which was so perversely preventing them from carrying on the fight. They seemed already to have recovered from their fatigue, and looked as bright and keen as if they were about to start on a campaign instead of being perhaps not more than half-way through a very big battle.

Once or twice the fog lifted for a tantalising second or two, enabling us to catch a glimpse of the winding Tangho flowing far away beneath us. Then, at four o'clock, suddenly, there came a great puff of wind from the west, tearing into shreds the mist-veil, and transforming it from a blinding obstruction into many trailing streamers of radiant, silvery vapour. As a fair landscape may instantaneously be flashed by a magic-lantern on to a sheet which until then was vacant, ugly and meaningless, so now the blank wall of mist in one second made way for many chequered patterns of dark green crops, golden river sand and trembling blue water, all framed about by innumerable tall, spiked, pyramidal mountains of jade (*see* Sketch XVIII.).

No sooner did the fairy-like panorama of mountain, river, plain and flying mist start to our eyes than it drew from the Japanese a thundering salute fired by the eighteen field guns on the ridge to my right, for there in the middle of the scene were the principal actors, a retreating army apparently caught in a trap. We could clearly see the Russian camps on the flat sands near Amping; camps which were being hurriedly struck before our eyes, and we could distinguish also long columns creeping slowly up and down the right bank of the river like leaden *Kriegspiel* blocks being pushed by a hesitating player over the map. Even more exciting and more significant was the sight of a narrow, dark line spanning the Tangho, towards which these columns were evidently making their way. Under my glasses this object revealed itself as a trestle bridge crowded with troops, whilst a brigade at least seemed to be waiting at the eastern end for its turn to cross and put the broad river betwixt them and the Japanese. Eight or nine miles to the north of us a big fight was in full flame over all the valleys and ridges leading down from the Kosarei ridge to Amping, and it was clear that Kigoshi's Brigade of the Twelfth Division was pressing down at best speed in hopes of cutting off the rear-guard of the Russians.

The whole of the Second Division had plunged down the mountain side the moment the fog lifted. But their field guns were fully five and a half miles distant from the bridge, and were practically out of range of even the nearest Russian infantry, so the Japanese infantry could not look to much assistance from them, seeing that it was not possible to advance them any further without making a road. The mountain battery which did such good work yesterday was, however, available, and followed the advancing Second Division as fast as it could.

Soon after 5 P.M. the firing seemed to slacken in the valleys north of Amping, and large columns of Russians debouched from them, making for the bridge and for fords in the river.

At 5.30 it looked as if there was a fair prospect that the artillery of the Twelfth Division, and perhaps some of the infantry of the Second Division as well as their mountain battery, might get within range of the bridge before the bulk of the Russians could get across it. Had they succeeded, a second Beresina tragedy would have overwhelmed nigh on a Division of Russians. There was still an hour and a half of daylight and almost anything was possible. But as these thoughts crossed my mind, two batteries of the enemy's artillery unlimbered on the open sand, close by the main camp which was now nearly struck, and almost immediately I saw eight white puffs of smoke over a point of the northern ridge down which the Twelfth Division was pressing; then a couple of groups of four just to steady the Second Division, and steadied they were! The Japanese either halted, or advanced double-slow time, whilst several great masses of Russians emerged from behind a low bluff by Amping

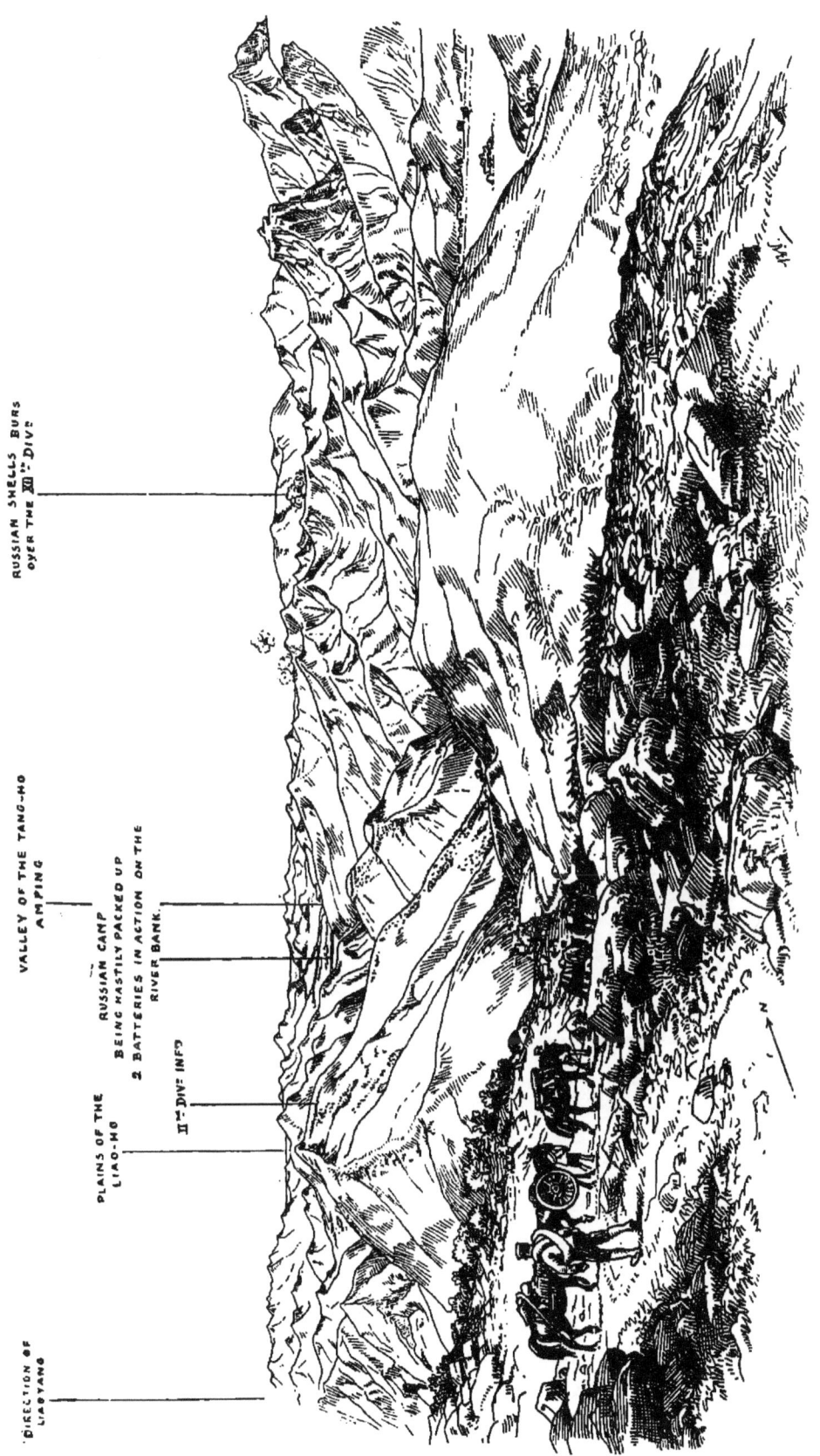

BATTLE OF LIAOYANG

FIRST GLIMPSE OF THE PLAINS, AUGUST 27, 1904
THE 2ND DIVISION 1ST ARMY ADVANCING TOWARDS THE TANG-HO

XVIII

## The Russians Retire

and forded the river. The enemy had now practically got clear away.

At 6.45 P.M. a single horseman appeared galloping over the sand on the right bank of the river for all he was worth. I cannot imagine what he can have been doing. The Japanese must be rather uncomfortably near him. However, he escapes. This is the last of the Russians on the right bank of the Tangho. The great Marquis Oyama has been duly obeyed.

Meanwhile several Russian batteries were firing heavily and covering the retirement. Yet another exemplification of the power of artillery when unopposed by artillery, culled this time from a successful withdrawal by the enemy. When I got back here, tired and wet, but extraordinarily happy, I found —— in much anxiety about my long absence. Evidently he thinks I should not have gone off independently, even with Headquarters' permission. However, nothing can disturb my equanimity on such a day as this. He tells me that the Guards have also been able to advance to-day, and have occupied Sanjago and Kohoshi.* It seems that the almost victorious Russians who were surrounding Asada and repulsing Watanabe were forced to retire on account of the success of the Second and Twelfth Divisions. Nevertheless, Kuroki is not quite happy about his left, and he therefore marches early to-morrow for Roshisan, whence he will be able to keep in personal touch with the Imperial Guards. I am to go with him.

To bed, therefore, although it is with reluctance that I prepare to loose my grip of the exciting consciousness that I have to-day seen the most stupendous spectacle that it is possible for mortal brain to conceive.

* Sanchiakou and Kaofengtsu (*see* Map XXII.).

Asia advancing; Europe falling back; the wall of mist and the writing thereon.

ROSHISAN,* *August 28th*, 1904.—Started at 7 A.M. and marched with Kuroki and all the Headquarters Staff, heading westwards towards Roshisan. It was a lovely day, and as we rode through a very mountainous picturesque country I saw two eagles quartering the ground in search of prey. During halts on the march to rest the horses I wrote down the fragments of conversation which follow:

"The enemy had some remarkably good chances of attacking on either flank, but lost them all through want of initiative. On our left he did manifest some energy, and thereby made us feel exceedingly uncomfortable. Marshal Kuroki had foreseen this danger and took it upon himself to express to the Marquis Oyama a strong opinion that the army of Manchuria should detach some special body of troops to watch our left flank during the movement we were ordered to undertake. The Generalissimo did not, however, accept this opinion. It was probably necessary to refuse the request, but it does seem a pity that our left flank could not have been shielded, if not directly then indirectly; if not tactically then at least strategically. Suppose the attack of the Second and Fourth Armies had hung fire from any unforeseen cause, then several Divisions of Russians could have been moved up the main road against our left! However, all is well that ends well, and certainly the enemy missed his greatest opportunity by neglecting to deliver a stroke against our exposed right and right rear from the direction of Penchiho (*see* Map XXIII.). Marshal Kuroki had never felt happy in his mind about this detachment of

* Langtsushan.

Russians, which consisted of at least one regiment of infantry, one battery of field artillery, and several thousand cavalry, and he disliked the idea of leaving it behind him at Penchiho in a position so threatening to our advance. He had therefore worked out a complete scheme for breaking up the Russian detachments both at Chaotao and Penchiho, but at the very last moment, and with the utmost misgiving and regret, he was forced to abandon the idea and turn all his attention to the task of co-operating with the Fourth and Second Armies. However, we might have spared ourselves sleepless nights, for the formidable Penchiho contingent has retired quite inoffensively and quietly with the remainder of the troops towards Liaoyang.

"During the night of the 26th, the enemy in front of the Second and Fourth Armies began to fall back from Anshantien. We only got the news at 6.23 P.M. on the 27th—yesterday. This movement was entirely unexpected, and had never seriously entered into our calculations. We, in common with the rest of the world, I imagine, recognised Anshantien to be quite the best defensive position which could be found between Kaiping and Liaoyang. It is also a matter of common knowledge that the enemy had expended an immense amount of energy, time and money in adding to the natural strength of the place by field-works and defences of every description. We would not of ourselves venture to ascribe so important a withdrawal of the enemy to the merits of the First Army, but Marshal Marquis Oyama, in his telegram announcing the retirement, specifically says that it seems to be due to the highly honourable battle fought by us on the 25th and on the 26th, and that he therefore has pleasure in giving us his congratulations. So great a compliment must spur us to still greater exertions, and accordingly, Marshal Kuroki issued orders to our army last night that they must form up to-day, at all costs and regardless of the enemy's position, with their right resting on the Taitsuho by Shobioshi and their line running thence through Daisekimonrei down to Shosansi on the left."

About midday we arrived at our destination, Roshisan, quite an important village—almost a town. I was told off to my quarters in a farmhouse half a mile away from headquarters, which is inconvenient. There was heavy fighting going on four or five miles to the north, but I could not get permission to go out to it. The firing, I was told, was due merely to the retiring Russians fighting a rear-guard action, the details of which did not concern the Headquarters Staff. In vain I represented that a rear-guard action was just the very description of fighting I most especially wished to study. I was informed that my horse was very exhausted, and so, although he had just tried to buck me off, I did not argue the point any further, as I saw that, for some reason or another, it was considered undesirable that I should go.

I was glad afterwards I had been able to submit with a good grace, for at 6.30 P.M. a kind young officer, who evidently had felt for my disappointment, came in to see me and to console me by giving me the latest news.

The first and most important item was that at midday, just as Marshal Kuroki arrived at his quarters, he was handed a telegram from Oyama's Chief of the Staff informing him that the Second Army hoped to reach that day a line extending from the Shaho[*] to the

[*] Not to be confounded with the Shaho north of Liaoyang.

river Liao, and the Fourth Army a line extending from Tentauyuan to Tsaofantun. The First Army must, therefore, conform by pressing on without a moment's delay to the south bank of the Taitsuho, and there prepare to make an immediate crossing.

These instructions constituted what may fairly be described as a tall order. The First Army was at the moment facing north-west, and was engaged in fighting with the enemy, over a front of some twenty miles, amidst the most broken, difficult terrain it is possible to imagine. It was no light task to break off the struggle or to give a fresh direction to a front so extended. Nevertheless, my young friend made light of all difficulties, and laughed at the long face I had pulled in sympathy with the dilemma in which I felt his chief must now be placed.

Modifications to the orders issued last night have already been issued, and are to the following effect:

The Guards are to take up a line from Mokabo to a hill a short distance north-west of Yayuchi; the Second Division are to occupy Sekishoshi with their main force and push out their left until it gets into touch with the Guards: the Twelfth Division are to make good Shobyoshi and are to be prepared to cross the river between Kuyentai and Sakan. My friend added, and I wrote down: "These are our intentions, but it depends, of course, upon the enemy whether they can be carried into effect. I may tell you that at headquarters they are not very sanguine that the Guards can now possibly succeed in carrying out their part of the programme, seeing that only an hour and a half ago the enemy was fighting hard and did not seem inclined to yield even one yard of ground, whereas our men must drive them back at least six miles if they are to bivouac according to their orders. Our chief is, however, more hopeful that the Second and Twelfth Divisions will be able to do their share of the business."

It was now half-past seven, and I begged my visitor to stay and have something for the good of my new house. He smiled and said he had already been too long away from headquarters, and that he must get back to where he could combine the operations of working and eating.

I asked him if he thought he could get me permission to ride out and see the Guards fighting through to their position to-morrow, but he acknowledged that, in anticipation of some such request being put forward by me, he had been instructed to advise me to content myself with going over the positions held by the Guards and Russians on the battle of the 26th. "It will be far more valuable for you," he urged, "than to be scrambling about under shell fire seeing a few groups of infantry executing manœuvres of which you will not understand the full meaning. You have Colonel Hume with the Guards Divisional Headquarters, and he will keep you informed as to the details of the fight. If you go out with an officer of the General Staff to-morrow morning and inspect the positions, some one from headquarters will be sure to see you on your return and tell you how the battle progresses in other parts of the field."

Fortune has been my guide and staff during this pilgrimage through Manchuria, and I can but follow her blindly and hope for the best. I did not therefore even struggle against my fate and tried to swallow my disappointment as if I were enjoying its bitter flavour.

ROSHISAN, *August 29th*, 1904.—A message has come over to say that, if I will defer my start for the battlefield until 11 A.M. and call at headquarters on my way out, I will be posted up in all the latest news.

—— is in low spirits to-day. He says, "*C'est le moment fort délicat.*" I think our *moment délicat* was the 26th instant, and that prospects improve with every mile of our advance, for the three armies are now almost in touch, and support should surely be forthcoming from Oyama if we find ourselves in a place too tight for us.

10 P.M.—I saw one of the Staff on my way out to the battlefield, and took down the following, verbatim:

"Before you visit the scene of the struggle of the 26th between the Guards and the Russians, I am authorised to give you some further instruction. All goes well. Notwithstanding the sudden change of plan which was sprung upon us by Manchurian Army Headquarters at midday yesterday,* the Twelfth Division was last night able to make good its new point without much fighting. The Headquarters and main force of the Second Division were not so fortunate They were delayed by fog to begin with, and then they found very few practicable fords over the Tangho. Moreover, the Russians offered a stubborn resistance, not only to the crossing, but also to the further advance up the hills on the western bank of the river. Consequently, General Nishi's main body has only succeeded in making good a hill a very short distance to the north of Sandiasi (Sketch XIX.).

"The left brigade of the Second Division (Matsunaga's Third Brigade) has, however, had much better luck. It made a night attack on the enemy north of

* See Orders on p. 67.

Sandiasi, and after some stiff fighting captured that position. Not content with a success, which would have been considered brilliant at the beginning of the war, Matsunaga managed to press on in pursuit all through the night, climbing lofty mountains and scrambling across ravines until, just as dawn was breaking, he occupied the highest peak of the Sekimonrei range (marked 243 on Map XXII.). In answer to our warm congratulations he has just sent back a message, saying that from this captured peak he can see the promised land stretching out before him, and the fair city of Liaoyang itself encircling the famous pagoda (Sketch XX.). In fact, he has become quite poetical!

"Lastly, we come to the Imperial Guards, whose progress has been disappointing. They vigorously attacked a Russian brigade which lay across their line of advance at Weizugo,* but the enemy had three successive prepared positions and offered a stubborn resistance. Consequently, the Guards have only succeeded in reaching a line, Shihodai-Shosanshi, and cannot at present get any further (Map XXII.). They report, moreover, that the line they were ordered to take up, namely, Mokabo-Yayuchi, appears to be the very position selected by the Russians for more formidable defences than any yet encountered. However, we shall see about that later on. Meanwhile, the Guards cavalry, working wide on their left, has got into touch with the cavalry of the Fourth Army at Kunshintai. Thus, you see, good and evil fairly balance one another.

"The Twelfth Division has done all that they were asked to do. The main body of the Second Division has fallen short of its objective by six miles, but, to counterbalance this shortcoming, Matsunaga's Brigade has exceeded its orders, and instead of merely linking

* Chinese, Weichiakou.

up with the Guards, has seized a commanding point considerably in advance of their right.

"The Imperial Guards Division is the only one which has not succeeded at any point in carrying out its orders. There is no help for this, and more cannot be expected from any troops than to fight three actions against a strong rear-guard, within as many miles, and to win them each time. It seems probable, too, that the threatening advance of Matsunaga behind the left of the troops engaged with the Guards will facilitate to-day's advance. On the whole then, Marshal Kuroki is well satisfied.

"You must not forget that each of our Divisions is faced by a Russian Division, and that the enemy have moreover two full Divisions in reserve. We have lost comparatively few men the last two days, but we lost 2000 on the 26th instant. The Second Division suffered severely in the night attack. For instance, the 4th Regiment lost its Colonel and the three Battalion Commanders.

"To-day the Fourth Army will advance to the line it was thought they might have occupied yesterday, viz.: Saka (Shaho) to Shuisenpu (*see* Map XXIII.). The Second Army should certainly reach the line from Shaho to the river Liao. It is desired by Manchurian headquarters that the First Army should take up a line from the right of the Fourth Army at Shuisenpu to the end of the mountains on the south bank of the Taitsuho at Kotagai.* But the enemy is occupying this very line of mountains from Shuisenpu by Mokabo, and his trenches follow the crests of the ridges in a north-easterly direction down to the Taitsuho at Kotagai.

"The position of the enemy would be enormously

* Chinese, Houtachieh.

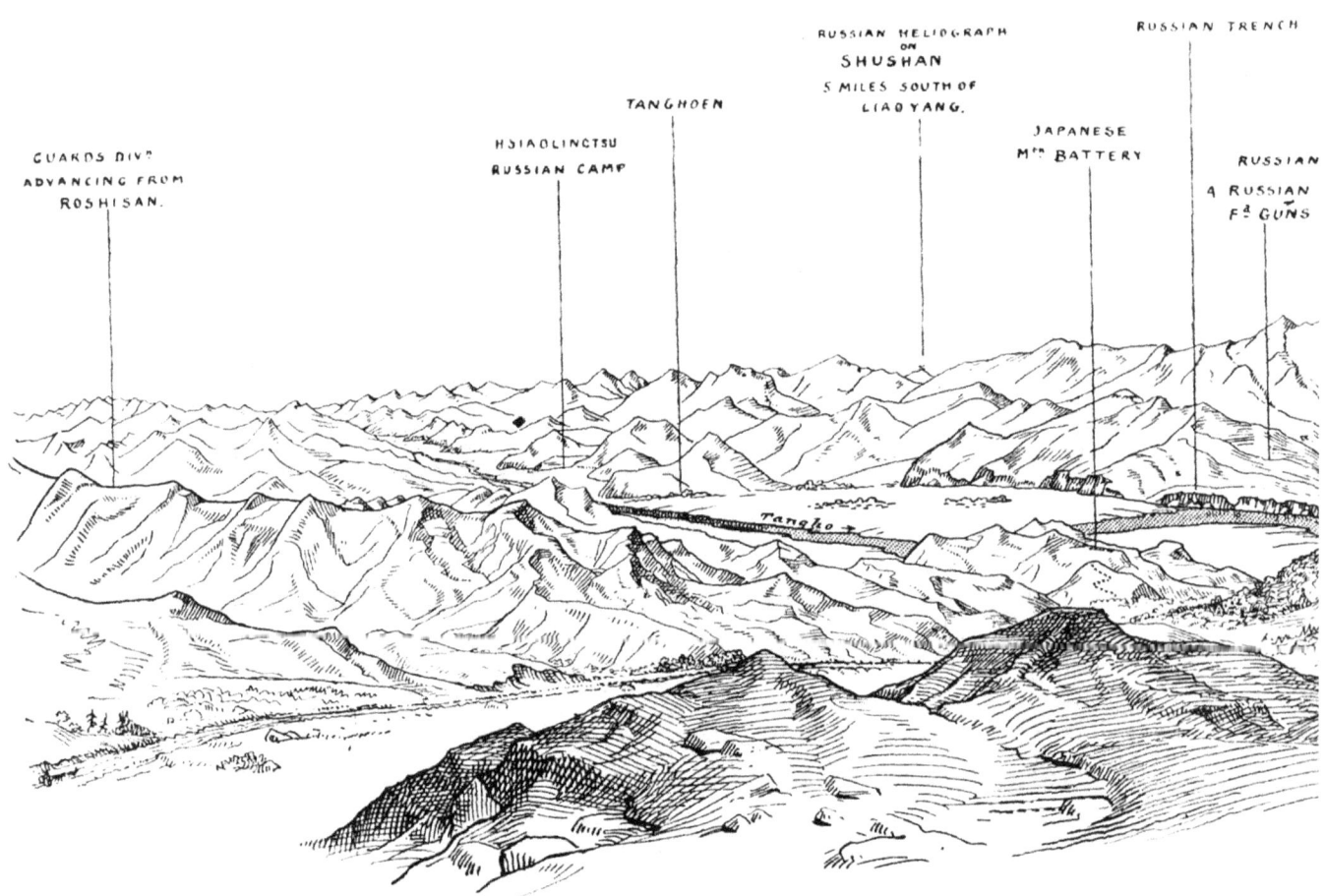

RUSSIAN REAR-GUARD
VIEW OF THE POSITION IN FRONT
THE 2ND DIVISION CROSSED THE

XIX

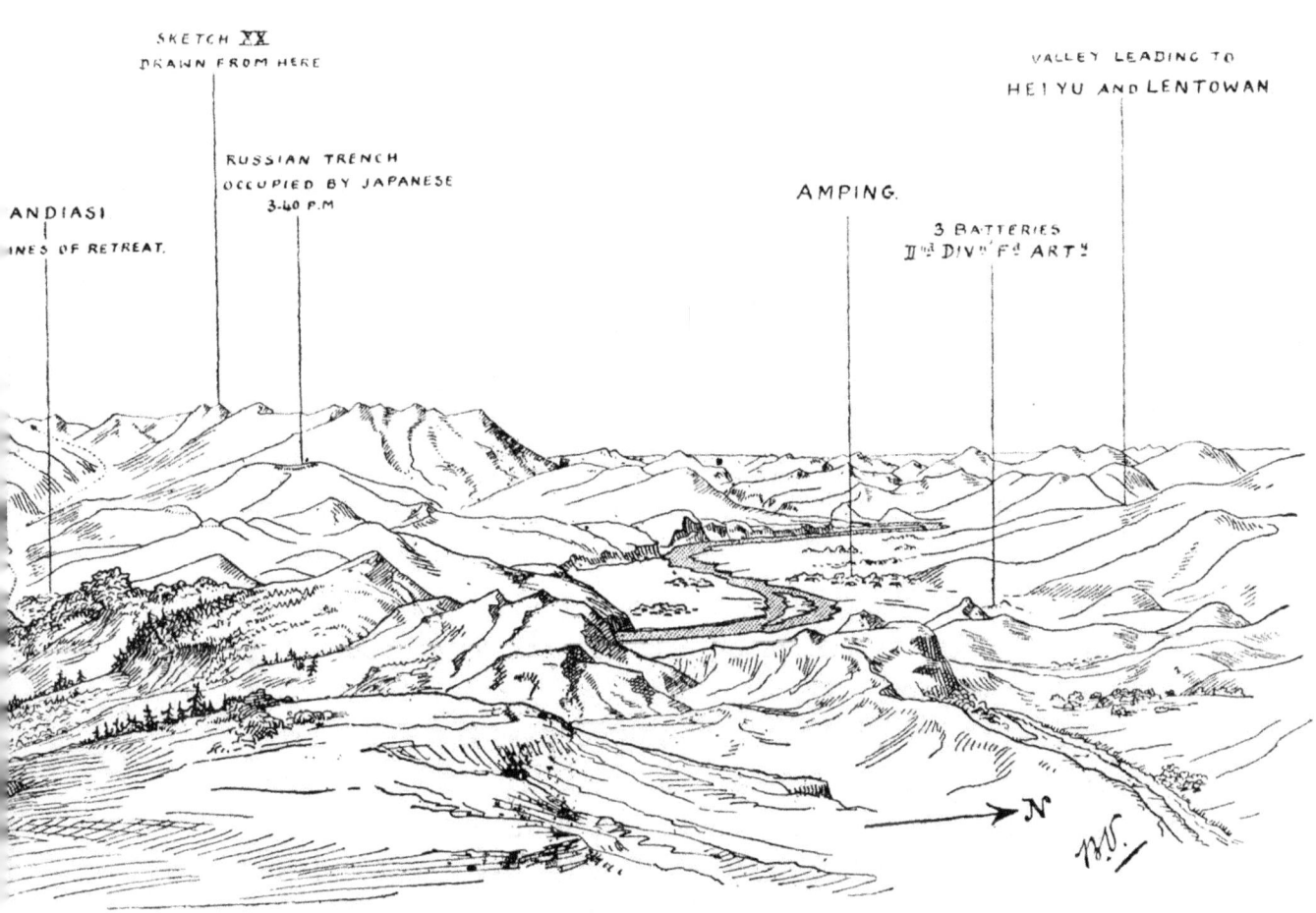

...CTION, AUGUST 28, 1904
THE 2ND DIVISION 1ST ARMY
NGHO BETWEEN SANDIASI AND AMPING

strong if the First Army stood alone, but the Fourth Army has very favourable ground in front of it, which should facilitate a turning movement of the right of the Russians in front of this army. The problem now to be solved is, will the enemy defend his present line, or will he fall back on Mukden? Supposing he retires to the north, he would have to face the probability of losing a considerable force in order that he might save the bulk of his army.

"Prospects would be bright were it not for the fatigue of our soldiers, amongst whom the Guards have now been moving and fighting for five days and nights without respite, and the other Divisions for four days and nights. The enemy imagined that, after the desperate fighting of the 26th, we would not press on so fast as we have contrived to do until now. On previous occasions, we have paused for a while after each encounter, but this time we have pushed on day and night, and we have the good news from Chinese sources that the greatest confusion and disorder prevails amongst the Russians on the road between Haicheng and Liaoyang."

Thereupon I took my leave and passed a very interesting day in going over the Russian entrenchments and the battlefield of the 26th generally.

I shall not burden my diary with any technical descriptions beyond saying that the Russian gun-pits and trenches were very complete and thorough, many of them being lined with sandbags, and having covered approaches leading from the rear. The terrain is more open here than it was on the centre and right, but I am becoming increasingly certain, as I gain in experience, that defence lines of the forbidding, precipitous type are in truth generally more open to attack than a simple, gently rising terrain which furnishes those who hold it with a wide, smooth field of fire and good positions for their guns.

I have now thoroughly examined the country held by the Russian centre and right, extending over a distance of perhaps fourteen miles. I have also seen, at a great distance it is true, the lofty Kosarei ridge held by the Russian left, which is, however, so conspicuous and distinctive that it is comparatively easy to form an idea of its features without any close inspection.

The conclusion I have come to after thus mastering the ground, is that the Russians made a fatal mistake in taking up the line Yoshirei–Yushuling to fight the battle of the 31st of July (*see* vol. i.).

The Yoshirei position, with its great spearheaded salient enclosing the Towan valley, did not naturally afford a symmetrical or cohesive line of defence, although certainly General Keller made the best of it, especially by his clever disposition of his artillery. Then again, the Yushuling position, with Makurayama as an outwork, was decidedly awkward and ill-knit to hold against a determined attack. But the great semicircular line of defence from which the Russians have just been driven was immensely strong and offered nothing which could fairly be called a weak spot to an assailant from the south. I think, then, that it would have been wiser of Count Keller and Turcheffsky to have fought their battle of the 31st on the line selected for the battle of the 26th August. Had the Russians acted thus, and resisted as stubbornly as they did at Yoshirei, I greatly doubt whether the Japanese would not still be fighting hard on the wrong side of the Tangho.

No doubt it may be objected that, when Count

Keller was attacked on the 31st July, he was thinking rather of offence against the Twelfth Division than of defending himself. Indeed, once might-have-beens make their speculative entry, argument becomes as endless as a recurring decimal. Still, this much is certain. The Russian positions on the 31st of July were unsatisfactory in many ways. Those from which they have now been ejected are exceptionally perfect and strong.

I have a message from headquarters telling me that to-morrow the Twelfth Division will not move, but will simply reconnoitre on both banks of the Taitsuho and complete its preparations for a crossing. The main part of the Second Division is also to stand fast, as it must wait for the Guards to fight their way up into line.

The only fighting that is to take place to-morrow, unless the Russians advance, is to be a big attack by the whole of the Guards Division, supported by Matsunaga's Brigade of the Second Division, on the enemy entrenched north of Mokabo. I am further informed that as I acted so philosophically in face of the refusal to let me go into the battle yesterday, the Marshal Kuroki is pleased to direct that I may go off to-morrow with Colonel —— and ride *via* Kohoshi and Shihodai\* towards Mokabo.† I am authorised to approach as close to Mokabo as is compatible with keeping clear of rifle fire.

Such a permission, giving me almost unlimited discretion as to my movements, sounds almost too good to be true.

\* Ssufangtai.        † Menchiafang.

## CHAPTER XXII

### WITH THE GUARDS DIVISION

ROSHISAN, *August 30th*, 1904.—Wet, tired, hungry; all my belongings lost, and in return a little English fox terrier gained.

But I must begin at the beginning.

We started at 9 A.M. and rode northwards for some fourteen miles—at a great pace, according to Japanese ideas. Fortunately, my companion was just as eager as I was to get within radius of the fighting. At last we entered the shell zone and found the troops hugging the sides of the valleys and creeping and darting along in real South African style, instead of marching down the path in the usual columns of route. Our guide here turned to the left, and we clambered up a height about one and a half or two miles south-east of Mokabo. On arriving at the summit we found we were about one mile north-west of another similar high mountain on which were two Japanese batteries firing an occasional shell to the northwards. An extraordinary number of Russian shells were bursting, apparently very much at random, over all the ground. The enemy evidently had not located the Japanese batteries, for although a good many shells did fall about that mountain a considerably greater number were bursting harmlessly on the mountain upon which ——, myself, and an officer from the Guards ammunition column were the only living beings. A few came from the north; first a faint far-away whirr passing with swift crescendo into a furious shriek, and ending in flash of flame and loud explosion, whilst the released bullets, like a flight of twittering birds, hissed past our ears or buried themselves amongst the stones at our feet. Others, the majority, drove down upon us with a solemn musical sound from the east, but these were fired at extreme range, and the bullets had lost their sharp and vicious note and buzzed heavy and slow like so many harmless bumble-bees. In no case could I see the enemy's batteries. All the country looked melancholy and dark.

I felt to-day as if a tragedy was being enacted: such is the effect of mere weather on the mortal framework which is to our sensitive souls what the barometer case is to the changing needle.

The whole of the valleys north of us were at intervals shrouded by the smoke of the *rafales*. Under this rain of projectiles the Japanese batteries kept very quiet, being unwilling, I imagine, to draw upon themselves a more accurate and concentrated fire. On the top of the mountain from which the two batteries were firing, I counted nine individuals in waterproofs (for it was raining), and made them out to be the foreign military attachés belonging to the Guards Division.

I could see very clearly the firing-line of the Japanese about 3000 yards to the north. It lay along a rounded cultivated ridge about one-third of the way up to the Russian trenches, which looked uncompromising and grim. The distance between the Japanese and the Russians cannot here have been more than 300 yards. The firing-line itself was thick, and it was shooting for all it was worth, but I noticed some supports come up over the exposed ground in rear to reinforce, and they crossed at a fast double and in very open order. In fact, they moved more as individuals than as a formed body, and if they had not been so numerous, I should have thought they were ammunition carriers. The officer of the ammunition column told us that the troops we saw were the 3rd Guards Regiment, and that the 29th Kobi was also fighting in front of us. No one knew how the fight was going, but he opined that these two regiments had got into a very tight place. Just as we were speaking, the Japanese batteries on the hill to our right rear opened a brisk fire on the Russian trenches. Before a dozen rounds had burst, I saw, to my surprise, the occupants clear out and bolt back over the crest line. Nevertheless, for a very long time the Japanese could make no advance as the ground to their front appeared to be enfiladed from Russian trenches further to the east.

At half-past three, however, the time had evidently come, and I had the great luck to witness an assault at a distance where I could distinguish through my glasses the individual men more clearly than on either the 31st of July or on the 26th instant. There was no formation, unless little groups of from six to a dozen men working quite independently could be called formation. What happened was that the face of the slope was suddenly covered by a loose mob which, when regarded more closely, was discovered to consist of very small parties extended at five or six paces interval, all going best leg foremost up the hill and devil take the hindmost.

I was rather too far to be able to say positively that there was no firing, but there could have been but little, as all these groups seemed to mask one another completely. The artillery had already cleared the trenches, but other works further to the east were still held by the enemy, and even after getting into the position some of the Japanese had had to evacuate it again and take up better natural cover a short distance in rear. Had there been many dead left behind by the assault I think I must have seen them, but I noticed no one fall, and I believe there can have been hardly any loss. Now the Japanese were certainly under infantry fire at medium range when they covered the last 100 yards to the trenches, so their immunity does not say very much for the accuracy of the Russian musketry. It is not fair, of course, to be positive on such a point from the safety of rocks nearly two miles distant. The ground may have given more cover than it seemed to give, or the Russians may have been under heavy infantry fire from other troops I could not see. All I can do is to give my honest belief each time and then at the end I may hope to convey a trustworthy general impression. Applying this rule to the case in point, I cannot help thinking that our own fellows would have taken very heavy toll of the assailants under identical conditions.

Prospects seemed bright for the Japanese, but obviously the Russians were still in a stubborn mood. I was looking at the crest of a mountain, with a tumulus on its western shoulder, which formed part of the Russian position, when suddenly I saw a line of some two hundred men step shoulder to shoulder on to the sky line and into the field of vision of my glass. I uttered an exclamation, and took my eye off to point them out to my two companions. Next moment I looked again, but not a soul could I see. Evidently these were Russian reinforcements who had dropped into a trench on the southern side of the crest line.

For a long time, ―― had been growing restive, and now he insisted that he would get into trouble if I did not make a start on our return journey, as he had promised to bring me back to headquarters by a reasonable hour. There was no help for it, and I had to tear myself away as best I could from a fight half fought.

Soon after starting on our long ride home, we came across a little white English fox terrier being worried by a huge pariah dog. A Chinaman had just driven off the monster with a stone, and the plucky terrier, though bleeding from the throat, was joining furiously in the chase of the pariah which was quite ready to fasten on to it again if given a chance. I whistled. Instantly the little beast rushed to my horse, enchanted once more to see a European amongst all these Asiatics. The Chinaman seemed inclined to make some claim, but I put my horse into a brisk trot, and the small creature followed me quite gaily. After we had travelled a mile or two, whilst she was running ahead of me, some evil recollection seemed to cross her mind, for she sat down suddenly by the roadside and raising her head set up the most forlorn and miserable howl I ever heard in my life. I felt indeed sad for this poor little atom. It was pitiful. However, the pang of grief passed quickly, and soon she was running and jumping about as cheerfully as ever.

Our horses were dead beat, and our road very soon got blocked with transport and detachments of troops and all the impedimenta of a great army. Before long it grew dusk, and so in heavy rain we floundered along, amidst crowds of men and vehicles. At last

I could see no further than ten or fifteen yards, yet, whenever I cast my eye back I was aware of a white dot threading its way close at my horse's heels, in and out of hordes of Asiatics, clinging on to the one European, who, like itself, was a stranger amongst the multitude. Twice we had to cross the Tangho, here two to three feet deep and 100 yards wide. Through thick and thin my small fellow-country dog stuck to me nobly. The first time she swam the broad river, although it must have seemed to her as boundless as the ocean, but the next time I got Sergeant-Major Watanabe to hold her before him on the pommel of his saddle. So, in course of time, namely, at 9.40 P.M., we reached our house, and found all dark and still. But there was a cart drawn up before the gate, and our entry was effectively barred. After shouting for a long time we roused the household, and were informed that, by order of the General Staff, our entire kit had marched away to Amping, twelve miles distant, at three in the afternoon.

Here was a fine predicament! Horses dead beat! Ourselves soaked, tired and hungry; heavy rain falling, and not the smallest chance of getting to Amping that night. I was very sorry for myself, and also more so for my new chum. I felt she must think I had lured her on with false pretences, and I am sure she expected to find a nice Russian lady, with tea and cakes, waiting for us by the side of a warm stove, after so painful a journey. Eventually we resolved to try and beat up some one at Roshisan, and we managed to make our horses crawl back as far as the village. Here we have fortunately found a Post Commandant, a very kind man, who has taken us in and given us a splendid meal of rice, tomatoes, and Russian tinned meat, washed down with *saké*. He has also lent us each a Government blanket from his quartermaster's stores, and our wet things will dry upon us during the night.

KURODANI (*near* LENTOWAN), *August* 31*st*, 1904.—Started for Amping at 9 A.M. Our horses were still dead beat, after their thirty miles yesterday, and hardly able to crawl along. We took four hours, therefore, to do the twelve miles, and when we got into Amping village at 1 P.M. we found our kit in the act of starting again to follow the headquarters on here, where we are quartered on the left bank of the Taitsuho. Taking out some barley for the horses and some rice for ourselves, we let the cart go on, and halted for a couple of hours' rest.

To my intense surprise, I found that the Chinese farmer who was our host could talk some English; he also seemed to know at once that I was a British officer, and hurried off to bring me his Chinese Bible, of which he was immensely proud. He is a pupil, so he tells me, of Doctor Westwater, of Liaoyang.

I asked him what he thought of the Russians.

He said they were kind men who paid for what they took, but that they were somewhat wanting in humanity. As he had in the same breath informed me that they did not do any harm, I could not quite follow him. At last, however, by the help of —— and Sumino, I made out that his true meaning was, "The Russians are somewhat wanting in the quality of being human." I was amused, as this is precisely the accusation Occidentals bring against the Chinese.

When I caught up Headquarters here at 5.30 P.M., I found them decidedly anxious and preoccupied. I was naturally full of my own small adventures and observations on the left of the army, but the moment was obviously ill suited for bagatelles of that sort. However, from the few minutes' speech I secured, I gathered I had been fortunate—if, indeed, it can be said to be fortunate to witness a misfortune—when I went to the Guards yesterday.

It seems that the 3rd Guards and the 29th Kobi, whom I had seen so gallantly take the greater portion of the enemy's trenches, had received no assistance from any of the other corps in their vicinity, and that they were eventually driven back by the Russians, who have now re-occupied all their previous positions. The Guards, far from having any idea of renewing the assault, are entrenching themselves as hard as they can against a counter-attack.

This is a *contretemps* not only unexpected, but at the present juncture peculiarly deplorable. For the plan by which (as I hear for the first time) Kuroki was to concentrate the whole of his army near Huankufun,* on the north bank of the Taitsuho, by the 2nd September, has now been abandoned.

It had been reckoned that by this date the Fourth Army would have advanced far enough to be able to relieve the Imperial Guards, so that they might close in and cross the Taitsuho with the rest of the First Army. Had the scheme worked out smoothly, then, with his own army complete and with the co-operation of the Umezawa Brigade from Penchiho, Kuroki could have led 50,000 veteran and victorious troops in a tremendous onslaught on the Russian lines of communication. But the Fourth Army has not come as far as Kuroki had expected, and I daresay, although I did not venture to make such a suggestion, that the Guards

* Chinese, Huankufen.

have not come as far as Marshal the Marquis Oyama had reckoned on. It is naturally quite impossible to bring the Guards away, as they are all that stand between the Russians, who have victoriously repulsed them, and the communications of the First Army. As soon as Kuroki crosses the Taitsuho, only the Guards Division and Matsunaga's Brigade of the Second Division will be available on the south side of the river to prevent the enemy at Mokabo, or east of it, from marching right down to Amping. But it is impossible to accentuate a risk which is serious enough already by still further weakening this Japanese containing force. Otherwise Kuroki would be positively inviting the Russians about Mokabo to come down and cut his communications.

It can be understood then how disappointed every one here feels about the failure of the Guards, which renders it necessary for Kuroki to make his perilous plunge minus their support and that of Matsunaga's Brigade. It is not the habit of the Japanese to attribute blame; not in the presence of foreigners, at least, but I can see that there is no sort of tendency to criticise the Guards. On the other hand, no one can understand how it has come about that the Second Division did not support them with Matsunaga's Brigade. It seems that Matsunaga looked on yesterday and never fired a shot to help the Guards to hold their own. Matsunaga himself is a splendid fellow, and no doubt there will be a satisfactory explanation forthcoming in the course of the next day or two.

Meanwhile, it may be noted that this check to Kuroki's left would not so very much have mattered had the plan of the battle been based on correct assumptions regarding the enemy.

If Kuropatkin is going to put his back to the wall at Liaoyang and fight the decisive engagement of the campaign, as has hitherto been assumed by the Japanese, then there is no extraordinary cause for hurry, and the concentration of the First Army at Huankufun might almost as well have taken place on the 3rd as on the 2nd September. But now a new and unforeseen factor has all of a sudden obtruded itself. Kuropatkin is not going to stake Russia's destinies on the issue of a single great battle. This time he is not going to repeat the tactics of the Yalu and sit still whilst around him the Japanese General Staff spider spins her web. Last night he made up his mind to retire! *

Such is the opinion of our Headquarters to-night,

---

* Some remarks made later on this subject by a very well-informed Staff officer supply an interesting comment on this part of the diary, especially as there seems to underlie them an intention to anticipate adverse criticism. He said: "It was on August 30th that the event took place which prevented us from making our pre-arranged attack on Liaoyang. That is to say, the attack could not be carried into effect on the lines we had carefully thought out, and we simply had to push off into pursuit from whatever positions we were occupying at the moment. I do not know what Kuropatkin may have reported in this connection, but it is a fact that on the 30th the enemy began to retire. From the positions held by the Second and Twelfth Divisions we could see the enemy on the south bank of the Taitsuho falling back on Liaoyang, whilst two or three of his Divisions were crossing the river and moving northwards. From the position held by the Guards we could see also that the enemy from Koraison was also retiring on Liaoyang. Finally, from information received from Marshal the Marquis Oyama the enemy seemed to be falling back even from Liaoyang itself. If this evidence was not already quite conclusive that Kuropatkin was in full retreat, I might adduce the further fact that from hill 186 we could see the railway north of Liaoyang, along which trains were passing in the direction of Mukden, at intervals of five or six minutes. Therefore, whatever the Russians may now pretend, we actually, with our own

and on it they have based a fresh scheme in substitution for their original carefully weighed plan of operations.

Put into a few words, the latest arrangements provide for the immediate hurried crossing of the Taitsuho by Kuroki at the head of little more than one-third of his army. Indeed, there is no help for it, supposing that he must forthwith take the fateful step. Obviously, the Umezawa Brigade cannot leave Chaotao without first driving the Russians out of Penchiho, and cannot therefore co-operate for several days. And I have already shown how the Guards, and Matsunaga's Brigade of the Second Division cannot possibly march

eyes, did see them on August 30th retreating as fast as they could. The question we now have to solve is, what course under such circumstances should have been pursued by the Commander of the First Army? It seemed clear enough that he was bound to abandon the plan of attack he had so carefully prepared, and that, however hazardous and difficult such a movement might be, he must instantly despatch such a force as he could lay his hands upon across the Taitsuho. The Second and Fourth Armies were also compelled to depart from their well-thought-out schemes, and simply pursue the Russians as best they could. It was under these circumstances that the Marshal Kuroki ordered the Twelfth Division and half of the Second Division to cross the Taitsuho at Lentowan. The only possible excuse for so small a force putting a swift and deep river between them and their friends was that the enemy was retreating. Kuropatkin determined to retreat, and began his preparations for that purpose on the evening of August 29th. If it were true, as Kuropatkin has reported, that his army began to retreat on September 3rd, then he could not possibly have carried it out in so masterly a manner unless he had first defeated the Japanese armies."

As this is a very much discussed subject, I thought I would settle it once and for all as far as the Japanese are concerned. Accordingly, I took an opportunity during the winter of consulting the Chief of Staff, Manchurian Armies—General Baron Kodama—and he replied to my question, "Kuropatkin determined to retire on the night of August 31st."

away eastwards leaving the Mandarin road open to an advance southwards by a victorious enemy with whom they are still in close contact. Instead of 60,000 men then, Kuroki must content himself with 20,000. In common with Cæsar's Rubicon, the Taitsuho of Kuroki may offer no insuperable barrier to the mere movement of the troops, but once they set foot on the further bank their commander commits himself to play for the highest stakes. He need not burn his pontoon boats, for the enemy's shell will do that for him fast enough if his forces prove insufficient to maintain their ground.

It seems that all the main points of this new scheme, based upon Kuropatkin's retreat, were settled on the 30th, and the Twelfth Division were ordered to cross the Taitsuho at Lentowan that same night, and then to move northward down the right bank of the river until they found a good position to cover the passage of Okasaki's Brigade of the Second Division. The Twelfth Division have carried out their orders. Much to the discredit of the Cossacks, they were permitted to do so without any trouble or hitch. But the Headquarters Staff are hardly recovered yet from the fright they got during the night when the large force of the enemy opposite Shobyoshi and Sekishoshi,* amounting to more than a Division, were reported, erroneously as it turned out, to be threatening a forward movement. We know that in ordinary life actions which appear small and trivial in themselves may yet have the most far-reaching effects. In war, however, the truth of the principle is much more immediately recognisable.

On the night of the 30th, the whole of the Twelfth

* Chinese, Shuangmiaotsu and Shihchutsu.

Division was definitely committed to the crossing of the Taitsuho, and the main body of the Second Division had concentrated by 10 P.M. at Kosojo* for the purpose of following the Twelfth Division to the Lentowan ford by way of the Henyu. The lines of communications of both these Divisions crossed the Tangho at the same spot, Amping. Matsunaga's Brigade was twelve miles to the south-west, assisting the Guards to contain another of the enemy's Divisions, and the Guards themselves were still further away in the same direction. Absolutely the only troops available to make face to the enemy's Division on the heights beyond Shobyoshi and Sekishoshi were four Japanese companies—two near Sekishoshi and two a little to the north of Shobyoshi. If a Russian brigade had come down from its position and overwhelmed these four companies, or even if one Russian battalion had marched round their left into the valley of the Tangho, then in neither case was there anything available to defend Amping from a *coup de main* but masses of camp followers and supply columns.

Small wonder, then, that the Headquarters Staff are in no mood to appreciate the recital of my adventures, which to myself had appeared so interesting and important.

A bold stroke at Amping by the heavy force of Russians, from whose undefeated front the Japanese had begun to clear as soon as it became dark, would have cut Kuroki's forces clean in two and, even if eventually repulsed, would have probably so destroyed and disorganised his transport as to put the First Army out of action for several weeks to come.

* Chinese, Kusaocheng.

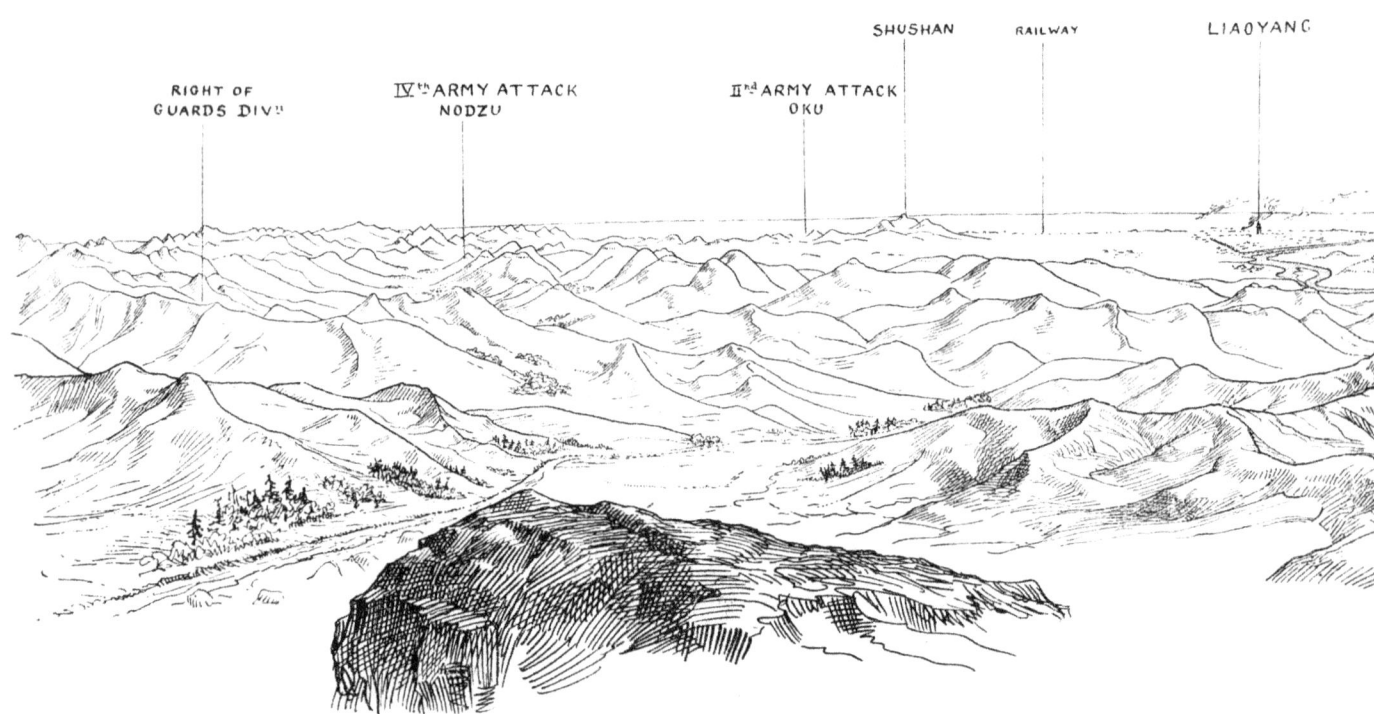

The Battle of Liaoyang as seen

XX

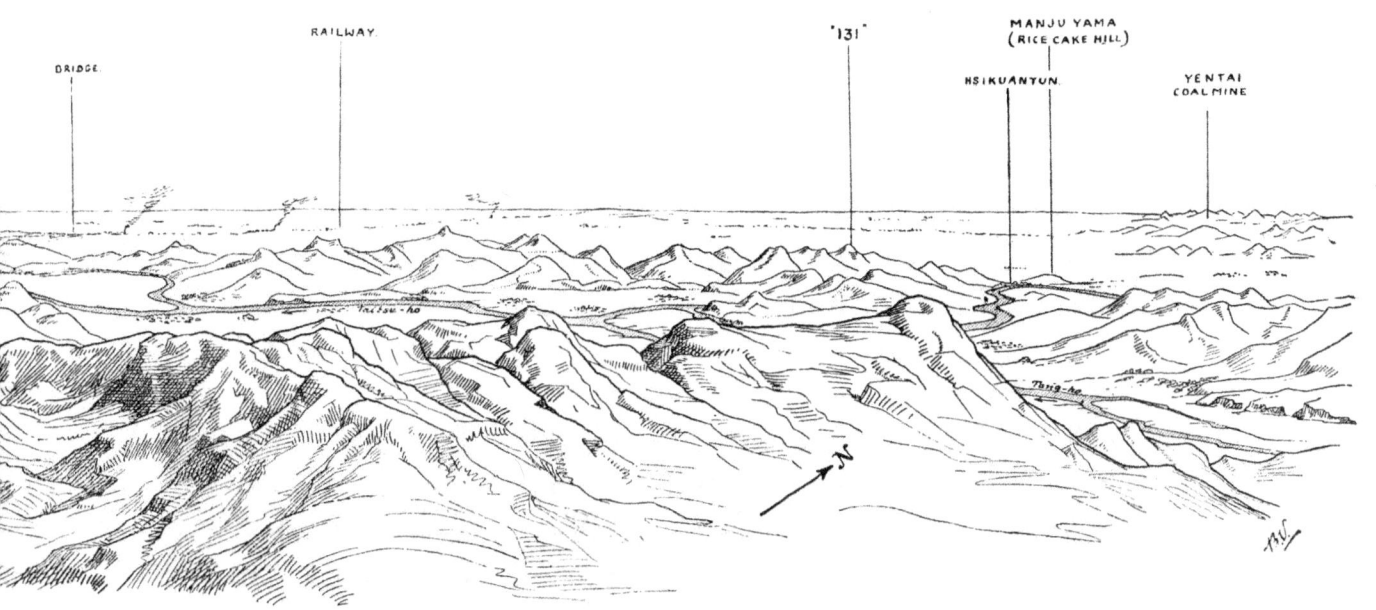

on August 30 and 31, 1904

## CHAPTER XXIII

### KUROKI CROSSES THE TAITSUHO

As I have several times criticised the Japanese for being over cautious, it is only fair to draw attention to the enormous risks Kuroki took upon himself last night. To cross a river in face of the emeny has been considered a delicate military operation since the days of Germanicus, but when, in addition to the dangers of flood and fire in front, a powerful force of the enemy is posted in a strong position on the near side of the river within five miles of the proposed point of crossing, then indeed the attempt makes heavy demands upon the audacity of the General.

Kuroki fully realised his danger. It had been intended that the Second Division should have attacked and carried the Russian positions on the high ground immediately south and south-west of Sekishoshi as a necessary preliminary to the passage of the river. The entrenchments, however, look very formidable, and it seems certain that Kuropatkin has given the order to retreat which will imply their early evacuation. It has been decided, therefore, to leave the Russians alone, and, relying upon their presumed lack of initiative, to trust four companies of Japanese infantry to contain them.

Never was presumption better justified. The Russian Divisions remained immobile. The Twelfth

Division crossed at Lentowan before daybreak, and advanced northward up the right bank as soon as it was light to cover the crossing of the Second Division. To-day they have swung round westwards, following the river, and are now facing the Russians at Huankufun with their left resting on the Taitsuho and their line running round in a semicircle to cover the Swallow's Nest Hill (*see* Map XXII.). Whilst the Twelfth Division were getting into position, Okasaki's Brigade began at 9 A.M. this morning to ford the river near Lentowan, and by 1 P.M. they had all got through safely to the right bank. The Field Artillery were forced to wait for a bridge and meanwhile took up a position to assist the deployment of the army on the northern bank, and, if necessary, to check any aggressive movement from the west.

I could learn nothing about the progress of the Second and Fourth Armies, but I was told that, whilst I had been away from headquarters, orders had been sent to General Umezawa which were calculated to bring him into our sphere of operations before very long. He had been at Chaotao in command of a mixed brigade of Kobi, with which he had been watching Penchiho, where a small force of Russians had remained after the retirement of the bulk of their troops on Liaoyang. Umezawa has now been directed to attack Penchiho on the night of the 30th, after which he is to march westwards and join hands with Kuroki to the north of the Taitsuho.

The situation, then, as far as I can ascertain it before turning in, is something like this: Kuropatkin is said to be retreating northwards on Mukden as fast as he can. Nevertheless, a big force of Russians are entrenching themselves amongst the Kuyentai hills. From their position some five miles to our west, on the other side of the river, they have been firing heavily but very wildly, much of the shrapnel bursting high or wide of the mark. On our left, the Imperial Guards have gained a little ground in the direction of Mokabo, but at Bohodai on their right they and Matsunaga's Brigade of the Second Division are still sitting down opposite the position they were driven from on the 30th. The 29th Regiment of Kobi, however, Kuroki's reserve on the 26th, which he had sent from Lienshankuan to help the Guards in their difficulties, has now been recalled and is to join the Second Division as soon as possible on the north bank of the Taitsuho. Under Kuroki's direct orders, Okasaki's Brigade of the Second Division and the whole of the Twelfth Division have taken up a position near Huankufun.

KANKUANTUN,* *September 1st, 1904.*—For the seventh morning in succession earth and air are trembling to the thunder of guns firing at all distances and in every direction. —— tells me that a pontoon bridge has been built during the night, and that we are to follow Kuroki across it.

We started at 7 A.M., and after marching a short distance our road divided, one track leading to the left, apparently to the river, the other going half-right. I felt sure we should take the road to the left, but —— was even more positive we should go to the right. We did so, and after riding two or three miles we came to the high ground overlooking Lentowan, where there was no bridge! I could not resist saying, "I told you so"—a phrase which, agreeable as it may be in the

* Chinese, Houkwantun. At this time, although I did not know it, Umezawa on the extreme right had captured Penchiho (*see* Map XXIII.).—I. H.

utterance, is never quite worth the eventual cost; and so there developed a marked coldness. I did not, however, so much regret the loss of time, as we happened to arrive just as a company of Japanese infantry was crossing the ford. The water came up to their armpits, and it seemed to me that they must be firmer on their feet than Europeans, not to be carried away by the current. Rough, broken hills came down to within half a mile of the ford. I presume they were picqueted by Japanese troops, but they look to me as if they had been expressly made by Providence to facilitate a protracted opposition to the crossing by such troops as the Cossacks have until now been supposed to be.

Retracing our steps to the parting of the ways, we now took my road, and arrived after a few hundred yards, at a very fine pontoon bridge, which took only one and a half hours to construct. We crossed, and then, turning west, scaled a tumulus-shaped hill of about 150 feet in height, crowned by the half-ruined battlements of a Chinese fort, called the Swallow's Nest.

It was now almost noon. Kuroki and his Staff were here, but, with very mixed feelings, I saw that the military attachés with the Second Division and half a dozen of my friends, the journalists, were also on the ground.

The first to greet me was Vincent. I have rarely seen any one so disreputable. He had slept in a muddy puddle by the roadside, and, to judge by what he had carried away with him on his clothes, he must have left it as clear as crystal. He looked very pinched and thin, and the seat of his breeches had been repaired with a large piece of a Russian greatcoat.

He knew nothing of the general situation—nothing

whatever; but he had collected a lot of valuable notes concerning the advance of his own Division.

A few minutes later, I passed him again. I could not imagine how his whole appearance seemed to have been transformed into one of radiant beatitude until I saw in his hand a tin which reminded me of happier days. I said, "Good heavens, Vincent, what is that?" He said, "It is an empty tin of raspberry jam Maxwell of the *Standard* has just given me." I exclaimed, "Did Maxwell give you an empty tin of jam?" "Oh, no," he replied, "I mean it is now empty." And so it was; not even a stickiness dulled the polished bottom of the tin, which, as I told Vincent with some bitterness, was certainly by far the cleanest thing he had about him.

After all, the stream of information did continue to flow without apparent interruption.

The first item was good, namely, that Umezawa's Brigade had duly captured Penchiho on the extreme right of the army. The next concerned the positions of the enemy, with whom we were in contact on the northern back of the Taitsuho, and certainly we could not have wished for a finer view of these positions than we got from our Swallow's Nest (*see* Sketch XXI.).

Immediately to the south, at our very feet, the broad and rapid Taitsuho ran due west for some three miles, when it turned northwards and, making a complete semi-circle the arc of which would measure about two miles, flowed away to the south out of our sphere of action. Where the river takes its turn to the south, it washes the steep lower slope of a mountain marked on the Russian map 131. This 131 is obviously an ugly fellow to tackle; and on his southern spur are guns, and the crest lines are entrenched

"Swallow's Nest Hill" and the Pontoon Bridge across the Taitsu, September 1, 1904

in several places, though not, apparently, very heavily. From 131 a long, low feature runs out northwards, and ends in a flattened hillock perhaps fifty feet high, which the soldiers have christened Manjuyama, or Rice-cake Hill. Just beneath the slight *col* which connects mountain 131 with Manjuyama, nestles amidst its orchards a fairly large village called Hsikuantun. Beyond Manjuyama the ground is fairly level until, some two and a half miles to the north-east of it, a curious five-headed hill about 200 feet high—Gochosan by name—rises up out of the luxuriant crops. North of Gochosan a long ridge continues for about four miles, ending in a round hill with a small house on the top of it which we were told overlooked the Yentai coal mines. The whole plain is a mass of high kaoliung crops.

It is desperately tedious to write so much description, but I shall never succeed in my report unless I get the lie of the country firmly fixed in my own mind, and the only way of doing so is either to live here for a week or to put it all down direct from nature.

To gain a general idea of the scene, it must be noted that at the Swallow's Nest Hill we had just emerged for the first time for four months from endless ranges of mountains. Looking north, south, east or south-west the familiar spiky pyramids still stood with stately ranks unbroken, but, apart from the outposts formed by Mountain 131, Manjuyama and Gochosan, the whole country to the west was an undulating and apparently open plain. I say " apparently open," because, actually, the kaoliung crops, from eight to twelve feet high, gave it all the tactical characteristics of dense forest.

The Russians, in force unknown, were holding a

semicircular position with their right on Mountain 131, and their line running north-eastwards thence by Hsikuantun, Manjuyama, Gochosan. Our own First Army—as many of them, that is to say, as had crossed the river—were spread out beneath us like a fan. Okasaki's Brigade of the Second Division was on the left, and had been endeavouring to work up to 131 and Hsikuantun since 6 A.M.; the Twelfth Division was on the right and had already at the time of my arrival made good its footing on the Gochosan hill.

Twenty-four Japanese guns had come into action at 6.30 A.M. from entrenchments dug during the night on a low ridge running north and south some 500 yards to the east of Huankufen (*see* Sketch XXI.). There were hundreds of Russian shrapnel bursting in *rafales* of eight over and beyond these guns. The enemy's batteries had ranged on another ridge about 400 yards beyond their real objective. Some trees grew upon the further ridge, and no doubt helped the common optical delusion whereby from a distance two features merge into one, and the intervening valley escapes notice.

All gunners are aware of their liability to go wrong from this cause, but the Russian practice of ranging in the air with time shrapnel instead of on the ground by percussion shrapnel, undoubtedly gives greater scope for such mistakes. Anyway, the Russian *rafales*, so savage in their seeming, were no more dangerous to the artillery against which they were directed than a Crystal Palace fireworks display.

General Kuroki himself told me that at 9 A.M. he had received a message from Oyama's Chief of the Staff—

Kodama—telling him that, since the 31st, the enemy had been retiring in front of the Fourth Army, who had, at daybreak to-day, captured Hsinlitun (Map XXIII.).

Simultaneously, the Second Army had occupied an important hill west of Hsinlitun with its right column, whilst the next Division still further to the west had carried Shuisenpu after losing very heavily. It seems clear, therefore, to Kuroki that the Second and Fourth Armies have made a most important advance, and he concludes that they must by now be in hot pursuit of the enemy. He is further confirmed in his view by a message which came in at mid-day telling him that the Guards had occupied the range north of Mokabo at 11 A.M.

Kuroki is radiant. The great moment of his life has arrived. He has only to burst through at Manju-yama and Mountain 131 to fix himself astride the railway to Mukden, which can be clearly seen, looking westwards over the village of Hsikuantun, bearing its busy trains northward. Several of the Staff have reminded me, as if I needed reminding, that to-day is the anniversary of Sedan. How strange if history should repeat itself! The hopes of the Japanese run high, and anything seems possible. I have sent the following cable: "First September. Since previous telegram six days nights incessant hard fighting, marching, entrenching. Troops sleepless last three nights, but Kuroki giving enemy no respite and by crossing Taitsuho fair prospects securing fullest results great victory."

Faithfully as I believe my cables have reflected the spirit prevailing at the moment amongst our allies, there is some bad luck about them from the Japanese

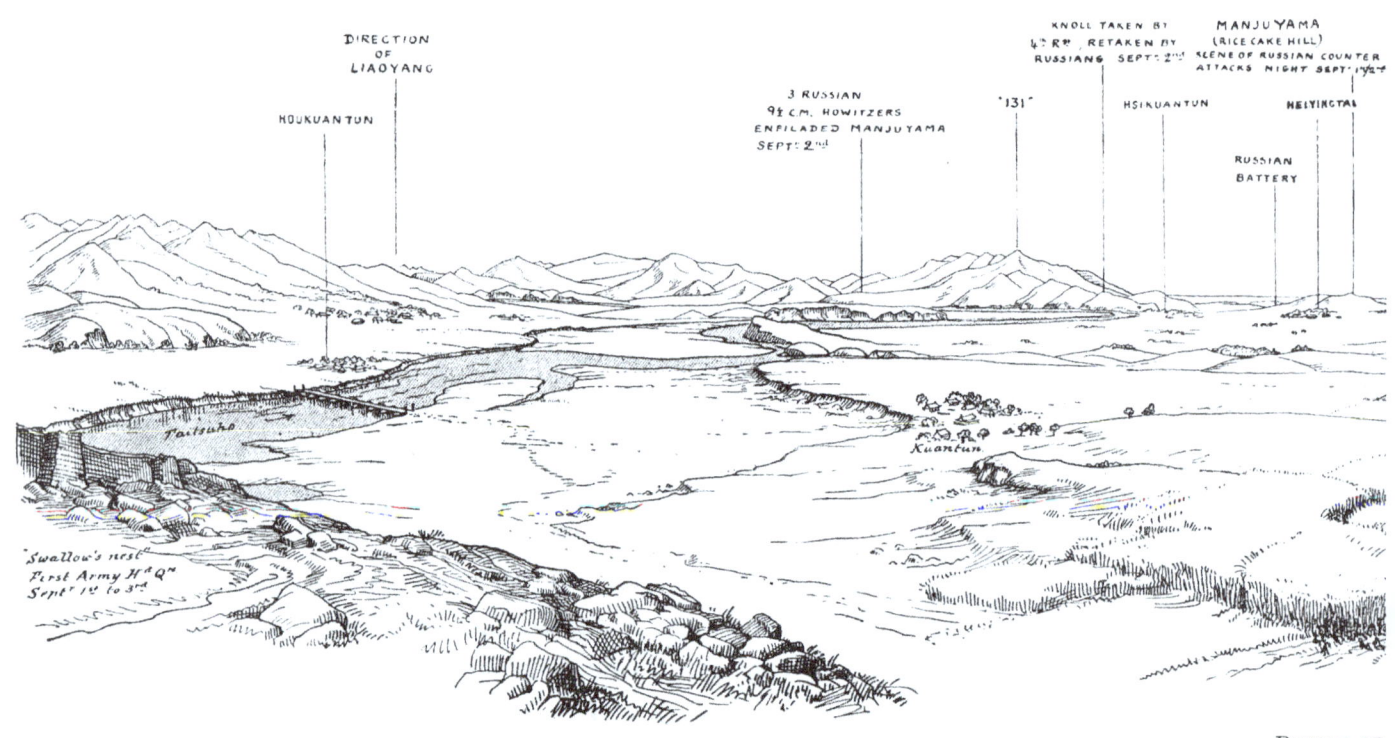

BATTLE OF
VIEW FROM "SWALLOW'S NEST HILL" LOOKING

XXI

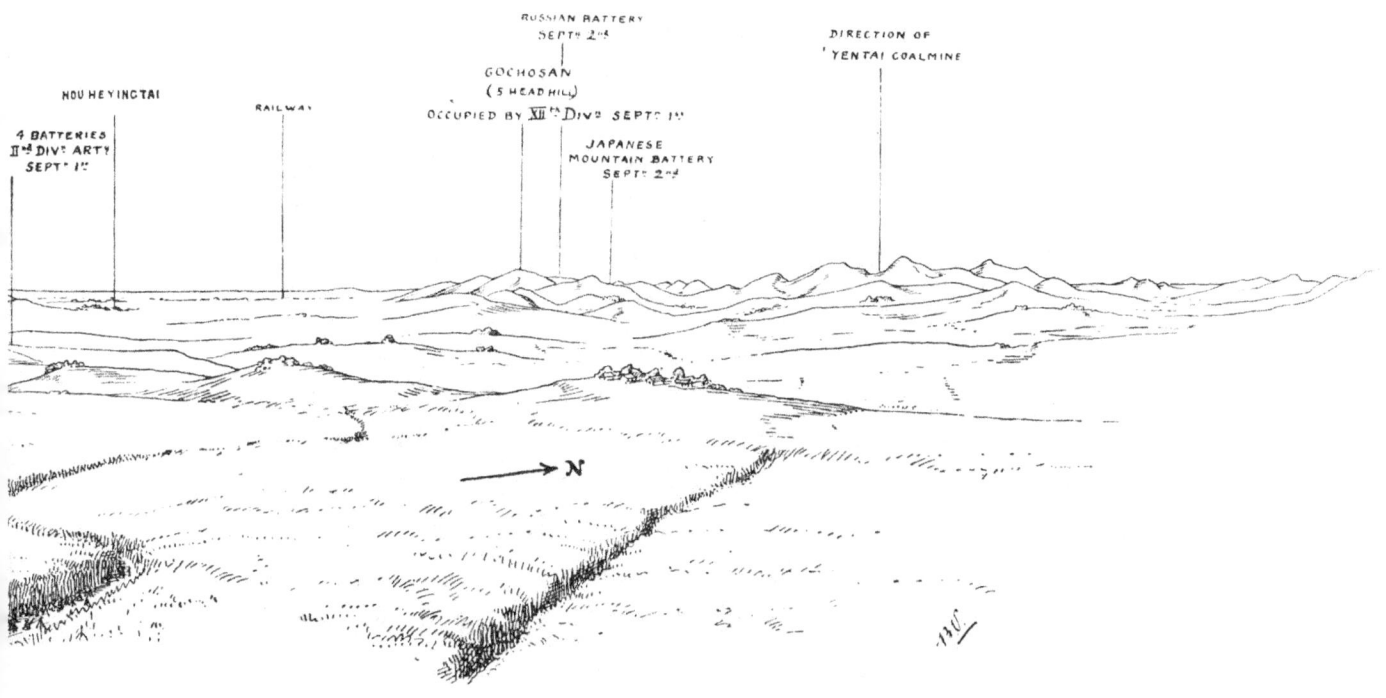

LIAOYANG
WESTWARD TOWARDS MANJU YAMA SEPTEMBER 1, 1904

point of view, and certainly there seems danger that they will bring bad luck to me.

At 1.50 a message came in, couched in somewhat alarming terms, to say that a Russian column two miles long was moving down from the neighbourhood of the Yentai coal mines, and threatening to roll up the right of the army.

Such information does not tally with the view that the Russians are in full flight, and I note a great change in the mood of all my friends. Lieut.-General Inouye, commanding the Twelfth Division, advises Kuroki to suspend his advance westwards until measures can be taken to probe the full significance of this threatening movement from the north.

Okasaki, however, had committed his Fifteenth Brigade too far to the attack of Manjuyama to be able either to stand fast or withdraw. So, at least, he chose to put it. He therefore informed Headquarters that he had asked the officer commanding the Second Division artillery to support him, and that he had also begged General Inouye to permit the mountain guns of the Twelfth Division to fire at Manjuyama. The request for the assistance of the Mountain Artillery was granted, but the officer commanding Second Division said that if he was to shell Manjuyama he must move up 1000 yards nearer the hill, a very difficult business, even with the kaoliung to conceal his movements, and necessitating the digging of fresh gun-pits in advance, which must take time.

To a British soldier it is most interesting to note that, although his own Divisional Commander, Lieutenant-General Nishi, was somewhere on the field, Okasaki did not hesitate to send direct to the officer commanding Second Division artillery, who was not under his orders, to ask him to carry out a vital, although dangerous, movement; also to mark, learn, and inwardly digest the fact that the artillery commander never dreamed for a moment of standing off on any mere point of punctilio.

When British merchants find their commercial supremacy threatened by the Germans, they appear very often to think that it is their Government or their workmen which are to blame; so, at least, I judge by what I have often seen written. It may be so. But it would be a bad sign for our army if we hesitated freely to acknowledge that in the ethics of militarism we have an immense amount to learn from the Germans. Okasaki's confident appeal to the officer commanding the Second Division artillery; the generosity of Nishi and the willingness with which the guns advanced, all this is pure evidence of German teaching grafted into Samurai unselfishness. German formations may be too close, according to some opinions; their trust in the sabre and the lance may be *vieux jeu* according to the views of a few conscientious critics; but no one who studied 1870 and recognised the loyalty with which German generals supported each other; who has considered how ungrudgingly assistance was rendered, whether asked for or not, irrespective of the corps or even of the army to which such units belonged, can doubt that in these respects we stand far behind the Germans of thirty-four years ago. If any one does doubt it, let him study some of our South African battles carefully, and then read the story of Spicheren and Wörth.

From all I can gather, it is clear that Okasaki is the leading spirit of the attack now in progress and, generally, in the decision to maintain the offensive on the left, threaten what may on the right. I think Kuroki, Inouye, and Fujii would all prefer to refuse their right and centre until the situation on the right flank has been cleared up, but the bold commander of the 15th Brigade sees only the enemy interposing between him and the railway, and has flung to the winds their prudence as well as his own. Feeling themselves more or less committed by the calculated Nelsonian impetuosity of Okasaki, Kuroki and his Staff have accepted the challenge of fortune, and are doing all they possibly can to ensure him success. The Shimamura Brigade (12th) of the Twelfth Division has been promptly ordered to wheel northwards, and has taken up a position about Gochosan to meet the two-mile Russian column coming from Yentai. Under cover of this flank guard, the Kigoshi Brigade of the Twelfth Division has closed in towards the 15th Brigade to support Okasaki's attack, and all available guns have received orders to lessen their distance from Manjuyama so as to shell it at effective ranges.

By 4.30 P.M. the Japanese guns were furiously pounding this hillock. The slight entrenchments were not deep enough or solid enough to stand such treatment, and as the clouds of black smoke from high explosive shell mingled with the snowy puffs of the shrapnel and settled more and more closely over Manjuyama's brow, I saw many of the defenders evacuate their shelters and run desperately back in hopes, often falsified, of escaping with their lives over to the far side of the crest.

At 5.30 the opinion was freely expressed on the Swallow's Nest hill that the Russians would be forced by such a fire to evacuate Manjuyama completely. But not a bit of it; at 6.30 they were reinforced, and at 7 P.M. word came back to say that in face of the cross fire of the Russian artillery from positions north-west, west and south of Manjuyama, there seemed small prospect that the Fifteenth Brigade would be able to work up to within assaulting distance in daylight. From two or three officers I heard the half-anxious, half-indignant remark, " the Guards should be here with us; we ought never to have crossed without the Guards." The situation is now no longer viewed through rose-coloured spectacles, but still Kuroki is full of good hope of breaking through to-night, and all that can be done is being done with that end in view. Urgent orders have been despatched to Umezawa to move on Yentai so soon as he has captured Penchiho*; Matsunaga has been directed to leave the Guards and to complete the Second Division by bringing his Third Brigade to join Okasaki's Fifteenth Brigade; even the two companies of the Second Division who had been left at Shobyoshi have been hurriedly summoned up from the south bank of the river.

As the sun sank below Manjuyama crest, sending out strange red streamers of light into the northern sky, the volume of the musketry increased until it surpassed in its violence anything I have ever heard. The artillerymen on either side worked for their lives round their bellowing guns and sent continuous streams of shells shrieking through the deepening gloom. In the fading light every flash of gun or bursting shrapnel showed up against the dull red background of the sunset like those vivid sparks which coruscate here and there on the surface of a sheet of molten metal as it cools. But the night

* By this time it was already captured.

came on apace and then all became still and very dark.

10.30 P.M.—I returned to Kankuantun at 9, but have been on the roof of my house for the last half-hour. For at about a quarter to ten, just as the moon rose, the firing broke out again on Manjuyama even more furiously than at sunset. The mountains and the river banks and the houses re-echo to the continuous, angry, growling sound of the musketry. The most bitter fight is illuminating the slopes of the hillock, and I could see its shape outlined by innumerable little dazzling specks, showing the thousands of rounds which were being fired. Hundreds of human souls are passing away yonder where the hill-side flashes flame. I feel very much afraid, and wish I had some one by me to hold me by the hand.

1 A.M.—The noise of the battle murders sleep. The flashes of the rifles are now like those sparks which break in clusters from the dark cylinder of a dynamo, and on the night wind, mingling with the interminable fusillade, comes an occasional low, tremulous, very human sound—it must be—it can only be—the shout of those that triumph blended by kindly distance with the heavy groans of the fallen. How can I sleep when less than three miles distant men with rage and death in their hearts, with haggard eyes and trembling hands, are struggling for the mastery with fire and steel? I am deeply depressed by the events of to-day, which disclose a half-hearted, dangerous plan of operations. If we fail to-night at Manjuyama, we may be pushed into the river to-morrow, or driven off our communications on to Penchiho. It seems to me that Kuropatkin can keep Oyama in play as long as he likes, first with his fortifications, secondly with

the Taitsuho; long enough anyway to swallow us up completely. To do the big thing we are here aiming at we need every man of our army, and at the very least a full Division of the Fourth Army. What madness induced me to send that sanguine cable this morning before realising how much of our force we were leaving on the south of the river?*

* I am tempted to cut out this faint-hearted reaction from my previous over-confidence, but as I am dealing with my impressions just as they arose I feel I have no right to suppress my mistakes.—I. H.

## CHAPTER XXIV

### MANJUYAMA

KANKUANTUN, *September 2nd*, 1904.—Rose finally at 4 A.M., after a sleepless night, and, crossing by the pontoon, again climbed the Swallow's Nest hill. No one had arrived there yet except one, a junior officer of the General Staff, and he told me the Headquarters had passed a bad night, but that Okasaki has captured the hill all right, although he has suffered great losses. The grisly phantoms of last night have vanished in the cool grey light of morning—thank God!

It seems that so long as yesterday's daylight lasted an assault had been impracticable. Before storming such a hillock as Manjuyama, exposed to the enemy's gun fire from three directions, it was necessary to consider, not only the primary cost of the assault but also the position of the stormers if successful. Exposed to such a terrific shell storm as it would have been in the power of the enemy to concentrate upon them, they must have been blown to bits long before they could dig themselves into comparative safety. We were mistaken, then, yesterday evening in thinking that the intensity of the musketry meant that Okasaki was seriously trying to effect a lodgment on Manjuyama.

As soon, however, as the crepuscule had deepened into the profound obscurity which last night preceded the rising of the moon, he advanced his brigade through the kaoliung to within rushing distance.

Each battalion moved with one company in line, leading, followed at close interval by the other three companies in section columns at deploying intervals. The direction was kept by the compasses of the officers. The signal for the onslaught was to be the rising of the moon.

It was nearly 10 o'clock when the first pale moonbeams stole across the battlefield, and no sooner did Manjuyama's ridge emerge ghost-like at that summons from the darkness than the 30th Regiment under the brave old Colonel Baba charged into its northern face with a tremendous Banzai yell. They made good their footing, and then came the turn of the 16th Regiment, which also dashed in fiercely, and effected a lodgment on the hillock's southern slopes. But the Russians here were stout fellows, although not very numerous or strongly entrenched, and those holding the central part of the position were not at all inclined to say Amen to a Japanese Banzai. Till midnight, confused and passionate fighting took place backward and forward over the shell scarred features of this little Rice-cake hill, about which hour the last handful of the Russians holding on round a small tumulus on the summit were fairly forced back into the surrounding sea of kaoliung.

Hardly had the Japanese realised that they were masters of the position, when two of the enemy's battalions made a determined counter-attack against the right flank of the 30th Regiment. Had these two battalions come as a reinforcement a few minutes earlier, whilst their own men were still maintaining their grip of the summit, the results of the night's fighting might have been different. As it was, the counter-attack was repulsed after half an hour's fighting, leaving a lieutenant-colonel and many others dead behind on the ground.

The great danger, the advance of the Russians from the Yentai coal mines against the unsupported Shimamura Brigade covering the right flank of the assailants of Manjuyama on the Gochosan hills, has never come to a head. The enemy in this quarter have shown no determination. They had opened fire at long range, first with a couple of field-guns, and afterwards with a battery; they had done a little long-range infantry skirmishing, and that was all.

Umezawa had found it necessary to advance northwards beyond Penchiho towards Pingtaitsu (Map XXIII.), so as to drive off the enemy completely, before obeying his orders, and turning westwards.

Matsunaga's Brigade of the Second Division is on its way back from co-operating with the Guards, and should arrive here before mid-day, The Twenty-ninth Kobi has actually arrived, and has already joined Okasaki.

Such was the situation as explained to me early in the morning. On account of the kaoliung, I could see no infantry except the Russians on 131 and Japanese on Manjuyama and Gochosan. The muffled, booming sound of a heavy cannonade came faintly to our ears over Mountains 131 and 151, which interpose between the Swallow's Nest on which we stand and Liaoyang, where soon we hope to stand (*see* Sketch XXI.).

Kuroki and his Staff turned up about 7 A.M. They seemed in good spirits. Kuroki admits he could not close his ears to the fusillade about Manjuyama, but, when it ceased, he says he felt so confident of a

Japanese victory that he was able to sleep soundly till sunrise.

News has come to hand from the Second Army to the effect that they intend to push on to-day to the south bank of the Taitsuho. The Guards also report that the Fourth Army has made such progress as to relieve them of any fear lest the Russians still facing them should take the initiative.

Under these circumstances, General Kuroki feels bound to redouble his efforts so as at least to keep pace with the progress of the other armies. He has therefore ordered the Guards to march northwards, cross the river near Kaochintsi and attack Mountain 151, which lies immediately south-west of Mountain 131, and is similarly covered from assault by the Taitsuho flowing along its steeply scarped southern slopes. All is possible if the Russians are on the point of retiring, and if Okasaki, as Kuroki mentions in the same order, is at once going to take Mountain 131; otherwise, the task seems impossible—unless, indeed, the Guards, like ducks, can first swim the river and then fly up the precipitous face of the mountain.

Just at this time, namely, 8 A.M., I saw the first step being taken by Okasaki to capture 131. Several companies of his infantry* worked up apparently from Hsikuantun village, and effected a lodgment a little way up on the northern spur of the mountain. This feature does not run up in one continuous slope to the summit, but is broken into three successive waves or knolls. At present the Japanese are clinging very closely to the lower of these under features.

It was whilst I was watching this plucky detachment that the Russian guns began a *feu d'enfer* against

* Three companies 1st Battalion 4th Regiment.

Manjuyama. From north, south, and west they rained shells on Okasaki and his men, who could only lie low and send up to us a melancholy message saying that an advance beyond Manjuyama was impossible owing to the strength of the enemy about Heyentai and Safutun, and that it was becoming very necessary to do something against the Russian artillery. Certainly this is so; but even the batteries which had again advanced during the night to the north-west of Huankufun cannot locate the enemy's guns, which are firing indirect, probably from behind kaoliung crops. Moreover, as Lieutenant-Colonel Kurita said to me the other day, every shot fired from a Japanese gun takes a day off his life, and although our friends are none of them likely to tell me so, I strongly suspect that after all the shooting of the past seven days they have not any superabundance of shot in their lockers.

Meanwhile, the General Staff are delighted that a commencement has been made in the taking of 131, and have sent (at 9 A.M.) these orders to the commanders of the Second and Twelfth Divisions.

(1) The main force of the enemy is retreating towards Mukden. The Umezawa brigade* is advancing on the coal mines, and the Imperial Guards on 151.

(2) The First Army is to pursue the enemy with its main force.

(3) The Twelfth Division will pursue towards Sandoha.† The Second Division, after taking 131, will advance towards Lotatai.

Kuroki's confidence is certainly magnificent. Matsunaga's brigade has now (9.30 A.M.) crossed and marched on to assist Okasaki, but the men are dead-beat

* From Penchiho.
† Chinese, Santaopa (*see* Map XXXV.).

General Kuroki and Staff on "Swallow's Nest Hill" North of the Taitsu-ho on September 2 during the Battle of Liaoyang

GENERAL KUROKI IS SHADING HIS FACE WITH ONE OF THE FANS WHICH EVERY SOLDIER CARRIED

and will not be able to do much for the next twenty-four hours. To judge by the firing, there is hard fighting going on between the Shimamura brigade and the Russians north of Gochosan, and Kuroki and his Staff look in this direction much longer and more earnestly than they do at the shelling of Manjuyama or at the Japanese companies clinging to the spur on 131, so I daresay our fate is being decided even now as I write. One thing is of good augury; as the morning wears on the sound of the firing to the north comes more and more faintly to our ears.

5 P.M.—Welcome news has come in from Shimamura showing that the menacing Russian column from the north has been swept away by the Twelfth Brigade, Twelfth Division, with unexpected ease. It seems that the five hills of Gochosan are separated by about a mile of low country, full of ravines and covered with crops, from a long bare plateau about 100 feet high, half a mile broad, and three and a half miles long, which stretches northwards as far as the Yentai coal mines. Super-imposed upon this plateau are two or three groups of round bare hills about 100 feet high, and standing, therefore, full 200 feet above the sea of kaoliung which wraps the whole face of the plain in its mantle of invisibility.

In the early morning, the Russian column two miles long (which has developed, according to the prisoners' reports, into a brigade of infantry and a considerable force of Cossacks under General Orloff) began to move off the Yentai plateau against Gochosan. They took no precaution to cover their advance by reconnaissance or scouting parties, and permitted the head of the column to be caught in close order amongst the low broken ridges and ravines near the village of Taiyo and between the two ranges of hills. Here the Russians were defeated and were rolled back in great confusion, part of them to the west and part backwards on to the colliery plateau. Later on, in some way not yet understood, Shimamura again got round them, probably by taking advantage of the kaoliung, and drove them clean off the field with hardly any loss to his own gallant brigade.

I gather that neither the Russian infantry nor Cossacks displayed on this occasion their usual tenacity. The Headquarters Staff consider it a marvellous piece of good fortune that, just where the threat was most formidable, the instrument should have proved so inferior. They believe these men of Orloff's are all reservists.

It is certainly curious that the Japanese, marching for the first time into an intricate country, which the Russians nevertheless should have at their finger-tips, are able to surprise and out-manœuvre their enemies with so much apparent facility once they trust themselves out of their trenches.

So much for the danger to our right wing from the north, which has now been brushed away by the excellent Shimamura, and indeed it was fully time, for things have not been going by any means so brilliantly here. The Japanese guns are silent, or very nearly so, either because the enemy's artillery is too powerful for them, or else because they are running dangerously short of ammunition. Consequently, the Russian guns are free to devote their entire attention to Manjuyama, and it is being so pelted with shell that Okasaki and his gallant Sendai lads will need all their constitutional absence of nerves to enable them to stand their ground much longer. Worse, the companies which reached the lowest knoll of 131 at 8 A.M., and which afterwards succeeded in getting as far as the second or penultimate point on the ridge, have now been fairly *rafaled* off the mountain. It was about 4 P.M. when they withdrew to Huankufun village, having to a certainty lost very heavily,* and then we were all able to see Russian reinforcements darting from one patch of kaoliung to another, and coming over the northern spur of the mountain in little thick mobs as if they meant to attack Manjuyama from the south. The sight woke up the Japanese guns and, by a spasmodic effort, they steadied this advance with shrapnel, and then, continuing their fire, drove it back over the spur or up again towards the summit of the mountain.

I see so much, so quickly, that, by putting points one after the other, like beads upon a string, I succeed only too admirably, I feel, in turning the most marvellous things any man has been so lucky as to see into a series of unarresting, commonplace details. Now this repulse of the Russians by shrapnel, when baldly stated, seems almost meaningless, and yet if I could give even a dim idea of what occurred no one would ever forget it. First, hundreds of little grey mannikins swarming forward over the spur of Mountain 131; next, the thunder symphony played by all the Japanese cannon; last, the crowd convulsed, tossed about like autumn leaves before the gale, until all the poor atoms were blown back in heaps from whence they came. Imagine a swarm of ants entering eagerly by an open door until the housewife seizes her broom and sweeps them out in tortured, struggling clusters; remember

* Extract from next day's notes:—The 4th Regiment lost 270 men out of their detachment of 600 before they withdrew from 131 at 4 P.M. yesterday.

that these are no insects, but living human beings; and then perhaps some dim idea may be formed of one small incident in the passion-play of to-day.

Having done so much, the guns quickly relapsed into long periods of complete silence, punctuated by brief intervals of very desultory and obviously feeble fire. With good reason. The Russians have fifty or sixty guns in action somewhere near Tatsurenko,* as well as forty guns firing hard from the neighbourhood of Safutun. In addition, there is a battery and, worst of all, three howitzers on Mountain 131, and another battery concealed in the kaoliung some two miles due north of Manjuyama.

The Headquarters Staff were in the gloomiest mood I have yet seen them. It was not, as far as I can diagnose their feelings, because they fear they are in imminent danger of being overwhelmed. I believe their chief dread of positive disaster passed away with the flight of Orloff before Shimamura.

It is rather rage and bitterness at feeling themselves impotent, whilst they see in the far distance trains puffing northwards, and great columns of troops and transport moving towards Mukden behind the shield of the two or three Divisions who are facing us. They are grieved also for the troops who are almost worn out, and who are not able to cook their rice under the terrible artillery fire.

Towards evening this fire increased to the maximum compass of 100 quick-firing guns.

The Japanese artillery was dead silent.

I have no words left to convey an impression of the fire of 100 quick-firers discharging their unlimited ammunition at top speed. To chronicle that the guns pealed faster and faster until the separate reports merge

* Chinese, Talienkou (*see* Map XXII.).

into one long-drawn roar; to explain that the air seems alive with bursting shell, or to speak of hurricanes of shrapnel and the whistling of their bullets, is hopelessly, miserably, tame, inadequate and paltry. I will confine myself, then, to the matter-of-fact statement that, if I were struck deaf and blind to-morrow, it would be a consolation to me for the rest of my life that I had heard and seen the great cannonade of to-day.

At 6.30 P.M. things grew quieter, and, tired out with my last sleepless night, I have returned here.

KANKUANTUN, *September 2nd*, 1904, 10 P.M.—All day long the battle has raged, but with singularly little material result beyond, I imagine, that each passing hour sees hundreds perish for the Mikado or the Czar.

The relative positions of Russians and Japanese on the north bank of the Taitsuho have hardly altered at all since yesterday, and what I have to write up now chiefly concerns the bloody, devilish combat which raged for the best part of last night over that shell-scourged, corpse-strewn monticule, Manjuyama.

Last night I slept profoundly till I was awakened at 3.30 A.M., and never heard a sound of the mortal conflict going on, only some four miles distant. But I felt as soon as I got on my horse, and rode through the village, that there was something in the air—that some new dread, anger or weariness, had spread through the dark hours.

Methought many of the soldiers crossing the pontoon bridge from north to south looked at me with strange glances, less friendly than usual. I felt glad, for once, that I had an officer riding by my side.

Is this the product of my own over-strained imagination? Partly, perhaps, but not entirely, I am sure. The First Army is being strained to breaking-point, and under that strain, although the officers are as polite as ever, some of the men show signs—very subtle signs, but still discernible to the object—that they are not inclined to be too discriminating in drawing a distinction between Russians or any other foreigners. "What a fantastic theory," some might say, "to build up between the differences of a smile and a scowl!" Well, be it so, my friends. As an old Highland officer used to say to my father, when he was getting worsted, "I canna argue, but ye're wrang."

When I reached the Swallow's Nest fort I got no invitation to come and hear the news; nor did I have the opportunity of exchanging one syllable beyond "Good morning" with the pre-occupied Headquarters during my stay on the hill.

My first intimation of the events of the past night came from a wounded soldier, who said he had left Manjuyama with his bayonet wound some hours ago, and that he could not say for the life of him whether then or now it belonged to the Japanese or the Russians.

The next was a statement made by another wounded soldier, who declared that neither Russians nor Japanese had retreated from Manjuyama, but that the Japanese must certainly be still in possession, for the Russians were all dead.

The next was from an Adjutant who said: "The Second Division had a terrible time last night. If the Russians had been able to maintain their grip on Manjuyama, the whole of Major-General Nishi's command (Second Division) would have been ruined. I would like to see two more bridges built forthwith, and the Guards brought over as quickly as possible."

Then I got something more authoritative from a

person attached to the Staff, to whom I shall be for ever grateful. Putting his information together with the result of Vincent's talks with many non-commissioned officers and private soldiers in Okasaki's brigade yesterday evening and last night, I find that no less than five desperate assaults were made by the Russians on Manjuyama.

The first was in connection with the attempt I saw being made from Mountain 131, when a battalion I could not see attacked simultaneously from Heyentai with the bayonet.

The second was by two Russian battalions against the left of the 30th Regiment; an assault which was so fierce and sustained that the brigade reserve had to be called up before it could be repulsed.

The third occurred only a few minutes later, when two more Russian battalions attacked the 16th Regiment, and actually made good the top of Manjuyama. Eventually they were driven down again at the point of the bayonet, but only fell back to a point about 100 yards beyond the bottom of the hill, whence they kept up a very hot fire on the crest. Some brave Russians now crept up the western slope unobserved and flung magnesium fire-balls on to the hill. The Japanese trenches were thus rendered clearly visible, and the enemy's fire became intolerably deadly. The men tried to put out the lights by flinging stones at them, but to no purpose. Then a soldier stepped forth from the ranks in the good old Samurai style, calling out his name and regiment, so that it was heard above even the terrible din of the musketry, and quietly set about extinguishing the fatal lights with the butt end of his rifle. I have not yet got his name, but they say he was not killed.

The moon had not yet risen, and in the intense darkness the opposing lines had become so intermingled that it was not possible to tell friend from foe even by the flash of the rifles. But dark as it was, it was evident enough that the Russians were still full of fight, for away to the west the band of a regiment on the march was plainly audible, and nearer to Manjuyama another battalion was loudly singing the National Anthem.

Seeing the urgent necessity of getting his men properly in hand before worse should befall, Okasaki told his bugler to sound the cease fire. The order was unhesitatingly obeyed by the whole of the Fifteenth Brigade, although many of the officers and men felt that by doing so the initiative was being surrendered, and a great advantage being given to the enemy. So the Japanese lay still under a grievous fire, and meanwhile Okasaki and his officers tried to pull together their broken and disordered line, and fit it to stem the impending wave of humanity which might, at any moment, sweep up again out of the surrounding darkness.

It was at 10 P.M. that it came, breaking in fire and smoke and steel full against the right of the 16th Regiment. Once more the Russian scouts had crept up in advance, but this time instead of fire-balls they flung into the trenches numerous hand-grenades, the size of oranges, which blew men's bodies to pieces. Then came the bayonet charge heralded by a terrifying shout, and it seemed as if all was lost, for the Japanese were driven over the crest and half way down the eastern slope of the hillock before they could make a stand. But here the solid 16th Regiment, aided by all the available reserves, clung on desperately. Now many a hero breathed his last amidst his fellows, as the soldiers fought it out with their bayonets, the big men rushing furiously head down, the small men alert and wary, never losing a chance. Half an hour the death grapple endured, and then, once more, the Russians fell back, leaving yet another 300 corpses strewn on those fatal slopes.*

The last or fifth assault came on at 2 A.M. against the 30th Regiment, and was more easily repulsed. But old Colonel Baba saw behind the retiring lines of these stormers another dark, slowly-creeping mass already enveloping both flanks of the hill, and threatening, by its mere momentum, to carry away everything if once it broke loose against his men. It was doubtful if the defenders could stand another grand assault, and the only chance seemed to be to anticipate the Russians and to make a vigorous counter-charge before they attempted to storm. All reserves were called up and, led by the 30th Regiment, some six battalions of Japanese were launched against the Russian left, which broke, and the whole of their massive column rolled back in disorder on Safutun.

If Orloff's easy defeat yesterday inclined the Japanese to depreciate their enemy, the fighting of last night has again raised the Russian prestige far higher than it has ever stood since the battle of the Yalu on May 1st last. It is admitted on all hands that victory or defeat hung evenly balanced in the scales during several hours. Had it not been for the arrival of Matsunaga's brigade, Manjuyama would have assuredly been lost.†

* Including the Colonel of the 123rd Regiment, and his handsome grey charger.

† The following is extracted from an entry made several weeks later:—A junior but responsible Staff officer, having remarked to me, "We should never have repulsed the enemy had not Matsunaga's brigade arrived by then. If we had not had the help of

It is curious how the tacit consent of either side has frequently bestowed upon some obscure corner of a battlefield an importance which no one could well have foreseen, or is even able entirely to explain afterwards in the light of actual events. Mountain 131 and Gochosan were obviously vital tactical points, but who would have suspected that an insignificant, turtle-backed hillock like Manjuyama,* was to be a scene of such carnage, and the turning-point perhaps of an historic battle. Certainly the Russians with Manjuyama in their possession could have brought up their guns on to the *col* which joins it to Mountain 131, and thence have supported a further advance of their infantry by direct fire at medium range, instead of by indirect fire at long range. But although such a consideration might present itself invitingly to the student of the map, it is in actuality very greatly discounted by the kaoliung, which conceals the movements of infantry and cavalry across the plain as well as a moonless night, and renders artillery action of any sort very much a matter of chance.

The same drawback lessens the value of Manjuyama as an infantry position. Had the harvest been gathered,

---

Matsunaga's Brigade, I think myself the fight might have had a different ending." I felt rather puzzled, as Major-General Okasaki had personally told Captain Vincent that Matsunaga had not been engaged at all on the night of the 2nd–3rd of September. I, therefore, begged the highest available authority to be kind enough to explain to me the true state of the case. He said: "Matsunaga did not fire a shot, but his arrival as a reserve to the Divisional General enabled him to send every man of Okasaki's into the firing ine instead of keeping some of them in hand under his own orders." —I. H.

* About 75 feet high, 300 yards long, and 20 yards broad on the top.—I. H.

this hillock would have afforded a very fine field of fire. With the crops standing there is no field of fire, for it is obviously impossible that any one can see from the top of Manjuyama more than a very few yards beyond the foot of the slope. What then is the value of a field of fire when the objective cannot be located even approximately? *Per contra*, any one who chooses to climb Manjuyama becomes instantly visible from any rising ground over the whole battlefield. I believe it is this very conspicuous visibility of the Rice Cake Hill which is causing both sides to concentrate their efforts upon it. Companies, Russian or Japanese, when launched out into the bewildering sea of kaoliung, instinctively converge upon Manjuyama as moths fly towards a candle, and many of them with the same results. Something more or less similar took place at the battle of Fredericksburg, when, on December 13th, 1862, Burnside seemed deliberately to select Marye's Hill as a suitable point upon which to hurl division after division to its destruction. Presuming the commander to have been sane, there is no possible explanation for such a negation of all the rudiments of tactics, except that the fatal hill stood out conspicuously and arrested the attention of a brain which was, for the moment, incapable of cool reflection. It is my firm belief that, in the present instance, the Russians would do much better to leave their montecule alone and content themselves with holding its Japanese defenders by a little gentle skirmishing.

From Manjuyama to Gochosan is a distance of 2½ miles, the whole of it thickly covered with giant crops. This gap between Okasaki and Shimamura is filled by three of Kigoshi's battalions—all he has to spare, as one of his two regiments has been sucked into the maelstrom of the Manjuyama struggle. One battalion per mile; that is rather weak! Had any of the Russian attacks, which fell with such sledge-hammer violence upon the entrenchments of Manjuyama, been piloted by capable officers through the dense kaoliung half a mile or so further north they must inevitably have pierced the defensive line, and even now, to-night, if they will only push boldly in anywhere between Manjuyama and Gochosan they should smash right through, at least, in the first instance. In that case, Okasaki at Manjuyama will have Mountain 131 on his left flank and a force of Russians marching and fighting in rear of his right flank under cover of the kaoliung. I think he must in that case fall back, and Shimamura, too, would begin to feel isolated at the Yentai coal-mines, so far away from the pontoon bridge.

The Guards could make nothing of Mountain 151, as was to be expected, seeing that the Russians were in a practically impregnable position, and that Okasaki could not take Mountain 131.

These poor Guards are always getting very hard nuts to crack. I believe they have spent the best part of the day lying on the south bank of the unfordable Taitsuho, being fired at from 151, without making any serious attempt to cross, by which inaction, I think, they show their wisdom, considering the artillery and other conditions prevailing at present. Meanwhile, an order went to them two hours ago, telling them to leave a brigade of artillery and its escort at Shobyoshi, so as to deter the enemy from vacating Mountain 151, either to reinforce another part of the field or to take the offensive, whilst with their main force they march round first east, then north, to join Headquarters at Kankuantun.

## MANJUYAMA

On the whole, neither Guards nor Second Division have been able to do more to-day than to maintain their ground. The only important movement made by the First Army has been carried out by Umezawa with his mixed brigade. On August 30th he had received orders to capture Penchiho, and then to move westwards, to join hands with the Twelfth Division to the north of the Taitsuho. In pursuance of these instructions, Umezawa captured Penchiho at daybreak on August 31st. On September 1st, he received more definite orders, telling him he was to march across the mountains and endeavour to surprise Orloff in the vicinity of the Yentai coal mines. Accordingly, he moved north-west of Penchiho on the 2nd instant, and was on the point of marching definitely west for the colliery hills when he heard that a fresh force of Russians had appeared to be north of Pingtaitsu. Bold as he is said to be, Umezawa could not afford to march off the ground leaving an enemy in the act of descending upon his communications, and so he had to retrace his steps and attack. The result was a brilliant little victory, and the retreat of the Russians to the northwards (*see* Map XXXV.).

Umezawa has now been able to carry out his orders, and joined Shimamura at the coal mines at 1 P.M. to-day (September 3rd), having left two battalions and two guns at Pingtaitsu to contain the defeated Russians.

Before I close my record of the great events of the past twenty-four hours, I must note a remark made to me to-day, on the Swallow's Nest hill, by a civilian of sorts, who has a brother commanding a battalion of the 12th Regiment. He said, "I fear we have no genius for commerce. Our only method of getting on in the world will be to go continually to war and exact very heavy indemnities as the price of peace." Captain Okada, who overheard him, went for him thus: "That is a very bad sentiment of yours. Mr. ——! If Japanese say such things, no wonder that a yellow peril theory finds ready acceptance. You assure a foreigner that we Japanese must sell our blood for money, but I assure him that such a thing no true Japanese would ever do!"

Mr. —— then became abashed and remained silent.

*Midnight.*—We are next door to Headquarters in the village, and going out just now for a minute before turning in I knocked up against young ——, who has given me an interesting postscript wherewith to round up my record of this eventful day.

It seems hardly credible, but the First Army has been entirely cut off from all communication with Oyama and the Second and Fourth Armies from yesterday night until a few minutes ago. The wires were cut, as it was only natural to suppose they would be cut, and then the Japanese armies, separated by only twenty miles of mountainous country, were unable, although it was a brilliant sunny day, to talk to one another. Here the much abused British army may take comfort and realise how all its past thirty years promiscuous fighting has not been time so entirely wasted as some of its critics would like it to suppose! There is nothing more trying to the nerves than isolation, and the cut wires go far to explain the unmistakable tension which existed during the day on the summit of the Swallow's Nest hill.

Now a few minutes ago communications were restored, and Headquarters have just heard that the Second and Fourth Armies have not been able to occupy all the defences on the south side of the river until 5 P.M. this evening.

Poor General Kuroki! Owing to the breakdown in the signalling arrangements and the consequent severance of communications, he had to act upon instructions many hours old. These had been his warranty for believing that the other armies would reach the river by the evening of the 2nd, and now it turns out that they will barely have reached it by the evening of the 3rd.

This is rough on the First Army, which has shed its blood too freely in the firm belief that it was lagging behind in the great pursuit, and could not comprehend why, when pressing on to cut off the enemy's retreat, it should have found itself so suddenly on the very brink of destruction. A dozen British soldiers with a couple of heliographs would to-day have saved the Japanese many hundreds of lives that were wasted in attempting the impossible.

## CHAPTER XXV

## LIAOYANG

K ANKUANTUN, *September 4th*, 1904.—Heavy smoke this morning, which came drifting over from the Liaoyang direction and mingled with the river-mist until it produced a very colourable imitation of a London fog.

Headquarters were delightfully cordial and forthcoming to me to-day, and did their best to supplement my news gleanings of yesterday. I found that I had already got my facts fairly well arranged, the gist of what I now heard being as follows:

"If we had advanced yesterday, the enemy could have enveloped us with four times our strength. It is very lucky indeed that Kuropatkin did not come and develop a great attack upon us with superior force at any time since the day before yesterday. On the evening of the 31st we intended to play with the enemy until, by getting Matsunaga over from the Guards, the Second and Twelfth Divisions should be complete. We then meant to leave a screen against the Mountain 131 whilst we pushed straight against the enemy's front for the railway, *viâ* Heyentai and Safutun. When, however, we learnt that Orloff with nearly a whole Division was in a position to operate against our right flank from the coal mines, we became stricken with paralysis, as it was altogether too risky an operation for any commander to push his force into a hole leaving the enemy in superior force on both his wings. Thus our General felt himself most disagreeably embarrassed all day yesterday.

"Beyond all doubt the Russians have had twelve or thirteen Divisions available to crush us had they felt fully determined to do so. But they have shown a great deal of vacillation, and until now our good luck has certainly been almost past belief. I suppose Kuropatkin still thinks we have six Divisions. Five minutes ago" (1.45 P.M.) "Marshal Kuroki received a report from the Second Division saying that they had occupied Mountain 131, which will enable us to pivot round with 131 as a *point d'appui* for our left, and who knows but that we may yet succeed in cutting off some of the Russians. I must now go, but before you close that favourite companion of yours, just write down in it for thought in future years that, on September 1st, Nishi* had only the 16th and 30th Regiments with him. In the afternoon came the 29th Regiment, and then on the evening of September 2nd Matsunaga arrived with the 4th Regiment.† Each reinforcement appeared upon the scene only just in the very nick of time to save us, so if ever in days to come you wish to teach troops the imperative necessity of doing whatever they have to do, whether it be marching or fighting, with *all* the energy and *all* the force at their command, you can tell them the touch-and-go story of little Rice-cake hill and preach the moral afterwards as much as you like. The text is good, whether you take it from the Russian point or our own.

* Lieutenant-General Nishi, commanding the Second Division.
† This does not quite correspond with my own conclusions as given previously, but the Japanese staff officer's statement had better be accepted as accurate.

"Yesterday, and the day before yesterday, the General Staff had no appetites. But although it may be that we shall all be accounted failures, yet I feel very certain that our attacks, and the bold face we have put upon the situation, since we first began to get into difficulties on September 2nd, are the true causes which have forced the enemy's troops on the south bank of the Taitsuho to pass over to the north bank, whereby the Second and Fourth Armies have captured the forts of Liaoyang. Thus the *rôle* of our army has been fulfilled, at least to the extent of one half.

"One more word, lest you begin to think of me only as a lecturer on solemn matters. Yesterday a military coolie had been taking rations to Manjuyama and was picking his way back under such a heavy fire as even great warriors do not often hope to encounter. At last a shell burst just at his feet, covering him with dirt, but, by some strange accident, leaving him uninjured. Instantly he stooped down, and picking up a stone flung it into the smoke, crying out, 'There, you devil—take that!'"

I saw but little more of interest from my perch on the Swallow's Nest. The Second Brigade of Guards under Watanabe joined Headquarters at mid-day. The fire of the enemy was rapidly dying out, a battery near Safutun being left almost alone in its activity. Moreover, the evacuation of 131 could only bear one interpretation, and accordingly the General issued these orders at 2 P.M.:

"The First Army will now pursue. The Second Division will advance to Lotatai. The Twelfth Division will get into touch with the right of the Second Division and will march on Sandoha, leaving a portion of their force to occupy the coal mines and to keep a look out for the enemy north of them. Major-General Watanabe, with his Brigade of Guards and the 29th Kobi, will take up a position at Heyentai and hold fast there as a general reserve. The commander of the army will also go to Heyentai."

A messenger was sent to Asada and the First Brigade of Guards, who were marching round by Amping, to aquaint them with the commander's intentions. At 5.10 P.M. news came to hand that the Second and Fourth Armies had at last occupied all the enemy's positions south of the river Taitsuho. The commander of the Guards Cavalry also sent in about this time to say that, as the enemy had now evacuated 151, he had made good the low ground between 131 and that mountain. As all the dominating features of the battlefield were now in Kuroki's hands, he decided to spare the Asada Brigade of Guards a forced march and sent them permission to halt the night at Amping.

Before dark, Umezawa from the coal-mines reached Sanchatsu (Map XXIII.), where he is now engaging the enemy's rear-guard, consisting of an infantry brigade and two batteries.*

*In a temple just below Manjuyama, September 5th, 1904.*—I seize the propitious moment of a half-way halt to write up this insatiable note-book. Started at 4 A.M. and marched through Huankufun towards Manjuyama. Much delayed by transport along the roads and on the pontoon bridge. Had a talk with a wounded soldier in the village whilst —— was making

---

* The hostile forces got into contact at 3 P.M. and carried on a sniping and skirmishing contest until past midnight, no particular damage being done to either side. For the closing scenes of the pursuit and a few simple comments on the battle, see pp. 128 to 140. —I. H.

inquiries as to Kuroki's whereabouts. He said the men all loved the war, and cared nothing for hunger or fatigue where the renown and authority of the Emperor were concerned. When they were wounded or sick they had only one wish, and that was to be allowed to rejoin their companies. He also told me that the Russians had stretched an enchanted wire in front of Manjuyama, and that if any Japanese soldier was unlucky enough to touch it his head flew off his shoulders that very second. His remarks might appear bombastic or high falutin to any one who did not hear them, but as a matter of fact they were spoken quite simply and with matter-of-fact conviction from the heart.

About 9 A.M. it began to rain heavily—a regular thunder plump. We rode for refuge to this temple just short of the eastern slope of Manjuyama, and here we have found Kuroki and the General Staff forming a somewhat remarkable group.

"My tables—meet it is I set it down."

In the temple are figures of Buddha and his disciples, whose fine serenity contrasts with the fevered energy of the mortals at their feet. One of the disciples is serving as a peg from which hangs Prince Kuni's dripping waterproof. General Kuroki is seated between His Imperial Highness and Major-General Watanabe, commanding the Second Brigade of Guards, on the one side and Buddha himself on the other. A couple of planks fixed up between the Buddha throne and a chair have been made to serve as a rude table. Across these planks is laid a map, upon which Colonel Matsuishi, vice-chief of the General Staff, and a young assistant, are busy with pencil and india-rubber entering the positions of our troops at the moment. Now a senior Staff Officer advances from the background and squatting, down upon his heels, Indian fashion, explains the situation on the map and discusses it, eagerly, with Kuroki and General Watanabe, both of whom put on spectacles to see more clearly. They say nothing and the Staff Officer says a great deal. Occasionally Kuroki punctuates a pause when the lecturer stops for want of breath by an approving nod. It is now 9.30 and I feel rather sad as they have told me nothing yet. They look fairly happy, but not exactly radiant or triumphant either. I hear guns in the distance firing very steady and slow; I should imagine some 9 or 10 miles distant. So soon as the sun comes out I ought to see something from Manjuyama.

*Safutun, evening.*—I saw nothing from Manjuyama, but I saw too much upon it. All along the crest were Japanese trenches. No corpses; only many stains and shapes of clotted blood which even the thunderstorm had not been able to wash away. But when I stepped forward and viewed the western declivity my heart for a moment stood still with horror. Never have I seen such a scene. Such a mad jumble of arms and accoutrements mingled with the bodies of those who so lately bore them, arrested, cut short in the fury of their assault, and now, for all their terrible, menacing attitudes so very, very quiet. How silent; how ghastly; how lonely seemed this charnel house where I, a solitary European, beheld rank upon rank of brave Russians mown down by the embattled ranks of Asia.

A stone pillar on the crest of the plateau was simply plastered with lead, and Vincent, whom I met shortly afterwards, told me that he had learnt from a Japanese soldier that throughout the night of the 2nd it had been mistaken for "some brave Russian." Marching on towards the west, we found the roads almost knee deep in sticky mud in which, like flies in jam, several batteries of Japanese artillery were feebly struggling. Another instance, if, indeed, one were wanted, of how seriously the Japanese gun is under-horsed, notwithstanding its lightness. All the infantry had to march along a narrow slippery raised path to the right of this quagmire. About a mile beyond Manjuyama, I came upon a dead Russian soldier lying right across the path, holding his cap in his hand. Thousands must have stepped over his body, but no one had yet found leisure to bury him. He was a very handsome boy of about twenty; singularly dark, and on his face was a slight smile as if he was dreaming some happy dream.

*Fenshan village (three miles north-east of Liaoyang). September 6th, 1904.*—Started to march here at 8 A.M. A bright, glorious morning, and so fresh as to be almost cold. After walking some four miles I drew up at a little clump of pine-trees about fifty yards to one side of the road. Shortly afterwards the Headquarters Staff rode by, and an important personage seeing me, left the *cortège* and came out to pass the time of day. I asked him if he was pleased. He thought for some time before he answered, and then said, "*à moitié.*" At this moment my little fox terrier, which now answers to the name of Rooski, began to chase a goat, and in the confusion another officer took the opportunity to whisper to me, "*Un tiers seulement.*" After Rooski had been reprimanded, my friend resumed:

"The enemy commenced his real retreat on the night of the 3rd. To bring off *un grand coup* we must have attacked and forced our way through the

Russian flank guard during daylight on the 2nd. We took the mamelon Manjuyama on the night 1st–2nd, but when it came to the continuation of our westerly movement next morning we found ourselves badly in want of the help of our Division of Guards. So great an enterprise demands careful preparation in advance, and we were not ready. Moreover, Marshal Oyama was already inclined to think that our First Army had been too venturesome and had sent us positive orders that we must be careful not to commit ourselves too far. By September 3rd the opportunity had passed, as we were then faced by a very superior force."

I was then asked if I had been given any account of the progress of the pursuit since the issue of the orders by Kuroki at 2 P.M. on September 4th.* I replied that I was sure the women and children in London knew more of what was going on than I did, marching along in the kaoliung, devoured by curiosity, and only supporting my ignorance by the persistence of my hopes of obtaining some such windfall as an interview with some officers of high degree. At this he seemed well pleased, and getting out his note-book spoke as follows: "Well, the fact is, the Divisions found themselves unable to carry out the orders we issued to them at 2 P.M. on the 4th instant. The Divisional Generals received them before 3 o'clock in the afternoon, but neither did the Second Division advance to Lotatai, nor did the Twelfth Division get into touch with the right of the Second Division nor march upon Sandoha. Not at once, that is to say. Not as had been intended. The Second Division did not begin its march until almost dusk. Both brigades lost their way in the kaoliung, and, after struggling in vain for some time

* See p. 124.

to make head against their difficulties, lay down where they were to await the morning light, having covered some two or three miles only instead of the six which was expected of them. The Twelfth Division did not commence its advance until after 10 P.M. and soon took the village of Sho-Tatsurenko.* (*See* Map XXII.)

"To avoid the kaoliung the subsequent advance was made along the raised embankment of the railway, by following which they hoped to arrive at Sandoha, their objective. Hardly had they progressed a mile, however, when they were charged into, full tilt, by a Russian column, which came tearing down the embankment with loud cheers. No one has been able to give me any just idea of subsequent events. Apparently, the Russians fought furiously, although without much discrimination. Through the kaoliung, at random, companies rushed about wildly with their bayonets at the charge. On the Japanese side also there was much confusion and some loss, and the advance was entirely arrested.† By daybreak the Russians had withdrawn, and without cavalry our

---

* Chinese, Hsiao Talienkou.

† Extract from an entry made on September 13th: "Captain Jardine, who was with this brigade, tells me that whenever one side charged the other side always charged to meet them. To a listener the effect was extraordinary. A hot musketry fight might be in progress, when suddenly the Russians would sound the charge. Instantly all firing would cease on either side, the Japanese cheering wildly in answer to the drums and bugles of the enemy. The Russian cheer 'Hoorah!' the Japanese, on such desperate occasions, cheer 'Wa-a-a!' The impression given by these cheers, mingling with the rattle of the drums and the clangour of the bugles, was more melancholy than martial, sounding like a prolonged wail of grief ascending from the troubled earth up into the dark heavens."— I. H.

Twelfth Division had no longer any chance of bringing them to book.

"Yesterday, Umezawa with his mixed brigade advanced from his position immediately north of the Twelfth Division as far as a line facing north-west through Sankwaisekisan* (*see* Map XXIII. or XXXIII.). Here he was engaged by a regiment of infantry, a regiment of lancers, and two batteries. He was not able to make much impression on the enemy. He may still be fighting and may do some good; but I fear not. The battle, in fact, is over, and the First Army has not captured many prisoners or guns.†

"It is these self-same guns which have made it too difficult. Also I must say the Russians made a fine retirement. They did not run away in too great haste, I assure you. There was no disorder, and every mile or two they halted and re-formed their ranks, and then continued the retirement in echelon, moving from one point of vantage to another.

"However, from the fact that the enemy did not commence his retreat until the 3rd, it is plain that he fell back simply because he was beaten. If Kuropatkin had merely meant from the first to fight a delaying action, he would have had all his arrangements organised to that end, and would certainly have started sooner. It seems, then, probable that, if the Fourth Army had not taken the great redoubt and pierced the Russian line to the south of the Taitsuho, Kuropatkin would have massed troops against us and attacked us in overwhelming force on the north side of the river. Equally probable is it that, if we had not stormed and held Manjuyama, Kuropatkin would have sent another

* Chinese, Sankuaishishan or "Three Great Rock Hill."
† The First Army captured no guns.

Division south of the river and have assumed the offensive against Oyama. But as the Japanese were successful and equally threatening on *both* sides of the river, all movement was paralysed except that of retreat."

Having spent a whole delightful hour, extravagant to himself but profitable to me, the great man gave his bridle rein a shake and disappeared, whilst I followed myself more slowly, congratulating myself upon the fountain of knowledge I had so opportunely struck.

There is scope for a fat volume on the battle of Liaoyang, and although my stock of indelible pencils will not carry me very far in that direction, I feel I ought to make an effort to sketch in, however lightly, some of my general impressions.

The first point which strikes me is the clear, simple, and direct character of the Japanese strategy, carried out though it has been on a grandiose scale. I think it is Clausewitz who says that in war everything is simple, but the simple is the most difficult. The Manchurian campaign will probably be quoted hereafter as an instance in point. I believe that Liaoyang was selected as the point of concentration for the three armies from the very outset of the campaign, and that all arrangements throughout were subservient to the end of doing precisely what we have just attempted to do here. True, no scheme of strategy can ever be independent of the actions of the enemy, and several times since the battle of the Yalu it has seemed likely that modifications would have to be introduced. Only a few weeks ago our Headquarters thought the battle might be fought at Kaiping. A fortnight ago, giving Kuropatkin credit for a skilful use of his chances, they were sure Oyama would have to fight at Anshantien,

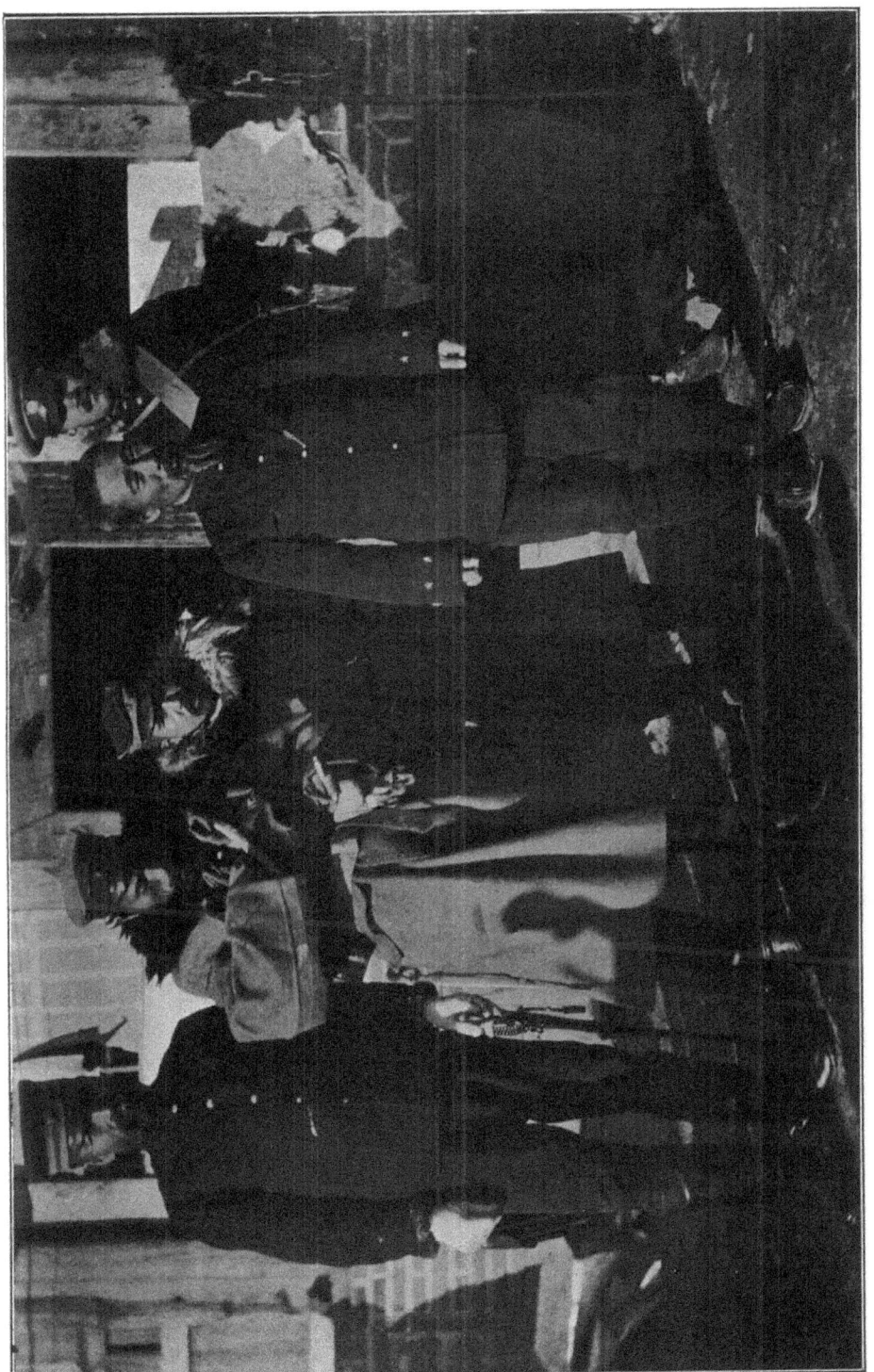

Col. Kani  Capt. Hishikari  Major-General Umezawa  Capt. Jardine

THE COMMANDER OF THE "MIXED BRIGADE"
ON THE RIGHT OF THE 1ST ARMY

and the First Army at Amping. Only after August 26th did they dare permit themselves to hope that the great event would, after all, take place at the predestined spot.

But variations such as these do not affect the general spirit of the scheme, which was that the three armies should keep quite distinct, on separate bases and lines of communication, advancing slowly and methodically in strict combination, preserving approximately equal distance from Kuropatkin's headquarters, but drawing nearer and nearer to one another as they approached him, so that, at last, on the actual battlefield, wherever that might be, they should find themselves clasping one another's hands in a semi-circle round the enemy. Here we find reminiscences of the scheme of the Prussians which led up to Königgrätz, especially in the fact that, in either case, concentration before entering upon the tactical area was practically impossible for geographical reasons.* It is natural enough that the Japanese should have copied Von Moltke's method of concentration on the battlefield as they are essentially German-taught strategists. In comparing the two schemes, however, it must be remembered that things are not quite as they were thirty-eight years ago. Strategically, no doubt, the dangers and advantages of such a plan remain substantially unmodified, but tactically the prizes of a successful concentration are greater whilst its realisation is more difficult. The reason the prizes are greater is that, with magazine rifles, smoke-

---

* Von Moltke, however, had reasonable grounds for believing that with his more rapid mobilisation he could concentrate the Prussian Army in the enemy's country before the latter could interfere. This scheme was nullified by the King, who, for political reasons, arrested the advance after the strategical deployment had been completed.

less powders, and an artillery which carries five or six miles, an army half surrounded, even if only by an equal force, finds itself at a great disadvantage. A mass is no longer able to break through a thin line as used to be the case when weapons only carried a few hundred yards, and an attack against an enveloping force can, owing to the very long range of firearms, be received by a flanking fire wherever it endeavours to push against the concave formations of troops which have advanced from dispersed bases.

The reason the difficulties of realising such a scheme are greater than they used to be is, again, because of modern armaments, which facilitate the holding of a strong force, for a time, by a much weaker force. Thus, if the commander of the concentrated army has prevision and quickness to take the situation in time, it is easier for him than it used to be to delay, and hold off at arm's length one portion of the converging armies with a comparatively weak force, suitably disposed in an entrenched position, whilst he vigorously employs the great bulk of his troops to overwhelm the other portions. In old days this game could be played on an area of a few square miles, *i.e.*, on the battlefield itself, but now guns and rifles carry so far that action should be taken at an earlier stage, and the effort should be made when the converging forces are at least twenty miles from one another.

From this point of view, Kuropatkin should, at all costs, have hung on to Anshantien with a strong delaying force whilst bringing all the troops he could muster, including his reserves, up to the right bank of the Tangho on the 26th to stake victory or defeat on the issue in that part of the field.

It may plausibly be objected that Oyama would in

such case have found out what was happening, and would have rushed Liaoyang before Kuropatkin could get back after repulsing Kuroki. But this is just my point; defences such as those of Anshantien cannot be rushed nowadays in five minutes, even by superior numbers.* If no other example were available, that of Kuroki's helplessness to break through the Russian rear-guard on September 4th, although he saw his enemy slipping away to the northward, would be fairly conclusive. Moreover, Liaoyang would not have been at the mercy of a successful assailant of Anshantien. After those defences came the outer Liaoyang position, then the inner circle of forts, and when the city itself should fall, was there not the great Taitsuho flowing deep and strong just to the north of it with all its bridges in Russian hands?

Some may think it would have been preferable to have reversed the process, and to have delayed Kuroki whilst fighting the battle of the war at Anshantien, which would then have culminated in a tremendous counter-attack against Oyama. I do not agree; but this is a matter of opinion. The remarkable point for consideration is that it appears doubtful if Kuropatkin ever fairly faced the problem. Certainly no one here can say whether he intended to hold Kuroki and defeat Oyama, or to hold Oyama and defeat Kuroki. Indeed, difficult as it is to believe such a thing, it almost seems as if Kuropatkin had failed to grasp the full significance of the Japanese strategical scheme, although its general course, together with the final tactical envelopment, stood up like a live creature out of the map. Otherwise how is it possible to account for the fact that Mountain 131, Manjuyama, Gochosan, and the Yentai

* See note on p. 144.

colliery hills were not, to some extent at least, previously prepared for defence.

One six-inch gun on the top of Mountain 131 would have altered the whole course of the battle on the northern bank of the Taitsuho. Two shells would have driven Kuroki and his staff from the very convenient Swallow's Nest hill. The pontoon bridge would have been in jeopardy. The Second Division Field Artillery would have been completely exposed, and the troops entrenched on Manjuyama would have felt a succession of 100lb. high explosive shells fired at that distance and angle almost unbearable. Even the Japanese mountain guns which fired with such effect from the southern side of the crest of Gochosan would have been taken in reverse and easily driven into the kaoliung by a six-inch cannon on 131. I do not presume to say the Russians should have profited by the experiences of the British army. But why not accept a lesson from the humble Boers? Bulwana was just as difficult a mountain to haul a big gun on to as 131; Lydenberg and Laing's Nek far more difficult. Two thousand men will make a cannon climb like a chamois, and if it is lost after it has done its business—why—what matter? Cannon are not keepsakes, but killing machines.

Still more surprising to me is the inexplicable failure of the Russians to oppose the crossing of the Twelfth Division at Lentowan. Surely no better opportunity has ever offered itself for the employment of a force such as the Cossacks are supposed to be. We have actually adopted the words *Cossack post* into our official military phraseology, so excellent do we consider the Cossack theory of watching and guarding a line of country. Under the most elementary system, there should have been no difficulty in obtaining information of the Japanese crossing the moment it began; indeed I have it on sure authority that the movement was not conducted with any exceptional secrecy or silence. Once the alarm was given, the mounted troops are not worth their salt who could not, before morning, have been swarming in the hills to the east of the river from whence, although they might not have been able to arrest the progress of the Division, they could most certainly have very seriously harassed and delayed its advance.

The conception actually entertained by Kuropatkin must remain obscure until reports are received from the Russian side, but it certainly appears as if he merely cherished the barren intention of putting a sufficient force at Amping and Anshantien to repulse the attacks of Kuroki and Oyama. But conceptions should be based on the principle of smashing the enemy. A wise Government will forgive even failure to the general who suffered defeat from the vaulting ambition of his plans. But the general who waits on events, endeavouring to be safe everywhere, preferring to lose a chance rather than run an avoidable risk, is only a good general from the enemy's point of view.

When Kuroki had a success on August 28th, and made good on the 27th the right bank of the Tangho, Kuropatkin began to lose his calmness. Obviously he had visions of the First Army making a forced march behind him into Liaoyang. Instead of sending back merely a Division to steady Kuroki whilst he himself gave Oyama battle at Anshantien, he retired the whole of his troops, who could not have been improved by the process, and bundled them up within a radius of four or five miles from Liaoyang. He thus encouraged the Japanese to an extraordinary extent (a fact I can personally vouch for) and enabled them to realise their long-planned, greatly hoped for, tactical concentration.

The battle was now more than three parts won by Oyama, but even at this stage a stroke of good fortune put a great chance again into Kuropatkin's hands. The Taitsuho rose in flood, denying its north bank absolutely to the Second and Fourth Armies, and hindering the tactical concentration which had appeared for a moment to be achieved. One Russian Division with some brigades of artillery and Cossacks to patrol the banks would have been sufficient to hold Oyama in check for the moment. The balance of the vast army was available to fling upon the top of Kuroki. It is improbable that the coming century will produce a crisis so deeply fraught with fate. Would the Russians merely use the swollen river as a means of escape, as Moore used the Esla during his retreat to Corunna, or, would they seize the goods the Gods had sent them and make the river a pivot of manœuvre for a great counter-stroke against the First Army? For one terrible moment it did seem as if Kuropatkin was actually going to put his fortune to the test and let the Russian soldiers have a real good fight—no piecemeal encounters; no bottled-up reserves, but every man in the firing line, like Kuroki on July 31st or August 26th. But no: just as the fate of Empires was trembling in the balance, there began that retreat on Mukden which took the heart out of the Russians who were still holding their ground and renewed all the energy of the exhausted Japanese. The Commanders of the First Army played their part here whole-heartedly;—tooth and nail, no reserves—every officer and man fighting like a wild cat. The Russian Commander never flung his whole army into the business *con amore*, as Skoboleff I am sure would have done, in the true adventurous neck or nothing style.

I began with the strategy; I will end with the tactics. The Japanese tactics realised the true ideal of employing every single man (except the cavalry), and of carrying out the general idea in accordance with the probabilities, careless of minor risks or defeats. The Japanese leaders fought throughout on the lines of Napoleon's maxim that the moral is as to the physical as three to one. The Russian leaders acted differently. Tolstoi says the army is everything; the generals are nothing. Napoleon affirms that in war it is the man who is wanted; not men. Into such company my own small opinion dares not intrude itself.

A Russian private has in him the proper soldier's stuff; give him something clear, simple, and definite to fight for, and his dead bear witness how resolutely he can make the assault. But, by messing troops about (a heart-breaking process, for which our own men have an explicit but quite unmentionable expression), by withdrawing them prematurely and hurriedly from elaborate defences; then yielding the battlefield on account of the loss of one or two non-vital positions; it is easy to turn an army of heroes into an army of hares. I think it is an infinite credit to the Russian privates that they seem to have, to a great extent, resisted the demoralising tactics of their leaders. Not that I mean to try and gauge the weight of the importance of the part played by *moral* in our last battle. I had as lief attempt to prove that a bishop was a better form of national investment than a battleship. But it will be generally accepted that the Japanese armies after the events of the past month must have had some advantage here, and the more I think the more certain am I that it was not strategy or tactics, or armament or information, which won the battle of Liaoyang for Oyama, but that it was rather the souls of the Japanese troops which triumphed over the less developed, less awakened, less stimulated, spiritual qualities of the Russians.

Let no Briton, however, presume to think that the Russians will not learn a vast deal nationally as well as militarily, by this war, or that they will necessarily in their next campaign display the same want of brilliancy and determination in their highest ranks or of manœuvring and shooting power in the lowest. Manjuyama has convinced the Japanese Army that the hearts of the Russian soldiers are in the right place. This is the great thing. The need of intelligence and of higher individual training must have been driven into the consciousness of the Russian Army by its sanguinary defeats, and in the ranks, even now, there is no lack of powers of endurance or of moral strength. Russia will survive Manchuria. An empire whose soldiers can die as the Russian privates died at Manjuyama is "no deid yet" as a 92nd Highlander private inscribed upon the tombstone of his battalion which had been buried in effigy on the sad day when, in 1881, the War Minister then reigning murdered its ancient and honourable number.

10.30 P.M.—A man of the Guards cavalry has just come in with a message to say that my baggage-cart and baggage have been destroyed by a Russian shell, which killed three men of the escort and the horse, and wounded a fourth man badly. It seems a strange thing that such an accident should happen to me out of all the First Army. I never knew such luck, but after all I suppose I ought to rejoice that I was not marching with the unfortunate escort.

FENSHAN, *September 7th*, 1904.—The remains of my kit came in here at 1.30 A.M. to-day. There is going to be a court of inquiry. The orderlies tell different stories. Some say the shell was fired by the Russians at the cart and hit it. Others that the cart went over a blind shell and burst it. I suspect myself that one of the escort picked up a shell and then carelessly let it drop, a pernicious trick indulged in by soldiers of all armies.

FENSHAN, *September 7th*, 1904.—All my kit has been riddled, bedding, clothes, reports, note-books—nothing has escaped. The most serious damage is that caused to my gum boots, my new khaki coat, and forage cap. I daresay a bicyclist may be able to patch up the rents in the gum boots as if they were tyre punctures, but the coat is past praying for, and I had been saving it up religiously for my call upon Oyama, whenever the fortune of war should be pleased to give us admission to Liaoyang. However, I have one consolation. I always picture the Devil roaming about and waiting his chance against me, armed with a great bow and a quiver full of arrows. Most of them are quite harmless to my particular individuality, but here and there is a shaft winged with black feathers, and these have power to work me deadly hurt. When the Fiend can be tempted into discharging one of his black arrows for the sake of some mere material injury, such as the loss of a bet or a mischance to my worldly goods, then I thank Heaven it is no worse and breathe more freely.

FENSHAN, *September 8th*, 1904.—Rode into Liaoyang. Mr. Masuda has washed my coat and done his best to sew up the holes in it, but I could have executed the repairs as well myself with a brad-awl and some string.

I found our attachés with the Second Army still in the state of tutelage from which we emerged directly we left Fenghuangcheng. They were confined to a radius of some 800 yards. I have heard a great deal about the Second Army, but I shall leave the south bank of the Taitsuho strictly alone, as the affairs of my own army give me more than enough to think about. After comparing experiences, I was offered a magnificent meat and bread luncheon. Colonel Haldane apologised for the quality of the bread, which was, so he said, inferior!!! I nearly dropped dead. This *recherché* luncheon spoke more eloquently than volumes of dry military literature as to the advantages of campaigning in combination with a line of railway.

I went on to pay my respects to the Marshal Oyama and General Kodama, his Chief of the Staff. What a difference does war make in the status of a general! In Tokio, Oyama and Kodama were grandees, certainly, but still hardly so exciting to encounter as, for instance, the Prime Minister, the leader of the Opposition, or a personage about the Court. Here, they are demigods, there is no doubt about it. Without an effort they can fill my note-books to overflowing with good things or send me empty away to Fanshan, or for that matter to Dalny or Japan.

I was kept waiting a couple of minutes in a small room furnished in European style when the door opened and Oyama, Kodama, and Fukushima walked in. Oyama was dressed in khaki, with tight Bedford cord pantaloons, and slippers. He looked remarkably well. He made me seat myself in a huge purple velvet armchair which had been Kuropatkin's, so they said. Then champagne and large Manilla cigars were handed round. When I saw the champagne I said, "I cannot restrain my smiles on seeing the face of an old friend." When this sentiment was translated, it happened to make a Japanese poem of exactly the right number of syllables. Oyama was greatly pleased, as he is a bit of a poet himself. In drinking my health Kodama said: "We must crack the next bottle at Mukden." I was questioned about my own adventures and a good deal also about the feelings of the First Army, on which subject I felt it prudent to say as little as possible. I asked Marquis Oyama if he was pleased with the result of his operations, and he replied: "Moderately; the Russians have managed their retreat too cleverly."

I told them the story of my misadventure with the Russian shell and about our soldiers of the First Army having had to eat their rice uncooked. They asked me if I had tried it. I said, "yes," on which, genuinely astonished and distressed in their hospitable souls, they exclaimed: "What! a British general make his dinner off raw rice!" I replied: "I did not make my dinner off it; I tried one grain to see what it was like, and that sufficed for my wants." This disposed of the incident and seemed to put them all into high good humour.

No one could have been brighter or cheerier than the redoubtable trio, and I did not know till I got back here again that General Fukushima had lost his son in the battle. It is the Japanese code of manners that no personal sorrow or calamity should be allowed even in the smallest degree to influence ordinary social duties or the manner in which they are conducted. Here was a case in point.

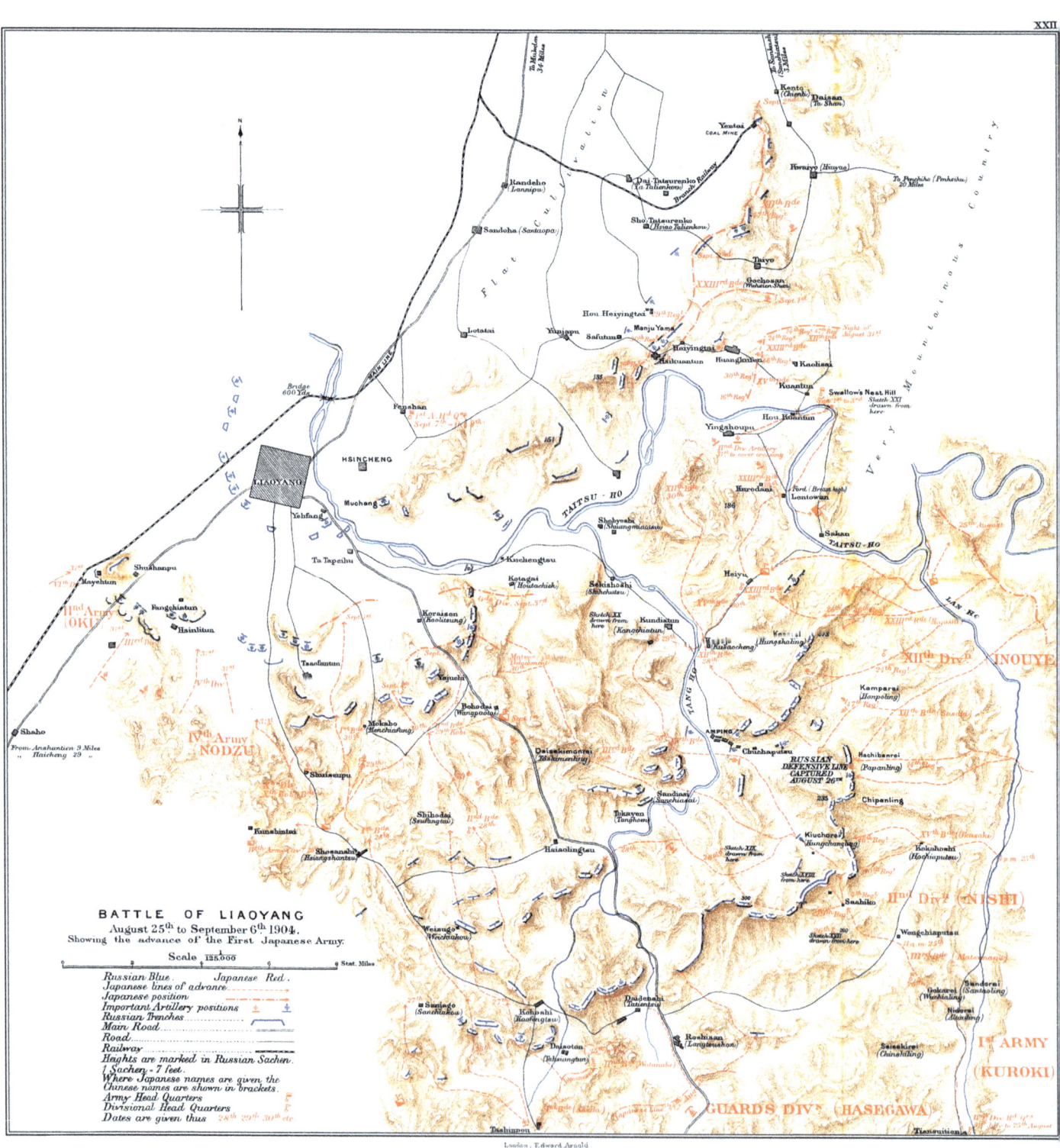

BATTLE OF LIAOYANG
August 25th to September 6th 1904.
Showing the advance of the First Japanese Army.

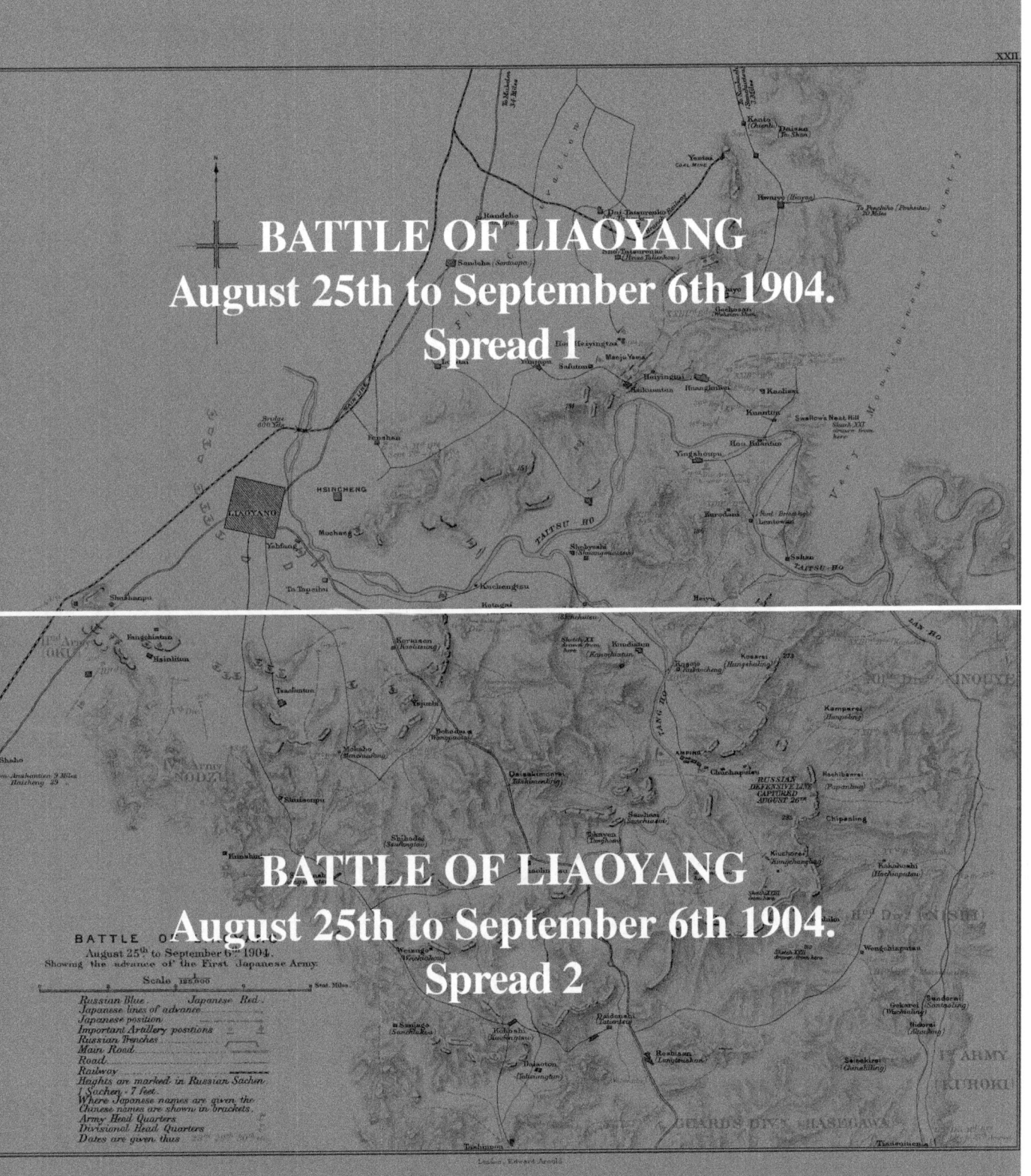

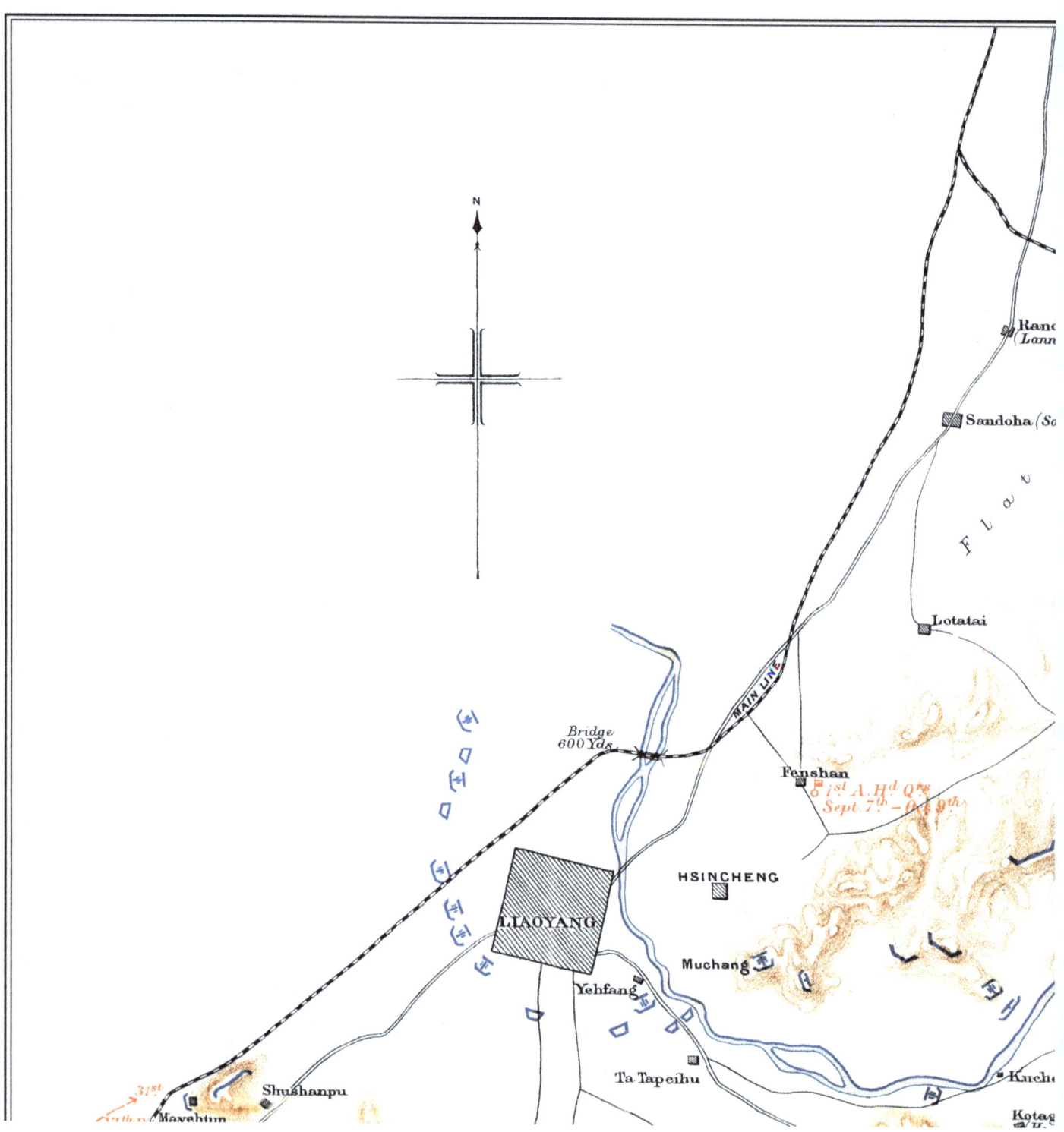

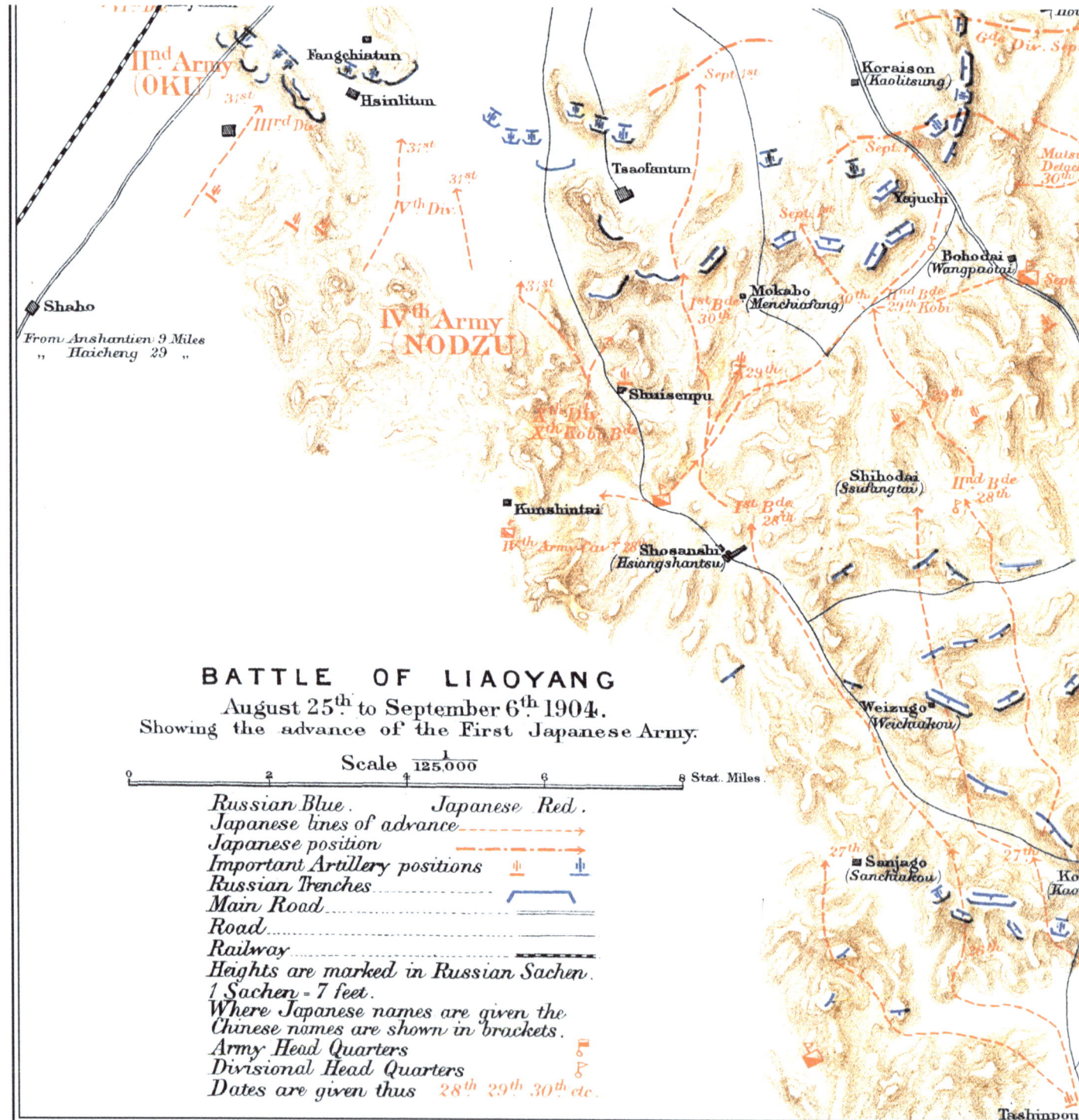

When I took my leave they came out with me to the doorstep and pointed out the big, canvas-roofed shed adjoining the house. It was intended to provide shelter for the escort of a generalissimo, and they said: "Is it not thoughtful of Kuropatkin to have made such convenient arrangements for us?" Then a final salute and I was off.

It was late when I got back, and I found Headquarters had been so put out by the action of one or two of my friends, the journalists, who had overstayed their leave of absence, that they had telegraphed orders to all the outlying military attachés to come in from their Divisions to Headquarters. So we shall be a big troupe again, just as we were in the days at Fenghuangcheng, which now appear so distant.

By the way, I must not go to bed to-night without first chronicling the remarkably fine dinner I had to-night, enriched as it was by the Chinese cakes and bread, apples, pears, and grapes I bought on my way back through Liaoyang.

### NOTE TO PAGE 135

The Ashantien position was 9 miles long; exceptionally strong against any frontal attack, and not easily to be turned. True, a gap of 12½ miles separated its eastern flank from the equally advanced Russian section of defence at Langtsushan, and into this gap the Japanese Tenth Division from Hsimucheng (Tokubokojo) appeared to be advancing. But the country to be traversed was so impracticable that the Russian troops on the spot should have been strong enough to resist any Japanese advance from that direction. The right of the position, which rested on low hills rising out of a sea of kaoliung to the west of the railway, was almost equally difficult to manœuvre against. To turn this western flank part of the Second Army must have made a *détour* through the kaoliung, exposing themselves to all the danger of surprise and counter attack.

# CHAPTER XXVI

## SOJOURN AT FENSHAN

FENSHAN, *September 10th*, 1904.— My brother attachés have come in, all very fit and full of news. We have a room to ourselves, thank heaven. They have seen and made notes of all the details of the combats of their respective Divisions, and I have got the run of the operations from the Headquarters point of view, so, between us, we ought to be able to produce some fairly useful reports.

I have just heard an account of a sermon preached a few days ago to the Imperial Guards by a Buddhist priest. He spoke for three-quarters of an hour, making the most of one of his rare chances. The sermon was so good that he frequently made his audience roar with laughter. He inculcated the Buddhist view of the insignificant value of life, and the folly of clinging to it too eagerly, by telling the men a story of two friends meeting in the street. After the usual salutations, one friend asked the other after the health of his most honourable father. The reply was that the father had just been drowned, which cast rather a damper upon the conversation. Plucking up courage, the man whose father had been drowned asked his friend in turn as to the health of a favourite uncle. The reply was that the uncle had also just been drowned. This time the friends could hardly help laughing. Thus they discovered two things : first, that death could not be so terrible after all ; secondly, that the sea was the most dangerous place in the world.

"In arriving at such a conclusion," said the preacher, "they were only partly right, for you, my brave friends, being many of you seafaring men, are well aware that the sea is by no means so specially dangerous as appears to have been too hastily supposed. The moral of my story is that the place of every one's death is pre-ordained, and that as one place is actually just about as dangerous as another, there is nothing in nature or in philosophy which should incline a man to go less boldly into a fight than into his bed at night. In neither case should he for a moment trouble his head with any trifling consideration as to whether he will come out of it alive or be taken out of it dead. I do not, of course, presume to speak to the Imperial Guards about any fear of the enemy. But I refer rather to the fear some of you may have that by some personal negligence or rashness you may possibly do something to injure your country or the Emperor. I tell you, fear not at all. If your intentions are right, then your actions will be right also."

Referring later on in his discourse to the temptations of the world and of the flesh he said : "A man may awake in the morning and long very much for an Osaka cigarette to smoke, or for a delicious sweetmeat made of red or white beans. If the powers of evil are very strong within him, he may even hope it will rain very heavily, so that on that day at least no exhausting march will be possible. During peace-time, when each of you is his own master, such thoughts are merely weak and rather contemptible, but in war-time they are absolutely wicked and unworthy of a Japanese soldier. Should your mirrors reflect such thoughts as these, then, indeed, as the poet finely says, you will see an ugly thing. Such ideas are Tokio ideas; fit only for Tokio and much to be fought against and regretted even when they occur there"; from all of which will be gathered that there is quite a family resemblance between the sermon of a Buddhist priest and a Church of England parson. Only, on the matter of military virtues, the Buddhist assumes a much loftier standard than the good Padre would venture to take up.

On the other hand, let no one imagine that the Japanese soldiers are immaculate lambs when it comes to the ordinary civilian qualities. I will not enumerate their lapses from the narrow paths of virtue, for it becomes not a guest to notice even the peccadillos of his hosts. But there are just a few, and I am not sure, without further inquiry, what view the Buddhist priest would take of such derelictions. Probably he would disapprove, but not to the same extent as might be imagined from his diatribe against what to us alas! are very venial sins of the self-indulgent or unmanly type.

FENSHAN, *September* 15*th*, 1904.—We are leading a very quiet life, writing our official reports of the battle, and reports also on all sorts of fancy subjects: cavalry, artillery, &c. &c.—for we feel we must earn our pay.

Jardine came in two days ago with fine accounts of the storming of the lofty Kosarei mountain on the night of August 25th–26th by the intrepid Kigoshi, and with even more exciting stories of the confused night-fighting in the kaoliung, near the Yentai coal-mines, on the night of September 4th–5th. We have all talked over the failure of the Japanese to make any effective pursuit, and our small committee, at any rate, have granted them plenary absolution. The First Army had been fighting nine or ten days and nights, and had lost very heavily. Had the Russians stood they would have attacked them again; but as the Russians were removing themselves, every one was only too glad to have done with them. If Kuroki's energetic orders had been addressed to fresh troops they might have been acted on with corresponding energy; as it was, neither executive officers nor men were burning to maintain contact with the receding zone of the Russian shrapnel, and they tacitly acted on this disinclination, feeling especially justified by the fact that their own under-horsed guns were unable to come up through the mud to support them. Thus it came to pass that, instead of starting soon after 3 P.M., the Divisional Commanders deliberately delayed until darkness; thus they got lost in the kaoliung, and thus the Russians, who are said by the Japanese to have been still full of fight, were able to get away without loss to their dignity or to their *matériel*.

No task is more agreeable to the armchair critic than to pounce upon the slackness of an army to take full advantage of a victory. The comfortable man sitting by his fire after a good dinner sees through the illuminative spectacles of a glass or two of port wine that one more trifling effort—a mere nothing compared to preceding struggles—would produce incalculable results. Next morning he takes up his pen and lets drive. Probably he is wrong. When two evenly-matched armies fight for several days and nights there is not often much to choose between the condition, moral and physical, of victors and vanquished. Just one hair's breadth of difference, possibly, if it could be traced, in the behaviour of a drummer, bugler, or simple private would have completely reversed the fortunes of the day. Nevertheless the irrevocable word "retreat" has been uttered by the Commander of one army, and the other army, which had, an hour previously, felt quite at the end of its tether, realises its victory. The experience is not easily forgotten, and, therefore, I feel able to urge with all the more conviction that, in such a moment of joyous reaction and expansion, troops do not respond very easily to orders to plunge themselves again under the showers of musketry and shrapnel.

We have a fairly decent room here, but the house is situated on the lowest-lying part of Fanshan, and the roads consist of alternative stretches of filth-pools and quagmires of sticky, smelly mud, over which we hop gingerly on stepping-stones till we arrive at a spot where, in some previous dynasty, one of these aids to progression has been removed. Then it becomes a case of skip, jump, flounder, and swear.

Our village is plumped down in the middle of a vast plain covered, up to within a yard of its walls, by magnificent crops. Even the very housetops are hidden under the insinuating grip of luxuriant cucumber and pumpkin plants, and bring forth an opulent harvest of green and golden gourds. In the courtyards the sunflower is the Chinaman's favourite. Here it grows to a height of fourteen feet, and often bears a blossom two feet in diameter. Englishmen accustomed to violets and roses and such like poetic trifles might think I had over-estimated the size of my sunflower, but fortunately I am not an uncorroborated Marco Polo, but am backed up by those who have measured. Sometimes the plain reminds me, especially by its flatness and clumps of large spreading trees, of the country round Lucknow; only the crops are five times more luxuriant, the houses ten times more substantial and prosperous.

FENSHAN, *September 15th*, 1904.—I have had a great score over Hume, Vincent, and Jardine. In the afternoon they all rode off to Liaoyang to buy pears and apples whilst I remained at work. At 3 P.M. —— came in and said that Colonel Matsuishi, Vice-Chief of the General Staff, had just received a cable ordering him to go back to Tokio to take up an important post at the War Office. It would be a nice little attention, therefore, he thought, if I would offer him tea and cakes that afternoon to celebrate his departure.

"That is all very well," I said, "but where are the cakes?" "Do not trouble yourself on that score," said ——, "I charge myself with the details of the entertainment." It sounded like a fairy tale, but I wrote over to Matsuishi, who very cordially accepted.

Shortly afterwards some soldiers appeared and decorated the room, and then Matsuishi arrived with Colonel Kurita and one or two other German-speaking Staff officers. Every one was at once put into an exceedingly good temper by the appearance of a light, well-baked gingerbread cake. It was so large that I thought at first some of it might be left over for my brother attachés, but very soon it had entirely disappeared. To the amazement of the company, —— then produced a bottle of gooseberry champagne, which turned out to be the bottle I was to have drunk to celebrate the fall of Port Arthur, and when the teacups had been filled with the bubbling, liquid amber, I proposed the Stonepine's health (Matsu, a pine; Ishi, a stone). This was my first attempt at public speaking in German, and it went abominably badly. After the usual things, I added: "I hope when Colonel Matsuishi returns in great honour and glory to take his seat with the Headquarters Staff in Tokio he will not forget his humble friends here, and that he will, on some suitable occasion, explain to the rulers of the army that, although we may sometimes be a little troublesome, we should not on that account be considered either wicked or dangerous (*vielleicht sind wir zuweilen etwas mühsam, aber nicht böse oder gefärlich*)." Matsuishi sat a good long time, and then made an excellent little speech in German with a word or two of English or French thrown in, saying how hard it was to leave comrades in time of war, but that duty must at all costs be done.

The evenings are now becoming quite cool and fresh.

FENSHAN, *September 17th*, 1904.—Yesterday I went to call on General Oku, the Commander of the Second Army. Although younger than Kuroki, he is still a Japanese of the old style. Whereas the dominant expression of Kuroki's face is that of dreamy benevolence, the chief impression conveyed by Oku's features is one of masterful brightness and intelligence. He was dressed in English khaki serge, and wore a tuft on his chin, French fashion. Last year he represented the Japanese army at Delhi, and he showed great interest in hearing about my life in Pretoria, and my relations with Lord Kitchener when I was his Chief of the Staff. When he had had enough of me he sent me off to inspect his battlefield, under charge of a selected officer, and I had an interesting day. Colonel Haldane has to deal with this part of the business, and I will only note down that I can understand now why Oyama did not make better progress in his attempt to turn the Russian right.

It is evident that after rain the plain to the west of the railway must have been practically impassable for artillery, and only passable with the utmost difficulty by cavalry and infantry. Therefore, the main successes were gained by Nodzu and the Fourth Army on the higher, stonier ground to the east of the railway.

In a quarry not far from here some Japanese soldiers had found a horse abandoned by the Russians. It had fallen down from a considerable height and was quite insensible. Its body was not yet cold, however, and a Chinaman passing by declared that, if there was any life in it at all, he would make it get up. He was allowed to make his experiment and, producing his knife, he cut something out of the corner of each of the animal's eyes. He then gave the horse a good kick, and it immediately stood up. The Japanese Veterinary Officer says that the Chinaman has not injured any vital part of the eye.

Marshal Oyama and General Kodama did me the high honour of calling on me to-day.

Later on I had a long talk with an officer from our own Headquarters, the first we have had for some ten days or so. He has given me a complete list of the Russian forces opposed to us during the battle of Liaoyang, with which I shall not burden these notes. Indeed, I have not the energy which would enable me to go over all the old ground again, but some of his remarks are certainly worth entering.

For instance, after giving me the detail of the enemy's troops, he went on to say: "There is no doubt that Kuropatkin felt great confidence in this big army, and was most anxious to bring off a counter-attack on a large scale. But once he had committed himself to a retreat from Anshantien, Marshal Oyama's pursuit was so quick and so persistent that he had no time to pull himself together or to make the necessary redistributions.

"So, likewise, were we too quick for him here, in our passage of the river, and the Russian defences on Tsaofantun and Hsinlitun were only commenced as we got within artillery range of them. Under so great a pressure, Kuropatkin had not time to reflect or to judge the situation calmly, and he could not even feel certain of the whereabouts of our main force. The wide frontage on which we maintained our right confirmed him in his incertitude, until, finally, he determined that safety would best be consulted by retiring without committing himself to his contemplated decisive counter-attack.

"By the evening of September 3rd, there were only 5000 or, at the most, 6000 Russians in Liaoyang itself. You can realise how fortunate we were that the remainder of the great army was for the most part engaged in falling back on Mukden instead of in pressing us back upon our bridges.

"Lieutenant-Colonel Fukuda has told you, in terms perhaps unduly sarcastic, that the First Army could make no use of their cavalry.* It was the same with the cavalry on the south side of the Taitsuho. Major-General Akiyama commanded the mixed Brigade of Cavalry, but although he was supported by field-guns,

---

\* Lieutenant-Colonel Fukuda, speaking of the action of September 3rd, had said: "Even at a supreme moment such as this there was, however, one group of men who were idle. This was the cavalry. So they were employed to go back to the river and cook food for their companions of the infantry."

machine-guns, and infantry, he could accomplish nothing against the right of the Russian Army. The Cavalry Brigade in question had two men wounded. As you know, we were very nervous about our right flank during the fighting on this side of the river; not only from Orloff at the Yentai coal-mines, but also from a point a mile or two further to the east. A convenient valley runs thence by which an enterprising Russian cavalry commander might have made a dash right down upon the Swallow's Nest Hill and the pontoon bridges. Naturally we had done what we could to provide against such an enterprise, and the hills to the north of the Swallow's Nest hill were picqueted with two battalions of Kobi, but these were far too weak to cover the whole of the ground effectively. We were rendered specially uneasy by the knowledge that, although Kuropatkin might overestimate our strength, the commanders in immediate contact with us must have been aware of our weakness. For the passage of the river by the Twelfth Division was watched by small parties of Russian cavalry, who fell back without firing a shot. The infantry then expelled them altogether merely by advancing, and so the two battalions of Kobi occupied the hills without any trouble or skirmishing."

Putting together the map and the foregoing statement, British officers will understand better than by any long-winded treatise how entirely different are the methods of the Cossack from those of the Afridi or the Boer.

The Japanese are, as I had already more than surmised, not happy about the general results of the battle. My visitor went on to say:

"Until mid-day on August 28th, when, at Roshisan,

we received orders telling us to cross the river earlier, and in less force, than we had originally intended to cross it, the operations of the First Army had been crowned with complete success. It will ever be our greatest pride to recall the achievement of Kigoshi's Brigade of the Twelfth Division when they scaled the precipitous ridge of Kosarei on the night of August 25th–26th. Some of the cliffs were so sheer that the soldiers had to bend down, like boys playing leap-frog, for quite a long time, whilst the remainder of their companions made use of their backs as stepping-stones. All the soldiers laughed at such an arrangement and said that Marshal Kuroki had made his army first like ducks to cross rivers, and now he was turning them into ladders to scale mountains. But towards the end of the continuous battles which ensued, these same merry men fell asleep in the midst of the heaviest fire, and when the enemy grew very close indeed their officers had to go round and shake them violently before they could be awakened. And now, having struggled to the very last stage, overcoming difficulties and hardships, we have failed in co-operating as we should have done with the other two armies, at which we feel much ashamed.

"Nevertheless, it is wiser, perhaps, to remember that things might have turned out even worse than has proved actually to be the case. At any rate, we deceived Kuropatkin as to our strength, partly by our wide extensions, partly because we assumed the strongest possible offensive, although we were so desperately weak. But the game was dangerous. The more we bluffed the worse our beating would have been had Kuropatkin's eyes been opened instead of remaining, as they did, tightly shut; and this is what we may put on the other side of the balance when we feel too much ashamed at our failure.

"Perhaps Heaven was, after all, bestowing upon us a special blessing just when we were most inclined to be downcast. Be this as it may, the 31st, the 1st and the 2nd, were the days when above all others in my life my dinner had least savour."

FENSHAN, *September 19th*, 1904.—It has suddenly become as cold as an English mid October. I went into Liaoyang to-day at 1.30 P.M. to feast with the Marquis Oyama at 3 P.M. The feast proved historic, inasmuch as it was the first occasion on which all the army commanders had met since the outbreak of the war. At one moment Oyama, Kuroki, Oku, and Nodzu were in a little group all by themselves. General Nodzu was of a frank and genial appearance. General Oku looked keen and forcible.

The three Imperial Princes—Kanin, Kuni, and Nashimoto—were also present. Prince Kanin is slight and very handsome. He looks every inch the *beau sabreur*.

One and all they were most friendly. Every one I have spoken to this afternoon has apologised for our hardships and want of food. There is no occasion. We are stout and well-liking and I trust do credit to our rice. I think, too, that every keen soldier would prefer to be credited with a perfect indifference to hardships. What we do appreciate is military *camaraderie* and the friendship of our hosts. Marquis Oyama told me, in French, that General Kodama was not present at the feast because he had gone down to Port Arthur to try and expedite matters.

When I came back I found a very nice letter awaiting me from General Teraoutsi, the War Minister at

Tokio, in which he also spoke feelingly about hardships and hunger. I must reassure him on this point.

FENSHAN, *September 22nd*, 1904.—Yesterday I concocted an answer to General Teraoutsi, in which I fully opened my heart to him. No one can censor a letter to the War Minister, I should think.

To-day I have been to call on General Nodzu, commanding the Fourth Army. He has taken up his quarters in a house standing in a pretty Chinese garden belonging to one of the wealthiest residents of Liaoyang. The general received me most kindly. Champagne and cigars were forthcoming to season our short conversation, after which I was packed off with a staff officer to inspect the scene of the triumph of his army. I will excuse myself from narrating a story which does not fall within my own legitimate sphere of observation. It is difficult to understand how troops could have been driven out of such positions as those held here by the Russians, except by pre-supposing a great superiority of numbers which the Japanese did not possess. The redoubt and trenches were immensely strong, except that they all lacked head-cover, and without head-cover troops are apt to crouch down and fire at random. Indeed, I saw in several of the redoubts to the south of Liaoyang marks of where the muzzles of the rifles seemed to have been resting against the earthen parapet, thus lending some colour to the theory that at once time in the action the defenders had been shooting high.

We were told how in one assault about twenty Japanese got into a redoubt and were cut off there. The Russians in the redoubt bandaged up their wounds and sent them all back again.

After my study of the ground I went to have tea in Liaoyang with a good missionary and his lady, Presbyterians both. Hume, Jardine, and Vincent had also been favoured with invitations. The missionary was unadulterated Scotch, and his wife was a Scots-Irish lady. We all enjoyed ourselves almost to excess. It was an exciting moment when we found ourselves seated at a table spread with snowy linen and groaning to be relieved of its weight of scones and of sponge cakes. Hume and Jardine fairly astonished this table, Vincent and I did our modest best.

Our hosts told us many interesting things about the Chinese, who are their pupils, patients, and friends, and also about the Russian occupation.

The Chinese were at first genuinely glad the Japanese had supplanted the Russians, as the former had won the highest reputation for themselves throughout Northern China by their admirable discipline and general behaviour during the Boxer troubles. Since their arrival, however, the Japanese have been looting chickens, and the Chinamen have already changed their minds, and sadly quote one of their own proverbs to the effect that "The grandmother has left us but grandpapa has come in her place." The missionaries themselves seemed to have liked the Russians very well. Up to the very last the latter had been absolutely optimistic. They were always ready to own up that their intelligence was bad, and that they knew very little about the Japanese movements; but they said that did not matter. The missionaries paid a handsome tribute to the behaviour of the men in Liaoyang.

FENSHAN, *September 28th*, 1904.—We are becoming luxurious and semi-civilised now that we have got on to the railway line. The Headquarters have been exceptionally hospitable and kind this last week, during which I have been busy writing reports.

A member of the Staff came to see me to-day. He gave me a number of details about the Manjuyama fighting, and explained the artillery firing we occasionally hear to the north of us, by saying that there are two Russian Divisions on the right bank of the Hunho who indulge in occasional skirmishes with Umezawa's brigade and with our cavalry patrols.

He went on to talk about Port Arthur. For weeks not one word has been uttered on the subject. He said that the semi-permanent forts, one on each side of the main road to the north of the town, had now fallen into the hands of the Japanese. The waterworks, which lie between these forts and the main forts, have also been captured, and to-day the 11-inch howitzers brought over from the coast defences of Japan begin to shell the town. These howitzers have a range of 8000 yards, and great confidence is expressed by the Commander of the Third Army—General Nogi—in the efficacy of their huge shells.

The next work which has to be taken is a permanent fort, situated on the east side of the main road within 4000 yards of the town. I said, "If it is a permanent fort, its capture may take a very long time," and I was told, "Never mind; it will be taken in the shortest time possible, even if our men have to tear up the masonry ramparts with their finger nails."

FENSHAN, *September 29th*, 1904.—I started at 2 P.M. to call by appointment on another missionary and his wife, and I found a big Free, not a wee one, who is said to be able to hold his own even with a red-beard Chinese bandit. He has been here many years, and is a considerable power in the land. He confirmed what his brethren had already told us as to the eagerness with which the Chinese had been looking forward to the advent of the Japanese. The prevalence of such a sentiment had been of enormous value to Oyama, as it had inclined the inhabitants of the theatre of operations to conceal everything from the Russians. Silence, impenetrable as a prison wall, had surrounded the intelligence bureau of Kuropatkin. On the other hand, as an example of the perfect information conveyed to Oyama, I was told that, on the last day of the battle, the Japanese had thrown thirty shells into the Yamen which had been the Russian Headquarters until a day or two previously, when, luckily for them and their records, they had changed. Now, however, that grandpapa had actually come, the poor Chinese had found in him a close relative of the Old Man of the Sea. The main reason why the Chinese were beginning to think more kindly of their former rulers was that the Russians were extraordinarily generous and liberal, whereas the Japanese were considered by the shopkeepers to be stingy. I may parenthetically remark that I do not think the Japanese are at all stingy. Only they have not got the money; and although this does not prevent a European from spending it, our allies have not yet caught the trick of conjuring with credit.

Another reason was that some of the Japanese were inclined to bully. I heard a story of how a Japanese soldier was having a dispute with a Chinese shopkeeper who kept a booth in the main street of Liaoyang. Suddenly the soldier took his rifle by the muzzle and, with its butt, in one fell swoop swept to the ground the whole of the man's lemonade, cakes, sweetmeats, tea, stirabout, and all the rest of it. There were any number of Japanese about who saw the occurrence and did nothing, so my informant went up to the Chinese soldiers and asked them what they were posted there for if they were not to protect their own people. Eventually he shamed four of them into coming forward to arrest the soldier. Meanwhile his fit of passion had passed; he was sorry for what he had done, and some of his fellows begged him off, saying it was a dispute about change, and that the Chinaman had not given him back his dues. The missionary, as was befitting, improved the occasion by pointing out that a difference of opinion about a copper was no sufficient reason for destroying a man's whole stock-in-trade, and that the worst of permitting rage to obtain the upper hand was that it caused the man whom it has mastered to lose all sense of justice or of proportion. Here, apparently, the matter ended.

I must interpolate here another commentary. Exceptions prove the rule, and I believe the story I have related is very much of an exception. The Japanese soldiers are kindly and respectable men with, as I have often written down, a very high sense of the military obligation to be upright, and chivalrous, and contemptuous of money. If this story had concerned a Japanese shopkeeper of the smaller sort, then I should not have been so much surprised. For these latter, lacking as they do the high ideals fostered by a military training, are apt to be overbearing and avaricious, qualities which may prove a handicap to them when it comes to colonising Korea.

A third cause of the disillusionment of the Chinese is the number of refugees who are now flocking into Liaoyang from the north, where all their villages have been occupied by the Japanese troops. Even where a portion of the houses have been reserved for the owners the Chinamen still insist on sending away all their women. It is not that the soldiers have been guilty of misbehaviour, or even of undue familiarity, with the celestial damosels. It is simply because the code of modesty of the Japanese Army differs from that which is accepted alike by Chinese and Europeans. Modesty assumes different guises in different countries, as well as in different ages, and here, in Manchuria, thousands of poor women are leaving their homes and crowding into the towns lest they should have their vision blasted by seeing a little Jap soldier splashing in his indispensable bath. When it is explained to a Japanese that it is indecent to strip off his clothes for a good wash in the presence of ladies he is genuinely shocked at the immodest ideas which, in his opinion, must underlie such a frame of mind. Even a Japanese, however, cannot altogether escape from the same troublesome modesty, and he is outraged beyond words if he sees, for instance, a European kissing his wife good-bye on a railway platform.

A fourth and last grievance is that, with winter coming on, the Japanese have often burnt doors and windows of Chinese farms in order to cook their rice.

As communications improve, the men will get a regular allowance of fuel and leave doors and windows alone. The British, at any rate, can throw no stones at soldiers who borrow furniture to boil their soup, and I have yet to see the officer whose respect for *meum* and *tuum* is so fanatical that he will let his men starve with hunger and cold whilst such luxuries as furniture adorn the adjacent dwellings.

## SOJOURN AT FENSHAN

According to the missionary the Russian soldiers were not easily demoralised—not, at least, for long. Their temperament was too mercurial. For a day or so after a defeat every one would be sunk in doleful dumps. Then the band would play, and by night there was a sound of revelry, during which the army would forget all its woes and become once more invincible. There is something, to me, very attractive in these traits of Russian character. I prefer the philosophy of the gay Cavalier to that of the sober Roundhead. Ever since Shakespeare immortalised the sentiment special allowances have been made for the warrior, and often have grave magistrates on the bench remembered that—

> "A soldier's a man
> And life's but a span
> So let the soldier drink."

But, after all, it is the business of a soldier to hold his life in fief for his country, and what is the value of war unless it burns up and destroys the corrupt vices which thrive so luxuriantly on peace and civilisation? Where, as at Liaoyang, and, in a lesser degree, at Capetown, the luxury is too rank to be completely consumed, then it is a bad look out for the army itself, as well as for the nation which produced it!

It was during the brief period of depression following the battle of the Yalu that Kuropatkin had railed back his stores to Mukden, but when the reaction had restored confidence the stores were all brought down again to Liaoyang, where their ashes are still warm. The foreigners with the Russian army considered Keller and Stakelberg the best and most energetic commanders, although the Russians themselves used to class them rather as thoughtless individuals of the St. Petersburg drawing-room type.

After this visit we went over to our former hosts, where, notwithstanding our outrageous appetites, we had once more been bidden to tea. Here we met three young ladies who were doctors. At least, one of them was a full-blown doctor; the other two were, I think, aspirants. Of course they were all Scotch—they always are in these impossible places.

The principal doctor was naturally pretty, but as a tribute to science she had brushed her hair flat and smooth, and had wound it into a hard and shining ball at the back of her head. I doubt if young women have any right to do this sort of thing. It is like a soldier who malingers by cutting off his trigger-finger to prevent himself from fighting. But now I am positively wandering. What with eating scones and drinking cups of tea, there was not much opportunity for conversation.

The lady doctor had been stopped once by twenty red beards armed with mausers, but when she explained that she was on her way to visit a sick woman they let her pass, not only unhurt but with full compliments. She saw them stop another cart immediately afterwards.

All the ladies were extremely annoyed with the British Consul at Newchwang, who had ordered unmarried missionaries of the fair sex to quit Liaoyang at the commencement of the war. They had thus missed the excitement and the opportunities for healing the wounded, and I shall be sorry for the gentleman if ever he falls into their hands.

FENSHAN, *September 30th*, 1904.—I went out, for a walk this evening with Rooski. Coming back I heard the band of the Guards, which was left behind during the fighting and has only just rejoined. Rooski, too, pricked up her ears and rushed off eagerly towards the sound of the music. Poor little doggie! Those strains must have reminded her of the Russian band-stand where, I am sure, she had been accustomed to receive caresses and cakes from all the gay company there assembled. But instead of finding anything so festive, she and her master were greeted by rather a depressing spectacle as soon as they turned the corner leading to the Headquarters.

Under the lee of a funereal clump of pines which marked a Chinese tomb, were collected the bandsmen of the Japanese Guards. The sun had set, leaving a dull red stain in the greenish western sky. Candles had been lit on the music stands, and flickered with a feeble gleam, whilst a selection of Scotch ballads which had suffered a Manchurian change in time and key and tune resounded dolefully through the empty streets. There we two sat on a Russian camp kitchen, and two ragged Chinese urchins looked on from the other side. No one else. Any number of Japanese officers and men were within a hundred yards of us, but when even the musicians do not comprehend the music they play it is too much to expect laymen to take much interest in the programme.

FENSHAN, *October 5th*, 1904.—Still busy in the morning with my report on lines of communication. I am also writing on the pros and cons of artillery dispersion or concentration as evidenced by the recent battles.

It has been quite decidedly cold for the past two days. The kaoliung is almost all cut now and is arranged in giant stooks, which are being carted away by degrees. These stooks, looking like lofty Indian wigwams, are so far apart that they would form no impediment to the movement of cavalry, and yet they give good concealment to anything which is over half a mile distant. What a chance they would give for dashing tactics on the part of the Russians! But the Cossacks, a sort of rude yeomanry, not knowing a word of Chinese, have evidently no aptitude for guerilla warfare, which requires either high training or else special conditions of life.

The bean crop is also being reaped. The result has been a great change in the tactical attributes of the *terrain*. On the whole, although no doubt the kaoliung was occasionally of help to the Russians, I think it is lucky for Kuroki that the battle of Liaoyang was got over before the country become so denuded as it will be shortly.

For the past four days there has been a steady flow of troops northwards. Such a movement seems to portend fighting, as it would otherwise surely be a very needless aggravation of the line of communication difficulties to remove men from the neighbourhood of the Taitsuho, where they can so easily be supplied not only by rail but also by water? Most of the soldiers we meet are clad in brand new blue serges, but they have now no numbers on their shoulderstraps, which really shows a great want of consideration on the part of the Japanese towards military attachés.

At 1 P.M. I went off with Hume to an entertainment given by the Guards Pioneer Battalion to celebrate the completion of a big bridge they have been making over the Liao river. It is an invariable Japanese custom to show hospitality on such occasions.

## SOJOURN AT FENSHAN 167

I am very glad I went. Kuroki was there with a great assemblage of officers, also the Taotai of Liao-yang, accompanied by some of his officials. For amusement we had a regatta in pontoons; the different companies competing and evoking much enthusiasm from their comrades on the banks. Heavy charges of dynamite were also exploded, killing numbers of fish. I secured a large basket full for our mess. Then came the feast which had, according to custom, to be served on the bridge itself. It adapted itself very well to our picnic, and I was much interested to see an entertainment given by a Japanese battalion to brother officers in other regiments and corps. The Guards Pioneers put their best foot forward, and all the officers from Lieutenant-Colonel to latest joined were as busy as bees. It was evident that the resources of the battalion were being taxed to the utmost. All sorts of receptacles were pressed into the service of the cuisine—mess-tins, canteens, ammunition-boxes, and wash-hand basins.

The dishes I have best cause to remember were dough dumplings of millet-flour, floating in a pink syrup something like raspberry vinegar; balls of minced-meat fried in batter; bags of apples and pears; an enormous caldron of stewed vegetables, and a wheelbarrow piled high with smoking hot rice. A truck laden with bottles of beer perambulated slowly across the bridge, getting sensibly lighter with each yard of its progress. In this delicious liquor the healths of the chief engineer and of the officer commanding the pioneer battalion were drunk with much enthusiasm.

Every one was friendly and familiar. All who spoke to me were astonished to see by my dusty boots that

I had walked. In spite of the marching powers of their own infantry, it is a ceaseless cause of wonderment to the Japanese when any one trudges on foot who might have ridden on horseback. In this respect they resemble the ancient Egyptians who were so puzzled when they saw the officers of the Roman garrison taking their constitutional up and down the ramparts of their fort. Junior regimental officers perforce take a great deal of exercise and keep very hard and fit, but as soon as a man gets on to the staff and is entitled to a horse he will not walk fifty yards a year if he can possibly help it. I have only met one single superior officer who is an exception to this rule; absolutely only one. He does like to take walking exercise for about an hour a day, and to this eccentric habit of his I owe many of my happiest and most profitable moments. Still, even he would never have dreamed of walking over here. For although I have come round by the railway bridge and have only marched some four or five miles yet, to hear my Japanese friends it might be thought I had covered myself with glory. I had to give a reason; to have explained that I walked for pleasure would have seemed incredible, and so I replied to their inquiries that I did it to keep myself thoroughly fit for the next great battle.

The First Army headquarters are not the men to miss a feast, and one of them told me, on the bridge, that the 11-inch howitzers had got fairly to work at Port Arthur, and had yesterday succeeded in knocking down the staff office of the Russian General in chief command. A counter-attack made against the Japanese left last night by one battalion was easily repulsed, as well as a similar attempt made against the right by half a Russian battalion. Still, the mere fact of the Russians making counter-attacks shows that they have some life left in them. Some of the officers here think that, as Port Arthur has held out for so much longer than any one had expected, Kuropatkin will very likely attack us. The Russians, they say, think themselves better than the Japanese in winter, and the pressure from St. Petersburg is very great. I wonder if this is true? Of course, if the St. Petersburg people try to force Kuropatkin's hand, Russia will deserve all that it will get. The Japanese are now entrenched up to their chins. Even as far back as this village, gun-pits and trenches have been dug on every commanding site.

FENSHAN, *October 6th*, 1904.—Sergeant-Major Sumino has told the interpreters and servants to pack all the attachés' kits into boxes so that they can be stored for some time, whilst the bare necessaries are to be put into one small bag. Great excitement, but —— absolutely denies that there is any prospect of a move.

FENSHAN, *October 7th*, 1904.—————still denies with oaths that there is any idea of a move on the part of any one, but we know he is not speaking the truth. Very vexatious; neither my new boots nor my warm coat have turned up in time.

9 P.M.—————has just been in. He says Headquarters are about to move thirteen miles to the north. Would I not prefer to stay quietly in this comfortable house and follow on afterwards for the battle? Headquarters undertake to give me ample warning. He then strongly recommended me to remain, as it was very doubtful indeed, he said, whether accommoda-

tion of any sort would be forthcoming in the neighbourhood of the new headquarters; not at least without a little time for making the necessary arrangements. I am afraid I almost lost that calm which, emulating the Japanese and trying to live up to their ideals, I have usually managed to preserve. "No!" I cried, "No! I will not let headquarters out of my sight; not for the sake of a comfortable house—not even for the sake of an Imperial palace!" So he flew off to consult with —— and ——, as he always does in these emergencies.

FENSHAN, *October 8th*, 1904.—The Headquarters march north to-day and we follow to-morrow. I only hope we are not going to miss anything. We have no idea whether we are going to see a Japanese advance or a Russian attack. A cable arrived for me from England to-day saying I was about to be offered an "important command," but nothing can be so important as my present work. I am reminded of my last day in Fenghuangcheng. The whole place is empty; only a few reservists are left in Liaoyang, where I have been to say good-bye to the hospitable missionaries to whom we British attachés owe such delightful tea-table and conversational reminiscences. A Japanese army disappears in one night as quietly as snow in a thaw.

## CHAPTER XXVII

### THE ARMIES IN CONTACT

TAIYO, *October 9th*, 1904.—Our baggage was ordered to start at 9 A.M., so to keep myself warm whilst the carts were being loaded, I went for a farewell promenade round the familiar homesteads of Fenshan. In the middle of my circuit I was surprised to hear the sound of brisk rifle-fire coming from the direction of Manjuyama. I feared the Cossacks might have worked clean round Kuroki's right flank, and as we were now all alone in the village I thought I had better get back to my horse so as to be prepared for all emergencies. When I told an officer of the staff who was to accompany us, he laughed and explained that the Chinese are taking advantage of the pre-occupation of the Russians and Japanese to run a little show on their own. Accordingly the troops of the Taotai of Liaoyang have chosen this moment to attack a band of Redbeards, who are showing fight in the valley between Mountains 131 and 151. I must deny myself the pleasure of being present. Imagine Lord Kitchener's feelings if he opened my despatch expecting an account of one of the decisive battles of the world and found instead an account of a Chinese scrimmage!

After marching for twelve miles to the north we reached this place, which is about two and a half miles

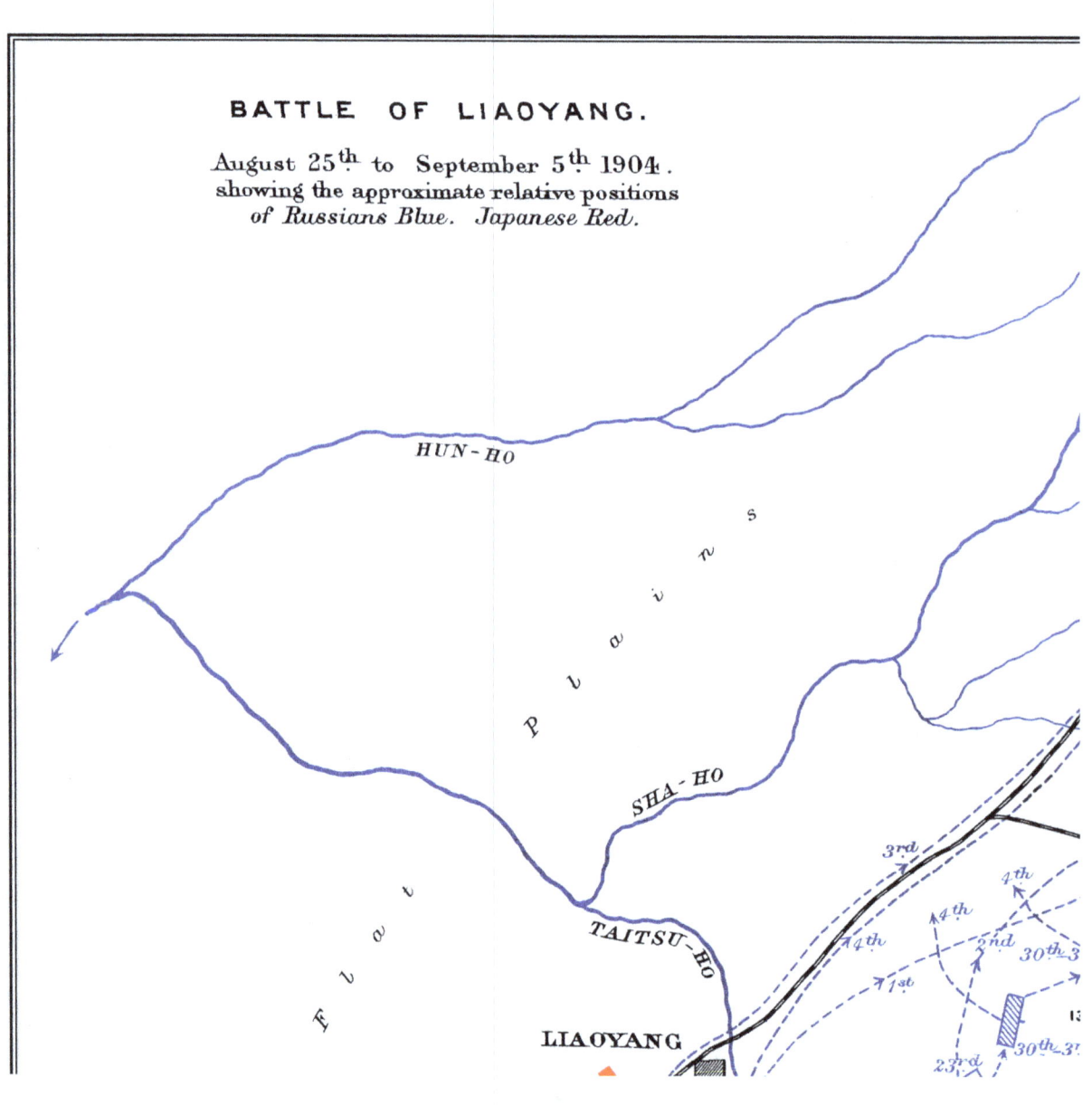

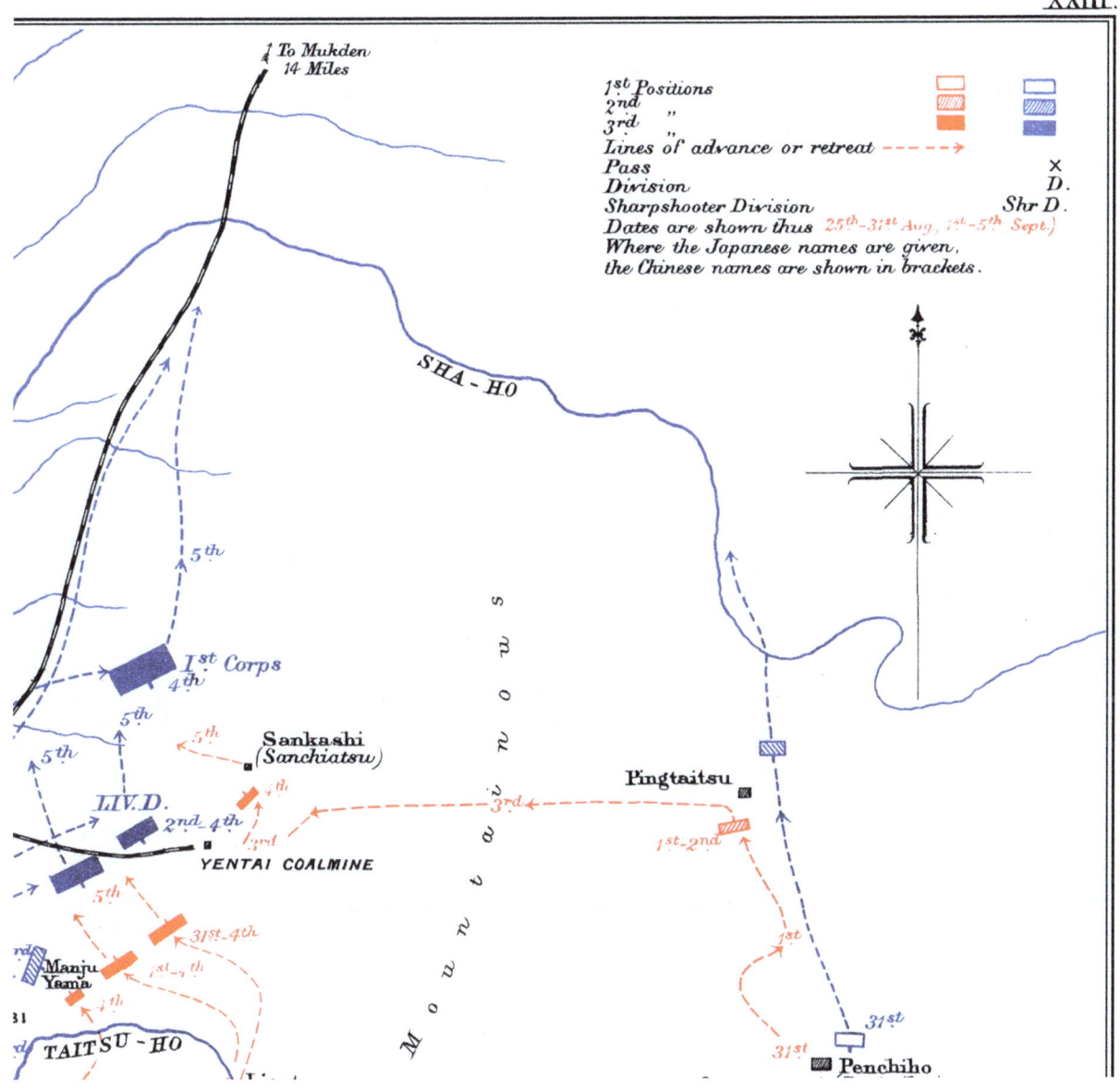

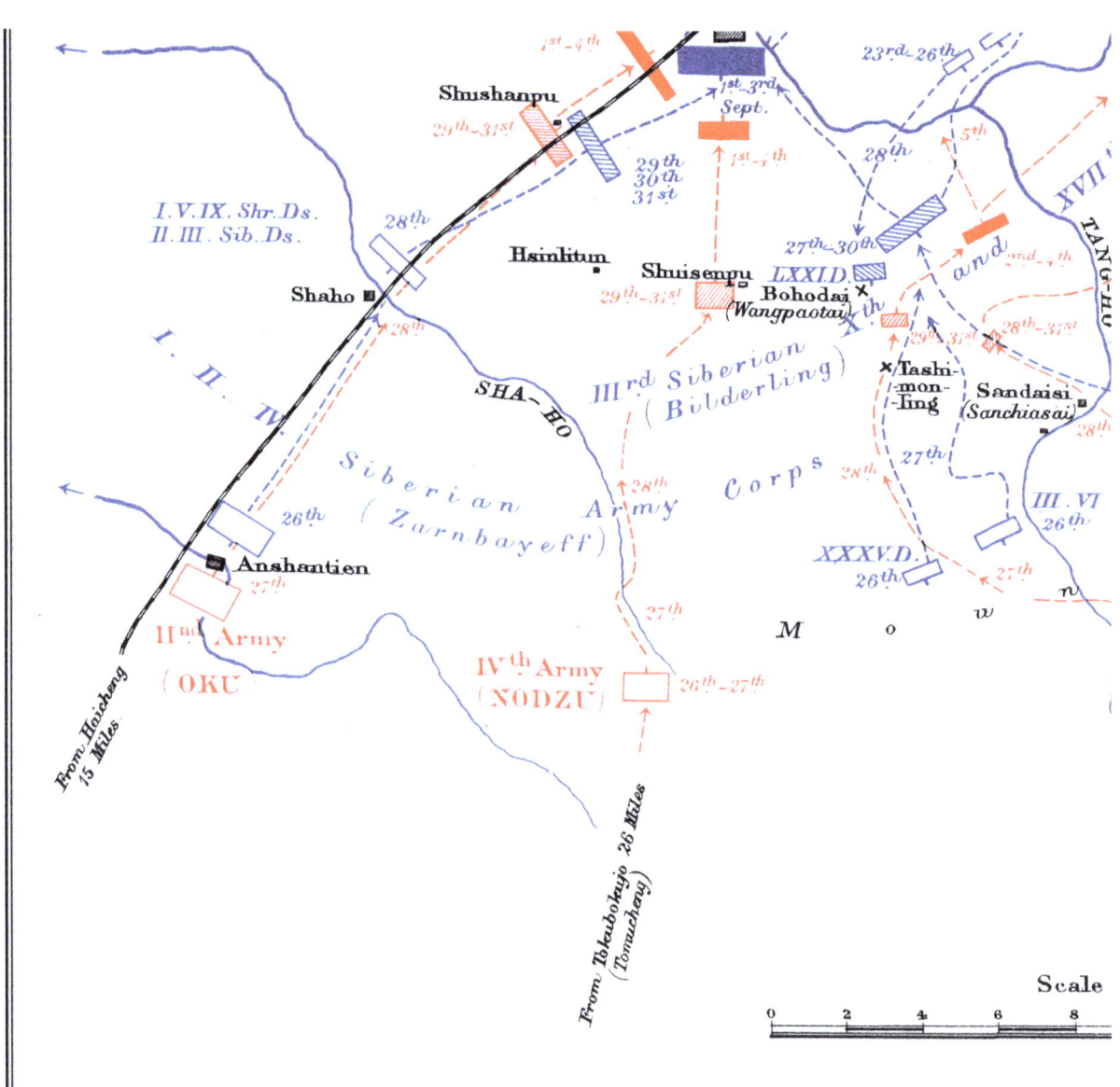

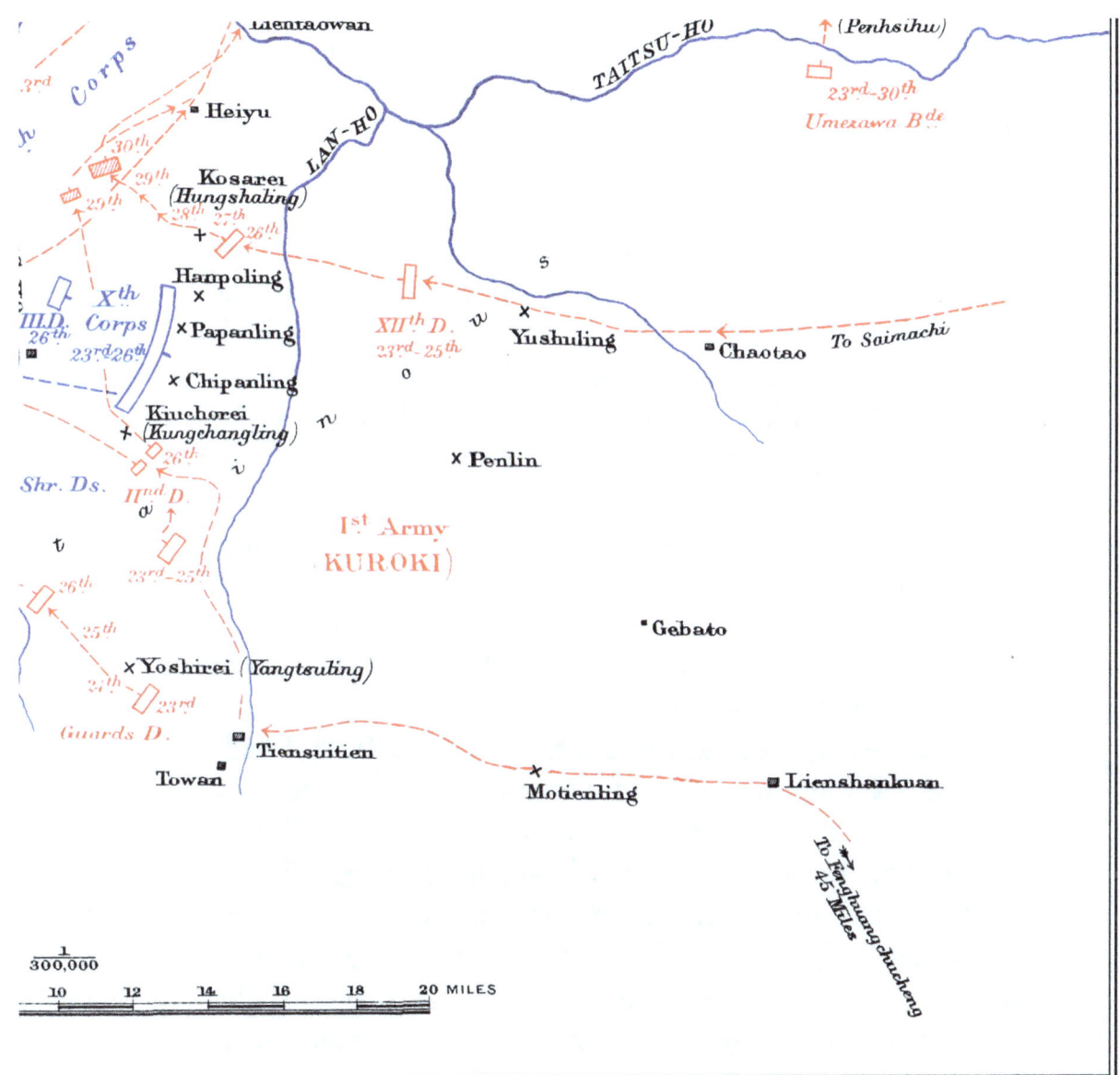

south of the coal-mines. The sound of heavy gun-fire is coming from the north-east.

Taiyo is a rambling village surrounded by the broken ground in which Orloff permitted his troops to be caught in their close formations on September 2nd. The owner of the farmhouse in which I am writing has just been doing some mule coping. He has a singular plan for testing the strength of the mules he is inclined to buy. Ropes are fastened to the mule's collar and six strong coolies hang on to these like grim death. The animal is then whipped up, and if it can overcome the resistance of the coolies it is bought; if not it is cast. Sometimes the coolies lose their footing and are dragged through the mud and trampled upon by the mules, greatly to the amusement of the women standing in the doorways, who simply shriek with laughter to see such jolly fun. The scene I have described may give some idea of the perfect indifference with which the Chinese continue their ordinary avocations at the very crisis of a campaign, even at the headquarters of one of the opposing forces.

9 P.M.—I got a message an hour ago from headquarters telling me that if I cared to come over they would be very glad to try and give me some idea of the actual, tactical situation. Needless to say I lost no time, and one of my kind mentors, resuming functions too long in abeyance, gave me about a quarter of an hour, which, if it does not tell me all I would like to know, reveals to me, at any rate, the gaps which have occurred in my knowledge of events since the battle of Lioayang.

The situation is of extraordinary interest. Although I had heard that the Guards, Second and Twelfth Division, stretched east and west in a line whose right rested on the Yentai coal mines and whose left reached the railway, I have never been able to hear a word of the Umezawa Brigade since they fired the last shots of the battle of Liaoyang at Sankwaisekisan * on the afternoon of September 5th. It seems that three days later Umezawa marched right away sixteen miles eastwards to Pingtaitsu, where he has been covering Penchiho against an attack from the north. (*See* Map XXIII.).

On September 17th an advance was made upon Pingtaitsu by a Russian force consisting of eight infantry battalions, eight squadrons of cavalry, and eight guns. The attack was delivered so half-heartedly that it was regarded as nothing more serious than a reconnaissance in force, but still it aroused Kuroki's anxiety, as he could not but recognise that Umezawa was dangerously isolated in the midst of the most mountainous district of Manchuria. Accordingly a couple of battalions were sent from the Twelfth Division to reinforce him. They joined at Pingtaitsu on September 19th, but hardly had they marched in when the Russians seemed not only to increase in numbers immediately in front of that place, but even began to work round to the east of it, threatening the important strategical point Penchiho, through which came all the munitions and supplies for the brigade. Orders were therefore sent to the General commanding the old line of communications between the Yalu and the Twelfth Division to push up any troops he could lay his hands on, through Chaotao, so as to strengthen the Penchiho garrison, but just as soon as each precautionary measure was taken it was met by a more than corresponding increase in the numbers of the

* Chinese, Sankuaishihshan, meaning "Three Great Rock Hill."

Russians facing and threatening to surround Umezawa. Kuroki had now done all he could do on the basis of his own resources. He therefore begged Oyama to permit the Guards on his left to be relieved by some other army so as to enable him to concentrate towards the threatened right or eastern flank.

Oyama consented, and ordered the Fourth Army to take up the ground to a point five miles east of the railway, thus releasing the Imperial Guards. Kuroki was now able to concentrate the Twelfth Division, and to retire it on Taiyo village, whilst he closed in the Second Division and the Guards. Thus, on October 1st, the Guards and Second Division formed the front line, which ran north-east and south-west for some five miles along the branch line of railway with its right resting on the coal mines (*see* Map XXXIII.). Three miles behind the right of this line was the Twelfth Division in reserve at Taiyo, whilst Umezawa was detached seventeen miles to the north-east at Pingtaitsu.

The First Army had now shifted the bulk of its strength considerably nearer to the eastern screen of mountains behind which trouble seemed to be brewing, and although, in mere measurement, Umezawa appeared to be as much out of touch as ever, yet, in reality, it was not so, for good roads ran out eastwards from Taiyo where the whole of the Twelfth Division lay available and concentrated.

On October 5th, the day I had met General Kuroki at the Pioneer bridge-building festival, when he and all his staff had appeared to be so singularly gay and *debonair*, reports from the front had been very disturbing, pointing, as they seemed to do, to some serious movement on the part of the Russians. So much was

THE ARMIES IN CONTACT 175

Kuroki influenced by his sense of an impending danger that he ordered a brigade and a battery to move northwards from the neighbourhood of the coal mines and occupy an important mountain* which lay six miles distant in that direction.

Next day news came in that the enemy in great strength had prevented the occupation of the mountain.

Until now strong reconnaissances had never been seriously opposed, and the denial thus given by the Russians to a brigade and a battery was considered a very significant sign.

Precisely at this juncture a fortunate accident put the whole situation beyond the region of reconnaissance and surmise. Near the Taling Pass (Map XXXIV.) a Russian staff officer had been killed in a skirmish, and on his body were found detailed orders by Kuropatkin to Stakelberg directing him to turn the right wing of the Japanese and then to march on Liaoyang!

The night of the 6th–7th was therefore spent by the headquarters of the First Army in anxious deliberation, and just as the discussion was at its height a trusted spy arrived reporting that very large bodies of the enemy had crossed the Hunho on October 4th and 5th, and that a heavy column was also certainly advancing from a point, Fushun, twenty-five miles east of Mukden, directly southwards.

Kuroki's mind was cleared of its last doubt. The Russian Grand Army was already well on the move. A message was instantly despatched to Oyama explaining the situation, and asking for orders especially with regard to Umezawa. The answer sent back by

* This was the mountain afterwards called Okasaki-yama. (Sketch XXIV.)

Manchurian Army Headquarters threw some doubt upon the reality of the supposed danger.

But General Kuroki did not feel himself absolved from responsibility by the scepticism of his superiors. How earnestly should British generals pray that they may be given his strength of mind in the hour of need.

Umezawa belonged to the First Army. His situation was hourly becoming more critical, and Kuroki felt bound to take the measures he considered necessary for his support. The question of what orders should be sent him cried for instant decision. For one hour the problem was eagerly debated. From the point of view of *moral* it would be infinitely preferable that Umezawa should hold on until the Twelfth Division should march out from Taiyo and join hands with his left. But before Kuroki could take such a decisive step as to march off the Twelfth Division to support Umezawa he must have some guarantee that his own left would, in case of need, be similarly supported by the other armies. At present these armies refused to realise the danger. Although their Headquarters had crossed the Taitsuho on September 14th and 15th, a large proportion of their troops were still far behind in the neighbourhood of Liaoyang. If their inaction were to prolong itself for another twenty-four hours, then, even with the best will in the world, they might be too late to support the main body of the First Army, weakened as it would be by the detachment of a third of its force. On the whole the risk was too great for an army commander to take upon himself without orders, and it was decided not to move the Twelfth Division on Pingtaitsu.

The next point for consideration was whether

Umezawa could possibly maintain his ground unassisted for two or three days. It was concluded that he could not do so. Orders were therefore sent to him to evacuate Pingtaitsu and to fall back upon Penchiho. The one consoling feature to set against the disagreeable necessity of having to direct a man like Umezawa to retire is that the whole front of the army will be influenced by this preliminary movement, and that it will cause the impending battle to be fought six or seven miles further south and nearer the Japanese base than would otherwise have been the case. Thus Stakelberg will probably be inveigled into coming a long way down into an intricate and broken terrain, where his heavy field artillery and numerous cavalry will lose two-thirds of their value in the entanglements of the mountains.

When Umezawa got his orders he was in contact with a superior force of the enemy, who were already beginning to surround him. He was forced, therefore, to stand fast until the night of the 7th, when he slipped away most cleverly as soon as it got dark, and got clear without having a shot fired at him. It is considered that Umezawa has made a fine opening by extricating himself so cheaply from the slow Russians. From the point of view of *moral*, there is all the difference in the world between an unmolested retreat and a retreat before an active pursuit.

I have been given the full orders issued by Kuroki at 2 A.M. on the 7th, but I shall file them separately. Their general purport is to the effect that the Twelfth Division should move from Taiyo eastwards towards Penchiho to fall upon the right flank of the two Russian divisions who are threatening it and to hold out a hand to Umezawa, who is endeavouring with very meagre resources to save it. The Second Division are to hold the country in the vicinity of the Yentai coal mines, and the Guards are to move round their rear and to concentrate and entrench in the mountains two and a half miles north-east of Taiyo. The position of the troops is still generally unchanged since this order was acted upon. At least, if it has changed I am not to be told anything more at present. For some reason or another the Guards and Second Division have changed round. We now have the Twelfth Division on the right stretching out as fast as it can towards Penchiho. The Second Division are on the left a mile or two north of the Yentai coal mines, and the Guards are in echelon in the centre a short distance in rear of the gap between our right and left wings. Oyama fully realises the situation now, and on the 8th instant he issued the simplest battle order that has ever perhaps been issued to so great an army. Here it is:

"The armies will concentrate their forces as much as possible in their present positions, and be ready to counter-attack the moment an opportunity arrives."

TAIYO, *October 10th*, 1904.—At 6.15 A.M. I was standing at the door of my house when the Second Cavalry Brigade under Prince Kanin came sounding down the street. As they trotted past to the musical clank of steel striking steel I was able to take a good look at them. The men were well turned out, and the horses looked in excellent fettle; they have not been long in the country. A few of the officers were conspicuously well mounted. It was raining hard, and the men were all wearing cloaks and aprons. The carbine was slung over the cloak, and they had a rolled *tente d'abri* behind the saddle. Under the saddle were two blankets, and attached to it were very large canvas saddle-bags and a canvas bucket. An officer of each regiment carried a standard. I hear the brigade is equipped with machine guns, but I did not see them. Prince Kanin, the officer whose looks I admired so much at Liaoyang, is their leader.

At 7 A.M. I attended with all the military attachés at Headquarters to hear Colonel Hagino deliver a short statement on the general situation. His discourse was interesting, not only to us but to several junior Japanese staff officers who stood with us, and who also wrote down the words of wisdom as they fell from the lips of the Chief of the Intelligence Section. I cannot imagine to myself an officer of Colonel Hagino's status in any European army deigning to trouble his head about a party of foreigners; still less can I see him dictating to them a careful little lecture just as a great battle is commencing. We Europeans and Americans may not be able to pick up as much information from irresponsible Japanese individuals as we might collect from men of our own kidney if we were campaigning with one another's troops, but I am certain, on the other hand, that in no army in the world would we receive as much official assistance in carrying out our work as we now do with Kuroki's command.

I mark this passage with blue pencil and turn down the leaf so that I may know where to find an antidote to my annoyance if ever in future I am again tempted to rail at petty restrictions and reticences. My outburst of gratitude is, it is only fair to add, not entirely owing to Hagino's lecture. At its conclusion I received some supplementary explanation of the situation which proved intensely interesting. As the informations I received are infinitely more valuable than the little I saw myself, I will write them down first in full and then, if I have time, I can add my own observations.

It seems that the play is rushing swiftly to its climax. The Russians are pouring down from the north, not only straight upon us here at Taiyo, but also on our comrades to the right hand and the left of us, as far as our breathless messengers have penetrated. Up to the present the hostile forces have not joined battle to our front, but the fighting may begin at any moment, and so close to us are the Russians that last night the whole of the First Army stood to its arms in attack formations.

Umezawa, in the east, is so far bearing the brunt of the attack and seems to be sorely beset. He and his brigade would probably be past praying for had the Russians come down like the wolf on the fold; had they developed even a touch of that audacious, head-long hunger for the fight which has so often been associated with successful military enterprise. Everything is vague as yet, and it is only certain that on the night of the 8th Umezawa was in desperate straits, almost quite surrounded by Stakelberg and Rennenkampf in greatly superior force, and that he was practically at their mercy. Had Umezawa gone under, then Penchiho and Chaotao with their supplies would also have gone by the board, and Kuroki himself might have been forced to move south-east with his whole army to deny the Lentowan ford over the Taitsuho to an enemy threatening Liaoyang.

Since his retreat from Pingtaitsu, Umezawa has been holding a lofty range of mountains from the Tumenling (pass) on the west, *via* the Taling (pass), to Penchiho on the east (*see* Map XXXIV.), where his right is well thrown back lapping round and shielding the town. He is, of course, far too weak for the task, but he must just do his best until the Twelfth Division can push far enough east to support him against the large body of infantry and cavalry who, under the orders of Stakelberg, are trying to turn his right. These troops have been more or less in touch with Umezawa since the 7th, but fortunately the Russians only commenced their attack at dawn yesterday, and then only at Penchiho, into which place Umezawa had just managed, on the evening of the 8th, to throw a reinforcement of two battalions and two guns. Still the position of affairs there must be very critical, if not desperate, for this morning the bad news has come to hand that during yesterday afternoon and evening two important outposts to the Penchiho defence line were attacked by the Russians and carried by assault.

Even more threatening is the news about Rennenkampf, who has crossed the Taitsuho at Weining and moved westwards down its left bank, cutting the communications between Penchiho and Chaotao and threatening the latter important depôt, which is only held by some two or three hundred men. The eastern line of communications is not immediately vital to the Manchurian Army, as a whole, but Kuroki cannot afford to lose it, and he has played his last card by despatching the Cavalry Brigade I have just seen to press on with all possible speed to Chaotao.

Evidently General Kuroki and his Staff are themselves somewhat vague about the progress of events opposite their right wing. For one thing, they have no maps, as the captured Russian maps upon which they have been mainly dependent until now do not show the Pingtaitsu or Penchiho country. As one of the staff ingenuously declared: "Our ideas of the theatre of war to the north of Liaoyang were bounded on the east by the Yentai coal mines; now we begin too late to realise that on our right hand there extends a very continent of mountains!"

Henceforth the British War Office will be able perhaps to pluck up spirit to defend itself with more energy when it is attacked by critics who, without too seriously weighing the financial and political difficulties, have exaggerated its responsibility for the want of good maps which made itself felt during the earlier stages of the South African War.

Having written so much I am interrupted by the loud, booming, double report of the Russian guns: one, two, three, four, five, six, seven, eight. Yes; certainly the Russian guns, and not so far off either.

Two or three miles north of Taiyo I arrived at a big conical hill due east of the coal mines and just above them (*see* Sketch XXXIV.). I thought I had found a splendid lookout post and began to climb up, leading my horse by the bridle, but on the summit were General Nishi and the Staff of the Second Division, who preferred my room to my company. It seemed a pity to retire, and so I advanced about three or four hundred yards beyond them to another likely looking hill overlooking a brigade of the Second Division artillery who had dug themselves in very snugly; luckily for them, for the shells were bursting over the gun-pits in strings with a succession of loud reports, raising clouds of dust about the batteries, but doing no harm to the men who lay flat under cover and attempted no reply. Five miles to the north the enemy were advancing. As far as I could see, namely, from Sankwaisekisan, a little to the west of north, to Shotatsuko to the north-east, the ground was alive with Russians (*see* Sketch XXIV.). No kaoliung here; no concealment, and there stood the Russians in solid masses—cavalry, infantry, and guns—formations such as I have not seen in recent years except upon the parade-ground.

The biggest mass, presumably a brigade, was below the big hill just due north of Sankashi, and must have amounted to 5000 or 6000 men in one solid block. Had the Japanese only possessed one or two of our South African Long Toms they might have had some fine shooting into the brown. The movement of such columns cannot be rapid, but it need not necessarily be so slow as that of the enemy, who alternated long halts with very short advances.

Meanwhile, I had leisure to look at the country. I found myself sitting on a detached conical hill, about 200 feet high. It formed one of the scattered western outposts of the continent of mountains which stretched eastwards continuously, ridge upon ridge, and peak upon peak, as far as the eye could reach. This mountain region has a sharp, distinct edge or ending, just as an ice floe ends sharply and decisively where it meets the sea, and to continue the parallel, just as the action of the water detaches many bergs which float by the hundred in the close vicinity to the pack and become rarer, and yet more rare with every mile's distance, so here the isolated hills become fewer and more scattered as the eye travels westwards, until, at last, out beyond the Fourth Army, the spacious plain runs out to the horizon in monotonous flatness.

Two of our divisions—the Twelfth and the Guards—and two of our brigades, Umezawa's and Prince Kanin's Cavalry, are swallowed up in the Switzerland of the Far East, which lies to the right. The Second

Division has half of its right brigade entrenched on Daisan,* on the very edge of the main mass of mountains. Daisan is due east of me, two miles distant, and it is about 600 feet high. The other regiment of this brigade (Matsunaga's) is at my feet in Kento village. The brigade of the renowned Okasaki is altogether clear of the mountains, and is entrenched on the bare plough of the plains, about one mile to the north of where I am seated, with its left (forming the extreme left of the First Army), resting on some low hills some two and a half miles north-west of me. (*See* Map XXXIII.)

At mid-day the Russian artillery became silent. It had not been able to draw the Japanese guns into a duel, and I do not think it had done much harm. By 1 A.M. the Russian infantry columns along the Shotatsuko-Sankashi valley had apparently got their correct intervals, and as heavy storm-clouds spread athwart the whole horizon ere they discharge their burden of lightning and of hail, so these dark masses began a stately deployment into long continuous lines, which made my heart sink with an impression of resistless strength and of a tremendous impending blow. This, too, although I tried to reassure myself by remembering how the eyes of an old Boer would have danced with joy to see his enemy advancing against him shoulder to shoulder, and although I knew that the formation was still far too solid to run the gauntlet of the Japanese artillery without being shattered in the attempt.

But now the long lines halted. Strange indecision! They remained motionless ten minutes; twenty minutes; and then I realised that they were entrench-

* Chinese, Tashan or great mountain.

ing, out of range of the Japanese! In that one moment all anxiety passed away. I cannot explain the sensation or instinct which possesses me, but there it is, and I feel possessed of great calmness, and the full conviction that the Russians have by their failure to come on, parted for ever with that moral ascendency which is the greatest of all the assets of an attack.

At 2.45 an officer's patrol which had been sent out by Okasaki to get hold of a low ridge east of Hanlasanshi,* about three miles to the north of us (*see* "V" Sketch XXIV.), was just anticipated by a superior force of Russians who, when they topped the crest line, found themselves within fifty yards of the retreating Japanese. In their eagerness, the Russians stood up on the ridge and fired heavily on the retreating party of some twenty men. These took to their heels and made record time getting to some cover 500 or 600 yards in rear—all except one man. When I first noticed this individual he was walking far behind his comrades, and at about 100 yards from the Russians. I thought the poor fellow was wounded, and kept my glasses upon him expecting every moment to see him drop. Suddenly he did drop; not as a wounded man but as a particularly lively skirmisher, behind a little grassy rise between two fields which gave him a little cover. Here he opened fire, gaily taking on 100 Russians at 200 yards range. After a minute or two he got up again, and under a shower of bullets which threw up dust puffs all about him, quietly sauntered into a small plantation some 100 yards further away, where I lost sight of him. No one was hit; or, at any rate, no one fell during the skirmish.

* Chinese, Panlashantsu.

After it was all over the Japanese guns opened at 1500 yards range on the ridge but made very bad practice, both range and fuse being too short. No soldier of any experience expects anything, even in a small degree, approximating to target practice accuracy on the battlefield. In 1879, the 92nd Highlanders were the best shooting battalion in India, and yet I saw 500 of their men fire three or four rounds each at one Afghan straggler clambering but slowly up a steep mountain at 400 yards range without effect. Still, I may frankly confess I have never seen any exhibition of marksmanship quite so deplorable as the shooting of the Russians on the occasion I have just described. When it fell dusk I returned to Taiyo rather disappointed at having seen no serious fighting. I fear it is my sin to love the noise of war, I do not quite know, though I often consider, what I shall say when I am called to answer for it at the long account.

## CHAPTER XXVIII

### OKASAKI'S DASHING ASSAULT

TAIYO, *October 11th, 1904.*—Guns booming and rifles volleying and rattling ever since the first grey streak of dawn. Have got orders that I am to participate with the others in a lecture Colonel Hagino is going to give us at 7 A.M., after which I am to separate from my friends and to accompany Kuroki and the Headquarters Staff who will now take the field. The other attachés are told off to work under the orders of that very exclusive body—the Second Division Headquarters.

8 A.M., *Coal Mine Hill.*—After the lecture I got little Nakamura, the interpreter, to accompany me here, where I have found the Headquarters. Kuroki was seated on a small yellow box belonging to the telephone section, whose terminal station is within ten yards of him. On his other side was a bearer section with its stretchers. The Commanders of the Artillery and Engineers, Colonel Hagino of the Intelligence, and Captain Saigo, the Adjutant, were in earnest conversation with Kuroki, and no other officer but myself was at that time present on the hilltop.

The great man got up and shook me by the hand, saying, "It is a very fine day"; not a very brilliant remark perhaps, but interesting from its very commonplaceness. Many men would have aimed at saying something adequate to the momentous occasion, but about Kuroki there is not even a suspicion of pose.

I said, yes, it was a fine day, and a pity so many fine fellows should have to die when the world looked so beautiful.

He replied, "To die in battle for their country is good fortune either for Russians or Japanese; and as to the fine weather, that is a good preparation for either life or death, as it has enabled them to snatch a little repose whilst lying out on the open fields and mountains all night under arms."

He then spoke the first few words on tactics he has ever addressed to me. He said, "Our infantry will not advance yet awhile. The enemy has only fallen back a short distance from before our right at Penchiho, and I do not like them to fall back any further at present. Therefore the Second Division and the Guards must not alarm them for their communications by a premature advance, and I am going to let the Fourth Army get into full swing on our left before we begin to move. The enemy has made a big attempt to turn our right, and now that his effort has been brought to a standstill, Marquis Oyama will perhaps have a chance of turning *his* right. Now that I have said so much, you as a General will only need to direct your glasses occasionally to the westwards and you will be able to discern as well as I can when we should make our start. How fast the artillery are shooting; I must watch them more closely."

Kuroki then sat down again on his yellow box, and remained quite quiet except when telephone messages or orderlies arrived, or when Hagino, map in hand, consulted with him. Then all the officers I have named squatted down, Indian fashion, in a tiny circle, and I looked the other way, lest any secrets were being ventilated.

It is now 8.25 A.M., and the violence of the cannonade surprises me even after my Manjuyama experiences. The Japanese batteries are in the same position as yesterday, all except one, which has advanced about 1000 yards during the night, and has dug itself deeply out of danger's way. A series of rafales are bursting just over these guns; a neat and curious sight. So much savage noise, and nothing to show for it but the sudden mysterious appearance in the air over the Japanese battery of a little white balloon, like the soap bubbles filled with tobacco smoke a kind uncle used to blow for me when I was a child. Then seven more balloons all in a line with the first, and so it goes on. The Japanese artillery is being held under to a great extent, but when it does fire, the guns are laid on Sanjoshisan, and the hills immediately to the south of it, making very good shooting at the crest lines, which are thickly packed with Russians. Boom! and then the long drawn out whirr of the tortured air as the projectile speeds on to its objective, until at last a small white cloud alights on the top of the distant mountain. It is still too misty to see very much on the plain.

9.15 A.M.—The mist has cleared. I see about a brigade of Russian artillery towards the bottom of the long spur which runs out in a north-westerly direction from Sanjoshisan, and one battery is firing from the north-east of Terayama. That is to say, I cannot see the guns—only the flashes of their discharge. But here, oh, splendid, soul-inspiring spectacle! Here comes the infantry at last. *Ave Cæsar, morituri te* *salutant!* Two long lines of infantry, arms sloped, bayonets glistening, marching shoulder to shoulder as if at a St. Petersburg manœuvre instead of across the Shotatsuko valley, whence they pass into the low-lying fields three and a half miles to our front, and are entirely lost to view. Drums are beating, no doubt, and colours flying, and every man in that mighty array feels himself a true hero, but it is lucky that the lines are still just a little far for the short-ranging Japanese guns, and that these guns are already pretty well mastered by the Russian artillery. It looks as if the Rooskis were coming on in earnest, and if that is so we shall have a real bloody battle, and make October 11th for evermore famous. The attackers should have one great advantage, inasmuch as they have already won the artillery fight. The Japanese gunners now, 10.15 A.M., are unable to show their noses. Oh, that some of our rulers could see what I see! Our guns are as near as possible on a par with the Japanese guns, and it is patent—obvious, glaringly obvious—that these have not a chance in the fair open field against the Russians.*

10.20.—I have just been told that affairs remain in a highly critical state at Penchiho, both in front of the Twelfth Division and on the right of Umezawa's Brigade. There is no idea now of the Twelfth Division falling, as it was originally intended to fall, upon the right of Stakelberg at Penchiho. There are other equally powerful bodies of Russians threatening the Tumenling and Taling Passes, and, far from attacking, the Twelfth Division are only hopeful that they may by great efforts be enabled to prevent the enemy penetrating between Penchiho and the Yentai coal mines. (*See* Map XXXIV. as well as Map XXXIII.)

* Modern guns have been issued to the British Army since this entry was made.—I. H.

Some Officers of the 12th Division Mountain Artillery

Stakelberg has a superiority of about six to one over the defenders of the extreme Japanese right. On the afternoon and evening of the 9th instant he had captured two lofty mountains—Mingshan and Shishan, which overlooked, and, to some extent, gave him a fire command over the Japanese trenches in front of Penchiho. (*See* Sketch XXX.) Instead of pushing on instantly and, under cover of the approaching night, making use of each of the captured heights as a fulcrum to break down all further resistance, Stakelberg rested on his laurels. Then two things happened.

That night three battalions and a mountain battery of the Twelfth Division, under command of Shimamura, one of the best Brigadiers in the Army, marched into Penchiho and gave a fine fillip to the spirit of the defenders. So much cheer did this reinforcement bring to their hearts that it was nobly resolved to let Umezawa's two battalions go back to their own Brigadier at Taling, where they were badly needed, whilst Shimamura with 3000 men remained to face Stakelberg's 15,000.

The second thing took place at 11 A.M. yesterday morning, up to which hour Stakelberg had been marking time until the mist should begin to rise. Shimamura, on the contrary, thought mist was just what he wanted to cloak his preparation for a mettlesome enterprise, and the very moment it showed signs of lifting he was ready, and, hurling 500 gallant soldiers at Shishan, snapped it back from its unsupported garrison before the enemy's masses could so much as set themselves in motion. This dashing feat of arms was performed in full view of both armies, and, like Robert the Bruce's historical whack on the casque of Sir Henry de Bohun, the incident must have exercised a marked effect on the fortunes of the day. Before armies close in mortal conflict their souls wrestle with one another spiritually, and thousands of intelligences strained to almost superhuman acuteness of discernment seek for some sign, and rarely seek in vain, for it is the nature of such signs to fulfil themselves.

When Shishan was taken, then, and not till then, did the giant begin to move, as Stakelberg's slow columns deploying into line commenced their ponderous attack. It is still touch and go out there, but the Headquarters feel more confident now that Shimamura has got back Shishan, for what that commander grips he will not be in a hurry to let go.

Another favourable prognosis is that Rennenkampf, who crossed the Taitsuho at Weining, has not advanced against Chaotao, where he might almost with impunity have dealt the First Army a severe blow, but has turned back northwards to attack or threaten Penchiho from the south. Between Penchiho and our coal mines the Russians are still hesitating in front of Umezawa and the Twelfth Division at the Tumenling and Taling Passes. They are in enormously superior force, and had they attacked directly they got into position, General Inouye, commanding the Twelfth Division, would never have dared detach Shimamura to reinforce Penchiho.

But it is easy to carry this same principle further. Had the Russians now menacing our main body with an attack come rushing down impetuously on the 8th instant, then Kuroki would never have dared despatch his Twelfth Division out to the east to help Umezawa, who must have been irremediably lost.

It seems that under our own orders issued at 10 P.M. last night we ought to be by now a mile or two beyond the line along which I can now see the Russians manning their shelter trenches. By now, in fact, the Guards to the east of Daisan mountain should have fought their way beyond Kamiriuka, and the Second Division, that is to say, the brigades of Matsunaga on the right and of Okasaki on the left, should be firmly fixed upon the height north of Shotatsuko. But here we are still much on the same line as yesterday. We are waiting, as a matter of fact, for the Fourth Army on our left. For Oyama's Manchurian army orders issued last night say specifically, so I am told, that the Fourth Army is to make a wheel to the right so as to drive the enemy off the main Liaoyang-Mukden road into the mountains. I think, though, that there is another reason besides the tardy advance of the Fourth Army to account for the fact that I am still perched on the coal mine hill when I ought to be five miles to the north of it, and that reason is to be found in the power and activity of the Russian artillery.

Whilst I was learning these details and committing them to paper, an officer had come in from the Second Division headquarters, who are on a hill close by, to say that Okasaki was anxious to advance against Terayama, but that he could not get any news of the Fourth Army on his left, so I may not have been correct in what I have just written about the hesitation being mainly due to the Russian guns. Okasaki is in the low hills two and a half miles to the north-west of us. An order is being sent back to him, through his divisional general, saying that General Kuroki can give him no news, but that he must understand quite clearly that he is absolutely forbidden to commit himself in any way until he gets into touch with the Fourth Army. Unless there is some very ugly mistake in the whole of the Japanese calculations the right of the Fourth Army must be within five miles of us.

Our position, and the lie of the country to the west of us, are ideal for the purposes of heliographic communication. Nothing could be better than a plain dotted here and there with natural signalling stations in the shape of detached hills. The sun, too, is shining gloriously, and we ought, in short, to be in close-knitted consultation not only with our own commanders and with Nodzu of the Fourth Army, but also with Oku of the Second Army, and with Marshal Oyama and Manchurian Army Headquarters. But we know nothing of what is happening outside Matsunaga's brigade on Daisan to our right and Okasaki's on our left.*

11 A.M.—The worst of writing on a battle-field is the necessity which it entails of constant contradictions. I have just been told that a telephone message came in from the Guards an hour ago, namely, at 9.40, saying that Izaki's First Brigade of Guards had captured a hill, called 242, without fighting, during the night, whilst Watanabe's Second Brigade had effected a lodgment at dawn on the southern part of Hill 238. (*See* Map XXXIII.) The capture of 238 was only effected after hard fighting, although there was no bayonet work, but only musketry. The Russians became silhouetted against the sky line at grey dawn, but the Japanese, who had worked up to close quarters, remained invisible in the dark valley, so that they had two to one the best of it. When selecting night positions

---

* There is a school of thought in Germany which deprecates signalling, as it is thought to lessen the self-reliance of commanders. But in this case, at any rate, the commanders were most anxious to communicate with one another.

the Japanese are more and more inclining to sacrifice the advantage of an extensive field of fire for the sake of forcing the enemy to cross the sky-line in his attack. Naturally the crest of the ridge is re-occupied directly it becomes daylight. We had arrived at a similar conclusion in the Western Transvaal towards the end of the South African campaign.* Major-General Asada, who has now been promoted from a brigade to command the Guards Division vice Hasegawa sent to be Commander-in-Chief in Korea, adds that he cannot carry out his orders in full or attack the enemy on the north side of the Kameriuka-Hakashi valley until his artillery is able to come up to his assistance. About this time I heard an officer say, but not to me, that it was too bad of our artillery not to put forth its full strength now that our infantry was advancing. But the poor old Japanese batteries are being simply smothered. The well-beloved guns cannot open their mouths. This is an exemplar of the weakest point of the Japanese— the inferiority of their artillery.

Soon after eleven o'clock an exciting message (as I could see from the faces of the staff) was received, the purport of which I did not clearly catch. From the talk of the adjutants it seems as if the enemy might be preparing to retreat. But notwithstanding very heavy fire, especially in the mountains immediately to the east, there is as yet nothing like general advance on the part of the Japanese.

12.15.—Just had a second cup of tea in a red lacquer

* I heard afterwards from Colonel Hume that in his orders for the attack, General Watanabe, who had no time to arrange for distinguishing badges, issued the following general instruction to the battalion commanders: "Japanese are short, foreigners are tall. There are no foreign attachés with the brigade to-night, so treat every tall man you come across as an enemy."

bowl. The movements of the Russians in the neighbourhoood of Shotatsuko and Terayama have for some time past seemed strangely undecided. Columns composed of the three arms march sometimes east; then counter-march and move north-west; two brigades hover to the north of Terayama; and again a brigade advances from Kamiriuka southwards towards Sanjoshisan. The fierceness of the artillery and rifle-fire continues unabated, and the Russians still keep a firm grip on Sanjoshisan on our right, and Terayama on our left. Neither side has any troops now in the open plain immediately to the north of the coal-mines. It is the hope of the Japanese that the Russians may be tempted to push into this vacant space, when they would be hemmed in and swallowed up very quickly, but I doubt if they will be quite so accommodating.

1.30 P.M.—I have witnessed a scene which I shall never forget as long as I live. For the last hour, Matsunaga has been making spirited efforts to reach Sanjoshisan, and his brave infantry have been streaming like a pack of hounds, now in full cry, now being badly checked, over the hills between Daisan and their objective. From my coal-mine hill I cannot see what is happening on the eastern watershed of these ridges, but the men working over the western slopes, and all their actions, stand out as clear as noonday against the rocky background. (*See* Sketch XXIV.)

Only two ridges lay between the Japanese and Sanjoshisan, but beyond that point they seemed quite unable to progress. Some time before mid-day Matsunaga reinforced his left from his brigade reserve in Kento village, and then at last he appeared to gain strength to press back the enemy a little further. On the last rounded ridge to the south-west of Sanjoshisan, and on one of the spurs running south-west from the main mountain were about two battalions of Russians, and they had some reserves close behind them in a wood. It was the fire from these battalions which was stopping Matsunaga's further progress. But now, in the most dramatic fashion conceivable, one more step forwards was about to be made. Exactly on the summit of the rounded knoll (called "Bayonet Knoll" on Sketch XXIV.) was an advanced post of some fifty or sixty Russians in a trench. They were engaged in a hot fire fight with Matsunaga's men on the southern prolongation of the same ridge at a range of 200 or 300 yards.

Suddenly I espied a Japanese section of perhaps twenty-five men darting along, and making their way in first-class shikari style from cover to cover along the, to me, fully exposed lower slopes of the ridge on which their enemy was entrenched. The Russian commander had made the fatal mistake of not throwing out a few men to cover his right flank. There was some broken ground at the foot of the knoll which would have given good shelter, and whence a small detachment could have enfiladed, and prevented the encircling movement now made by the Japanese. For these, daring greatly, worked right round and upwards until they suddenly emerged within fifty yards of the Russians, and actually in their right rear. The commander of the Russians drew his sword. He and all his men quitted their entrenchment and fell on with the bayonet whilst the detachment of Japanese rushed in to meet them. Then, just like a football scrimmage, except for the gleams of steel, the little mob of brave and desperate fighters worked slowly over to the northern slope of the knoll, leaving a trail of prostrate, motionless figures. The Russians were the more numerous, but help was at hand for the Japanese, though none came, why I cannot say, for their adversaries. Matsunaga's main frontal attack dashed in from the south, and soon all that could be seen of the late defenders of the knoll was a handful of poor fellows running with painful slowness in their long great coats over the open plough. They fled towards the north-west, becoming fewer and fewer under the fire of many rifles, which freely took toll of the survivors even as I looked, horror-stricken and yet fascinated by the tragedy of such a scene.

A very minor incident perhaps to chronicle so fully during a great battle. But there is value in small things just as much as in great. Any impartial soldier who saw what I saw would have been struck by the parade-like stiffness and inflexible immobility of the Russians which condemned them to be passive spectators of their own impending envelopment and destruction by the lightning-like initiative of the individual Japanese soldier. Then, small as was the affair, it might serve to recall to his memory a Latin proverb, and he might wonder if this was to be merely a chance example or whether it was a case of *ex pede Herculem*.

2 P.M.—It looks as if Matsunaga's men had shot their bolt in capturing "Bayonet Knoll." They are evidently under a very hot fire from the main mountain of Sanjoshisan and from the intervening ground, and are busy entrenching themselves just behind the crest line of the ridge they have won. Matsunaga has sent in to say he is having a terribly rough time, but his troops must now be within a mile of the Russian guns at the foot of the spur running north-

west from Sanjoshisan, so these last also must find themselves in a difficult position. I have only just heard that a message came in at 1.7 P.M. from the Guards saying the enemy was too strong, and that an advance beyond Hill 238 was impracticable. I can now see a Russian company who are trying to work southwards along the western slopes of Sanjoshisan. They have got into a ravine which forms a deep, yellow-coloured scar half-way across the flank of the mountain, and there they seem to stick. At this time I heard Kuroki exclaim: " I must insist upon getting clearer information about our own troops and those of the enemy."

2.40 P.M.—Beyond Shotatsuko * large columns of Russians are marching eastwards. They seem in some confusion, and the Staff declare that they can see single guns moving with them which is a very good sign, if true, only I cannot make them out. The woods and villages are on fire. All looks well.

3 P.M.—The Russians, instead of retreating, have come out of the burning woods beyond Shotatsuko, in two extended lines at an interval of 400 yards. Behind them is yet another line of company columns of sections. A great battle is being waged to the westwards by the Second and Fourth Armies.

3.15 P.M.—A grave decision has been taken. Okasaki has been granted permission to attack Terayama.† When Kuroki heard within an hour from Asada, commanding the Guards Division, and Matsunaga, commanding the Third Brigade, Second Division, that they were at the end of their tether, he must have felt some heaviness of heart on reflecting that, in the eastern area of combat at Tumenling, Taling, and

* Chinese, Hsiao Takou.
† Terayama is the Japanese for Temple Hill.

Penchiho, the outlook was very black and that his high hopes of relieving his overmatched right by a brilliant counter-stroke in the centre had fallen to the ground. There remained only his extreme left where Okasaki, fearless and true, a general good at need if ever there was one, might still, if qualities of great-heartedness and resolution would serve, achieve some exploit by which the soul of the Russian Commander might be shaken and daunted. True, it had been Oyama's intention that the advance of the Manchurian Army should be by a wheel to the right, and in pursuance of this intention the Fourth Army should have led the way by taking Sankwaisekisan before Okasaki moved forward. But the intention of a Generalissimo must sometimes give way to the imperious necessities of an Army Commander, and as Nodzu * made no sign and the shadows were growing long, Kuroki, with what anguish of mind no man will ever know, resolved to let slip his great warrior from the leash.

3.40 P.M.—The Russian artillery at the foot of the spur running north-west from Sanjoshisan is retiring one gun at a time. What between high explosive shell and rifle bullets they must surely have suffered terrible losses in holding on so long.† A column of Russians is certainly retiring over the big hill a little to the north-west of Shotatsuko‡ by the same path along which they made their advance yesterday.

3.45 P.M.—Okasaki's Brigade has begun to move against Terayama. It is as bad a place almost to

* The Commander of the Fourth Army.

† Afterwards I went over their position and I doubt if their casualties were very serious, although they had lost eight or ten horses. The guns had been in action just behind the crest line and most of the Japanese shell had passed over them.

‡ Afterwards called Okasakiyama.

attack as was the Boer position at Doornkop by Johannesburg. Looking, as I do, due north from the coal-mines, the country lies before me as plain as the palm of my hand, apparently open, flat, plough-land, unbroken except by a small rocky hill (Japanese Ishiyama) 2000 yards distant. Carrying the eye onwards beyond this rocky Hill there is a continuation of the level plain for 2500 yards as far as Terayama, although, on closer inspection, it becomes evident that, about two-thirds of the way across the open, a straggling village called Kokashi, should, by its orchards and houses, yield some concealment to an attack advancing from the south. The hill itself rises less than 100 feet above the plain, and is about 500 yards long, from north to south. It seems to be narrow at the top, about the centre of which stand the Temple buildings. A low ridge, slightly elevated above the plain, connects Terayama with the mountains on the north of the Sankashi valley, which are full of Russians. Just to the south and west of the hill is a sunken road, into which Russian troops have been seen dropping from view and evidently taking up their line of defence. Indeed, I can see them even now in places showing themselves clearly up to their waists notwithstanding the Japanese shells passing over their heads on to Terayama.

A natural cover such as this sunken road is much better than any extemporised field-work, inasmuch as there is no freshly turned-up earth to betray its existence to the hostile guns. But the Russians have quite thrown away this advantage by exposing themselves to view, not only on first entering the sunken road, which may have been inevitable, but now, when from every point of view except that of the Japanese, it is most necessary that they should escape detection. Even as I write the Japanese artillery are beginning to range on them, and it seems that not even the instinct of self-preservation can induce the Russian soldier to grasp the full value of concealment.

The main strength of the Terayama position lies, not so much in the hillock itself, the long narrow shape of which, pointing towards the south like an arrow, gives no breadth for the development of any volume of musketry upon the Japanese line of advance. Its strength lies rather in the perfectly flat glacis of 500 or 600 yards, extending unbroken to Kokashi village; in the enfilading fire which can be brought upon this glacis from the Russian guns at Sankwaisekisan, as well as from a battery to the north of Sankashi, and most of all, perhaps, in the sunken road I have described which runs north-westwards, passing within a few yards of the southern salient of Terayama, and covering the whole of its western flank.

8 P.M., TAIYO VILLAGE.—I was unable to write more on the field, as I could not afford to take my glasses for even one moment off the most headlong and dashing attack I have ever witnessed. In saying so much I do not wish to imply that it was a finer attack than that of the gallant infantry at Elandslaagte and of the Gordon Highlanders at Doornkop, by Johannesburg, for that would be impossible, but it was more swift and on that account more impressive.

A nation which can produce a whole brigade; that is to say, two regiments, or six battalions; every single individual of which eagerly rushes to seek the bubble reputation in the cannon's mouth; not one single individual of which is even a laggard, must be a great nation, and cannot be denied the palm. But I am anticipating. It was about 3.45 of the clock when the brave Japanese broke cover in one long line and headed due north. The men were almost shoulder to shoulder in single rank. The supports followed at about 200 yards, also in single rank, and behind them came the reserve in double rank. There was no firing. The rank and file marched with sloped arms and fixed bayonets and swung along steadily, almost solemnly, forward. Many bullets came flying over Kokashi village from Terayama and struck the plain here and there like the first heavy, stabbing drops of a coming thunderstorm, but still Okasaki did not open his ranks. It was God's mercy that the Russian gunners held off their shrapnel *rafales*, or, to speak more materially, it seemed to be owing to the efforts of the Japanese artillery that the outburst of the deluge was fended off for yet a little longer. All along the front of the Second Division the gunners sweated and laboured at their task until Terayama was almost obliterated from the landscape, swathed around in a pall of inky black smoke from the high explosive shell. Nor were the enemy's batteries north-west of Sankwaisekisan and north of Sankashi forgotten, and so furious and sudden was the fire attack made upon them that the Russians devoted all their attention to the Japanese guns, and could not, or, at any rate, did not, turn upon the infantry.

Now I noticed that the power of Kuroki's artillery had been augmented, and learnt that the guns of the Fourth Army had also joined in from their position on the low hills two and a half miles to the north-west of where I sat. I cannot tell the number of guns in action on either side, but certainly those of the Japanese were the most numerous. In spite of this advantage the Russian artillery slowly wrested back its superiority, until the fire in support of the attack again became spasmodic and feeble as heretofore. But not before it had to a great extent served its purpose. Okasaki's infantry had reached Kokashi without firing a shot themselves, and without, so far as I could see suffering any loss at all from the bullets which had been raising little puffs and spurts of dust about them as they advanced. As for the Russian guns, they had either failed to detect the commencement of the attack, or else they had been successfully distracted from their legitimate target by the Japanese bombardment.

It was soon after four o'clock that the Brigade Okasaki disappeared into Kokashi and into a village half a mile to the east of it called West Sankashi. Then there arose a continuous tearing crepitating sound, not very loud, and yet sufficient in intensity and volume to cause us all to shiver with excitement. To the ear of a civilian the noise might have awakened comfortable reflections of frizzling bacon; to a woman it might recall the bubbling of her tea kettle. But it stirred my own blood like the Valkyrie Ritt. It startled me like the sudden snarl of a wild beast. For I knew that thousands of rifles had opened magazine fire and were struggling at from 500 to 600 yards distance for the fire mastery, that fire mastery which, established by the one side would render the assault possible; established by the other must doom it to disastrous failure. Such sounds as these, wafted upon the evening breeze, bore messages of life and death; more—of victory or defeat to all who could grasp their significance.

For a long, long time the anguish of anticipation was spun out to the uttermost. A quarter of an hour passed, then another quarter of an hour; the General

Staff could hardly endure it any longer, but Kuroki remained confident and calm. Then another ten minutes. The tension became unendurable. The setting sun threw its reddish rays slantwise on Terayama, and showed it smoking like a volcano, but apparently quite lifeless. We could see the temple and the plain more clearly even than at mid-day. "Ah," said Kuroki; "he cannot get on. To-day we are stuck fast all along the line." In his voice was no tone of regret, no shade of mortification; at the most it could only be said that the actual words betokened some touch of despondency.

Hardly had he spoken when a sharp exclamation from an adjutant made me turn my glasses once more upon the deserted plain, and to my amazement I saw it, deserted no longer, but covered by a vast, straggling, scattered crowd of individuals, each racing towards the Russians at his topmost speed. The Okasaki Brigade was crossing the open to try and storm Terayama by one supreme effort; and the only English expression which will convey an idea of their haste is that phrase of the hunting-field, "Hell for leather." Bullets fell thick amongst those who ran for life or death across the plain, and the yellow dust of their impact on the plough rose in a cloud almost up to the men's knees. By what magic these bullets almost always struck in the vacant spaces, and very rarely on the bodies of the men, I cannot explain, beyond saying that it is ever thus with the bullets of a bad shooting corps. At the first glance it seemed as if there was no order or arrangement in this charge of a brigade over 500 to 600 yards of open plough. But suddenly I realised that it was not chance but skill which had distributed the pawns so evenly over the chess board. The crowd, apparently so irregular and so loosely knit together, consisted of great numbers of sections and half-sections and groups working independently, but holding well together, each in one little line under its own officer or non-commissioned officer. There was no regular interval. I should say that the lateral distance between men was anything between two and ten paces. The interval in depth is more difficult to determine, but it is safe to say that it was rarely less than ten or more than forty paces.

In certain respects the startling, sudden onslaught of Okasaki's Brigade resembled a Dervish rush, but with one marked difference, inasmuch as the formation was not solid but exceedingly flexible and loose, offering no very vulnerable target even to a machine gun. The speed was marvellous, and the men got across the plain more like charging cavalry than ordinary infantry. Some say that the leading sections paused once to fire. I did not see this happen. To the best of my observation the assaulting infantry ran 600 yards without the semblance of a halt, and as their leading files reached the sunken road they dashed unhesitatingly into it, right on to the top of the crouching Russian infantry! Next second the Russians and their assailants were rushing up Terayama slopes in one confused mob, the whole mass convulsively working bayonet and bullet and clubbed rifle as they ran. The hill was carried. Bravo! Bravo!! Bravo!!!

The whole thing was so instantaneous that the Russian artillery at Sankwaisekisan did not get to work until just as the last of the Japanese were clearing off the plain and closing in on Terayama. The guns north of Sankashi had fired, but in the agitation of the moment their shell were fused too short and burst high in the air. Their range must have been over 4000 yards, whereas the Sankwaisekisan guns cannot have been more than 3500 yards, and were absolutely in the prolongation of the left flank of the advance. The actual temple buildings held out for some ten minutes, and were then carried by the bayonet. But the Russians on the northern section of the hill were sturdy fellows who resolutely refused to budge. This is always the way with the Russians. Just when further resistance seems hopeless they begin to fight *à outrance*. Still, so long as the forlorn hope (if a rearguard may be called a forlorn hope) held on, there was a door being held open on the hill whereby reinforcements could enter. Two Russian battalions thought of making the attempt. They came down from the hills to the north looking formidable and bold until, on their entrance into the zone of conflict being greeted by a shower of shells, they thought better of it and sheered off. But their comrades, the little body left on the hill, still seem to be holding on to the last corner of the hill, and are making a very gallant fight of it, not so much, I fancy, in any hope of dislodging the Japanese as for the honour and glory of the Army and the Czar.

At 5.20 there was a discussion between all the Staff and Kuroki as to how the troops at Penchiho were to be fed now that the Cossacks had crossed the Taitsuho and were interposing between them and Chaotao, whence, until now, they had drawn their supplies. The question seemed to be considered very urgent and important. At 5.30 urgent applications for gun and rifle ammunition began to come in from all sides, and there were earnest consultations on the subject.

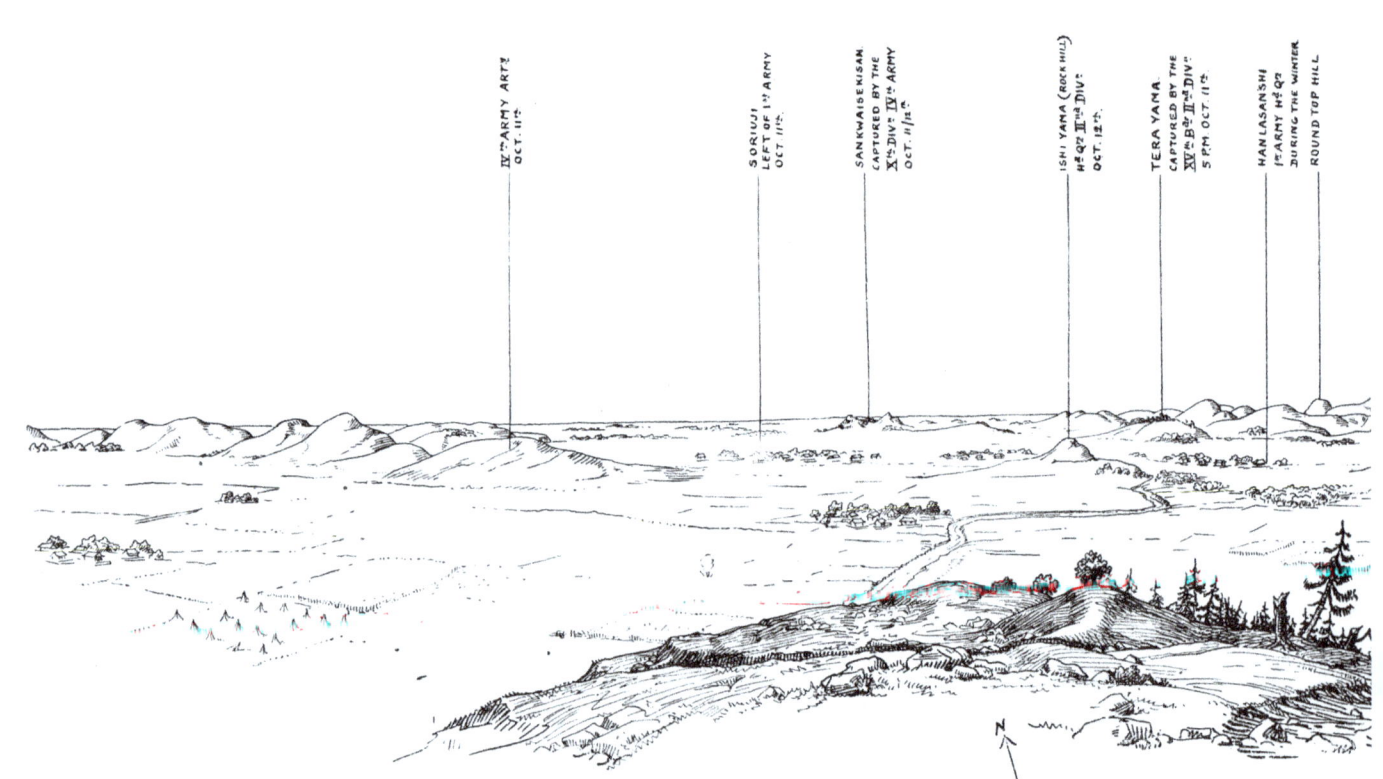

VIEW OF THE BATTLEFIELD OF THE SHAHO

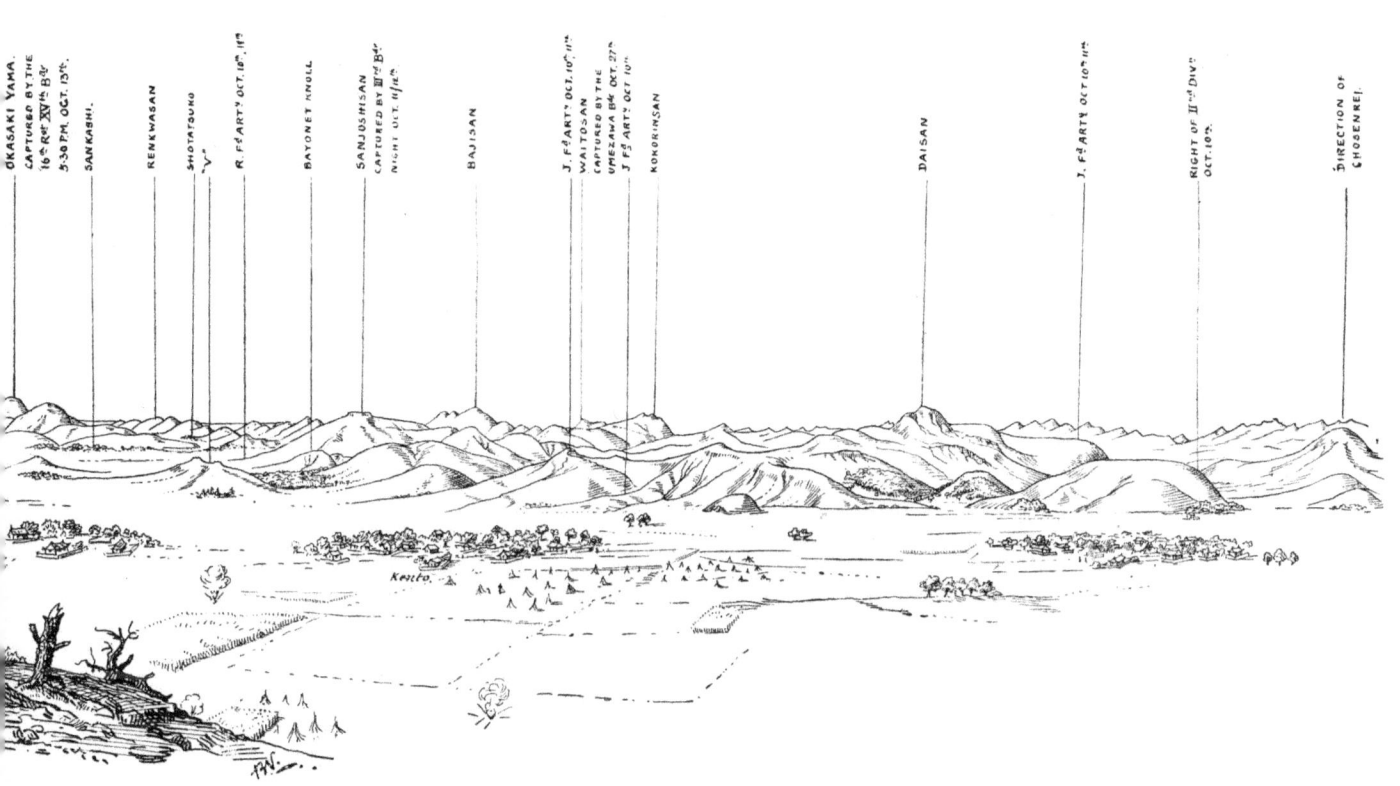

FROM YENTAI COALMINE HILL, OCTOBER 1904

The Russian guns were now firing heavily into Okasaki's Brigade on the south part of Terayama, both from the east and from the west. I left the coal-mines at 5.45 P.M.

So ends a day filled with the life and death of half an average life-time. I wonder what are the feelings which Kuroki conceals behind that impassive mask—his countenance? Brilliant as it is, Okasaki's triumph is not perhaps considered by him sufficient when he reflects that no other success has been scored, and that his right at Penchiho stands still on the brink of ruin.

## CHAPTER XXIX

### THE BATTLE CONTINUES

COAL-MINE HILL, *October 12th*, 1904, 8 A.M.—Again from this same hill the marvellous war panorama spreads out to the same Valkyrie orchestra of cannon and small arms. But the music is less strident. The battle is shifting to the north. The Japanese are holding Sanjoshisan and all the heights south of the Sankashi-Menkaho valley, and have clinched their hold on Terayama, which belongs to the northern heights, by digging themselves deeply into the ground. Before I left Taiyo, at 7 A.M., Colonel Hagino said to me, "To-day's fighting will be desperate, because the enemy has now been forced back upon the mountain tops to the north of the Sankashi valley, and we will have to deliver our assaults from the low ground." But I must hasten to add that he seemed rather to relish than to dread the prospect.

I am now with the Headquarters Staff. The amount there is to write about is simply bewildering and my fingers are half frozen by this eager, nipping air from the north.

The first thing I have to do is to knit up to-day with yesterday by putting down what I have been told about the eventful night which has just passed. Terrible fighting was taking place all along the line whilst I was comfortably sleeping at Taiyo, and the results have been on the whole reassuring. Nothing will ever persuade me that the Headquarters were not anxious and almost alarmed last night. But if they had courage and self-restraint to conceal their feelings from a casual observer (in which category I do not class myself), their bulletin to the army was even less calculated to reveal any touch of doubt or despondency. I quitted the General Staff on this same spot at 5.30 yesterday evening. By 6 o'clock they had talked over the situation and had issued the following orders, which were, I think, considerably more sanguine than their feelings:

(1) The enemy seems to be retreating on every side. A detachment from the Second Division will advance eastwards to attack along the front of the left wing of the Twelfth Division. The Japanese forces in the direction of Penchiho are still safe.

(2) I intend to-night to take the line from the east of Domonshi to the height north of Shotatsuko.

(3) The Guards and the main force of the Second Division shall continue their advance and carry out the objects of the First Army.

(4) The Twelfth Division and the Umezawa Brigade shall continue to carry out previous orders.

(5) The general officer commanding will be at Taiyo to-night.

The task of carrying out these orders should be lightened to Okasaki's fifteenth brigade on Terayama by the fact that the Fourth Army on his left has made an important advance during the past night and has captured Sankwaisekisan. General Nodzu * has then not only made good all his leeway, but has seized a point some two miles north of Terayama, and to that

* The Commander of the Fourth Army.

The Temple to the God of Children on Sankwaisekisan (Three Great Rock Hill).

extent has taken the lead in the great race to Mukden between Oyama's generals. An adjutant from the Fourth Army came up here half an hour ago and has given some interesting news about this fighting. Sankwaisekisan is five miles from us, a little to the west of north, and can be seen very clearly (*see* Sketch XXV.). I have also had a good account of the terrain from Captain Jardine, of the 5th Lancers, who accompanied the Second Cavalry Brigade on a reconnaissance to the Three Great Rock Hill (which is the interpretation of the Chinese name) on the 8th instant. Sankwaisekisan is not at all unlike Terayama in size or shape, but differs inasmuch as it stands alone on the flat plain with no broken or rising ground worth mentioning within several thousand yards of it. There are villages on the plain, it is true, but none nearer than half a mile except a few houses and walled enclosures nestling under the eastern flank of Sankwaisekisan itself. The rock rises quite clear and distinct like an iceberg from the ocean, or, more accurately perhaps, it might be described as resembling a mediæval warship sailing due south over a smooth sea of yellowish plough. The ship is lower in the waist than at the bows and carries a high-peaked poop. Set in the centre of the low waist are three buildings, evidently temples, enclosed by a fairly high wall.

I have described the Three Great Rock Hill* in some detail, although the exploit of its capture belongs to another army, and although I do not know very much about the conditions under which the attack was delivered. But I am tempted to depart from my principles by the strong family resemblance between Terayama, taken by Okasaki yesterday, and Three Great Rock Hill, taken by the Tenth Division, Fourth

* Sankwaisekioan.

Army, by night attack. Both commanders were under the obligation to occupy their respective hills, but Okasaki chose the day, and the commander of the Tenth Division preferred to await the fall of night. Looking with a calm and unprejudiced mind at the ground from where I sit, I freely confess that I would have acted as did the commander of the Tenth Division, and have made my advance across the level plain, if not in the dead of night, then, at any rate, in the dusk of evening or the misty grey of the early dawn. But a Japanese officer of high rank considers that the way in which these two commanders treated their parallel problems affords proof of the admirable audacity of Okasaki, which has been thrown into striking relief by the want of self-confidence of the captor of Sankwaisekisan.

All I know of the night attack at present is that it was carried out by twenty-three battalions, and that the leading battalions were in single rank, shoulder to shoulder; the supports a very short distance behind in line of section columns.* The advance began at 1 A.M. and got within 150 yards by 3 A.M. when the enemy opened with volleys. The Japanese did not reply, but crawled on quietly, on hands and knees, the bullets flying high, as is invariably the case at night, unless preparations are

* It transpired afterwards that there were six battalions in the first line in single rank, shoulder to shoulder. Eight battalions in support, in line of section columns at close interval, but with fifty yards interval between battalions, and nine battalions massed in reserve.

The depth between the first and second line was fifty yards; and 150 yards separated the second from the third line. The army reserve under General Nodzu was one and half miles in rear of the western flank of the attacking line.—I. H.

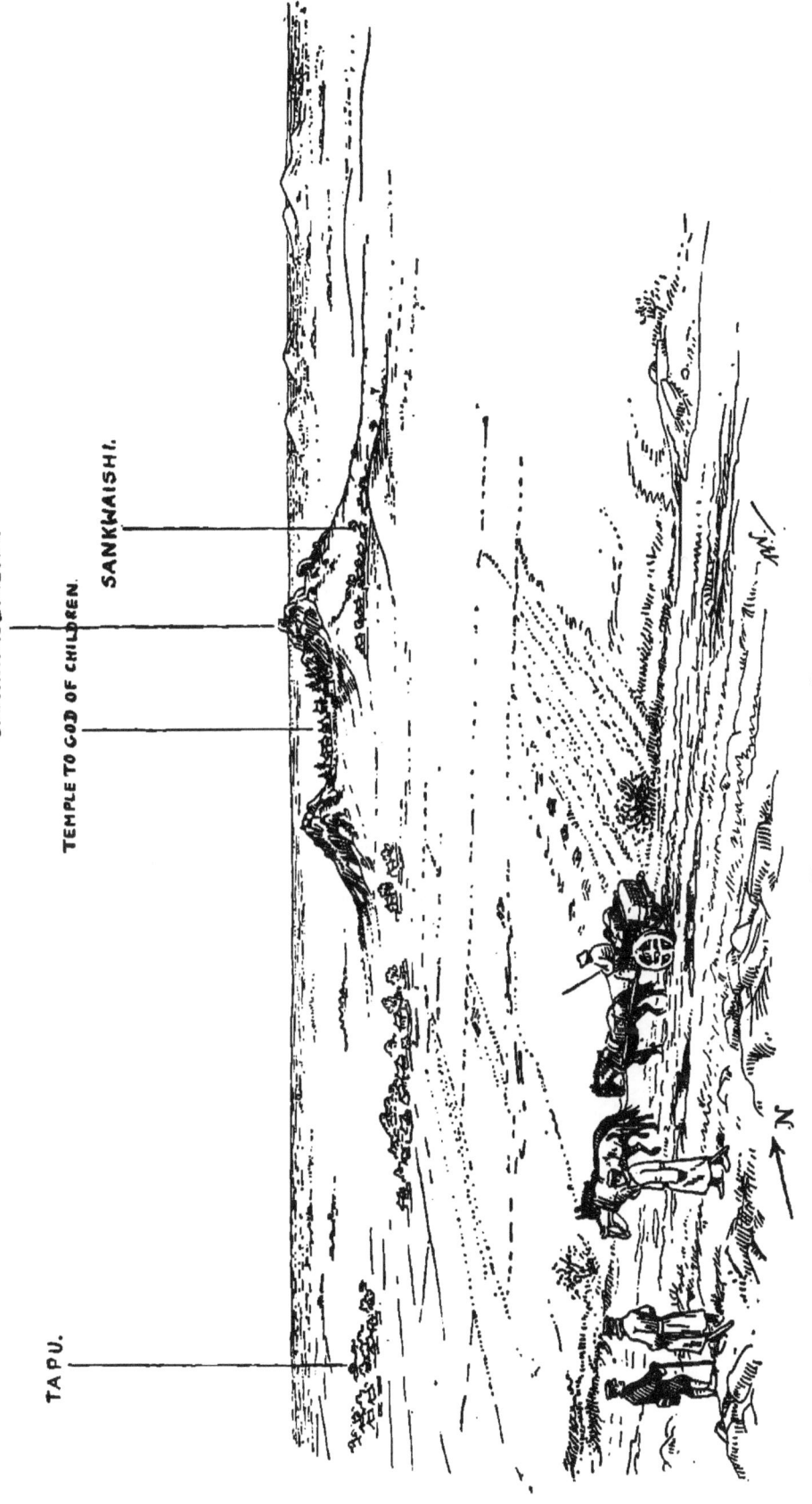

BATTLE OF THE SHAHO

SANKWAISEKISAN (THREE GREAT ROCKS HILL) CAPTURED BY NIGHT ATTACK BEFORE DAWN ON OCTOBER 12, 1904, BY THE 10TH DIVISION 4TH ARMY

XXV

made by stretching a string or wire in front of the defenders' trenches, under which the muzzles of their rifles can be placed. At 100 yards range, however, the Japanese could no longer be restrained from firing. The main part of the Three Rock Hill was captured by 4.30 A.M. after bloody and desperate fighting, but the Russians still held on in places, and defended the village even after it was blazing. In fact, it is said that the fighting is not yet quite at an end, and that groups of desperate Russians are even now struggling on in corners amongst the rocks, and refusing all temptations to surrender. However, to all intents and purposes, the hill is certainly captured, for I can clearly see the troops of the Fourth Army swarming about on all sides of it.

The Fourth Army* have lost 1000 men in this

---

* The following extracts from a subsequent conversation with one of the actors in the night attack make the story more complete: "Sankwaisekisan had been nicknamed by the soldiers *oni no uchi*, or 'the devil's mansion,' and as our proverb has it that the devil is a bad person to sup with, and his mansion was to us an unknown land, we all feasted heartily up to 11 P.M." ... "The regiment occupying the Three Rock Hill was a fine corps, with a great reputation, and they showed great nerve by withholding their fire until we drew very close indeed. ... It was the Alexander Third Regiment. The enemy's dead gave proof that they had freshly arrived from Europe, as their skins were quite delicate and white, not at all tanned as yet by the hardships of campaigning. They wore long frockcoats, which were absolutely new and unsoiled, and on their shoulder straps there was a crown." ... "The enemy still clung to the rocky parts of the hill and to the temple, and the firing continued as heavily as ever, more especially from the village. Major-General Marui, commanding a brigade, was wounded here, and the standard bearer of the Himeji Regiment was killed. Another officer seized the standard, and he was also shot. Then Colonel Yasumura, commanding the regiment, took it up, and in his turn he fell, being struck by a bullet from the wall. Thus there was no one left to command at this point, the colonel of the next regiment being

attack on Three Rock Hill, and Okasaki has lost an equal number in the day attack on Temple Hill. But the majority of Okasaki's losses took place, it seems, after he had captured the hill and were caused by the Russian artillery opening from east and west (as I saw them last evening) on the men who, in delivering their assault, had closed in on the hill, and then stood crowded upon it.

It is very difficult, therefore, to argue from the respective losses suffered or results gained which

further to the east. Then there occurred an incident of some interest. The adjutant of the brigade met the adjutant of the regiment and discussed the situation with him. They agreed that the village must be carried at once and at any cost, as a prolongation of the struggle would result in an excessive number of casualties. So they called out loudly in the night, "Is there any one here who will leap into that village and set it on fire?" Out of the darkness came the reply, "I, Captain Sumida, will command the troop which is determined to die; who will follow me?" And nearly 200 men closed in to his call and put themselves under his orders. All of the leading men were shot or bayonetted from behind the wall as they came up to it, but others managed to climb it and set fire to several houses. Amongst these houses they found a wounded lieutenant-colonel of the enemy, who was so badly hit that he could only stand with difficulty when he was put upon his feet. They told him that the whole Division was now round the village, and that one part was taken and another part in flames, so that he should go to the corner where fighting was still going on and order his men to surrender. He refused however, saying, 'I have orders to hold the village to the last, and therefore cannot surrender!' Near by they captured a non-commissioned officer, and said the same to him. He went into the village and spoke loudly to his men. At the same time the houses took fire. Whether it was because of the conflagration or from what the non-commissioned officer told his men, we cannot say, but the Russian firing from the village ceased. At 5 A.M. the Russians were still to be found in places. They fought bravely; in fact, some remained hidden in the temple caves and crannies of the rocks, and even in the Chinese water jars, and fired when the Japanese soldiers approached."

method—the day or the night attack—proved most successful. The highly-placed critic I have quoted seems very confident that Okasaki is to be praised for having staked all on a bold attack in broad daylight. So be it. But war is an uncertain game, and it seems to me that a couple of machine guns on Terayama and a quick, capable battery commander at Sankwai-sekisan might have changed the verdict which will now probably be pronounced by history, and have handed down Okasaki to posterity as having been over confident, whilst the prudence of the Fourth Army Commander would have been held up as an example to be commended.

One more point before I quit Terayama. In former wars I have, in common I suppose with other commanders of any experience, often had occasion to long for cavalry to launch at the enemy during some crisis of the struggle. Throughout the Manchurian campaign such a thought has hitherto never once occurred to me. Neither infantry has the slightest idea of permitting itself to be hustled by mounted men, and it has been apparent to the meanest military capacity that the cavalry could not influence the fighting one way or another except by getting off their horses and using their rifles. But yesterday, when I saw Okasaki's men streaming across the plain, in what I might call ordered disorder, the whole of each individual's faculties and energies concentrated on the enemy in front, I felt for the first time that a few Russian squadrons, adroitly led to within half a mile of the left flank of the charging Japanese might, by a combination of good luck and good guidance, have struck Okasaki's Brigade a staggering blow whilst it was straining every nerve and muscle in mid career against the rival infantry.

Obviously mere bravery and dash would not have sufficed for the commander of such a fire-eating venture. To succeed he must have been a man who was capable of keeping his cool touch on the fevered pulse-beats of opportunity until he felt the fateful second had arrived; then, flinging caution and judgment to the winds he must have had a big heart, iron nerve, and the devotion of his men to enable him to spur out of his ambush full tilt, not alone, but followed, as if he were a queen bee leading her swarm, by all his galloping squadrons. A rare type of man, and that is one reason amongst many why successful cavalry charges were not exactly of every day occurrence, even in muzzle-loading days.

My only excuse for this excursion into the misty realms of might-have-been is that all yesterday it was positively painful to see masses of Russian cavalry sitting idle in their saddles looking on whilst their infantry and guns were fighting so hard and so well that it seemed as if even a few hundred carbines or rifles must have sufficed to turn the scale.

To return to Okasaki. That best and cheeriest of Brigadiers has been busy all night improving upon his success of yesterday evening. The capture of Terayama was not fully completed until midnight as, after dark, there were two Russian counter-attacks, which were easily repulsed, although if they had come on whilst some of the garrison was still holding out on the northern point of the ridge, they might have been exceedingly dangerous. There was also a good deal of desultory fighting between a Russian regiment, which advanced westwards from Sankashi as it grew dusk with a band playing at its head, and the 29th Regiment of the Second Division. This combat also ceased about midnight, apparently by mutual consent.

By 4 A.M. Okasaki's Brigade was concentrated in Sankashi village and started off to attack the round hill called Suribachiyama * by the Japanese, who do not display much more originality than the Boers in their nomenclature of their landmarks. His men were just in the nick of time to anticipate the Russians who were marching up in the darkness from the western valley and some sharp fighting ensued in which the Japanese, being in possession of the crest line, had the advantage. Meanwhile, the 30th Regiment, which had been detached to capture Nanzan, had taken it without trouble (*see* Sketch XXVI.). At dawn they had handed over their prize to the Fourth Army and marched round in a south-easterly direction to take post in rear of the centre of their own brigade.† The highest mountain of the group, due north of Suribachiyama is still in the hands of the Russians, but every one hopes that Okasaki will soon have gained possession of it. He has now taken all the outworks of this mountain; Terayama on the south, Nanzan on the west, the rocky ridge and saddle on the west and south-west, and Suribachiyama on the south. There is only the one parent mountain left, and then, according to the opinion of the officers here, we ought to have a clear run in northwards. With luck we may then cut off the enemy who, under Stakelberg, are still causing

* "Rice Mortar Hill," a name also given to one of the most important points in the Russian defensive line on the North bank of the Yalu. See Vol. I.

† This small plan gives a better idea than any description of the precise situation at the hour these notes were written, namely, between 9 and 10 A.M. The Russians on the hill north of Suribachiyama, afterwards called Okasakiyama, were supported by comrades

218 A STAFF OFFICER'S SCRAP-BOOK

every one a great deal of anxiety concerning Penchiho and our right flank.

Due north of our coal mine hill then the battle is assuming a most favourable complexion. North-east the prospects seem equally fair. Matsunaga, whose Third Brigade of the Second Division seemed so completely brought to a standstill when I quitted the field last night, has now carried the great and formidable mountain of Sanjoshisan. The assault was made at 7 o'clock last night, and he did not win undisturbed possession until after a series of dubious and bloody encounters which endured until 1 A.M. At dawn he descended the northern slopes of Sanjoshisan, and is holding a village on the southern edge of the Kamiriuka valley. He is now under orders to cross the open and attack the enemy lining the opposite

on Round Top Hill and by batteries north-east of Shotatsuko and between Sekibioshi and Hamatang. In fact, they were so strongly fixed in their position that Okasaki did not dare tackle it until he could get more help from his artillery, and no further progress was made in this part of the field during October 12.

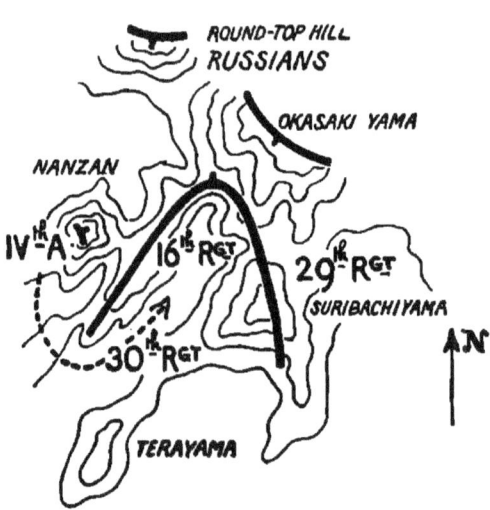

## The Battle Continues

hills. Verily the Japanese Commanders* do not hesitate to make calls upon the endurance of their troops. Matsunaga's brigade had stood to its arms all the night of the 10th-11th; on the 11th it had been the whole day under fire, and had been very hard put to it to hold its own; it had carried the combat on into the next night and had stormed a formidable mountain, stubbornly held. Now, the hardly tried brigade was to advance across a valley even more open and spacious than that traversed by Okasaki yesterday, and to dislodge the Russians lining the opposite hills; surely as difficult and dangerous a task as any soldier has ever been asked to undertake.

At 8.35 a message was brought in by an orderly from General Asada, Commanding the Guards Division. In it he announced that his left brigade under General Watanabe had as good as taken—"surely took," was the exact expression—the northern continuation of Hill 238 as well as Hakashi village. The message had been despatched at 6.30 A.M.

At 9.15 an adjutant of Asada's arrived with confirmatory information. He had left his General at about half past seven. He bears the good news of how Watanabe carried the Russian position opposite him by a combined frontal and flanking movement. It seems that at 2.30 A.M. Watanabe sent off the 4th Guards Regiment to make a circuitous march eastwards and debouch on to the big Kamiriuka valley, where they

* This order may seem to clash with the orders issued yesterday evening at 6 P.M., under which Matsunaga was to move eastwards along the front of the left wing of the Twelfth Division. But it was obviously impossible to move down the Kamiriuka valley eastwards until the enemy had been cleared out of the valley itself as well as from the lower slopes of the mountains on the north which completely commanded it.

were to capture the village of Hakashi, and thus threaten the retreat of the Russians who were about to be attacked by the other regiments of the brigade.* This regiment (the 3rd Guards) advanced at the same hour, 2.30 A.M., to drive the Russians out of the position which they had held all the previous day on the prolongation of the ridge 238. The point marked 238 (see Map XXXIII.) is the southern extremity of a long razor-backed ridge running north and south. The Russians were holding a position across the ridge with their flanks well thrown back, and were only some 300 or 400 yards distant from Watanabe when he started the 3rd Guards to attack them.

* As I subsequently learnt, Lieutenant-Colonel Iida, commanding the 4th Regiment, marched off as ordered, but got hung up and delayed by some bad ground. Before he could extricate himself, fighting broke out between the 3rd Regiment and the Russians on the ridge immediately west of him, and random bullets wounded some of his men. Not wishing to be drawn into the engagement, he edged more away to the east and by 4.30 in the morning debouched into the broad and level Kamiriuka valley. He now formed his battalions into line of section columns at twenty yards interval between companies, with one company in reserve, 100 yards in rear. In this formation he approached Hakashi when about fifty Russians charged out at top speed, cheering, and in the half light got within twenty yards of the 4th Guards before they discovered their strength. They then turned and ran back to Hakashi village for their lives, pursued by the whole of the 4th Guards, who, obeying an uncontrollable impulse, raised a mighty shout and pressed into the village at their heels. By the time the village was taken it was daylight and a company of Russians on a spur above it opened fire. The Japanese did not reply, but stormed the spur with the bayonet. Lieutenant-Colonel Iida now noticed fugitives from the direction of 238 crossing the valley to the west. Accordingly, he advanced close up to the village of Kamiriuka and, forming line facing west, he opened a heavy, long range fire on the fugitives from 238 and from Hachimaki Yama, killing large numbers of them.

One battalion * moved down the valley to the east of the heights held by the enemy with orders to turn westwards up the steep hillside as soon as they got level with their position. It was hoped that they would thus be enabled to turn the left flank of the Russians. Simultaneously another battalion was directed to bear right down upon the enemy in two parallel columns of route by fours. The columns moved northwards on either side of the very narrow crest line, and were not more than forty or fifty yards apart. The head of each column of route was covered by one section moving in single rank a few yards in advance of it. When the covering section got within 100 yards of the enemy they were fired upon, and then the columns deployed and returned the fire. The young officer says that at one time no one knew how the fight was going to end. There was terrible confusion, and the company commanders had lost control over their men who were broken up into groups firing in every direction, whilst Russians, as well as Japanese, were rushing about anywhere and anyhow with their bayonets at the charge. I can imagine that in a *mêlée* of such a description the Japanese would be more at home than any European, and that once the Russians broke their ranks their fate must have been sealed.

It will be weeks probably before I get any authentic, or at least authorised, account of the action, but I find more and more as I go on the value of a note put down upon the spot.†

* I heard afterwards that the formation adopted by this battalion was line of companies in section columns with one company as reserve fifty yards in rear.

† As I had correctly surmised, I heard no more about Watanabe's attack until long afterwards, and so, to make the story complete, I add a few extracts from entries made on a subsequent date. Colonel

At 10.15 a friend on the staff found leisure to come and have a short talk. He said, "I never have the courage to bring to your Excellency anything but good news, as you always write down whatever I say, and it is a sore trial to see misfortunes chronicled in the note-book of a friend." I replied, "With such an army as Kuroki's First Army I do not think you

Hume, attached to the Guards Division, is my principal authority. In the attack made by the 3rd Guards Regiment on the Russians holding the ridge to the north of 238, the battalion which moved down the eastern valley, and then marched westwards up the ridge endeavouring to turn the enemy's left flank, bore the brunt of the fighting. The battalion only consisted of three companies, one company being brigade reserve. As soon as their leader began to climb the ridge he was fired into at a range of less than 100 yards. Thereupon an order was given to the two leading columns of sections to deploy into line, the reserve company remaining in column. After firing three volleys the Japanese charged with the bayonet, but were repulsed after a severe struggle. The men fell back just below the shelter of the steep crest-line and waited at about ten paces distance from the Russians to recover themselves for a fresh effort. The reserve company was brought up to reinforce the centre, and then a second charge was made. This attempt also was repulsed after a peculiarly bitter and prolonged fight with bayonets and hand grenades. The Japanese say that never since their Civil War have they been met with equal determination. One section had been kept in hand to guard the right flank, and now it was withdrawn and sent in to reinforce the centre. It was the last chance, but it was successful. The whole line rose like one man and charged with a great shout, when the enemy gave way. The Japanese here lost ten officers and 200 men out of a total of about 600.

The 4th Guards battalion which advanced on either side of the crest line of the ridge, in double column of route by fours, was not so roughly handled, as it arrived after at least one charge had already been delivered by the 3rd Guards.

A feature of the fight was the Japanese trick of climbing up quietly under the steep crest and seizing the projecting Russian rifle from which they wrenched the bayonet. There were several cases here of Russians and Japanese who had simultaneously transfixed need fear that my note-book will be anything but a consistent record of success." From the conversation which ensued, I gather that Kuroki is in high spirits. He is specially delighted with the Guards; not so much because of the victorious assault of Watanabe's brigade on the left, with which I have just been occupying myself, as with the unopposed advance of their right brigade, under Major-General Izaki, to a position which threatens the retreat of the enemy in front of the Second Division. The destination of this column had been the hill north of Menkaho, which is called Sanjoshi Yama.* The order issued to it was coupled, however, with a caution to keep touch with Watanabe's brigade. As, however, Watanabe was delayed by the obstinate resistance of the Russians, and as Izaki encountered no opposition, the latter had to elect, after reaching Menkaho, whether he would hang back to keep touch with Watanabe or press forward to Sanjoshi Yama. He chose the latter alternative and occupied Sanjoshi Yama by daybreak, and by doing so, of course, lost all touch with Watanabe who had not yet occupied Hakashi. He is now advancing to a fresh position just north of Kokorinsan and Bajisan, and if the enemy in front of us do not make haste and retire, there seems to be a good chance that they may get caught.

one another on their bayonets. I remember the same thing happening in the Afghan War. The dead Japanese and Russians lay, for the most part, in two distinct lines less than ten yards apart.

The Russian trenches were not worthy of the name, being merely slight scrapings along the crest-line involving ten minutes work. Had their entrenchments been more thorough, it is very doubtful if Watanabe could have succeeded.

* To be distinguished from Sanjoshisan. *See* Map XXXIII.

At this moment our talk was interrupted by the sending of a message, which was for a Japanese almost an angry message, to the artillery to our front to open a heavier fire. Captain Saigo simply flew down the hill with this order. My friend then resumed, "The enemy are decidedly beginning to fall back upon Mukden; we are annoyed because the commanders, and especially the guns, are too cautious in pressing their advantage. We can plainly see the commencement of the retirement, but brigadiers are slow to grasp the situation, and the artillery are worse. Here are the Russian batteries by Renkwasan and Domonshi firing freely at Matsunaga's brigade, and our artillery does not bestir itself!" I asked if I was correct in my conclusion that the Japanese guns were overmatched yesterday. The reply was to the effect that the artillery had fully expected Matsunaga would have captured Sanjoshisan mountain before daylight, and had got out of their gun-pits and taken up a position in the open on that supposition. When they found that Sanjoshisan was still in Russian hands, they had to get back into their gun-pits, a proceeding which took them a long time. "However," continued my mentor, "that is no sufficient excuse. We had seven batteries of field guns here yesterday, and if they had been boldly and wisely handled they ought to have been able to have accomplished something considerable. Okasaki yesterday lost over 1000 men; Matsunaga over 600, and I verily believe that a smarter and bolder use of our artillery might have saved us many of these casualties. The Twelfth Division and Umezawa's brigade have been having even more desperate fighting than Okasaki and Matsunaga. They have lost 1800 men or thereabouts, but I will tell you about this later on."

There is no doubt that the Japanese guns are so deeply dug into the ground that they have become almost as immobile as guns of position. They take far too long in getting in or out of their pits, and I think the habit of entrenching imposed upon them by the superiority of the Russian artillery is tending to lessen their initiative and audacity.

At 10.40 a junior staff officer came and spoke to me most kindly, giving me his views on the situation. He is very hopeful that we will succeed in capturing the Russian guns to the north of Shotatsuko. He points out to me that the Fourth Army on Nanzan is now due west of them; that Matsunaga will be within shooting distance to the south-west of them as soon as he succeeds (as no one seems to doubt he will) in crossing the valley, and that Watanabe's Guards are due east of these guns, whilst the Guards' right brigade under Izaki are actually to the north-east of them. In fact, with any luck, Matsunaga's attack, when it comes off, will throw the Russians right into the arms of Izaki's brigade of Guards, who are by now probably at Bajisan, whence they can easily move across to Renkwasan, and thus capture not only the guns, but also, very likely, the bulk of the infantry. My informant seems to feel that the Japanese artillery is not doing as much as it might do. He has a strong theory that the guns of the defence must employ direct fire. Otherwise he does not think they can correct range and fuse quickly enough to cope with a sudden and rapid advance. On the other hand, he thinks the guns of the attack, when opposed by artillery, must always fire indirect. They have no difficulty about rapid changes of range, as the defence line remains stationary, and if they attempt to come into action within view of quick-firing artillery already in action, they would be destroyed before they could fire a shot. The theory is plausible. I must think about it.

11 A.M.—For the past hour, including all the time my friends have been speaking to me, a brigade of the Second Division's artillery, posted east of Hanlasanshi, and two batteries belonging to the Guards in action near Hakashi, have been expending much ammunition in their efforts (not sufficiently strenuous according to Headquarters) to silence the Russian guns. They have succeeded in overpowering one battery to the north of Shotatsuko, but the remaining guns, posted near Renkwasan and Domonshi, are not only unsilenced, but cannot be diverted from firing at Matsunaga's brigade, concealed in the village of Senkiujo. (Map XXXIII.) Senkiujo is hidden from my view by the mountain of Sanjoshisan, but I am told there are numerous walls and ditches and houses which should afford good cover until the moment comes when they must emulate Okasaki's Terayama exploit and make their effort across the broad Kamiriuka valley.

Whenever there was a moment's pause in the dull roar of the cannonade, I could clearly catch the far-off, insistent, drumming undertone which told me that long lines of riflemen were striving for the mastery, and that yet another great moment was approaching. For magazine fire cannot go on indefinitely, and so, sure enough, at half-past eleven o'clock, Matsunaga made up his mind to slip his men from the leash and face the open plain. I am actually cold-bloodedly writing as I watch the brigade dashing across the valley. I could not have done so much yesterday, but custom aids coolness. The right and centre of his attack is to a great extent concealed from me by Sanjoshisan, but I can see the left almost as clearly as I saw the assault of Terayama yesterday evening. The formations are much the same; that is to say, there appear to be no regular intervals or alignment, each man running on the devil-take-the-hindmost principle, and concentrating all his energies on being the first to reach the enemy's trenches. The Russian artillery have been firing indirect at a range of some 5000 yards upon Senkiujo village, and again, as yesterday, they are much too slow in switching on to the attacking Japanese, and continue to send shell over their head (presumably into the village which I cannot see) long after they have got well out into the open. Even now—11.35—when they do change their objective, the shrapnel usually bursts too high and is too scattered to be very destructive. On one particular spot, however, range and fuse have been corrected with some accuracy, and, as if acting on their own initiative, but probably in consequence of orders previously given, the little running groups gave this danger zone a wide berth by closing in to the right hand and to the left.

It strikes me that the character of this assault is even more completely individualistic than in Okasaki's attack of yesterday. I can see great numbers of men fall, presumably to fire or to get breath (as I do not think it possible that so many can have been hit), and yet I never notice a group or section halt and lie down together. It is difficult to be sure, as the moment a man lies motionless I lose sight of him, but I think the bulk of those who drop* down so suddenly must rise again very shortly to resume their advance. Otherwise, there would be gaps in the scattered crowd, whereas the men composing it still remain, on the whole, very evenly distributed. My belief is that the men are covering the half-mile of distance which separates them from their enemy in several rushes, but that each man chooses his own moment for the halt.

11.45.—I am sure now that Matsunaga is not attempting to cross the valley in one tremendous rush. If it were so he would have been in the Russian trenches ere now, or else in full retreat, whereas he has not yet made his effort and is only two-thirds of the way across. The firing is very heavy.

11.50.—The foremost of the Japanese are lying down firing at about 250 yards from the Russian trenches, which are on a knoll just north of the village of Zenshotatsuko. (*See* Sketch XXIV.) Others are joining them, and now, for the first time, the attack presents the normal appearance of a fairly thick firing line with a loose supporting body, I can hardly call it a line, some 200 yards in rear.

11.55.—The whole of the firing line has risen like one man and made the charge. Simultaneously the Russians are clearing out and falling back with some precipitation on to the main ridge.

11.57.—The Japanese are now swarming like an army of ants over and around the knoll of Zenshotatsuko. Matsunaga has effected his lodgment on the

* The losses only amounted to 235, so it is not possible that any large proportion of the men who seemed to fall on October 12th were hit.—I. H.

hills to the north of the Kamriuka valley. One more mighty step forward has been made!*

* I wrote this description actually on the spot as I saw it. Long afterwards I saw Matsunaga and he informed me that his attack was normal, except that he had forty yards interval between companies instead of six yards. He had, so he says, two battalions in the first line; the men at three paces interval, and the interval between companies already mentioned. At 1500 yards he halted seven minutes, and then advanced as fast as the men could run to 800 yards. During this period there was no check and hardly any firing. At 800 yards the line lay down, and opened magazine fire for two minutes. From thence onwards he advanced by rushes of companies. First right; next left; then centre double company. Between 800 yards and the position the supports doubled up and reinforced whilst the reserves closed in. At 250 yards from the position there was a slight check for half a minute, when the charge was sounded and the knoll was rushed with the bayonet.

No doubt Matsunaga is correct as to the orders issued, but the impression I received was one of far greater dispersion, depth and irregularity. I only saw the advance from 800 yards onwards, and then only the left of the line.—I. H.

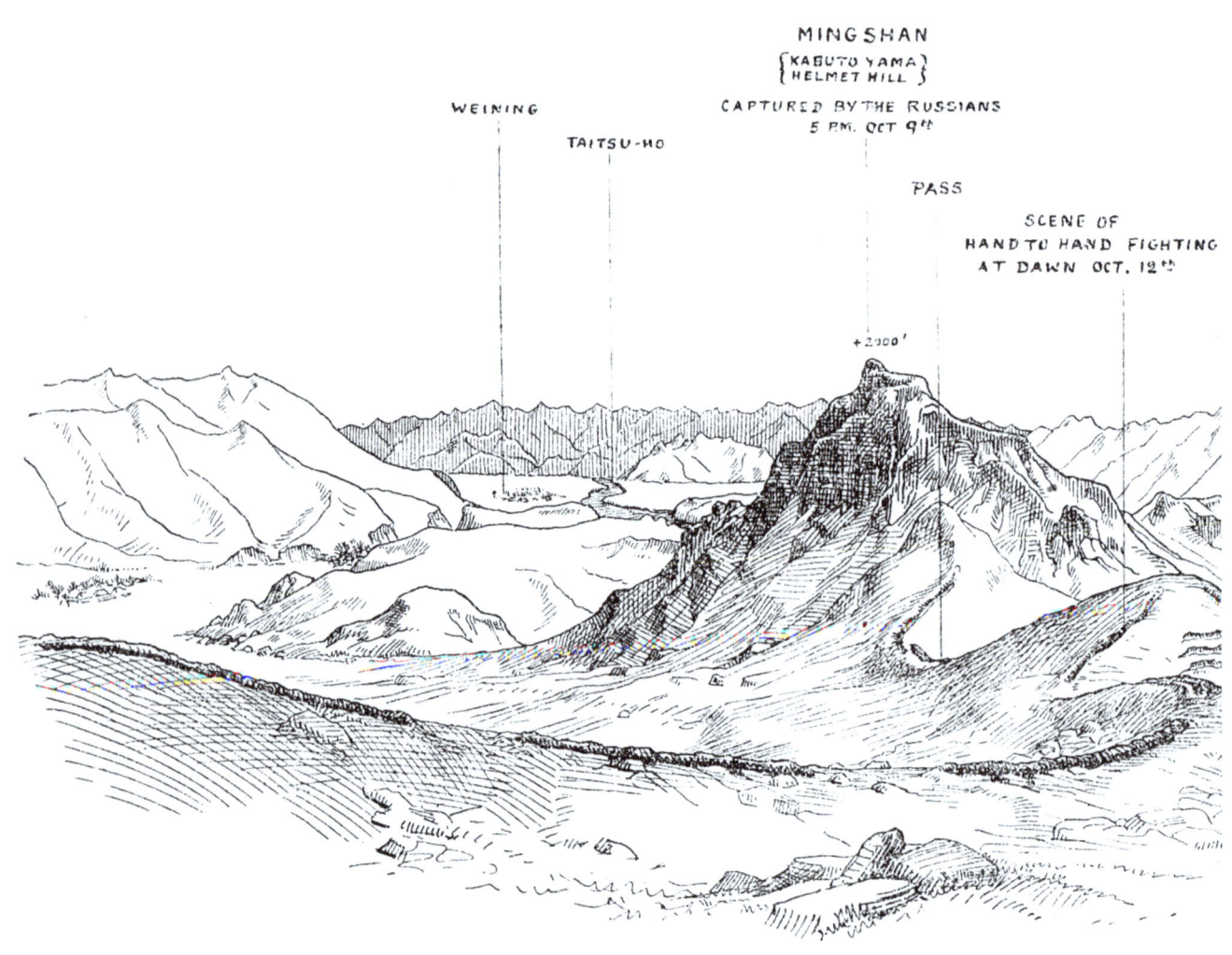

BATTLE OF

VIEW FROM HONDA YAMA THE RIGHT OF THE
DURING THE RUSSIAN ATTACK AT DAWN ON OCTOBER 12, HAND TO HAND FIGHTING TOOK

XXVIII

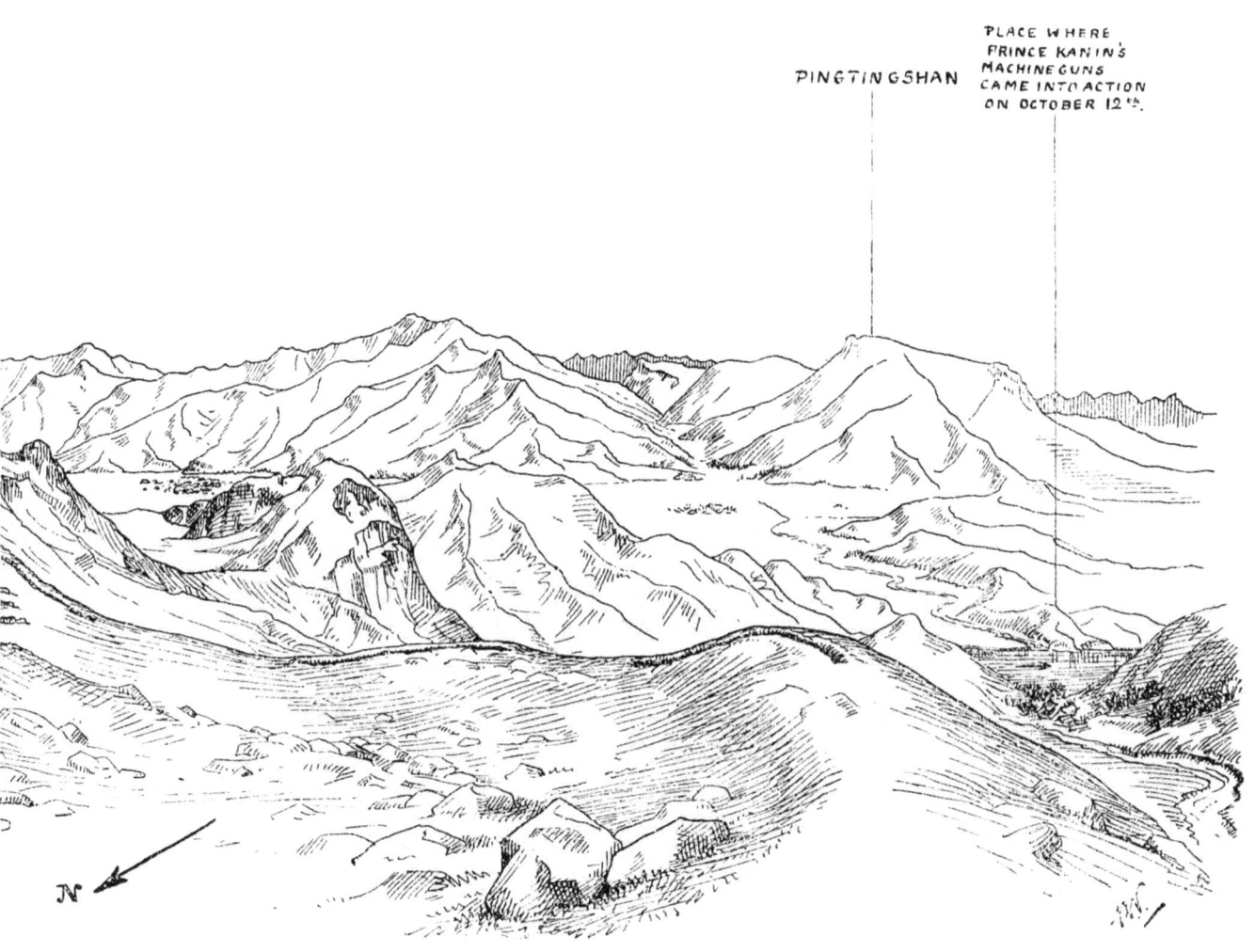

THE SHAHO

JAPANESE POSITION NEAR PENCHIHO (PENHSIHU)
PLACE IN THE TRENCHES IN THE FOREGROUND, BUT THE RUSSIANS WERE REPULSED

## CHAPTER XXX

### OTA'S SUN-FLAG

*Midday.*—General Kuroki is breakfasting together with His Imperial Highness Prince Kuni. All the Headquarters are in high glee; even, for them, quite boisterous.

12.45 P.M.—I have had another conversation with an officer who has come to sit by my side and is in great spirits. He says that an order has just been sent to Matsunaga bearing General Kuroki's congratulations, and directing him to march east as rapidly as possible and occupy the pass at Chosenrei. (*See* Maps XXXIII. and XXXIV.). If he can succeed, he will then find himself within eight and a half miles of the line of retreat of the enemy under Stakelberg and Rennenkampf, who are still making the most determined attempts to carry the Penchiho defences or to break through the Japanese lines by the Taling or Tumenling Passes between Penchiho and the coal mines. Nothing will bring these Russians back so rapidly as a good thrust by Matsunaga at their line of communications (just as the head of a snake must perforce shoot swiftly round the instant an enemy stamps upon its tail). My friend went on to say, "The heaviest of the fighting has taken place at Penchiho, where Major Honda and his small force have been winning great glory. Yesterday morning the Russians delivered a fierce assault under a covering fire from our captured

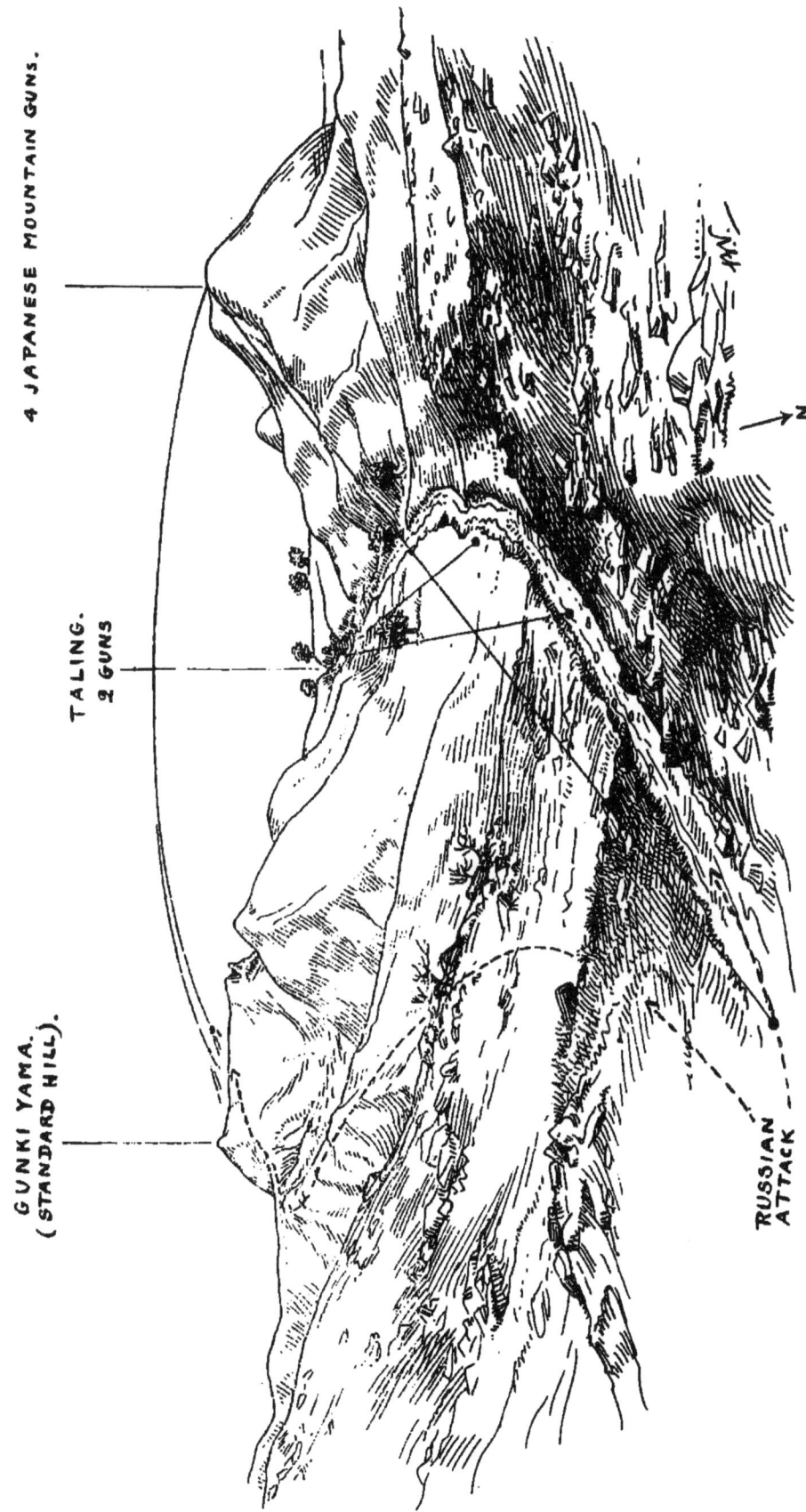

BATTLE OF THE SHAHO

VIEW OF THE TALING FROM THE ROAD BY WHICH THE RUSSIANS ATTACKED AT DAWN ON OCTOBER 12

XXXII

outpost of Mingshan, which lies within easy rifle shot south-east and commands that part of our line. The Russians kept trying to close with the bayonet, but Major Honda's battalion was just able, and no more, to keep them off with fire. Had it not been for the enemy on Mingshan, who were free during the conflict to fire directly down into the trenches, our losses would have been trifling. As it is, they have been very severe, but now, this morning, the bulk of the Twelfth Division and of Umezawa's brigade have arrived as reinforcements, and by working tooth and nail throughout the night our entrenchments are completed. It is well that it is so, for we have just got a despatch giving us some particulars of the greatest assault yet delivered, which took place this morning at 4 A.M. The Russians made their main attack at the very same spot, under protection of the covering fire from Mingshan, and lucky it was that instead of Honda's one weak battalion we had four strong, fresh battalions ready to receive them, behind good solid fortifications which had been finished just in the nick of time. For the enemy have never before, not even at Manjuyama, made so brave an effort. Above all, their officers behaved nobly and led the men on, running out well to the front and waving their swords to encourage the rank and file. But it was no use, for the assaulting formations were too solid to stand against our deployed line, awaiting them behind a well-constructed parapet. The Russian battalions were in quarter column, and only about one-eighth of their men could have used their rifles had they wished to do so, but as a matter of fact they trusted almost entirely to the bayonet."

Such a conflict calls to mind the advance of the Old Guard at Waterloo, and it seems clear that many of the Russian Corps still consider a rifle rather as a convenient staff on which to fix a bayonet than as the deadliest invention and prop of civilisation. Who can read Milton's "Paradise Lost" without wondering what would have been the result of the conflict between the embattled Seraphim if, instead of those "hollow engines," long and round, charged with old-fashioned black powder, Lucifer had suddenly unveiled 200 quick-firing, smokeless $18\frac{1}{2}$ pounders. Because Japanese as well as Russians occasionally like to revert to cold steel, do not let it be forgotten that Suvaroff's saying must now be reversed and that it is the bullet which invariably makes a fool of the bayonet provided only the trigger is pulled by a practised marksman.*

Continuing, my friend told me that the latest news from Penchiho was to the effect that the fury of the fighting had for the time being abated. There was, however, desperate work on hand both at the Taling and Tumenling Passes. At three this morning a regiment of Russians approached the Taling in close formation, but were easily repulsed by the fire of two guns when they got within 400 or 500 yards of the trenches. At 5 A.M. a regiment, perhaps the same regiment, attacked a table-topped hill † 300 yards in advance of the Japanese position, which it slightly commanded. The summit was held by an outpost of one company, and at the foot of the hill was the battalion

* Phrases have much to answer for. Often things only contain a half-truth when fresh coined, and in course of time these half-truths are apt to become wholly false. It seems to me sometimes as if this childish nonsense about the bullet being a fool has been as much responsible for the misfortunes of Russia as all her bad diplomacy and unsound strategy put together.—I. H.

† Called afterwards Gunki Yama, or Standard Hill. *See* Sketches XXXI. and XXXII.—I. H.

commander, Lieutenant-Colonel Ota, with a reserve of another company and the regimental standard.

Lieutenant-Colonel Ota's adjutant had previously been adjutant at the Military College, and was well known, therefore, in the army, and it was he who, hearing heavy musketry just before dawn, ran up to the top of the hill to try and discover the cause of the alarm. On gaining the summit he saw what he took to be a line of his own men showing up against the sky-line, and got within thirty yards of them before he discovered that they were Russians.. Hastily retreating, he informed his Commander that the outpost had been overwhelmed, and that the position was in the hands of the enemy. Dawn was now breaking, and disclosed the survivors of the outpost company still standing at bay half-way down the hill and exchanging fire with the Russians on the crest-line.

Taking the standard in his hand, Lieutenant-Colonel Ota advanced to reinforce the remnant of his first company. At the same time two Japanese guns, which had been kept back in rear for safety's sake during the night, had resumed their day position on another mountain top only 700 yards distant to the north-west of the pass. From thence, at a range of 700 yards, they blazed away point blank with shrapnel, sweeping the confined space afforded by the captured hill-top, upon which a whole Russian battalion was now crowded together. But Ota had no idea of waiting for the artillery to have its full effect, and, holding high the regimental colour, he boldly led his two companies up the face of the hill in counter-attack against the position he had lost. Immediately, he was hit by four bullets, and had just strength sufficient in him to commend the standard to the guardianship of his major, who also fell almost at once, desperately wounded, but handing on the sacred emblem to the adjutant, who, in his turn, dropped in his tracks to a Russian bullet. Last of all the Imperial ensign passed down to the hand of a private soldier of the first class, who led the last stage of the assault and planted the insignia of his regiment firmly on the corpse-strewn summit. As he did so, full in the face of the Russians thirty or forty paces distant, they in their turn gave way. The Japanese pursued to the crest-line and, looking down, beheld the two other Russian battalions coming up the hill. Officers and men of these reinforcements spread out their arms to stop their fleeing comrades and shouted to them to stand fast, but all in vain. The fugitives dashed into the serried ranks of their brethren and flung both battalions into inextricable confusion. The two companies fired into the struggling mass at seventy-five yards range, and in five more minutes the victory was conclusive.

Only quick decision won this fight; quick decision and the personal heroism of Ota and his officers. Can war be altogether bad when it inspires ordinary men to actions so touching and so sublime? No true soldier will ever hear unmoved the tale of the sun-flag of Ota. His heart will surely fill with thankfulness and joy as he thinks of the passionate devotion to the military idea which stands embodied in the silken rag now streaming to the winds of heaven over the outpost of the Taling Pass. Long may that brave standard be borne at the head of a gallant regiment, raising the generous enthusiasm of successive thousands of Japanese recruits. Long after its lustrous embroideries have mouldered into dust may the ideal it stood for be remembered by our people in England. May they all hear the story of Ota's sun-flag and learn at what cost this morning it crowned the scene of conflict

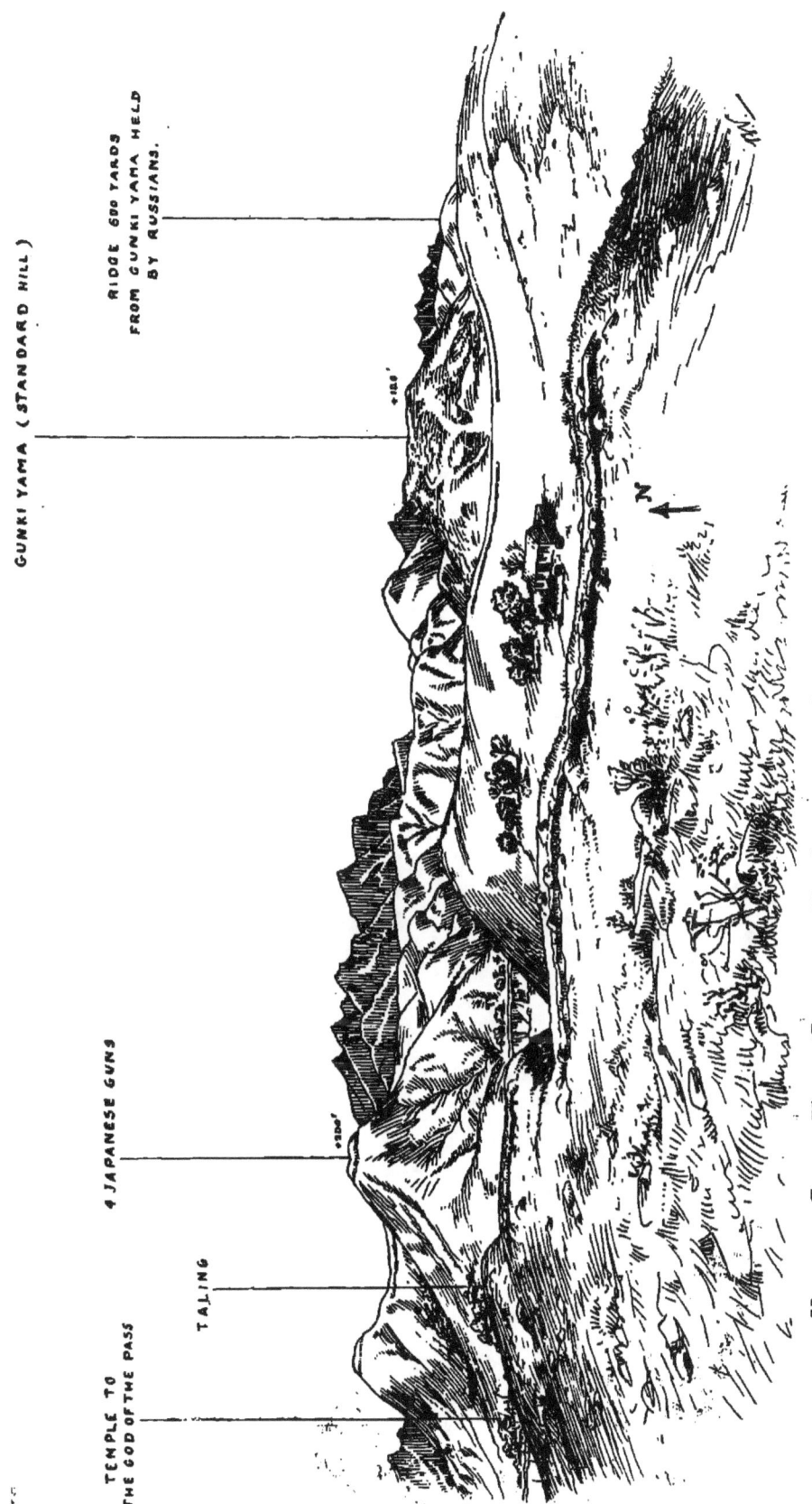

View of Gunki Yama (Standard Hill) from the Japanese Trenches at the Taling (Pass)

XXXI

where it waves free, the symbol of a mighty empire and the very incarnation of its glory. Dai Nippon —Banzai! *

In front of the Tumenling Pass there has also been some very severe fighting, and victory or defeat seem still to hang in the balance. Yesterday there was a heavy fire action in progress until dark, but nothing very decisive was attempted on either side. To-day at 4 A.M. the Japanese position was attacked all along its length with the bayonet. When the last news came to hand the struggle had actually endured at close quarters for two mortal hours, and it may be going on yet for all we know to the contrary. The Russians when repulsed only fall back a dozen yards or so into the dead ground below the crest-line, whence they throw hand grenades into the trenches, whilst the Japanese retaliate by hurling great rocks over the crest and down the slope along the top of which the Russians are lying. At one place the enemy actually succeeded in carrying a section of the trenches, but fortunately this part of the position was commanded by high ground at close range, so they were forced by fire to evacuate it again. My infor-

* I consider the Gunki Yama affair to be a very typical action. On the one hand, a big, unwieldy, inert regiment; and on the other, two quick, alert, independent companies. Had the Russian battalion commander, on taking the summit, at once detached a section to either flank to work round the slopes of the hill, these would have mown down the Japanese as they advanced up the ground (dead from the summit) to the assault. Or, had the regimental commander at once moved his other two battalions round the base of the hill, instead of straight up it, he might so have scored an important success. But the idea of piling together men on a small space of ground to make it secure is Spion Kop, *vieux jeux* and utterly damnable. Ota recovered, although one of the four bullets which struck him had pierced his chest. He received a fine Kanjo from Oyama.—I. H.

mant says "fortunately," for he imagines that if it had been necessary to deliver a counter-attack, "there would have been literally no men available for the purpose." As usual Kuroki remains undisturbed, though the crisis on the right is certainly grave. I presume he relies upon our successes here, and on the impending flank movement of Matsunaga, to neutralise any potential Russian gains in the Penchiho direction.

There is no news to hand about the Russians who crossed the Taitsuho at Weining on the 8th instant. But the important post and depôt of Chaotao is probably out of immediate danger as it was occupied by Prince Kanin and the Second Cavalry Brigade yesterday evening. The infantry garrison has also been increased from seventy to 350 rifles by sweeping in all the odds and ends within twenty miles distance. The Japanese have had extraordinarily good luck with their cavalry brigade. After sending them to Chaotao they seem for once to have lost some of their nerve, and to have hesitated to risk their last reserve against a wide turning movement. A counter order was therefore dispatched, telling His Imperial Highness to leave Chaotao to its fate, and to move southwards to Shakan on the Taitsuho, so as to cover the rear of the right wing of Kuroki's Army. The message miscarried, and now Prince Kanin and his cavalry have reached Chaotao, and, humanly speaking, have saved it!

An infantry battalion belonging to the Twelfth Division has crossed from Penchiho to the south bank of the Taitsuho, and is going to try and get touch with Prince Kanin's Cavalry, so that they may, in concert, operate against the extreme left flank of the Russians.

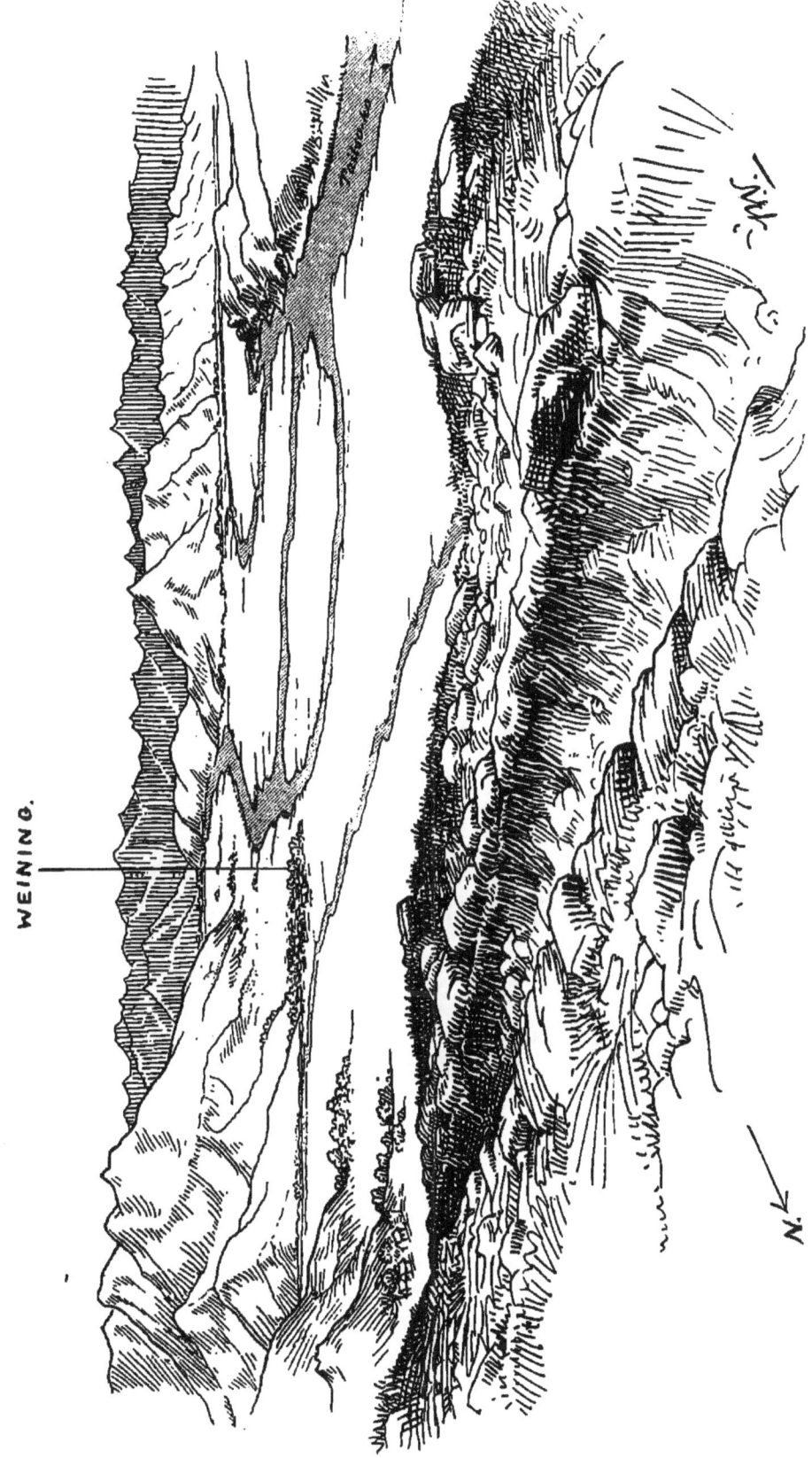

BATTLE OF THE SHAHO

XXIX

VIEW OF THE VALLEY OF THE TAITSU-HO NEAR WEINING FROM THE MOST ADVANCED JAPANESE TRENCHES NEAR PENCHIHO (PENHSIHU)

The garrison of Penchiho may now hope to be fed by its own line of communications. Yesterday the whole of its supplies had to be sent along the front of the First Army. Thus even a minor local success of the Russians along the front of the right of the Second Division, the Guards or the Twelfth Division would have resulted in the complete cutting off of the Penchiho supplies of ammunition and food.

TAIYO VILLAGE, 7 P.M.—During the rest of the afternoon there was not very much to note from independent observation. Matsunaga sent back at 3 P.M. to say he could not possibly march eastwards on Chosenrei until after dark, as the Russian guns commanded the whole of the Kamiriuka valley. About the time this message was received, the sound of very heavy firing came from the north-east. I think it must be caused by the right column of the Guards assaulting Bajisan. I saw several attempts made by Okasaki's men at various times during the afternoon to storm the highest mountain north of Shotatsuko, but on each occasion they had to double back to cover very quickly as soon as they had reached what is evidently a very deadly zone of fire at about 150 yards from the summit. These abortive attempts were not made by any large body or, apparently, by superior order, but merely by section or company commanders who thought they would have a try on the chance of finding a weak spot through which they might penetrate.

If, however, I have not seen much since Matsunaga's capture of the rocky knoll north of Zenshotatsuko, I obtained an intensely vivid and interesting account of a great cavalry success near Penchiho, when I went to say good night half an hour ago. The encounter took place this morning, and sets the minds of all the

Staff very much at ease regarding the course of events in that part of the field, as the whole of the 1500 Cossacks under Rennenkampf, who had crossed the Taitsuho at Weining on October 8th, have now been driven back eastwards, and communications between Penchiho and the south are once more open. But there is more than mere relief from anxiety to gladden the hearts of Kuroki and his Staff. A positive brilliant victory has been achieved. The enemy have been struck a deadly and more then decimating blow, and to add to the intoxication of the joyous tidings, the Corps which has added such lustre to the arms of Japan is the hitherto misprised Cavalry which —last but not least—was led by an Imperial Highness, the dashing Prince Kanin.

Although Chaotao lies only seventeen miles south of Penchiho, and was practically undefended * on the 9th and 10th, yet, for some reason which may be explained hereafter from Russian sources, the 1500 Cossacks with their battery of Horse Artillery attempted nothing decisive, but hung about between Penchiho and Chaotao as if waiting for the fall of the former place.

On the 11th, Prince Kanin with the Second Cavalry Brigade and six Hotchkiss machine guns arrived at Chaotao, and thus anticipated the Cossacks in making a raid which every one here has consistently assumed they must make if only for the reason that it seemed so easy and so desirable from their point of view, so unpleasant and mortifying from the point of view of the Japanese.

To-day, at 3 A.M., Prince Kanin marched on Penchiho (*see* Map XXXIV.). At the Senkin Pass he had a

* The garrison consisted of seventy infantry soldiers.—I. H.

skirmish and drove the Cossacks back northwards. As I have already noted, the Russians in their attack on Penchiho had been trying to envelop the place, and their extreme left had actually worked round along the river Taitsu due south of the defence line. Thus on the extreme Japanese right the defenders were thrown back like the lower part of the letter "S" along the tops of the mountains whose slopes ran down into the river, whilst the Russians with their backs to the river and their faces to the north were half-way up the slope still endeavouring to effect a lodgment on the crest-line. After the skirmish on the Senkin Pass, the Cossacks fell back as far as the Taitsuho, where they still interposed between the advancing Japanese cavalry brigade and their own infantry who, on the northern bank, were busily engaged with the defenders of Penchiho. On the nearer approach of Prince Kanin, however, the Cossacks shifted their position eastwards, still covering their unconscious infantry so far as to forbid the Japanese cavalry from making any attempt to cross the Taitsuho, but leaving it open to them to occupy some high ground on the southern bank which was within effective rifle range of the Russian Camp on the other side of the river.

Prince Kanin is not the sort of man who would miss good chances, and certainly on this occasion he seems to have unhesitatingly seized the ripe gift offered him by fortune. Stealthily manœuvring his six machine guns into position on a high and broken spur which ran down to the water's edge, he suddenly opened a hellish rain of bullets upon two Russian battalions who, at half-past eleven o'clock, were comfortably eating their dinners. In less than one minute

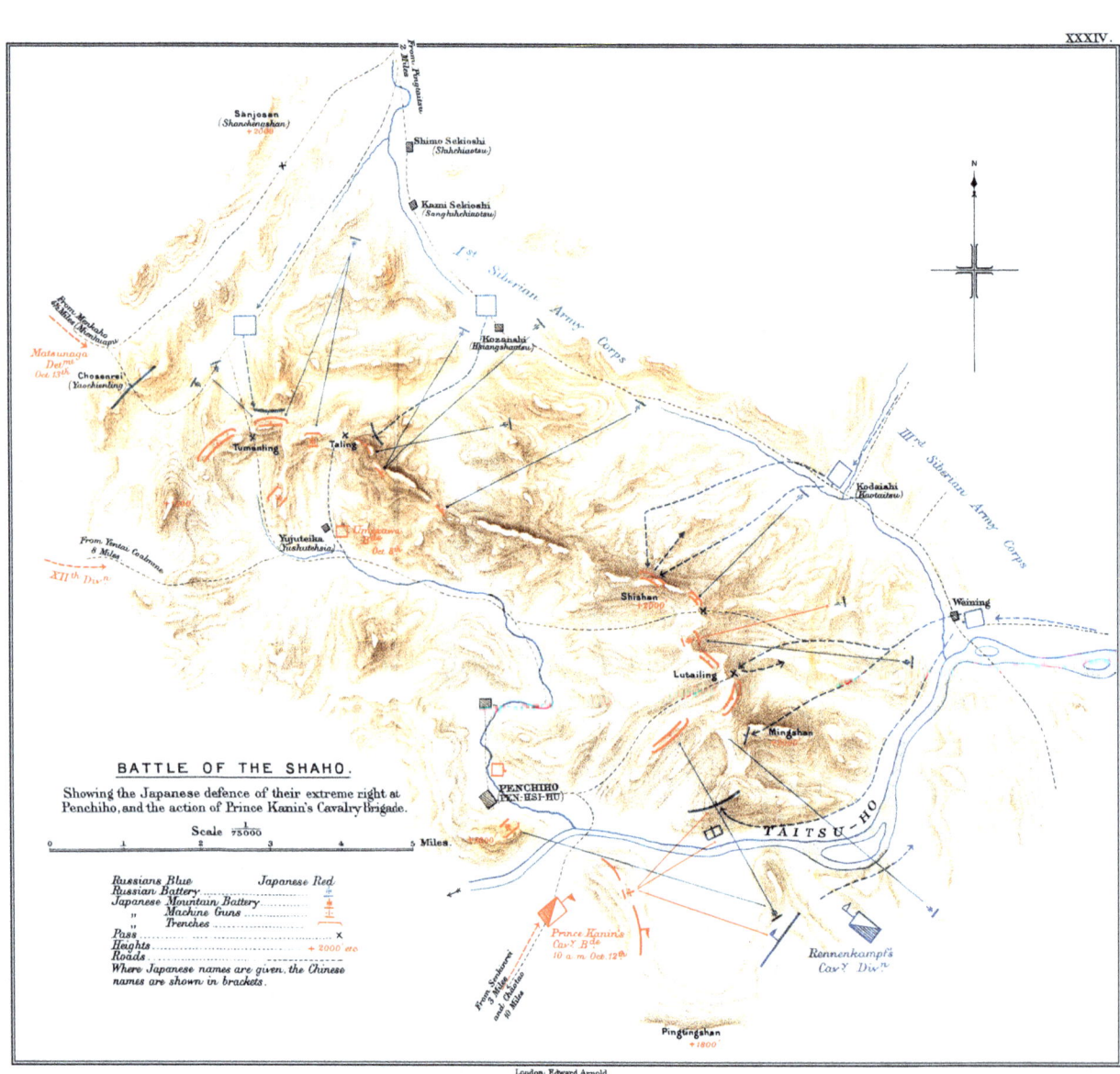

# BATTLE OF THE SHAHO
## XXXIV
### Spread 1

# BATTLE OF THE SHAHO
## XXXIV
### Spread 2

BATTLE OF THE SHAHO.

Showing the Japanese defence of their extreme right at Penchiho, and the action of Prince Kanin's Cavalry Brigade.

Where Japanese names are given, the Chinese names are shown in brackets.

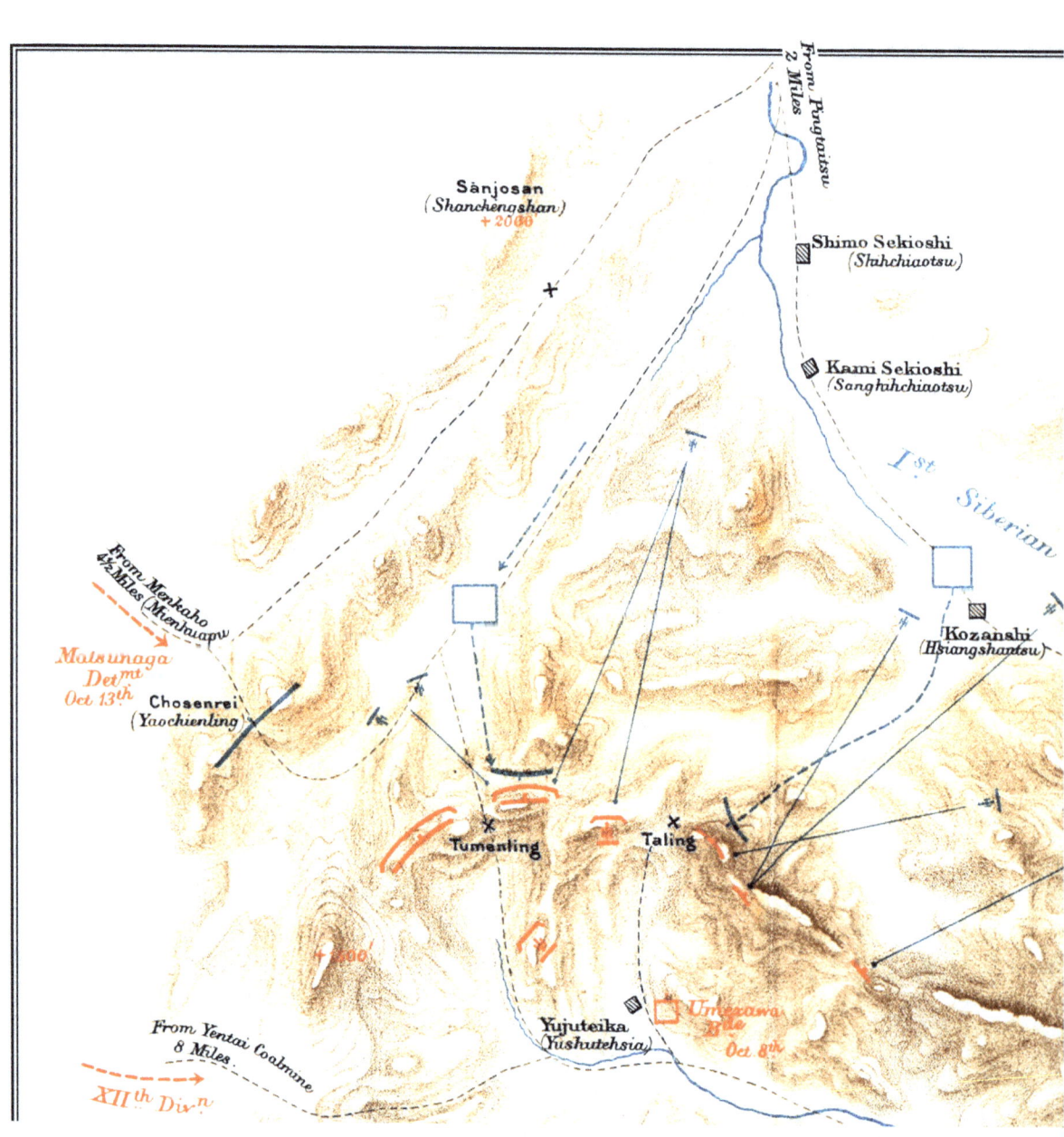

XXXIV.

Kodaishi
(Kaotaitsu)

IIIrd Siberian Army Corps

Army Corps

# BATTLE OF THE SHAHO.

Showing the Japanese defence of their extreme right at Penchiho, and the action of Prince Kanin's Cavalry Brigade.

Scale $\frac{1}{75000}$

0　1　2　3　4　5 Miles.

Russians Blue　　　　Japanese Red
Russian Battery..............
Japanese Mountain Battery............
　,,　　Machine Guns............
　,,　　Trenches............
Pass............×
Heights............+ 2000' etc
Roads............

Where Japanese names are given, the Chinese names are shown in brackets.

PENCHI
(PEN-HSI-

From Senkinrei 3 Miles
and Chaoiao 10 Miles

London

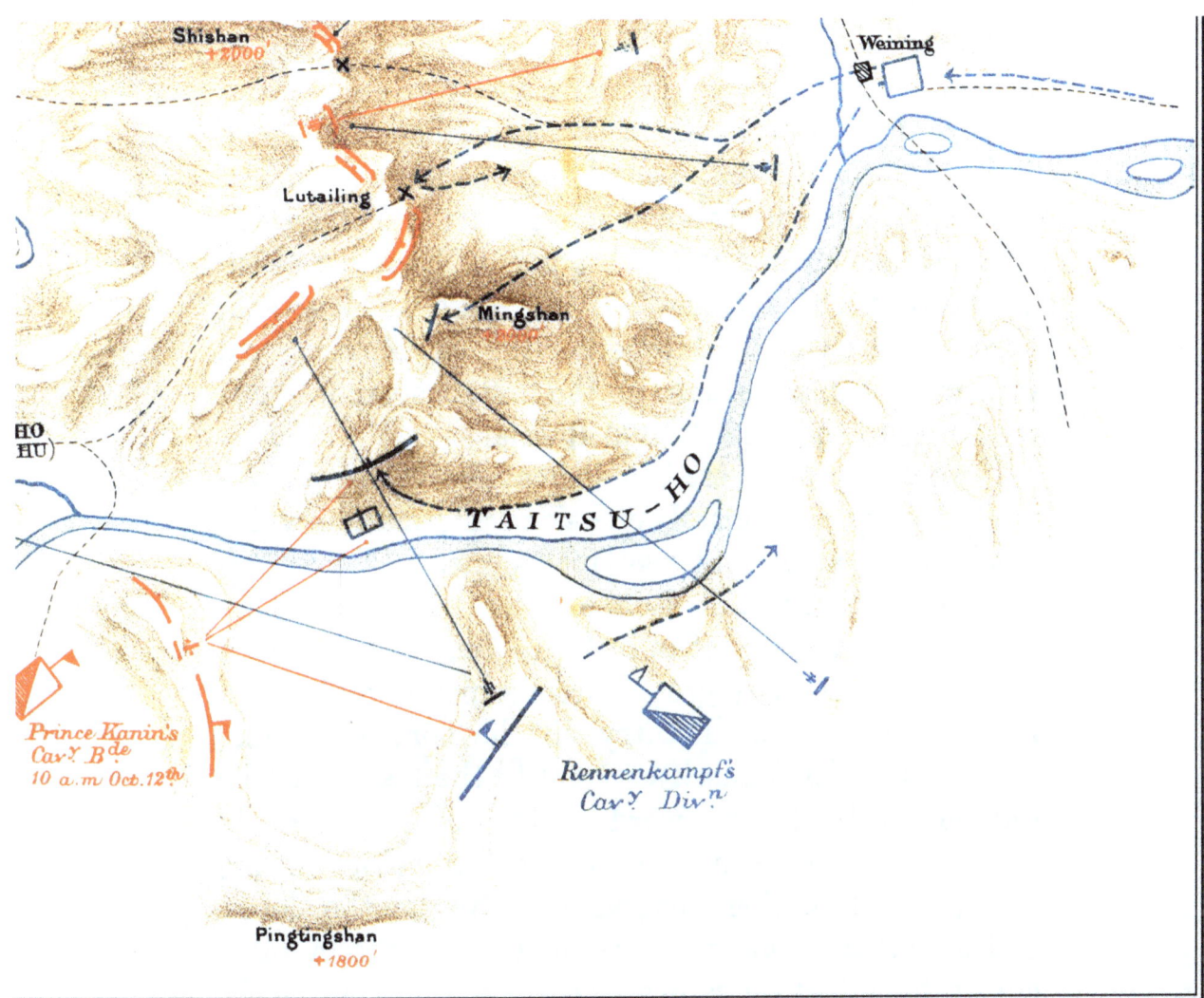

hundreds of these poor fellows were killed, and the rest were flying eastwards in wild disorder. Next moment the Maxims were switched on to the Russian firing line who, with their backs to the river and their attention concentrated on Penchiho, were fighting in trenches about half-way up the slope of the mountain. These, before they could realise what had happened, found themselves being pelted with bullets from the rear. No troops could stand such treatment for long, and in less than no time the two brigades of Russians which had formed the extreme left of Stakelberg's attack, were in full retreat. Altogether the six Maxims had accounted for, according to the first despatch, 1000; according to the second 1300 Russians.

It would be rash were I to dogmatise on the comparatively scanty and entirely one-sided information which is all that is at present available to me. *Primâ facie* it seems strange that Rennenkampf did not either elect to fight to the last in order to deny to the Second Cavalry Brigade any ground from which it might with impunity molest the infantry on the northern bank; or else (if he felt himself unequal to the task) that he did not at least send word to the infantry down in camp by the northern bank of the Taitsuho, warning them, as well as their comrades fighting on the slopes, to look out for squalls. Some may think the infantry should have had their own picquets thrown out on the high ground along the southern bank of the Taitsuho, but it seems to me that the infantry cannot well be blamed for supposing they were safe from sudden surprise in this direction when they believed themselves to be covered by 1500 Cossacks and a battery!

I ought to turn in so as to be fresh for to-morrow, and yet I ought also to write for several more hours if

I wish to record even feebly my impression of this day of days.

The Japanese are doing wonders—prodigies almost—and the Russians can nowhere resist them. Yet I have a strange feeling as if these Russians were like cotton wool—very soft at first, but getting harder and harder as they are pressed and pressed, until at last the force which is squeezing them finds it has got hold of a solid slab of gun-cotton, unplastic as iron and capable of exploding with terrific violence. Okasaki does not seem able to carry the round hill north of Shotatsuko in the same slap-dash style as he carried Terayama, which yet appeared to me far the stronger position of the two.

One more reflection. The Japanese artillery did not, in my humble opinion, distinguish themselves to-day as much as the other arms. When Matsunaga stormed the knoll above Zenshotatsuko a minute or two before 11 A.M., the hills to the north of it were covered with retiring Russian infantry. By this time the Russian guns north of Shotatsuko had been silenced, and those near Renkwasan and Domonshi could not range the Japanese batteries (*see* Map XXXIII.). With better signalling arrangements and good horses, I think that the Japanese batteries might have galloped up to effective range of the retiring infantry within a quarter of an hour of the commencement of their slow retreat up the slopes of the mountains, and have punished them severely. What actually happened to-day was that a message was sent back by an orderly and that the artillery began to move forward at 11.30 when all the retreating infantry were already getting under cover. Even then the guns seemed to advance desperately slowly, although the roads were good and dead level. The brigade on the right after all only advanced 300 or 400 yards to a spot under Sanjoshisan, where they had deep gun-pits ready prepared, and this although there was a splendid position 1000 yards further on where they might have shelled the enemy effectively, instead of at such extreme range that their shrapnel bullets could have had no velocity remaining to do much harm. The two batteries on the left went almost as far as Terayama, where they came into action on the open plough. Their advance was more pronounced and useful to the infantry than that of their brethren on the right, but even so, it was neither prompt enough, fast enough, or bold enough, according to my ideas—ideas which are shared, unless I very greatly mistake, by many Japanese officers.

I must now positively turn in. Vincent and the foreign attachés with the Second Division are here, and have spent the day on Terayama. They say it is covered pretty thick with Russian dead and wounded, mostly middle-aged, bearded men. On several of them were found prayer books in Russian presented by the British Bible Society. My American *confrère* says that we are a very difficult people to compete against—we deal out Bibles to one side and guns to the other. Colonel Hume, who has been with the Guards, has witnessed the scene of Watanabe's fight which I have tried to describe. I have got the facts correctly enough, so it seems. He saw a very exciting series of incidents where two Japanese batteries were running the gauntlet of fire along a short section of the road between Hakashi and Kamiriuka, on which a Russian battery in action near Domonshi had ranged to a nicety. On this one occasion the Japanese drivers managed to raise a gallop. Each gun or waggon went singly and, as it reached the dangerous spot, sure enough the *rafale* burst all round it. Finally, the old forge waggon came lumbering along, and the shells exploded so near to it that the horses, accustomed as they should have been by now to any sort of uproar, took fright and bounded, so that a man fell off the tail-board. He picked himself up, however, and ran off as if the devil was after him. One lead-driver was very cunning: he kept the corner of his eye in the direction of the enemy's guns, and the instant he saw the dust of their discharge, pulled up dead, twenty yards short of the danger-point, and thus eluded the eight shells which spent themselves harmlessly on the track just in front of his team. When all the excitement and firing was over, the casualties were checked, and it was found that in one battery only seven men had been hit, and in the other ten horses!

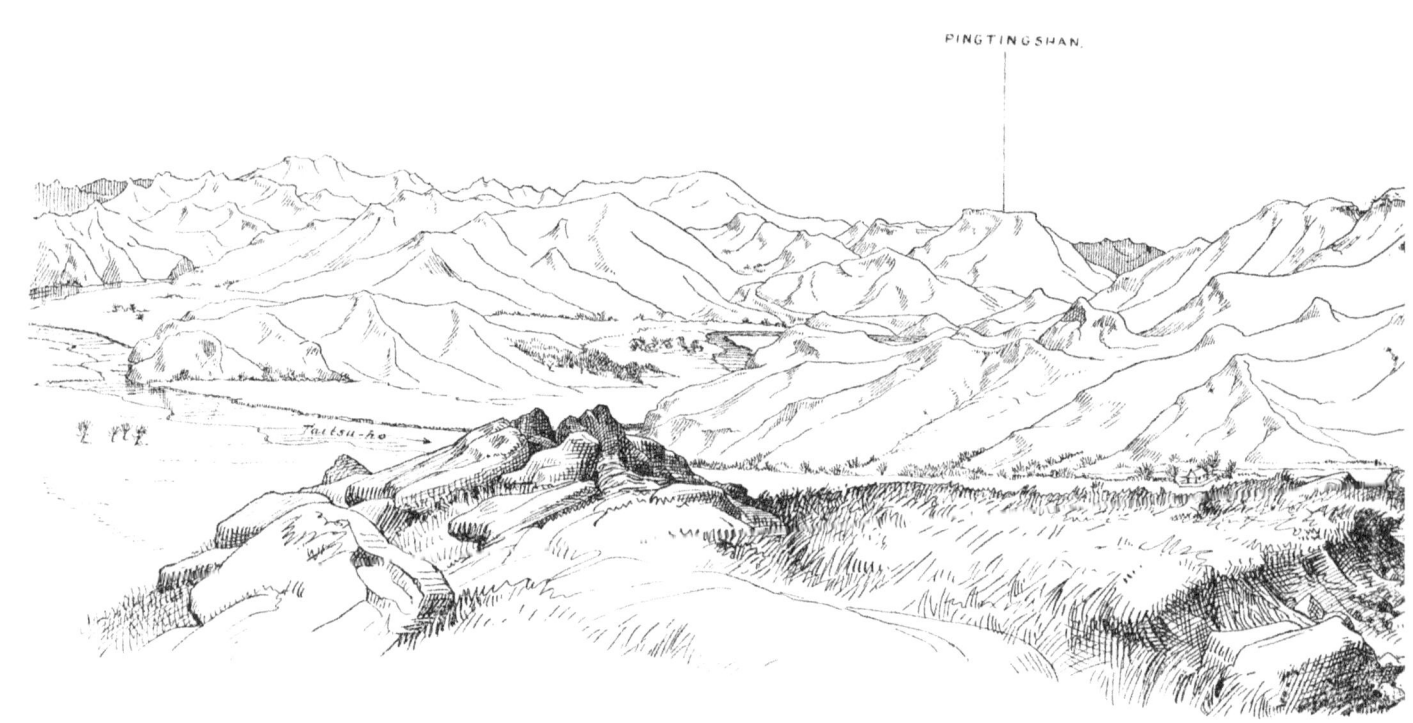

View of the Japanese Position near Penchiho

XXX

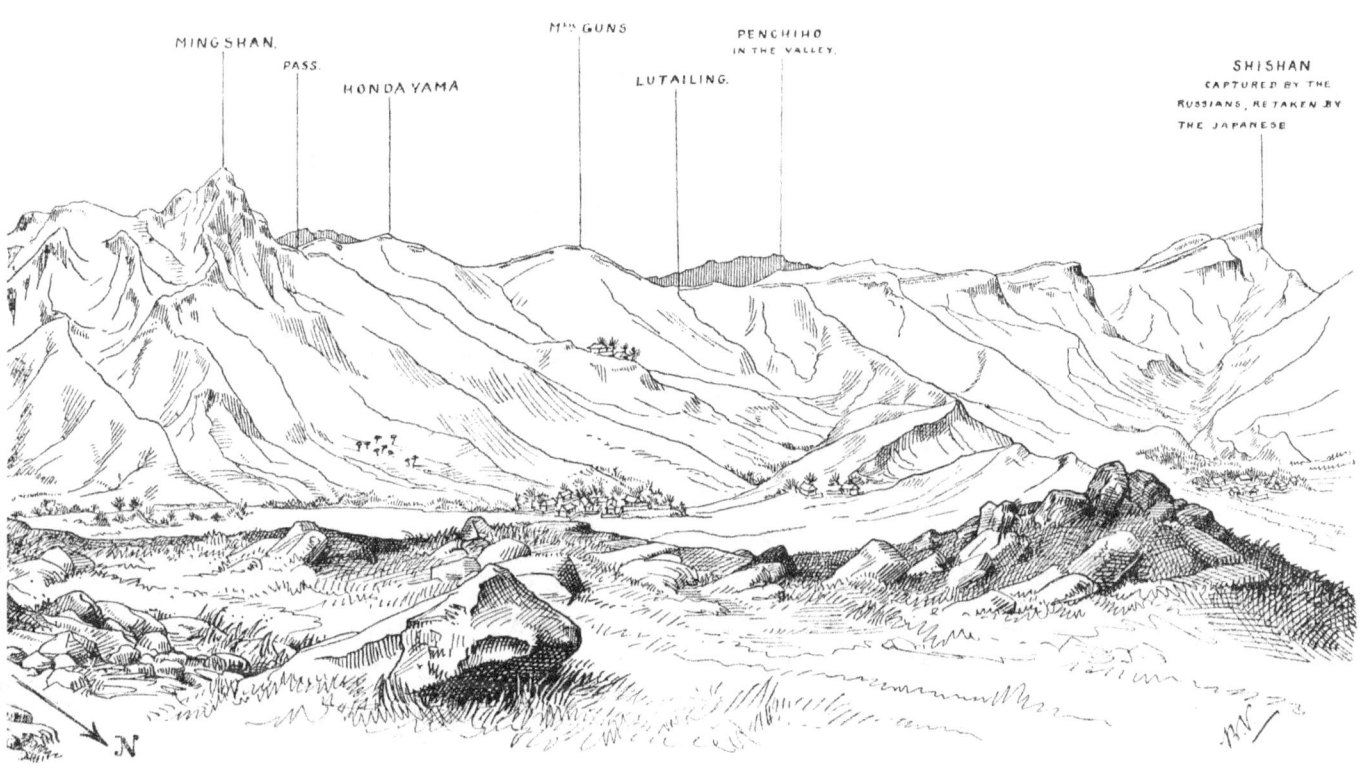

(Penhsihu) from the Russian Side

## CHAPTER XXXI

### THE ASSAULT OF THE TALL HILL

A HILLOCK JUST NORTH-EAST OF HANLASANSHI, 1 P.M., *October* 13*th*, 1904.—Last night, General Kuroki issued orders for a general pursuit of the Russians, and announced his expectation that the Guards Division would be able to press them back to the south of Hoshuho, whilst the Second Division would make good Wasoko. Commanders were enjoined to punish the enemy as much as they could during their retirement. But, so far as I can see, nothing of the sort has taken place. The Headquarters Staff and myself have pushed on to this rocky knoll whence we should get an extraordinarily good view of the advance when it does take place, but that is not yet. In front of us, just out of rifle shot, is Okasaki, apparently in precisely the same position as yesterday. Not a yard has he gained during the night, only, wherever his men happened to be at sunset, they have now deeply dug themselves in. The Fourth Army is still holding Nanzan and attacking Round Top from thence. Suribachiyama, the ridge joining Nanzan to the high hill to the east of it, and even the south-west skirts of the high hill itself,\* are in Okasaki's possession, but its summit is still swarming with Russians. The Japanese have a battery north of Sanjoshisan and one brigade on a spur south of Suri-

---
\* Afterwards called Okasaki Yama. (*See* Sketch XXVI.)—I. H.

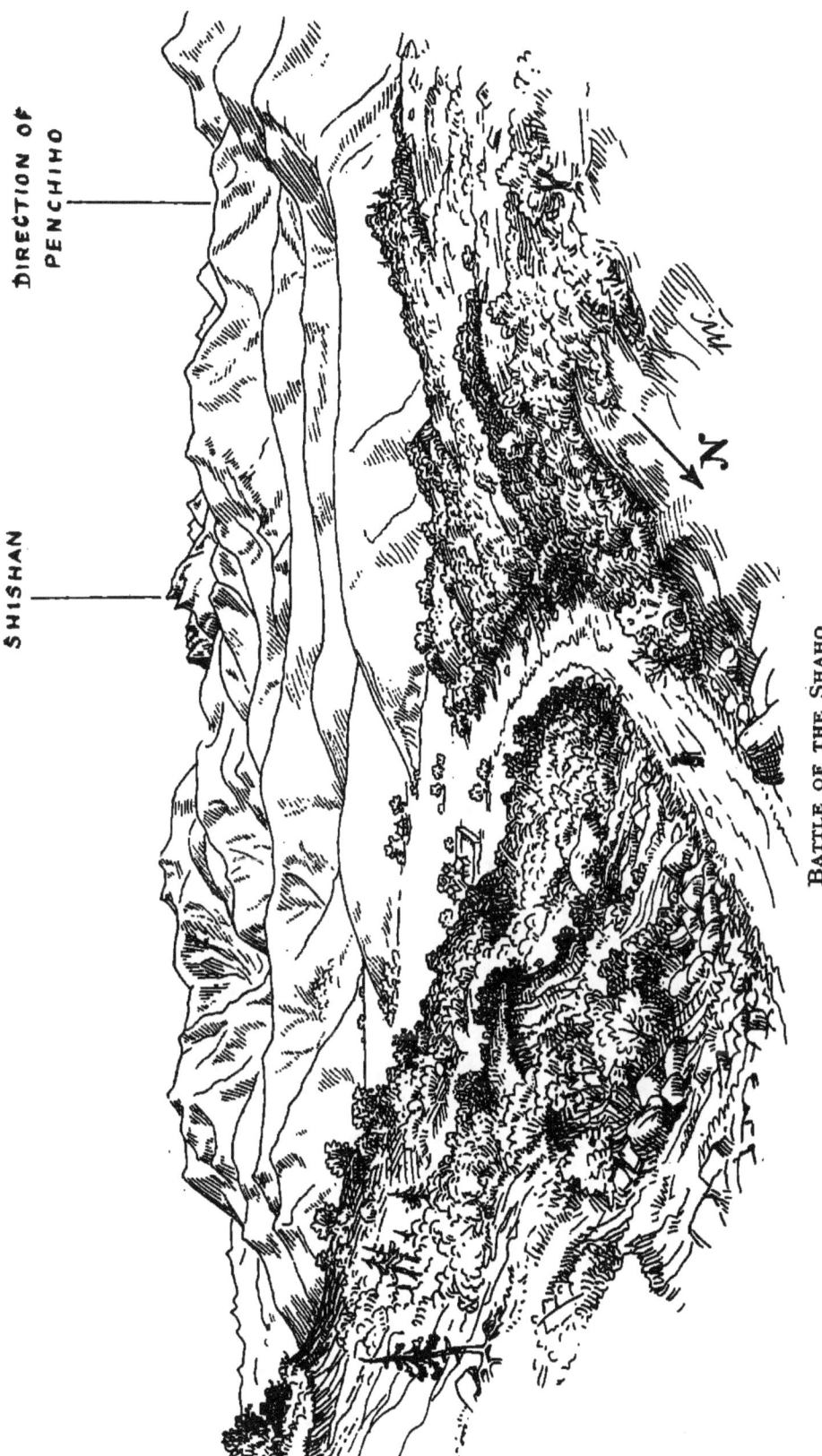

BATTLE OF THE SHAHO

VIEW FROM THE TOP OF THE PASS AT CHOSENREI (YAOCHIENLING) LOOKING TOWARDS PENCHIHO (PENHSIHU)

XXVII.

bachiyama. They are firing on the high hill. From its position the battery near Sanjoshisan is able to some extent to enfilade the Russian line, but the other three batteries are firing direct and cannot at such a short range and high elevation expect to do much damage to men below the crest. Howitzers, in fact, are badly wanted here. Strange to say the Russian batteries from positions near Renkwasan and Hamatang are firing either at Terayama or at the batteries south of Suribachiyama, or occasionally in our direction, but take no notice of the battery just north of Sanjoshisan which must, I am sure, be doing a lot of damage. Whenever Okasaki's infantry attempt any offensive movement, the Russians disregard the shells bursting among them and stand up to fire, so far with the result that the Japanese cannot get on at all.

Things are worse with the other brigade (Matsunaga's) of the Second Division, from which a long despatch has just come in by the hands of a Guards orderly. At 7 P.M., by which time the shades of evening completely hid their movements from the Russian artillery, they started for Chosenrei to intercept Stakelberg's retreat.* The rain came down in a perfect deluge, and the night was dismal, stormy, and dark as Erebus. Slipping in the icy mud, covered up to their waists with layers of congealed clay, the gallant fellows stuck to it until 5 this morning, when they found themselves within 200 yards of the Russians. They have made two assaults which have

* I heard afterwards that the Russians did apparently suspect that there was something in the wind, and made a sharp counter-attack just as Matsunaga was starting. Most fortunately it was not vigorously pressed, and Matsunaga was able to repulse it and continue his march with only half an hour's delay.—I. H.

been beaten off with heavy loss. Matsunaga sends in to say he is going to try again, and hopes for better luck next time.*

From the far right at Penchiho the news is more reassuring. The Russians are in full retreat. But it is a retreat as unmolested as that of Liaoyang. The

* At Chosenrei (Pass) there is a very steep ascent of 150 feet up a narrow ridge which blocks the valleys east and west (see Maps XXXIII. and XXXIV.). After the repulse of Matsunaga's second attack, one and a half Russian battalions appeared from the Shinkwailing direction and, occupying the heights on the north side of the valley up which the Japanese had advanced, threatened their retreat. Matsunaga held off this force with a portion of his reserve, and with nerve and indomitable resolution continued his assaults against the pass. The slopes were so slippery and steep, however, that his tired, mud-clogged troops sustained repulse after repulse until, in the evening, two Russian guns coming on to the pass opened fire, and four howitzers appeared on the sky-line near the Shinkwailing. The fighting continued until 9 P.M. and firing then ceased. Next morning the Russians had retired.

This night march and the bulldog fight at the end of it were a fitting conclusion to Matsunaga's exploits, which had commenced on the morning of the 11th and had gone on uninterruptedly night and day since then. If the western world is still curious to know the cause of the Japanese successes in the field, here, in the conduct of this small and unsuccessful operation, the secret may be read in epitome. How many brigadiers are there in Europe who are sufficiently confident in their chief and in themselves to accept responsibility with Matsunaga's pertinacity and nerve. After an exhausting night march up a long valley, he met the enemy posted across the head of it and twice made the assault without success. He then saw fresh Russian troops lining the northern heights of the valley up which he had marched, threatening to descend and cut off his retreat. Did he fall back? Far from it. On the contrary, putting away fear, he redoubled his efforts to carry the pass by assault. I admit that Sir Frederick Roberts fought the battle at Charasia under precisely similar conditions, except that the Russians would have given quarter and the Afghans would not. But Charasia took place long ago.—I. H.

Twelfth Division and the Umezawa Brigade are holding a line twelve miles long, and it is impossible to change in the twinkling of an eye from defensive to offensive formations, especially as the enemy are still making some show of attacking at the Tumenling and Taling Passes, where a heavy bombardment by their artillery is even now in progress. The Guards are endeavouring to carry out Kuroki's spirited orders. Asada has ordered his right column, under Izaki, to take Bajisan, and then to proceed to the capture of Sensan, a big mountain two miles to the north-west of it. The left column under Watanabe is to attack the enemy in the hills immediately to the east of Domonshi.

It now becomes apparent that the idea of countering Kuropatkin's attempt to turn our right at Penchiho by turning his right and driving him off the railway and Mukden into the mountains, has now been definitely abandoned. We are actually aiming at something bold in detail, and no doubt difficult enough, but infinitely less comprehensive and conclusive. There are two schemes simultaneously in operation. The one is to use Matsunaga's brigade to intercept a portion of Stakelberg's rearguard by cutting in on its line of retreat over the Chosenrei. The other is (with the assistance of the Fourth Army at Nanzan, and by moving the Guards from Bajisan to Domonshi), to envelop both flanks of the Russians who are fighting exactly in front of us here. If this is successful we may cut off their retreat and perhaps effect an important capture.

1.50 P.M.—We have no news yet from the Guards, but I now see troops moving along a ridge some four miles to the east-north-east, probably about Renkwasan. They are dodging from knoll to knoll, advancing very slowly with a Japanese flag at their head. These must be the Guards. I can also see some Russians, apparently only 300 or 400 yards distant from the Japanese standard, and shells from the Guards' artillery are bursting freely on the open hillside between the two forces. No doubt great deeds are being done out there, but when individuals show up no larger than a pin's head, excitement and sympathy are proportionately reduced.

2.20 P.M.—Kuroki expressed anxiety about the difficulties which were delaying Okasaki in his attempt to make good the summit of the tall hill two miles north of us.*

2.30 P.M.—Far away I see some 200 Russians making a counter-attack against the Guards.

2.35 P.M.—They have not got very far. Not more than one quarter of the way across the interval between the two lines. Still, the Japanese cannot get on.

2.40 P.M.—At several points brave individuals carrying little flags are advancing up towards the summit of the tall hill,† and about two companies have worked man by man to a small under-feature not more than 150 yards from the top behind which they are squeezed together, a little crowd, lying as flat as they can, whilst over their heads I know countless bullets uninterruptedly sing and whistle as they did at equally short range over the defenders of Waggon Hill.

2.55 P.M.—A battalion of Russians is swarming up a spur to counter-attack the Guards. The General Staff have sent an adjutant to gallop for his life to the Second Division Artillery south of Suribachiyama, to tell them to turn their guns that way. Before he

* Okasaki Yama. † *Ibid.*

## The Assault of the Tall Hill

had gone two minutes they did it of their own initiative, scattering the Russians a bit, but not checking them altogether; and now I believe the Guards are beginning to fall back.

3 P.M.—On the tall hill* events seem to be approaching a crisis. All the Japanese trenches are full to overflowing, and still men keep dashing out to them, and diving into these overcrowded gashes on the flanks of the hill. I am near enough to distinguish the officers very clearly by their swords. Several of them are standing up. The Russians on the top of the hill are also standing up to fire regardless of the bursting shells which fall by dozens at their very feet and conceal them from view sometimes for seconds at a time. The whole of the Japanese artillery is now blazing for all it is worth at the summit of the hill. Three of the batteries are in action close by Suribachiyama; a mountain battery is firing from Nanzan, and the battery just north of Sanjoshisan is specially busy, and is undoubtedly doing more damage than all the rest put together, as it is able to get an enfilading effect and to throw its shrapnel from left to right of the Russian line.

The Japanese are making the assault I verily believe! They have swarmed out of their trenches and have disappeared over the brow.

3.15 P.M.—A company has succeeded, at least for the moment, in making good the crest of the long spur running westwards from the summit (*see* Sketch XXVI.). But as soon as it topped the ridge it was met by a tremendous fire from Round Top Hill, and by an enfilading fire from the Russians on the main hill.† It seems impossible that the men should hold on, but they do.

* Okasaki Yama. † *Ibid.*

Suddenly a little cluster of flags breaks out into spots of colour in a slight depression due south of, and not more than forty or fifty yards distant from, the actual summit! The effect on the officers around me is electrical. The symbol of the heroic soul of their nation is almost touching the ranks of the Russians. They feel that actual contact with their talisman must be fatal to the enemies of their Emperor, and yet they tremble to think that this time perhaps it is decreed that fortune may fail them at the last. To myself, the anxiety of seeing the two forces within stone's throw of one another is almost unbearable. The Japanese know, I presume, where they have got to, but I doubt if the Russians, who are still shooting down the hillside, have any idea that their enemies are crouching close by to make their last spring. Meanwhile, another company has advanced straight up the southern slope to within 150 yards of the defender's line. It lies down to fire, but there is no friendly feature of the ground here to hide it. The Russian bullets knocking up the dust cover them with a light haze. They can endure no longer, and rush across to the long spur running westwards, leaving a trail of prostrate bodies. Here they fix themselves on to a part of the crest-line half-way between the summit and the spot whence the first attempt is still clinging on and exchanging a furious fire with Round Top. (*See* Sketch XXVI.)

3.30 P.M.—A message has come in to say that the Fourth Army on our left has entirely defeated the enemy, who are flying in disorder.

3.40 P.M.—The two companies I observed at 2.40 P.M. lying close behind an under-feature 150 yards from the summit have sent forth a little forlorn hope.

## THE ASSAULT OF THE TALL HILL

It consists of less than 100 men. Most gallantly they advance until they get to within a few yards of the summit, and then their hearts fail them and they rush desperately down the hill, leaving their dead behind them. At the same time the Russian shrapnel from the east-north-east and from Hamatang seems suddenly to find their fellows clinging on behind the under-feature. The spot has been badly shrapnelled for two minutes, and now, instead of about 400 men, there are only about sixty or seventy left, the rest having cleared off down the mountain side. But the men with the flags close up to the summit are still holding on, though how they can do it I do not know, as the shrapnel seems to be bursting right in their faces.

3.45 P.M.—An adjutant has come in from the Fourth Army saying that the Tenth Division, which was supposed to be pursuing the badly defeated Russians, has suffered a severe repulse. The Staff are bewildered, and do not quite know what to believe. At the same time another despatch has come in from Matsunaga at Chosenrei to say that all his repeated assaults have failed, and that he is being surrounded by the enemy. The Guards contribute their quota of ill news, for not only has their famous encircling movement been brought to a full stop, but their right column has been virtually defeated, and orders for its retreat were issued at 2 P.M.

Amidst all this, Kuroki keeps a stiff upper lip and only says it is the more imperative we should carry the tall hill * to our front. A staff officer remarks, "The whole of the First Army is in difficulties, but presently Okasaki will put everything right." All the same, an appeal for help has been made to Oyama, and

* Okasaki Yama.

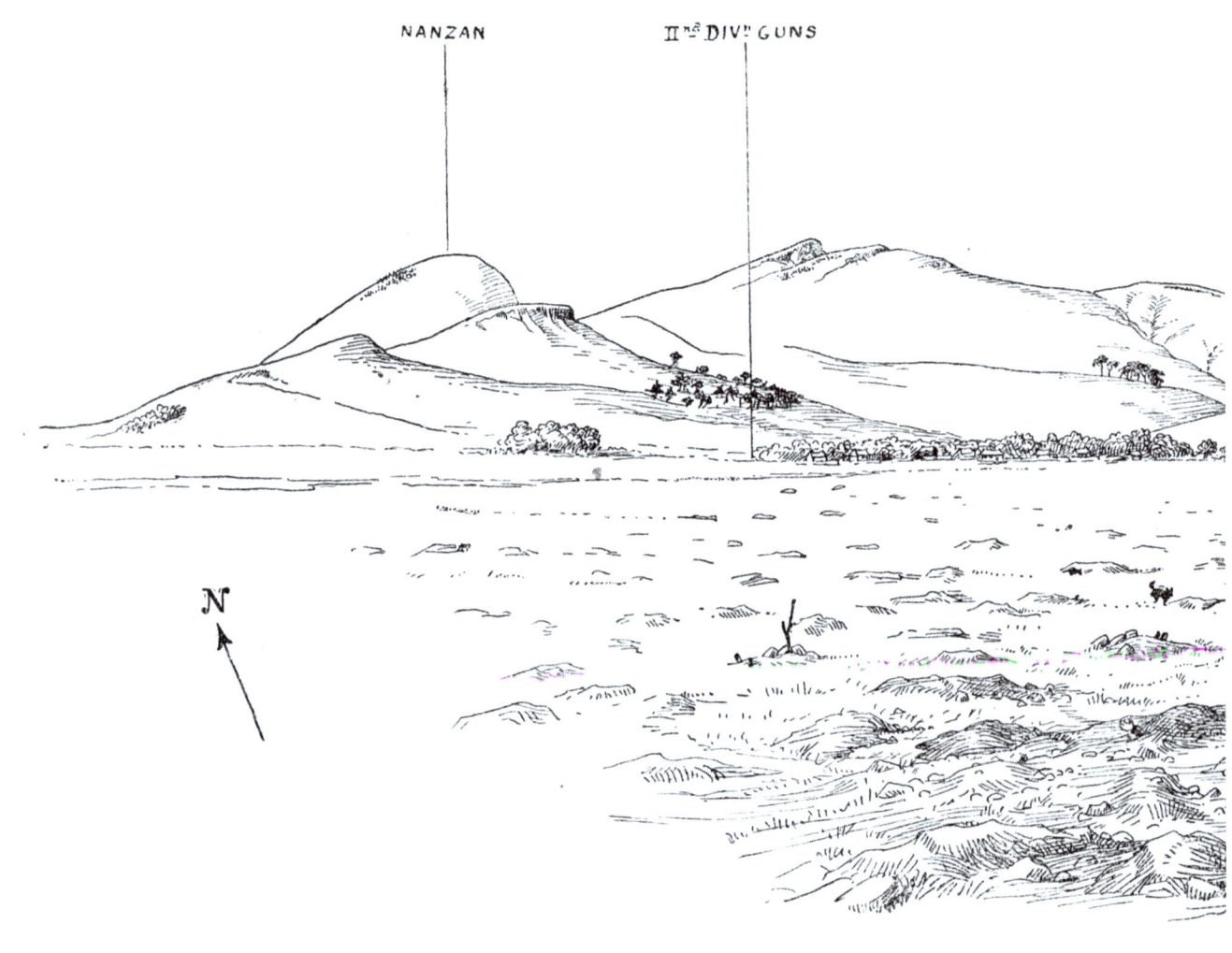

BATTLE OF

VIEW OF OKASAKI YAMA FROM THE POSITION OF
THE HILL WAS CAPTURED BY THE 16TH
THE FOREGROUND SHOWS THE OPEN PLAIN OVER WHICH THE SAME

XXVI

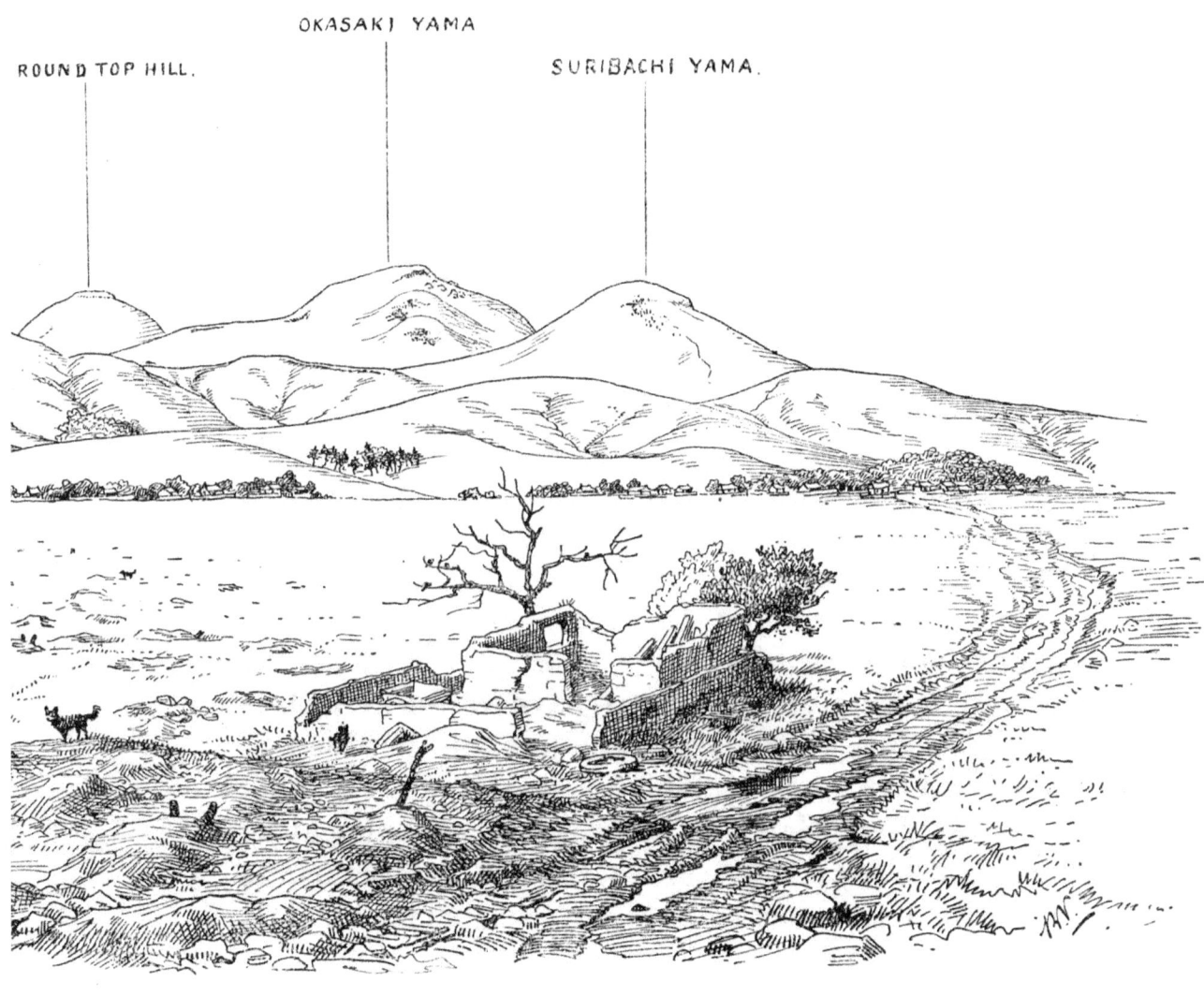

THE SHAHO

THE 1ST ARMY HEADQUARTERS, OCTOBER 13, 1904
REGIMENT, 15H (OKASAKI) BRIGADE 2ND DIVISION
BRIGADE ADVANCED IN THE ATTACK ON TERA YAMA, OCTOBER 11, 1904

he has responded like a noble Samurai, putting the Manchurian Army Reserve at our disposal, and now it is marching here just as fast as its legs can carry it over the ground.

4.45 P.M.—The hour is at hand. Beneath my strong glasses the Japanese in the little hollow just below the summit seem to stir uneasily and to prepare. On to the narrow space which separates them from the Russians the guns of both armies are pouring out shell by the hundred. The shell drop earthwards in rattling thunderclaps, releasing the awful Genius of War, who, in the shape of a tall, ghost-like pillar of smoke, stretches out his huge and shadowy pinions over the encountering hosts. The Russian shrapnel fly fast and thick just over the southern side of the crest-line. They are fused and ranged to perfection, and before they burst they cross a rain of Japanese shells pitching within ten yards of them over the northern edge of the same crest. Many a bullet must be finding the wrong billet when the two targets are only fifty yards apart. The hour has come. A handful of Japanese have leaped from their cover to fling themselves to earth within ten paces of the Russians. Unendurable suspense! Here I stand in safety, seeing Japanese and Russians springing up to fire point-blank into one another's faces, then crouching down to reload, then again rising for a moment to fire. It is too much!

I saw these things as clearly as if I were a part of them, and the sight of these little struggling figures silhouetted against the sky will never be effaced from my mind. For now the Russians rose in a line and, holding their sharp bayonets before them, charged down like mountain bulls. At their head was a gallant officer in a white coat, and his sword flashed as he waved it round his head. Down and back went the Japanese; the Headquarters Staff had to turn their heads away from the long-drawn-out agony of this struggle with bayonet and sword; but I could not, for I was lost in amazement. The foes had drawn apart, and stood facing one another at ten yards' distance. It seemed an eternity, and actually it must have been a minute. Then they closed again, and seemed to wrestle body to body, and parted again and threw rocks and thrust with bayonets and clubbed their rifles. But they did not shoot, or if they did it was only a very, very little. There were only some seventy Japanese, and perhaps fifty or sixty Russians. The crisis lasted full five minutes, and now the Japanese seemed beaten; several of them fell back; all was lost —No! the fugitives turned again, brave fellows! The Russians withdrew to their trench, the Japanese followed close on their heels, and the position was taken. From right and left reinforcements continuously worked their way up the hill side, and by half-past five o'clock the whole of the crest-line was thick with Japanese emptying their magazines against the retreating Russians, and firing at Round Top Hill, which was now being once more assaulted by the Tenth Division of the Fourth Army. The whole of the First Army Headquarters look taller and bigger men, as if a great weight had suddenly been rolled off their shoulders.

War brings with it many surprises, but I must say I never expected to see in a modern battle a long-drawn-out struggle with the cold steel carried on in broad daylight between men armed with modern weapons. It exemplifies the strong tendency of human beings to revert to primitive methods under the influence of any great pressure or strain. It might be the same with our own men under similar conditions, but I can answer for it that it would not be so with the Boers. Neither Russians nor Japanese can hold a candle to a Boer when it comes to the instinctive, deadly, panther-like quickness with which the hunter of the veldt can use a rifle at close range. In such a *mêlée* as that which I have just seen, a good Boer would have had an enemy on the ground for each of the ten cartridges in his magazine within some twenty seconds! The bayonet should have no fears for such a man. After all, a soldier with a bayonet is more easily stopped, and much less swift and terrible than a tiger. Yet there are men who will follow up a wounded tiger on foot for pleasure. But they are practised riflemen and have confidence in their aim.

7 P.M.—Round Top has been captured by the Tenth Division, Fourth Army, assisted by the fire of the Second Division, from the captured hill, now called Okasaki Yama in honour of the gallant brigadier. Okasaki himself and his troops are to have no rest, but have been ordered to take another hill two miles to the east by Renkwasan during the coming night. They are now starting.

The capture of Okasaki Yama relieves the First Army from a great danger. Since Matsunaga has been sent to Chosenrei (where he is still held up), the weakest point in Kuroki's line is that between the right of the Second Division and the left of the Guards. In fact, the gap of some three miles between them was at first only filled by two Kobi battalions, left behind by Matsunaga, afterwards increased to four Kobi battalions by the addition of the whole of Kuroki's reserve. Okasaki Yama was like a spear-head, pressing painfully against this weakly armoured spot. Had it not been taken before nightfall, it might have punctured an open wound in the Japanese line of battle, through which several Russian Divisions* might have penetrated into their vitals. I am sure that the sending of Matsunaga to Penchiho was worse to the commander of the First Army than losing a limb. If, however, I were asked whether the problematical results were worth so desperate a risk I, personally, with the limited information at my disposal, should say, most certainly not. The consideration of such a question is more suitable for an elaborate study than for my note-book, but, briefly, it seems to me that the best justification for detaching Matsunaga would be:

(1) That the Twelfth Division was in such a bad way that help must be sent them at all costs.

(2) That there was danger lest the Russians should break through the Japanese Twelfth Division, and thus cut the line of communication through while supplies had been sent to Penchiho since Rennenkampf had interrupted the Chaotao-Penchiho road.

(3) That Kuroki had a right to reckon upon Marshal Oyama's willingness to send him the Fifth Division and Second Battalion of Foot Artillery,† who should be here in an hour's time.

I doubt myself if, on closer examination, it will be found that any of these suppositions could be answered in the affirmative, and if so I think it must

* No less than four Russian Divisions were available, and with Okasaki Yama in their hands a night attack on and through Hanlasanshi must almost inevitably have succeeded.—I. H.

† This battalion of Foot Artillery was armed with old-fashioned $9\frac{1}{2}$ centimetre bronze mortars conveyed in the ordinary Japanese pony transport carts.

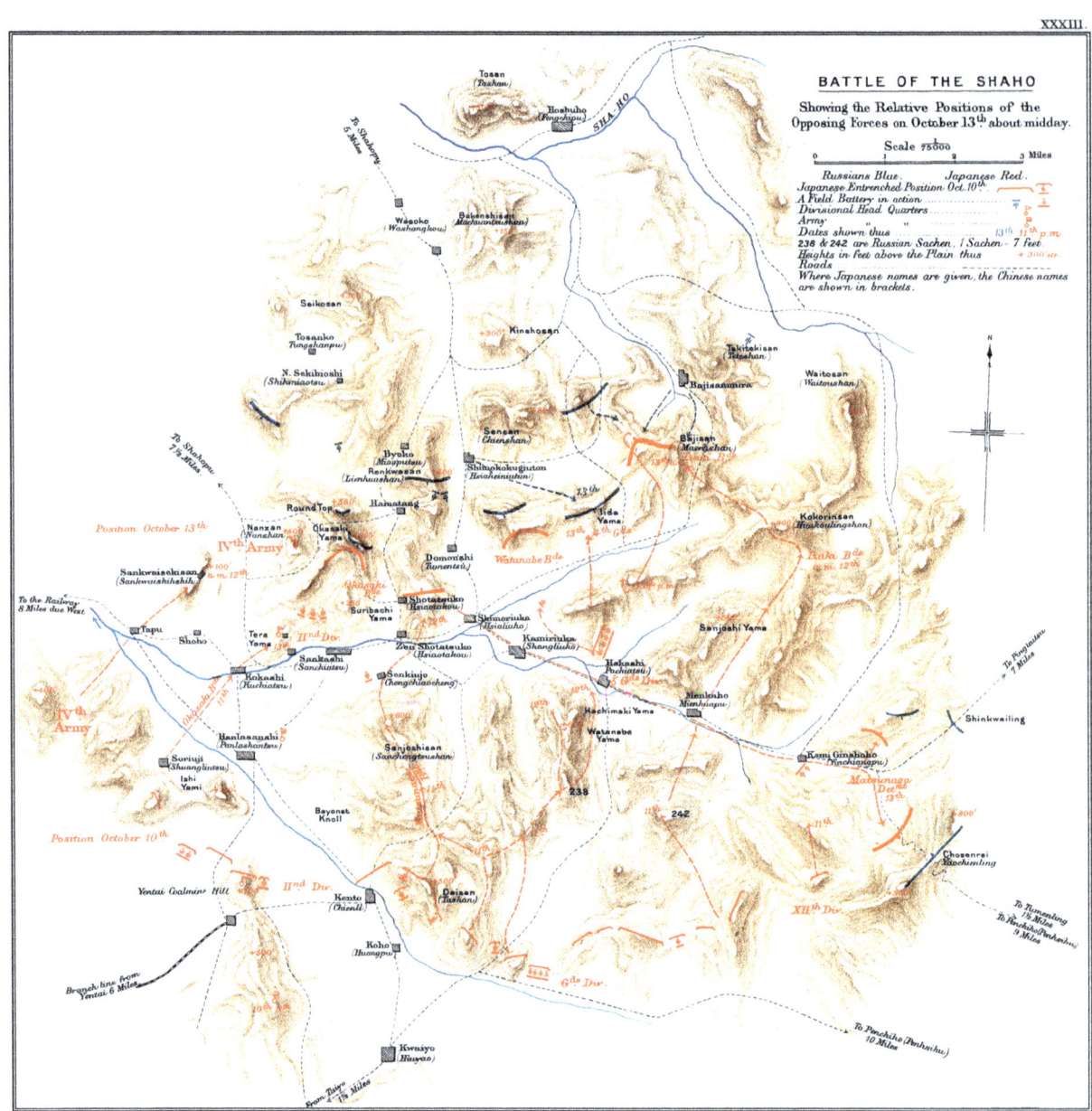

BATTLE OF THE SHAHO
XXXIII
Spread 1

BATTLE OF THE SHAHO
XXXIII
Spread 2

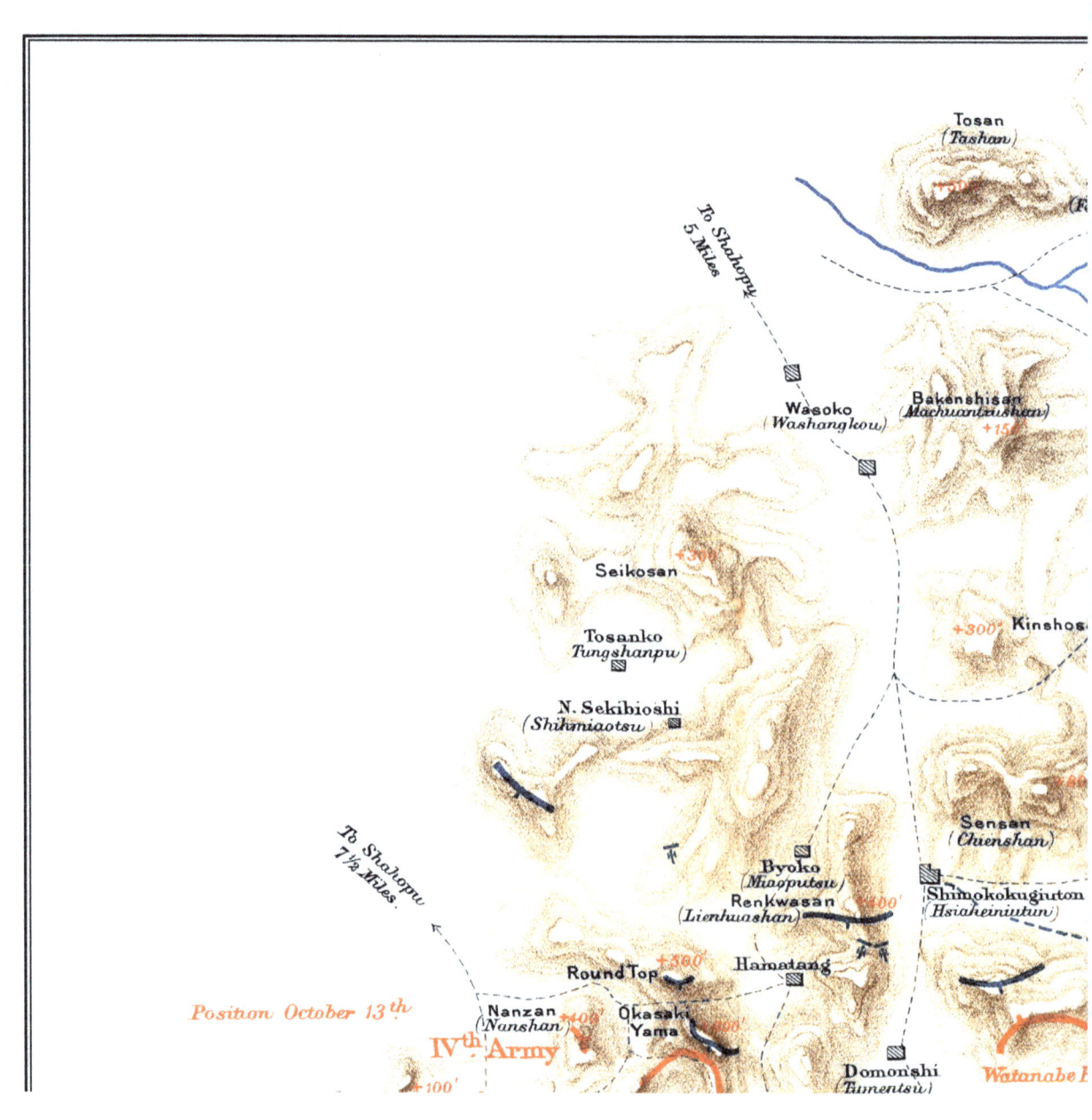

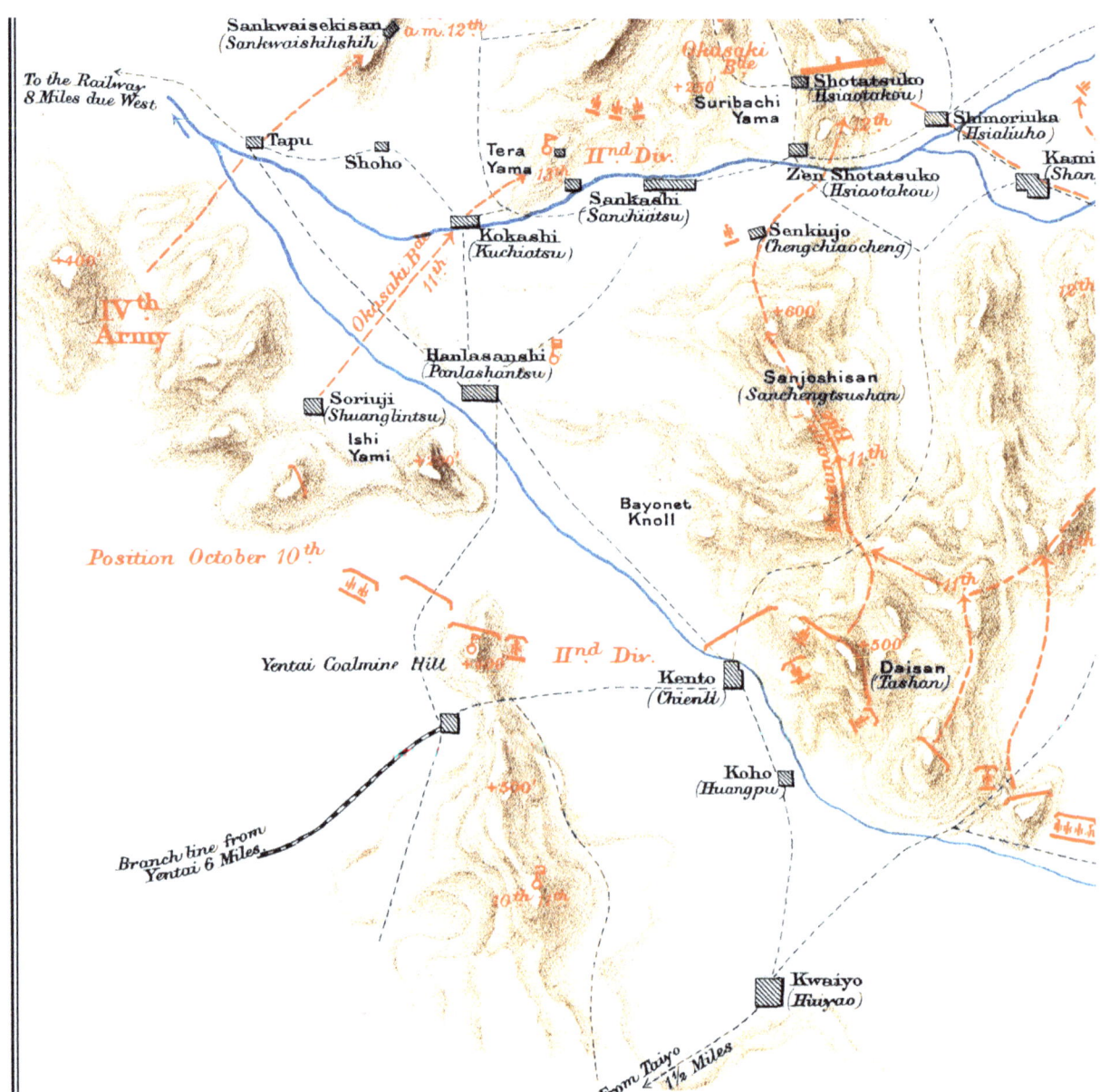

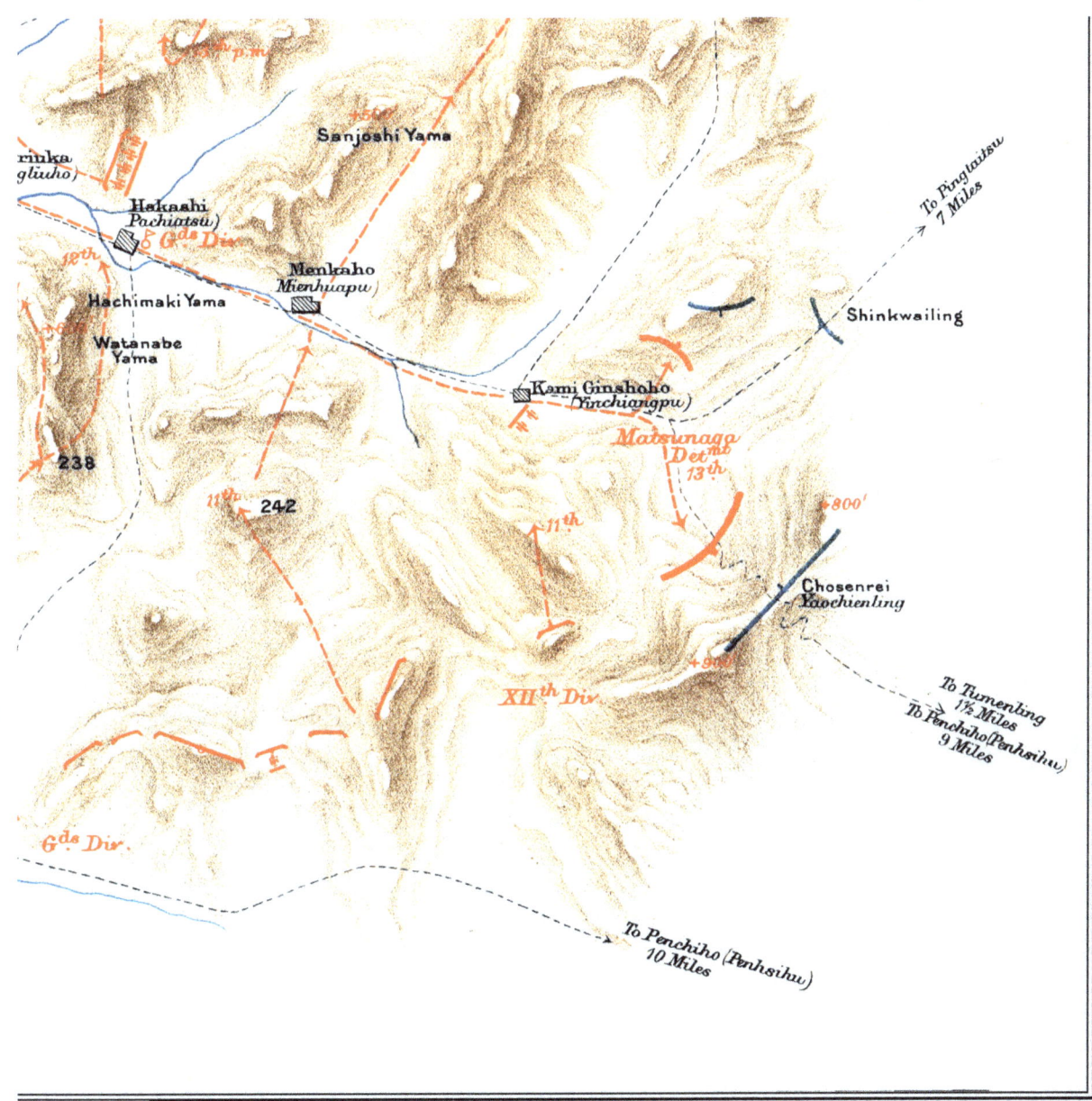

be admitted that the despatch of Matsunaga was one of those over bold strokes to which continued good fortune may sometimes tempt the greatest commanders.

By taking Okasaki Yama, Okasaki has again saved the situation, for, by nightfall, no other success had crowned the efforts of the First Army.

## CHAPTER XXXII

## THE RUSSIANS RECROSS THE SHAHO

*October 14th, 1904, 8 A.M. On the mound north-east of Hanlasanshi.*—The sound of the firing has receded northwards, and I can see nothing from here, but I have been told some particulars regarding the action fought by the Guards yesterday, which emphasise the importance of Okasaki's victory. As I have already noted, the left Guards column was to occupy the hills east of Domonshi, whilst the right column was to take Bajisan, and thence to attack and occupy the big mountain Sensan, from which the retreat of the Russians holding Okasaki Yama and the neighbourhood could have been cut off. (*See* Map XXXIII.)

The right Guards column of six battalions under Izaki, duly attacked and captured Bajisan, but when it endeavoured to force its way across the long, low ridge connecting Bajisan with Sensan, it came under fire from the north-east and north-west, against which it could make no progress. A Russian column then advanced through the village of Shimokokugiuton and made a counter-attack against Izaki's left, whose whole force was thus thrown on the defensive.

The left Guards column started at daybreak for the hills east of Domonshi, but found them occupied by the enemy in such force that, far from being able to attack, the column was forced to entrench and defend itself. Thereupon a large body of the enemy was encouraged to strike boldly at the gap which separated the right and left Guards columns, and in doing so occupied a small hill (now called Iida Yama), midway between the two, thus piercing the centre of the division. Not a moment was to be lost unless a disaster was to ensue. If the Russians on Iida Yama were reinforced they might either continue their advance and capture the Guards artillery, or else, striking out left and right, they might outflank and overthrow both right and left columns.

In this emergency the 4th Guards Regiment, who formed the Divisional Reserve under Colonel Iida were ordered to attack. Iida made a fine advance and effected a lodgment on the knoll which now bears his name. He could not altogether expel the enemy, but he arrested their progress and turned their thoughts away from further offensive action.

Meanwhile, the right column had been driven back by a Russian counter-attack from Bajisanmura,* and continued its retreat for several miles until it re-entered the general alignment which it had first quitted on the night of the 11th-12th, not too wisely I venture to think.†

At midnight, last night, the enemy began a general retirement, and the whole of the First Army, including

* Maerhshan is the Chinese name for Bajisan. Mura means village in Japanese.

† It is difficult to understand how the Japanese on the col between Bajisan and Sensan were allowed to retire without being very seriously punished. They were under fire from Sensan, and the Russians were in occupation of Iida Yama and advancing from Bajisanmura. However, they did get away quite comfortably.

the Fifth Division,* lent to Kuroki by Oyama, is now advancing on the Shaho.

10 A.M.—I have just had the privilege of a few minutes' talk with H.I.H. Prince Kuni. He was pleased to remark that whenever he came out in the morning he always looked first to see if the guns of the enemy were further off, so as to get an idea of how things were going. I said that to achieve the same result I always looked at the faces of the Staff.

I then got leave to go and see Terayama and Okasaki Yama. On Terayama the poor gods were out in the open; both the Japanese and Russian artilleries having combined to knock their abode about their ears. Three gigantic figures especially attracted my attention. They were surrounded by many wounded, and the gods themselves had been stabbed all over by the bayonets of the religious Russian soldiers (*see* Photo.). Altogether a very piteous sight, though the human wounded were being looked after to some extent. The sunken road on the south and south-west of Terayama had afforded the Russians admirable cover. I dismounted and got into it just to make sure my observations were correct from the Russian point of view. It is impossible to imagine more favourable shooting conditions. In most directions the Russian field of fire extended for a clear 1000 yards which was unbroken by even a scrap of cover, and at the worst point of the compass they had a clear 600 yards. In theory it seemed that the defenders had only to lay their rifles flat along the ground and pull the trigger to check any attempt at a *coup de main* like that of Okasaki on the 11th instant. However, it was not so in reality. The Russian dead

* The Fifth Division concentrated last night at Hanlasanshi and Kamiriuka.—I. H.

had not yet been buried. The majority had been killed by shrapnel, but there were a fair number of bayonet wounds also. In the road itself, where the dead were thickest, not many seemed to have been killed by rifle fire.

I next rode to Okasaki Yama. There were still some Japanese dead on the lower slopes. They were all young and looked like boys compared with the big, bearded, middle-aged Russians whose dead (not nearly as many as I expected) were chiefly on the summit. Whilst gazing around I met two soldiers of the 16th Regiment which had carried out the assault. I got into conversation with them through Nakamura, and found that one of them had actually taken part in the desperate struggle I saw at 5 P.M. last night. In answer to a question, he said he had used neither bullet nor bayonet, but had taken to stone-throwing. I asked him why he had done so, seeing it was surely quicker to load and to fire, and he replied that the Russians did it, and that it seemed at the moment to come more handy. I thanked the men, and said every one had yesterday admired the brave regiment. They said something to Nakamura in reply. He did not translate it to me, but I saw him smiling to himself, and asked him to repeat the remark. He then told me the soldier had replied it was an honour to his corps that it should have won the approval of a general of an allied nation. He was a particularly nice-looking boy with a delicate, well-bred face. The other was more of a round-faced country bumpkin. I only note down the incident to show that many of the Japanese private soldiers are perfect gentlemen.

On the scene of the hand-to-hand struggle I watched

Chinese Gods in the Temple on Terayama after the Capture of the Hill by the Okasaki Brigade on October 11

NOTE THE WAY THE IDOLS HAVE BEEN BAYONETED

yesterday with almost horror-stricken attention, there were a number of Russian bayonets. It seems that the Japanese soldiers were able to catch hold of them in the *mêlée* and twist them off. Another Japanese soldier searching about for mementoes here told us that the Russian bayonets were blunt and would not penetrate a thick coat. In proof of his assertion he picked up one or two and showed that the chisel-like edge had become quite dull. The Russians always manœuvre with fixed bayonets, and no doubt they are apt to become blunt under service conditions. Some arrangement will have to be made in future whereby it is impossible for an enemy to grasp a bayonet by the blade and unfix it.

From where I now stand it is easy, without being a great tactician, to see where the Russians made their mistake in yesterday's battle. They had a superiority of numbers, but they were unable, or rather did not seriously attempt, to make these numbers tell. Round Top and Okasaki Yama together did not afford room for the effective employment of more than a regiment. At the most, this terrain gave scope for one battalion on each summit and one battalion entrenched in support a little way down each northern slope. But the Russians had several divisions available. In the old days when weight and cohesion were everything, these might have been used in long columns like battering-rams to drive a hole through one small vital point in the enemy's position. Nowadays the way to employ superiority of force is by occupying or advancing over a wider front than the enemy, and so enveloping him. For it is certain that to cram more troops than can freely use their rifles upon a narrow ridge like Okasaki Yama is merely to offer up victims to the opponents' shrapnel.

There is doubtless a moral support in being surrounded by friends, but in proportion as comrades become corpses the confidence changes into dismay. In my opinion, then, the Russians were bound to clear for themselves a wider frontage, and vigorous counter-attacks upon Suribachiyama and Nanzan would not only have achieved such an object if successful, but even if unsuccessful would have distracted the plans of the Japanese and prevented them from devoting the whole of their deliberate attention, as well as their concentrated artillery fire, to the capture of Okasaki Yama.

At 1 P.M. I rode back towards the knoll north-east of Hanlasanshi. On my way I passed some of the new Fifth Division. The Fourth Army has no military attachés, and in passing along the ranks in the narrow streets of Sankashi I was naturally enough taken by the men for a Russian prisoner of rank.

When I arrived at the Hanlasanshi knoll, I found Kuroki engaged in conversation with an officer who had just come in from the staff of the generalissimo. He was quite the typical, army head-quarters staff officer. He wore a smart, new greatcoat with a fur collar and bright, polished buttons which made all our old garments almost rend themselves in envy and despite. As customary, too, he was received with a very special deference. He has brought us a copy of a proclamation issued by Kuropatkin to his army, of which I am to have a translation. Its general tenor is that he was sorry not to let his army stay and fight it out at Liaoyang, but that a better opportunity had now offered. I am sure the Japanese think precisely the contrary.

I hear that the whole of the Russians are now in retreat, and that on our right Matsunaga has joined hands with the Twelfth Division, and is in full pursuit. Also that last night Okasaki had some more stiff fighting near Renkwasan. As soon as it was dark he moved north-eastwards across the valley to the east of Okasaki Yama. The Russians were posted on a hill just to the west of Renkwasan. They held their ground with determination, and again bayonets and hand grenades superseded the bullet, more legitimately than in the daylight contest on Okasaki Yama. Eventually the Russians were driven off, and they fell back on Hamatang. It is said that Marshal Oyama has written a Kanjo* for Okasaki.

5 P.M.—There has been a lot of thunder and icy rain, which must have caused the troops very great discomfort, and must have killed off hundreds of wounded who might otherwise have had a chance.

HANLASANSHI, 10 P.M.—We are all together again in a Chinese hut. Apparently the Russians have only fought rearguard actions to-day, and are now all across the Shaho. The Fifth Division got to Waitosan on the Shaho by 2 P.M. and wished to push on. Kuroki was inclined to consent, but Manchurian Army Headquarters would not hear of it. Amongst other things found on the top of Okasaki Yama was the sword of the brave Russian officer who led the charge down the hill. The point was encrusted with blood for about three inches, so the poor fellow got it well home into some one before he fell.

And so the great battle is over. What an experience! My mind refuses to take it all in, and I am sure I have stored up food for reflection for the rest of my life.

* A Kanjo is a written approval, a much-prized reward for either a unit or an individual.

## CHAPTER XXXIII

### THE LITTLE MAN IN GREEN

HANLASANSHI, *October 15th*, 1904.—If any confirmation were needed of our information that the fighting is over for the present, it would be furnished by the arrival of a posse of workmen from headquarters who have begun to repaper the windows and clean the place up generally; a sure indication always of a halt of some duration. But there has been a good deal of firing in front of the Second Army, and I hear that they are attacking and endeavouring to force the enemy across the river at a place called Shakaho.*

I do not myself believe that Kuropatkin's scheme of putting the bulk of his troops on his left and endeavouring to turn the Japanese right at Penchiho was sound. Stakelberg apparently concentrated at Fushun, and meant by marching in a curve of 180 degrees, *via* Penchiho, to turn the Japanese right and arrive at Liaoyang. Mountains lend themselves to delaying operations by a weaker force, and it might have been foreseen that Umezawa, with what assistance he could get from the Twelfth Division, would be able, by taking up successive positions, to delay the progress of a force even such as Stakelberg's, which is said to have consisted of four divisions of infantry and a division of cavalry. Meanwhile, the right wing of the Russians would be exposed to the risk of being crushed

* Chinese, Shahopu, near where the railway crosses the Shaho.

by a direct Japanese advance along the clear and easy main road and railway, and by the routes leading northwards from the Yentai coal-mines. Had Stakelberg possessed a separate line of communications to the north-east or east, then perhaps Kuropatkin's scheme might have been worth trying. But this was not so, and Stakelberg's line of communications started, as a matter of fact, from his base to the north of Mukden. Oyama's idea was to advance left in front, and to endeavour to turn the enemy's right. By so doing he hoped not only to push him from the railway, but drive him altogether eastwards, into the mountains and away from Mukden and his communications which he could only then have regained by a long and circuitous march northwards. Oyama was content to run a fair amount of risk on his own right at Penchiho for the chance of so great a gain, feeling confident that any success on the direct road would quickly cause a halt to be called to a commander operating in circuitous fashion along a curve of 180 degrees. Oyama's plan fell short of complete success because the Russians fought stoutly and had too many troops still in hand on their right and centre, notwithstanding the powerful force they had detached to their left under Stakelberg.

To deal out destructive criticism, pure and simple, does not however appreciably advance knowledge. I will try my humble best then to put forward an alternative proposal. Suppose I had had the honour of being staff officer to Kuropatkin, what sort of a scheme of attack would I have drafted for his approval?

In brief, my plan would have been to concentrate the main Russian force near Hanlasanshi, whilst I merely played with the Japanese right by demonstrating against it with inferior forces just to keep it occupied. I would have opened the ball by making a night march with a special detachment with which I should have endeavoured to turn Marshal Oyama's left by the right bank of the Kongo. The force for this purpose would have been one infantry division and all the cavalry and horse artillery. Another of my columns would have marched south along the line of the railway, but the great bulk of my troops would have concentrated, as I have just said, on the line Hanlasanshi–Domonshi.* Full initiative must have been given to the commanders on either wing, as their communications would have been practically *en l'air*. Then at a given moment I would have thrust with all my energy and force at the Japanese centre, and must have broken it. Kuropatkin knew well the position of the Japanese divisions and their strengths before he despatched Stakelberg to the East. It was impossible to keep him indefinitely ignorant of their distribution. He knew then that he was in superior force, and that he was stronger generally opposite the Japanese right centre, but probably he did not quite gauge how weak, how very weak, was Kuroki between the Second Division and the Imperial Guards. Still, he must have realised something, and even if I had found myself his staff officer under the faulty conditions of the plan he actually adopted, I would have done my best to induce him to strike one good, downright blow just on the right of the Second Division, or on the left of the Guards.

It seems to me, in the wisdom that comes after the event, that the chief of the staff to Kuropatkin might have advised his commander on some such lines, and that if his advice had been acted upon the battle might

* Chinese, Panlashantsu-Tumentsu.

not, after all, have ended so very badly for the Russians, although certainly their advance on Liaoyang must in any case have been defeated. The fact is our First Army was at its very weakest between the Second Division and the Guards, and it was a touch-and-go affair on that part of the terrain until the night of the 13th. Up till then, if the Russians had come on with the four divisions which they had available on the line Hanlasanshi–Domonshi, and had *hardiment menés l'attaque de nuit, ça aurait réussi.*

The battle of the Shaho, which must, from every point of view, be considered one of the most important engagements ever fought upon this planet, will doubtless form a favourite text for the dissertations of able historians. Numbers will be checked and weighed in the balances of time and opportunity. Maps will be studied and masses of individual testimonies will be sifted and carefully checked. Not until then can any authoritative judgment be pronounced on the commanders and troops on either side. Still, it must also be remembered that time spent in careful investigations is not altogether time gained. During the next few months many fables will be invented and many individuals will have realised that it is to their advantage to confuse and darken the issues. I am therefore less inclined to apologise than perhaps I ought to be that I have ventured to set forth, here on the very ground, an opinion which is certainly as sincere as it is strong.

I have written the foregoing whilst waiting for an important officer in his quarters, in a small room in a Chinese Temple. The air is thick with cigarette smoke. An adjutant, who has been up all the previous night, sits at a table hardly able to keep his eyes open for sleepiness. On the kong, a small orderly-room clerk is squatting down like a statue of Buddha, writing orders with a paint-brush and indian ink, each character a masterpiece of art.

HANLASANSHI. *October 16th, 1904.*—Slight frost last night. A lovely day to be alive; a feeling emphasised by the surrounding battalions of dead on whom the earth does in truth lie lightly, so lightly that everywhere they seem to be struggling to escape and walk again on this beautiful autumn morning.

I have managed to secure a statement of the number of Russians actually buried on the battle-field up to dusk yesterday evening. Here it is:

| | |
|---|---|
| Left bank of Taitsuho . . . . . | 350 |
| Taling and Tumenling . . . . . | 500 |
| Heights north and south of Kamiriuka (Shanlingho). . . . | 600 |
| Heights north and south of Shotatsuko (Hsiao Takou). . . . | 1000 |
| Neighbourhood of Sankashi (Sanchiatsu). . | 600 |
| ,, of Seikosan * . . . | 300 |
| Various scattered spots . . . . | 300 |

This makes a total of 3650 dead who have actually received interment; but judging merely from my own observation in the immediate neighbourhood, the very least that can be added on for corpses still unburied is 10 per cent., making a total of 4000. According to

---

* This was the scene of a fight witnessed by Vincent on the 14th between the left of Okasaki's Brigade and the right of the Fourth Army, against a Russian rearguard packed very close upon a ridge. The ridge was swept from the south by artillery of the Second Division and from the south-west by the artillery of the Fourth Army. All the losses, practically, were caused by shrapnel. The number of dead stated to have been buried is corroborated in this instance by information I received from an officer of the 40th Regiment, who was actually engaged in the work.

recognised custom, the killed should be multiplied by five to arrive at the total casualties, which thus amount to 20,000.

The dead Russians in front of the Second and Fourth Armies are reported to be 4000, and on the same principle the total losses of Kuropatkin must number fully 40,000. As the action was, for the first time in the campaign, a *bataille de rencontre*, and as the Russians had not therefore the advantage of field works, the more extended formations of the Japanese and their intelligent use of the ground told heavily in their favour. They do not reckon their loss at more than 10,000, and they are in a position, which Russia is not, to replace these losses promptly. Man for man the Japanese reckon they can place troops at Mukden in one-third of the time in which the Russians can hope to do so. So at least they say, although I think the comparison is somewhat sanguine.

HANLANSANSHI. *October 17th, 1904.*—At the tail of all the self-congratulation of yesterday's entries, a small regrettable incident has crept, belated, half ashamed to show its face, but still, refusing to be altogether ignored. Yesterday, the Fifth Division marched back to rejoin the Fourth Army, leaving one battalion behind to hold Waitosan.* Last night a Russian regiment attacked the battalion and recaptured Waitosan after a stiff fight.

But this is not all. We hear rumours from servants and interpreters that the Fourth Army has lost ten guns. Ordinarily, I pay no attention to camp rumours, which are as numerous and fully as un-

* Waitosan (Chinese, Waitoushan) is called by the Russians "Temple Hill." This must not be confounded with Terayama or "Temple Hill," captured by the Okasaki Brigade on October 11th.

authentic with the Japanese armies as with our own, but a report of defeat and disaster is something new, and must, I think, have some foundation on fact.

HANLASANSHI. *October 18th, 1904.*—At 2 P.M., Colonel Satow came in, and said he was ordered to read us out an information.

The communication was as follows: "As the enemy was resisting very stubbornly at Shakaho (Shahopu) in front of the Second Army, the 5th Brigade of the Tenth Division, Fourth Army, was ordered to march against the left flank of the enemy with one Brigade of Field Artillery and one Brigade of Mountain Artillery. The brigadier crossed the river and attacked the left flank of the Russian position at Shakaho (Shahopu) on the 16th instant. As, however, the enemy held on with great determination, he received orders to retire. At that very moment the enemy attacked the Brigade in great force and fury. A confused, bloody combat ensued, which lasted long into the night. Both sides fell back simultaneously, but the Brigade found that in the course of the engagement it had lost nine field guns and five Mountain guns."

I am very glad indeed that the Japanese have told us their bad news so frankly. Satow delivered the message very well. I merely said, "Such incidents must always happen in war," and he bowed.

So far as I can recollect, this reverse is the first of its sort that has been suffered by a Japanese army for many years. There was no similar misfortune during the war with China, and there has been none, so far, in Manchuria.

HANLASANSHI, *October 20th, 1904.*—I had a long talk to-day with a staff officer, mainly about Port

Arthur and the effects of the eleven-inch howitzers. It appears they have hit the ships in harbour several times, and that once General Nogi can sink them some of his army will probably be brought up here.* The Eighth Division has arrived at Yentai Coal-Mines, and two more Kobi Brigades will also soon arrive in the fighting line. The enemy in our front are entrenching themselves heavily. It is the earnest hope of the Japanese that the Russians will soon sally forth and attack them again. The fact that Kuropatkin decided to come south and fight the last battle, instead of falling back and awaiting Oyama at Taling, north of Mukden, was the most splendid piece of good fortune that could possibly have happened to Japan. So the Head-Quarters here think it is not too much, perhaps, to hope that the Russians may repeat their mistake and have another fight; when it is impossible to say, of course, who would win, but when the battle would, any way, be finally decisive of the campaign, one way or another.

As regards the guns captured from the Fourth Army, it turns out that the loss of the brigade was only some 500 men. The guns were taken after dark, when they were in column of route. The Japanese opinion is that the Fifth Brigade went too far in the first place, and that in the second place the retreat could not have been well conceived or carried out from the tactical point of view. If a retreat has to take place by night it is obvious that the infantry must not fall back until the guns and train have got a good start of them. After that, when the main body of the infantry falls back it must still leave a strong rear-

* I omit all the Port Arthur news, as it does not immediately concern the First Army

guard behind it, and when, as in the present case, a comparatively small force has penetrated into the enemy's country, flank guards also become absolutely necessary. Had such principles been acted upon by the Commander of the Fifth Brigade on the night of the 16th-17th October, then, although the infantry were exterminated, the guns at least might have escaped. Supposing, however, that the guns had been captured after very heavy losses had been suffered, then no one could have said one word. But 500 casualties is not enough to set against the capture by the enemy of fourteen guns. The brigadier was too courageous— that is the long and short of it. The young officers of the First Army, on hearing of the disaster, say, "This is very wholesome and salutary for us all, and will teach us to be cautious on future occasions."

In the afternoon I went with Vincent for a walk, and we took the direction of the mountain Daisan (Sketch XXIV.) which we determined to scale. When we were still along way off we noticed the head and shoulders of a man against the sky-line on the summit. As a very extensive view can be obtained from the top of Daisan, it seemed possible that the Japanese might have posted a look-out sentry there; and so, as we have both had some narrow escapes lately from revolvers and rifles levelled at us under a misapprehension, we were careful to walk up in such a way as to give no reasonable ground for suspicion. That is to say, we advanced up the bare spur as ostentatiously as possible, took out our handkerchiefs and blew our noses and talked to one another, just to show we were not the scouts of the enemy. When a mountain gets very steep at the last stage of the ascent, however, the climber has not much breath to spare for such demonstrations, and that, I suppose, must account for the complete frustration of our precautions by the event. For, as we topped the crest line and stepped on to the little flat plateau at the summit, we became aware of a little Japanese figure in a greatcoat and uniform of a greenish hue sitting there, looking northwards through his field glasses. On hearing our footsteps he turned his head, and, seeing us for the first time, sprang to his feet, his face convulsed with terror. He had a long staff in his hand, and he kept striking the ground with its point and stamping with rage, evidently quite beside himself, as he endeavoured to edge away towards the shelter of a rock, from the other side of which he could, we knew, call for help to the picquet on the next hill and make a fuss generally.

Vincent talks Japanese fluently enough, and he tried to reason with our ally, telling him who we were and where we came from, but it was all of no sort of use; he might as well have addressed himself to the winds. The man was completely distraught. Never shall I forget the picture he made, or the alternating expressions of fear and fury which passed across his face. He looked, with his green clothes and his staff and his stamping foot and his mingled glances of horror and rage as if he had escaped from some fairy tale to torment us. At last I stepped forward—he would have struck me had I come within distance—and put my card, whereon my rank and name were clearly written in Japanese characters, on a big stone. I suppose the idea that raiding Cossacks do not first present their visiting cards to their intended victims must then have penetrated his mind. Any way, still keeping his staff raised in readiness to strike, he cautiously approached the stone after I had as cautiously withdrawn, holding my hands well outstretched so as to show that no treachery lurked behind my modest bit of pasteboard. Then, when from the corner of his eye he had mastered the inscription, he did at last become half convinced that we were not as we seemed, but, on the contrary, a pair of honest gentlemen out for air and exercise. He saluted, and we even had some conversation.

A military attaché must never lose an opportunity. Whether in love or war, recreation or work, he has to keep a sharp look-out not to lose the smallest chance of gaining information. So, as soon as we ascertained that our new acquaintance was a doctor, we questioned him about his hospitals. He told us he had been absolutely chock full ever since the middle of August. He had kept careful notes of the description of wounds in his own hospital, and had often discussed the point with his brother medicos; and he thought that if bullet wounds were put at 100, shrapnel wounds would stand at a ratio of about 20 and bayonet wounds at 2. He had been with the First Army since February, but he had never heard of our existence until now. Even after this agreeable conversation, our new friend was by no means at his ease. So he removed himself from our society as soon as he could politely do so, and afterwards we saw him deep in consultation with the non-commissioned officer and some men of a neighbouring post, who were all regarding us with much interest.

I have come to the fixed determination not to go out again without a Japanese soldier as escort. Two days ago, as I ran round a hillock to warm my feet, I had a loaded rifle pointed slap at me by a sentry, and I have always thought the habit of levelling firearms at people's heads unnecessarily dangerous. Yesterday a gendarme pulled out a revolver at Vincent, making him so voluble in Japanese that if only the examiner at Tokio could have heard him, he would have passed, I am sure, with honours; and to-day we have had the worst adventure of all. For there is not a shadow of doubt in my mind that had our doctor possessed a revolver, it would have been a case of shooting first and explanations afterwards. I am fond of adventures, and, at one time or another, a goodly number have come my way, but enough is as good as a feast. To be shot by a doctor would be a silly end to a life which has afforded me some interest. Ended by a doctor some day I must be, I admit. It is the common fate, but a pistol is not a legitimate weapon for the purpose.

## CHAPTER XXXIV

### BANQUETS AND REVELS

HANLASANSHI, *October 21st, 1904*.—A bitterly cold wind is blowing, although there is not yet anything specifically Siberian about the temperature—not more than four or five degrees of frost at most, I fancy. I went for another walk with Vincent, but after our experience of yesterday we made a sergeant-major come with us, although it was much against the grain. He thinks we are mad thus to clamber up and down mountains for no ostensible profit or amusement.

Our companion was in an unusually communicative mood. He would not admit that any soldiers were tired of war's alarms or anxious to seek repose in the bosom of their families, except perhaps a few of the city-bred men. I see that he considers it natural that a cockney should be less enduring in his patriotism than a rustic.

I am inclined to agree. A peasant cultivating even the tiniest patch of his own is in rather a different mental relation towards his country from a merchant who mainly makes money out of it, or a factory hand who draws upon it for wages. He owns a bit of it. I have seen stretches of a foreign country farmed on a big scale with machinery and hired labour and hard by I have compared it with a succession of small holdings. From the point of view of farming, there is no comparison. Cultivation on the grand scale brings most out of mother earth. But, from the point of view of humanity, there is no comparison either. The peasant owner is a man; a proud, strong, independent man, who has a stake in his country. Those are the fellows we want as soldiers; the yeomen who have been from the beginning of history and will to be its end, the very backbone of empires.

From the subject of the soldiers, our non-commissioned officer went on to remark that the Japanese nation would not feel they had received full value in the way of a war unless they had casualties totalling up to at least 200,000. He thinks the First Army is getting on very nicely, as one-third of those who embarked in February for Korea have now either died or returned sick to Japan. We do not regard our wars from such a standpoint; nor I fancy do the Japanese either; but it pleases him to say so, and certainly I have often had occasion to notice that, far from attempting to minimise their losses, our allies are, if anything, inclined to exaggerate them. I think our friend is spinning yarns for our benefit. He informs us that the people of Kyushu are of a fickle, fiery and impulsive temperament (*Ki ga michigai*). The Twelfth Division are entirely drawn from Kyushu, and they are desperate fellows for an attack, for when their blood is up there is nothing that will stop them. The best bluejackets come from near Shimonoseki and from Yamaguchi and Kigoshima. The best soldiers in the army, by common consent, are the Second Division from Sendai. They are men whose character is solid and reliable, and who are not too quick-tempered. Finally we were told that at the Penchiho night attack the Russians shouted out a sentence of Japanese which they had learnt by heart, "The Russians are coming, the Russians are coming!" "However," added our informant, "they did not come so very far after all." It is, perhaps, hardly worth while burdening my note-book with such bald chat, but just for once in a way it is as well to include a record of the opinions, queer, partial and uninformed as they may be, of a non-commissioned officer of cavalry.

In the afternoon I went over a Field Hospital belonging to the Second Division at Sankashi. There are altogether 780 of the Division in hospital, of whom only 30 are sick, the rest being wounded. Sixteen wounded Russians have been brought in, but all, except one, have been sent away. The doctor who took us round told us that more than one half of the wounds were from shrapnel bullets, and that there are only ten bayonet wounds now under treatment. Both these statements would, however, be misleading unless supplemented by the further information we received during our inspection, namely, that the excess of shrapnel wounds was mainly owing to the whole of Okasaki's Brigade getting bunched up on Terayama immediately after its capture, when they were subjected to a very severe bombardment; secondly, to the fact that the Russian bayonet with its thin weak shaft and blunt chisel point does not penetrate a thick coat, but almost invariably bends. We have all seen bent Russian bayonets lying about the scenes of conflict, so this is no doubt true, and must be a very encouraging factor to the Japanese *moral* when they come to close quarters with their adversaries. The pluck of the patients we saw was quite admirable. They are one and all burning to get back to their regiments; so much so indeed, that the doctors say they fret, and that their recovery is thereby retarded. The politeness of the brave fellows is almost superhuman. The sick, even those sick unto death, try to raise themselves on their hands and knees to bow to the foreign officers.

In the evening I met a friend on the Staff who had just come back from an interview with the Marshal Oyama. In the course of conversation, the great Marquis said, "If the First Army does not take any guns, it cannot expect a *Kanjo* (letter of appreciation), to which my friend, playing on the word, replied, "Your Excellency need not trouble, we will get our *Kanjo* (they must pay the shot) from the enemy."

HANLASANSHI, *October 25th.*—Jardine has returned full of information after a ten days' stay with a cavalry regiment. His first appearance was an awful shock, and he overheard the cavalry colonel utter the Japanese equivalent for d—— when he was told a foreigner had come to be attached to his command. Every one I think will have full sympathy for his sentiments. Nothing however could have been kinder than his treatment of Jardine. He and five other officers shared a small Chinese room 12 feet by 12 feet, and he was able, from the facilities placed at his disposal, to get an idea of pretty well everything that went on from orderly room and drill to reconnaissance and manœuvre.

To combine exercise with news, I took him with me for a walk to Bayonet Knoll, the little hill on which I saw the Russian detachment circumvented by a section of Matsunaga's men from Daisan. (Sketch XXIV.)

Looking over the ground I refreshed my memory of that dramatic little affair, and realised, even more forcibly than on the 11th instant, what a striking example it had furnished of the excellence of the Japanese soldier. His love of fighting and his individuality combine to render him almost independent of leadership and formations, once he has been fairly launched on the attack. The functions of the Japanese officers are mainly to administer and to instruct. Their leading is noble, could not be more dashing; but it is not really so necessary in battle as it is with most other nations. The question of formations is vital in Europe, because they are one of the instruments whereby commanders endeavour to bring their troops to the desired spot with a minimum of loss, and make available, at the right moment, the requisite weight of fire or steel to break through the enemy's defence. But, if every private soldier is absolutely determined to get to close quarters with his foe, and is sufficiently intelligent to use ground to the best advantage in doing so, then half at least, and the most difficult half, of the objects sought by drill, formations and leadership is already a national attribute. This is doubtless what was meant by a festive officer in the far-away days of Fenghuangcheng, when he insisted on how much more quickly the Japanese could turn a peasant into a soldier than the Germans.

10 P.M.—Colonel Satow has brought us a telegram saying that the Baltic Fleet has sunk one British ship and damaged two others in the Dover Straits. No one can understand what this means, and many disbelieve it.

HANLASANSHI, *October 27th*, 1904.—Hume has come back from seeing the Japanese recapture Waitosan from the Russians. As it projects well out into the valley of the Shaho, the Japanese should now be able to keep an eye on the proceedings of the enemy. Hume gave us a vivid account of a Russian officer rallying his men after they had fairly forsaken their trenches. He ran after them, stopped them, entreated them, and finally brought them back in a fine rush which recaptured the trenches, into which only about a dozen Japanese had so far penetrated. A gallant fellow! Let us hope he got the cross of St. George. There was a celebration to-day of the victory on Okasaki Yama. Okasaki himself rode a very fine captured Russian horse.

HANLASANSHI, *October 28th*, 1904.—An officer of the Manchurian Army Headquarters Staff rode over to see us, and to discuss the Russian Baltic Fleet and its strange behaviour. I do not think the incident will end in war, but many here are of a different opinion.

I was told that the captured Japanese guns had been used already to fire back at our lines along the Shaho. Also that two of them had been paraded through the streets of Mukden. I asked what was the attitude of the Chinese Governor, and was answered by a Japanese proverb, "He waits until he sees the colour of the standard."

HANLASANSHI, *October 29th*, 1904.—Nothing to-day but excitement about the Russian fleet and our fisher boats. The Japanese are greatly stirred.

HANLASANSHI, *October 30th*, 1904.—Baltics are flat to-day.

HANLASANSHI, *November 3rd*, 1904.—This is the auspicious date on which the Emperor celebrates his birthday. Immediately after luncheon, I put on my sword, and went round to congratulate General Kuroki and his Imperial Highness Prince Kuni. I found them both sitting in a little tent which was pitched in the courtyard of their house. The Prince unfortunately was suffering from a touch of influenza. We were having the usual sort of conversation, when everything was illuminated by the entrance upon the scene of the gallant General Okasaki, wearing all his medals and waving in his hand a small Japanese flag. He was, in fact, as gay and debonair as a man ought to be on his wedding-day. He gave his little flag, with a flourish, to Prince Kuni; he caught Vincent by both hands over some small joke, and shook him to and fro in pretended annoyance. In fact, he was essentially human and delightful, more like a vivacious Irishman in high good spirits than the reserved and very correct Japanese.

I told him he must go a bit slower in his victorious career, or he would kill the unfortunate foreign attachés who, hard as they may work with their pens and ink to keep pace with his exploits, were yet left hopelessly in arrears. He said, pointing to General Kuroki, "My instructions came from his Excellency; I passed them on to my regimental commanders, and they and their men carried them out to a successful issue!"

I asked him if some tea he had sent me long ago in a present had been grown in his own garden, when he laughed very much and said, "The tea was Russian tea, and the garden it sprang from was my sword."

When we got back we had a grand dinner, and went afterwards to the play, which was held in a Russian barrack-room. Our entrance disturbed the "turn" which was in progress, and the proceedings were still more interrupted by soldiers bringing us each a little bowl of claret, served with dried fish cakes and sweet biscuits. An English audience would probably have been annoyed, but the Japanese certainly were not. Then, to my surprise, Marquis —— rose, and, thumping on a table for silence, turned towards the audience and began to speak. I caught my own name, and then every one in the theatre stood up; so it suddenly flashed across me that I was being introduced to the crowd. I jumped to my feet, and bowed respectfully in every direction. This seemed to be all correct and in order, and the people were just about to sit down when the Post Commandant began a speech, saying that the foreign officers and the Lieutenant-General had done him a great honour in coming to witness his poor entertainment, and that he must apologise for its roughness, poverty, and general inadequacy for such an occasion, to which I made what reply I best could.

The curtain was a red blanket held up by two soldiers, who lay down on a given signal. Instead of rising, therefore, it fell, and the play then began; not exactly a play, but what the Japanese call a sword dance. The actor had to avenge his brother, and he went through a pantomime of adoring his sword and of killing a man with it. All this took a very long time, and was greatly appreciated by the audience. I admired the lightning quickness with which he whipped out the blade, and delivered the deadly sweeping cut from under.

Next appeared a Chinaman from the village, who gave us a love-song on a sort of zither. He played well, laying his instrument flat upon the stage, and striking it with two little hammers. He was a man of middle age, of an intellectual type of countenance. Indeed, a serene and noble-looking man. Some people think Chinese and Japanese resemble one another. I can only say that it is impossible to conceive any members of the human race less like one another than the Japanese warrior, with menacing gestures, waving, glittering sword, bare arms, and a wisp of white cloth knotted tightly round his temples, and, on the other hand, the mild and melancholy performer on the zither. After the love-song, Nakamura produced a great effect by coming out in front of the curtain and announcing, " A very, *very* pretty girl will now sing ! "

All things are possible, and there was quite a sensation. The curtain fell, and before us stood a brawny soldier of the line dressed as a geisha, who was received with a roar of amused disappointment. But he proved to be a dancer light as air, and sang, too, of love and cherry blossoms as if he had been to the manner born.

Last of all, a Chinese band took possession of the stage and fairly let themselves go. I never heard such a row. An earnest old man beat a drum even more conscientiously than the gentlemen with pince-nez who perform at Mr. Wood's concerts in the Queen's Hall; not intermittently, however, but continuously like the drum at the end of Tchaikoffsky's 1812 symphony. There were cymbals large and loud, and cymbals small and piercing. A big gong of the "come to dinner" sort. A small gong set in a frame and struck every half-second by a boy armed with a miniature polo stick. Two reed instrumentalists who, in their efforts to compete with the cymbals, blew out their cheeks to an extent I should not have believed possible. Either Chinamen have stronger lungs than Europeans or else the walls of their cheeks must be much more elastic. Last on my list, but not least in performance, was the player of what must certainly be the germ from which sprang our church organs. A powerful musician, scarlet and perspiring from his exertions, blew hurricanes into a thing which looked like an average-sized teapot through a pipe which resembled an average teapot spout. Round the teapot were set pipes, the longest about one foot, the shortest perhaps four or five inches. These had holes cut within half an inch of their base, just like the holes in an organ pipe. Altogether this astonishing band has, I believe, enabled me to realise the feelings of the Philistine who goes to hear Wagner because it is the fashion.

The end of all things was the entry of a body of stalwart line of communications troops, who marched in with steady tramp in double rank, halted, fronted, and sang the National Anthem,* in which we all joined, standing up at "attention" in our places.

COAL-MINES, *November 4th*, 1904.—General reaction after yesterday. Sumino tells me that arrangements are made when a free issue of saké is issued to the troops on such an occasion as yesterday to provide total abstainers with an alternative, so that it should not be possible to say the State was encouraging the vice of drinking. Thus yesterday three-fifths of the army refused saké and received in lieu a packet of sweetmeats. There is a camp rumour to the effect that Kuropatkin has destroyed all the bridges in rear of his army, so that the next battle must be a case of victory or death. This supposed desperate resolve is, however, somewhat discounted by the fact that within a couple of weeks the rivers will be frozen solid.

COAL-MINES, *November 9th*, 1904.—When I got up

---

\* The Japanese national anthem is difficult to translate. The literal English equivalent is as follows: "Dynasty of the Emperor, 1000 years and 8000 years, till pebbles lined with moss and became a big stone." I am sure it cannot be satisfactorily rendered into ordinary smooth English verses. But, greatly daring, I venture to submit a humble attempt to reproduce the idea and the swing:

The great rocks—the great rocks and the pebble stones
      Suffer change, sad and strange.
The Emperor! The Emperor and his dynasty—
      Gods divine—deathless line!

this morning at 7 o'clock I found the whole place in confusion, several fatigue-parties being busily engaged in covering the house with flags. It was the King's birthday, and by-and-by officers began to come in with congratulations, and even sometimes with highly acceptable gifts. At 8 o'clock Captain Tanaka appeared, bringing with him an enormous case of the best champagne as a present from the Marquis Oyama. So as to be first in the field he had started in the dark and bitter cold at 6 A.M. from Manchurian Army Headquarters. Another officer arrived conveying the felicitations of Generals Kodama and Fukushima. Next came Lieutenant-Colonel Kurita on behalf of General Kuroki, accompanied by the adjutant of His Imperial Highness Prince Kuni, and, in short, I found myself drinking the King's health in champagne and holding an informal sort of levée between the hours of eight and eleven. Tanaka was the last to leave, and he celebrated the auspicious occasion by dedicating to me three poems about Kuropatkin, which he signed "Tommy Atkins."

I will first give my English rendering; then the Japanese with the literal translations. The first verse is all a skilful punning play on the names of the leading generals. Thus Kuropato, the black pigeon; Oyama, big mountain; Kuroki, black tree; &c.

### THE ENEMY'S CHIEF.[*]

#### No. 1.

In the great mountain, by the eternal snows,
So far it is, a gloomy forest grows,
'Neath which dark bloodstains mark the fatal spot
Where the black pigeon felt the deadly shot.

---

[*] In Japanese Kuropatkin means Black Pigeon.

## Banquets and Revels

### No. 2.
He turned to gaze once more on Rama's shrine:—
O'er all its memories of mirth and wine
The same moon shone! He spurred his charger white *
And vanished like a snowstorm in the night.

### No. 3.
The mountains shake and shudder to their core,
As Echo spreads the cannon's hollow roar;
The pigeon, the black pigeon, wings his flight
For distant fields before the fall of night.

### No. 1.
*Kuropato* no bakuyei.
*Oyama* no *Oku* no *Kodama* ni
　osoreken
*Kuroki* hato yoyo
　*Nozumai* wo shite.

Far up in the great mountain in black trees he brought down a black pigeon with a small bullet.

### No. 2.
Furikaeri Tekisho ikami
Nagameken ikuyo
　minareshi ramato no
　tswki.

Turning back the enemy's chief gazes upon and sees how night after night used to look the moon of Rama's pagoda

### No. 3.
The black pigeon frightened by the echoes in the mountains flies to sleep "in the field" during the night.

At night a grand banquet was given in honour of our King. The walls of the dining-hall were decorated with Japanese flags, and also with the word "Hurrah!" done in huge Gothic letters by Nakamura. The letters were formed by pasting yellow kaoliung seeds upon a white background, and gave the effect of old gold.

* According to the Japanese, Kuropatkin always rode a white horse.

The table was gay with flowers and dwarf flowering bushes which the soldiers had constructed with infinite trouble out of brushwood, upon which (after bending it to the true artistic curves) they had stuck bunches of cotton wool and small flowers cut out of carrots. There were also any number of white and yellow roses most cunningly devised out of tissue paper.

After dinner and speeches we adjourned to the next room, and Nakamura gave a performance pretending to be something or some one. I forget exactly what it was all about, but I know he imitated animals and, in our exhilarated condition, made us laugh until the tears ran down our cheeks. All this time the band of the Imperial Guards, which had been sent down to do honour to the occasion, had been playing very vigorously, and it was to the strains of a polka that Sergeant-Major Watanabe entered the anteroom. He had been wondering for some days how he could pay me the greatest compliment, and he had determined that as I was there as representative of the Army of India, he would get himself up as a native of Hindustan. Accordingly he painted his face coal black, and put on a heavy fur coat, hair outwards. He looked extraordinary, and made us roar with laughter, and was altogether a great success, for he is ordinarily an austere man with very high standards of discipline and decorum. On entering, he presented me with his visiting card, on which was written " The Honourable Mr. India."

Next came Sergeant-Major Sumino, dressed as a fashionable Chinese lady, in a bodice and skirt of beautiful flowered silk. Then a soldier of the train made his appearance costumed as a geisha in wig and kimono, the latter only a red blanket, but so wonderfully manipulated with pins and strings that it caused the more sentimental to sigh.

Lastly, four band boys, attired as European ladies, appeared upon the scene, and danced a set of lancers with four bandsmen. Nothing could exceed the painstaking punctilio with which they ploughed through their figures. It was most amusing to see these extraordinary looking females working away in so solemn and correct a style at their frivolous task.

After this I thought it was full time for Lieutenant-Generals to go to bed. A child has to take itself off just when the fun gets fast and furious, and men over forty-five should learn to do the same. When I did turn in, it was with a strong feeling that nowhere in the wide dominions of the King had his birthday begun earlier or lasted longer than at the coal-mines of Yentai.

*November 23rd, 1904.*—Just returned from a luncheon with the Marquis Oyama and General Kodama.

I must say the latter is a marvel. He was ten hosts in one. Told stories. Roared with laughter. Shouted. Drank toasts with every one all round. I watched him and saw him in the midst of all his jollity, forced jollity, no doubt, but still extraordinarily well forced. I watched him, and I saw how, when Marquis Oyama occasionally took up the parable, or when, from some other cause he was free to drop out, his face fell instantly into lines of the deepest concentration and thought. Once I observed him casting his keen, penetrating glance over us one by one, sizing us up to a nicety I am certain. Somehow he brought to my mind the line,

"Ambition pale of cheek and ever watchful with fatigued eye."

## CHAPTER XXXV

### NAKAMURA ENCOUNTERS SANTA CLAUS

COAL-MINES, *November 29th*, 1904.—I heard yesterday that Okasaki was ill and was going back to Japan this morning. So I walked down after breakfast to see him off at the Yentai railway station. When I got there I was told that Okasaki's train would not start for some little time, but that the General was at the Post Commandant's house, and would be glad to see me if I cared to come up. I walked across at once and was shown into an empty room. After a few minutes the gallant General came in, and his appearance gave me a terrible shock. Last time I had seen him was upon the Emperor's birthday, when he was the very personification of careless, rollicking joviality. He had been through all his bloody battles and had emerged ever-victorious, without so much as a scratch. The most famous man, perhaps, in the Army. I can never forget him on that occasion bursting into the tent waving his little flag—so fit and jolly. And now, what was this? A grey, haggard figure in a long, full-skirted, shroud-like dressing-gown, with a small red cross worked upon the sleeves, whilst the whole of his head and neck, excepting just the face, were swathed in white bandages. He looked exactly like an animated corpse. He begged us to seat ourselves by the hibachi with his old familiar gesture, but

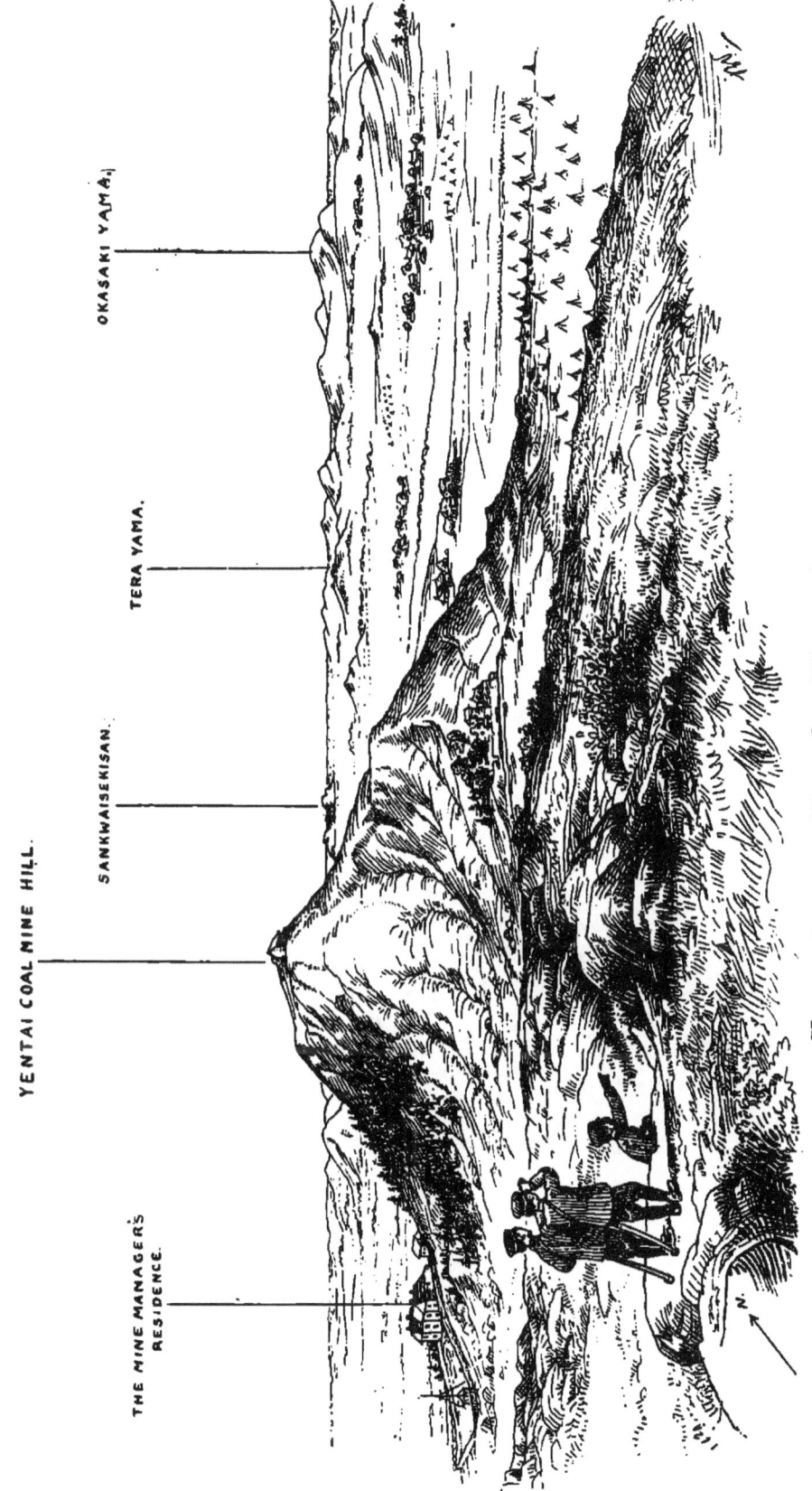

Yentai Coalmine Hill—Our Winter Quarters

we were horrified and could not. I just said, "I have come, General, to wish you *bon voyage* and *au revoir*." He said, "I have got this tiresome tumour, which my friends assure me will be better operated upon at Hiroshima than here; so I have yielded to their importunities and am going very quickly so as to get back again also as quickly as possible." This was very pitiable. I felt the sentiment of sorrow rise quite painfully in my heart. I said, "My General, we all await your early return, and until you come back you leave us, at any rate, the famous mountain, Okasaki Yama, the scene of your greatest exploit, by which to bear you affectionately in mind." The others told me afterwards that my remark seemed to please him, but I felt rather overcome at seeing the poor wasted body and drawn features of one who had been so *preux chevalier*—so famoused in fight—and could not notice much more. For we shall never see him again. *Sic itur ad astra*. Vanity, vanity, all is vanity, saith the preacher.*

*December 1st, 1904.*—Have spent a long day inspecting the 30th Regiment under the French-speaking Colonel Kawasaki. The men are living in excavations rather than in houses, that is to say, the roofs are only about two feet above the ground, whilst the floors are about eight feet below the ground. After luncheon the Colonel, pointing to the red slip with Chinese characters on it which was pasted over the door, said, "Every Chinese house contains that notice. The characters signify good fortune and happiness, and it is considered a good thing if the owner on awakening

* To the delight and surprise of every one, including the doctors, Okasaki did recover and came back again in the course of a few months.

in the morning lets his eyes first rest upon words of such good omen." Kawasaki went on to tell us that in one village a rich Chinaman with a fine house begged to be excused having soldiers billeted upon him on the plea that all the rooms were occupied by women and children. After some argument he was allowed to have his way, and a notice was being written out, in the ordinary course, with a paint brush and Indian ink upon white paper, to say that the house was privileged and that Japanese soldiers were forbidden to enter it. The Chinaman watched the preparation of this notice with great apparent interest, and when it was ready asked what was going to be done with it. "Oh," said Colonel Kawasaki, "it will be pasted upon the outside of your door." The Chinaman seemed much disturbed, and after some hesitation he begged that the paper might be destroyed, as he had changed his mind and would place his quarters at the disposal of the soldiers. On inquiry the Colonel found that black characters on white paper are just about as unlucky a combination as it is possible for a Chinaman to encounter. Presumably, if this villager ever reaches London town, his literature will be confined to the *Pink 'Un* and the *Westminster Gazette*.

COAL-MINES, *December 5th*, 1904.—The thermometer touched zero for the first time last night. There is a cave in front of our army which is occupied by the Russians at night and by the Japanese in the daytime. The Russians recently left the cave in a very dirty condition, so the Japanese wrote a note asking that their mutual abode might be kept cleaner. This note was deposited upon the ground, together with a bottle of brandy, when they marched out in the evening. Next morning the cave was clean, and a

[A Visit to the 30th Regiment in Winter Quarters at Shotatsuko (Hsiao Takou), December 1904

rouble was lying on the ground to pay for the brandy. There was also a note saying that in future the cave should be kept clean, but that all the same the Japanese were devils to kill all the wounded. Hagino is now inditing an epistle, with enclosures, showing the number of Russian wounded who are actually in Japanese hospitals. This also will be left in the cave post-office.

COAL-MINES, *December 8th*, 1904.—Bitter, bitter cold. I hear that the troops at the front are seriously embarrassed by the fact that the rice on its passage to the advanced trenches turns into ponderous marble blocks upon which a bayonet produces no great effect. Imagine being served up a chunk of marble for dinner with the thermometer at zero!

COAL-MINES, *December 9th*, 1904.—Two hundred ducks and chickens, our winter's store, were put on the roof by the cook last night, and they are all, every single one, frozen to death this morning!

COAL-MINES, *December 19th*, 1904.—Have been very busy report writing, and have had nothing special to record for a long time, except interviews and consultations regarding medical and transport questions. To-day we had a meeting to test the captured Russian rifles. The targets were of the ordinary bull's-eye pattern and the distance was about 600 yards. The stop butt was Ishi Yama. I little thought on October 12th that I should ever be firing a rifle against Ishi Yama myself! The Russian rifles are sighted for firing with the bayonet fixed, and we had to use them without a bayonet, which made the shooting most difficult. Luckily we were allowed two sighting shots, and after my second try I found it was necessary to aim about three yards below the target and about five yards to the left of it. The result was a splendid triumph for the British army. Colonel Hume won the first prize, tieing with a Japanese adjutant, and I won the second prize, clean. How delighted Lord Roberts would have been with our success, for we are both members of his old team which, in its day, has won some notable victories in India. I got a very nice prize indeed; a barrel of pickled cabbages.

I have now got a small Chinese boy, aged about twelve, to help to light the stove and clean my lamp. I asked him to-day if he liked Russians and he replied indignantly, "No!" Asked again, "Why not?" he said, "They have big noses and eyes." I suppose if bad boys in England were asked why they flung a stone at a Chinaman they might very probably say, "Because they have small eyes and no noses."

COAL-MINES, *December 22nd*, 1904.—Vincent and I have had a delightful outing. We went to a quiet luncheon, just our two selves, with General Kodama, Chief of the General Staff. Had a Cossack patrol passed that way there was nothing to show them that Yentai village was the abode of Manchurian Army Headquarters, except perhaps the numerous converging telegraph and telephones lines which centred at the brain of the military organism. No guards, no patrols, hardly any troops, just a common Chinese village. We were shown in at once to the quarters of the Chief of the Staff, quite a small building. The General's room was about twelve feet by fifteen feet. A Russian drum filled with charcoal embers was the hibachi, and the furniture consisted of one table, two broken-down chairs, and several boxes of maps.

I started by saying that I did not intend to ask any

The Officer Commanding the 2nd Division Field Artillery in his Winter Abode at Hamatang

questions about the present state of affairs, but added that if General Kodama would enlighten me on a few obscure points regarding the past events, his views would be of inestimable value.

His Excellency spent an hour and a half telling me all I wanted to know, and seemed in the best of spirits and full of keenness.

He showed me his left wrist, the bone of which had been injured in the Satsuma rebellion, and I was able to respond by showing him my left wrist, the bone of which had been injured at Majuba.

I told him I had that day received a request for an autograph from a small boy at Osaka, and he showed me a pile of applications from school children which, he said, he always met as far as he could. He produced a postcard written by his grandchild, aged three, wishing him a safe and early return. Then we began to talk about His Excellency's old life when he was Governor of Formosa. He was very much interested and pleased to narrate his experiences in that capacity, and he showed me a photograph of his house there, which is a stately and beautiful edifice.

At this stage luncheon was brought in. Very delicious. Soup, duck, Formosa oranges, Kioto cakes, and red wine. At 1.10 p.m. a wire arrived from Port Arthur, which General Kodama at once read out. It was to say that west of Sei-ho-han, where a peninsula sticks out into Pigeon Bay, one gun had been taken. The Russians tried a counter-attack, but failed.

I said to General Kodama I had brought him luck, and he agreed, saying that he had not expected this excellent news so soon. The point now captured should command the road by which supplies have until now been entering the town nightly from junks in Pigeon Bay.

After lunch we took our leave, very grateful for all the kindness we had received, and especially for the many useful notes we had obtained for our official reports.

COAL-MINES, *Christmas Day*, 1904.—I rode over this morning to make my salaams at the headquarters of the Second Army. I am sure the people at home, especially those in London, have not half as fine a day as we have here. There is a gentle breeze from the south and a bright sun, and under influences so genial the thermometer has risen to within four or five degrees of thawing-point, a temperature which makes our Arctic furs seem almost oppressive. The country was powdered with dazzling snow, and our ride across the bloody fields of Terayama and Sankwaisekisan was most peaceful and lovely to the view, although up against the soft southern wind a muffled cannonade kept ever rumbling and muttering from behind the rampart of the northerly ridge of mountains.

In the evening we had a great feast. Mistletoe in abundance, a wretched mockery under the circumstances. I thought of the previous year, and of how we all stood before the porch and draining our glasses flung them lordly (they were not ours) on the ground. The cold and frosty stars had twinkled above us, and in the intoxication of that sweet moment the absence of mistletoe passed unnoticed by all.

Each member of the company of foreign officers felt probably some such sad contrast, for the gaiety was forced, so at least it seemed to me. But one little figure was determined to be gay; truly gay, and not only in seeming. This was Nakamura, our interpreter, who climbed up painfully on to the side table, blinking like a young owl behind his spectacles, whence he delivered, with surprising boldness, the following oration:

"GENTLEMEN,—I had too much to read last night and was sitting up till it was very late. So I could not get up this morning, when a strange old man was standing in my room. I knew surely that he was Santa Claus. I jumped upon my bed, and respectfully but merrily bid him 'A Merry Christmas.' He was pleased, and handed me a letter, as well as a bag, to deliver to you. But when I saw the address on the envelope, it was written, 'Dear Children, Huangpu Coal-mine, Manchuria.' I was quite puzzled, for, as you know, there is no children in this house, and told him of that. He looked quite astonished, and stared on my face for a while. Then he laughed, and laughed heartily, and said, 'My child, do you think you are a grown up man?' I said, 'Yes.' 'Oh no,' he said to me, 'You are only a baby.' And again, 'Do you think General Hamilton is an old man?' 'Yes, I do, and he is the eldest of all.' 'No, no,' he said, 'he is also my boy.' I was quite stupefied, but he asked me once more, 'Do you think Captain Hoffmann is a large man?' I said, 'Yes, of course, he is so tall and big as Gorias.' 'Oh no, my child,' he said, 'they are all my children, and by dear children here I mean all seventeen people in this house.' When I thought I could understand him, he jumped upon his sledge and ran off to the northerly direction." (Hoots, jeers, and loud cries of "Spy! Spy!! He must have been a Spy.")\*

\* In our reports the stock phrase used to be that the Russians were retiring " in a northerly direction."

"Now, Gentlemen, here is the letter. Let me read it:—

"'DEAR CHILDREN,—I am much pleased, for you have been perfectly good through this year. I don't like to see two boys are quarrelling now. They are very naughty. I hope they will shake their friendly hands again before I will come next time. (Cheers.)

"'I left a bag with your good General' (laughter and whistling) 'Nakamura to open it before you this evening. Now goodbye, my children, I wish you a Merry Christmas!

"'Your old friend,
"'SANTA CLAUS.'"

The speech was received with rapturous applause, for we are all very fond of Nakamura, who is the most unselfish and obliging of interpreters. Simple as he seems and transparent, yet, as with most Japanese, there is more in him than meets the eye, and although he has served us continuously during the past eight months, no one had ever suspected him of being the possessor of so much courage and *esprit*. We were as much surprised, and almost as greatly pleased, as must have been the mother of Demosthenes when she heard him speak for the first time after his pebble practice on the beach.

COAL-MINES, *December 26th*, 1904.—Every one is very late in consequence of the number of last night's toasts. After breakfast, Nakamura came into my room with a large card, and begged me to write upon it a verse of poetry which should include his own name. He encouraged me to believe that if I could rise to the occasion, the card would be handed down as an ancestral heirloom in the Nakamura family. I cannot imagine

Sir Ian Hamilton and "Rooski," December 1904

a family of small Nakamuras, and I am greatly bothered by the name, but, in gratitude for his admirable speech last night, I managed to concoct this rhyme for him:

### TO THE ENGLISH INTERPRETER WITH THE FIRST ARMY

> You storm the bloody fortress ditch
> And otherwise defeat the Russian,
> But do it in a lingo which
> Sounds strange as English to a Prussian;
> 'Twere hopeless did we lack as sure a
> Translator as our Nakamura.

COAL-MINES, *New Year's Day*, 1905.—Had quite a quiet dinner last night. As the clock struck twelve America and Great Britain foregathered and drank a bottle of Oyama's champagne, exchanging affectionate good wishes for the prosperity of our mutual nations during the coming year. I doubt if people in England realise the special kindness shown by all Americans to British officers in foreign countries. They look upon us as a sort of Prodigal Mother, and kill the fatted calf accordingly.

I went over in the forenoon to pay my respects to General Kuroki, and heard that a Cossack officer had come out under a white flag and had received permission to converse for half an hour with a Japanese officer. It was stipulated that no military matters were to be discussed. The confabulation lasted three hours, and the Cossack says he will bring a dozen of his comrades with him next time. The language was French.

11 P.M.—Only a few minutes ago I was writing in the dead silence of the night wherein no one but myself seemed to be alive. I love such moments when

the last tiresome sounds of conversation have died away, and it is possible, for a brief interval, to enjoy the calm of reflection. Suddenly, up rose a strange, fierce song floating through the calm air of the spacious night. In cadence and tone it recalled the dervish chants which bade us prepare for battle in the memorable nights when we bivouacked on the banks of the Nile. This must surely be the pæan of triumph over the fall of Port Arthur. All the soldiers are singing . . . just as I realised what had happened, I heard hurried footsteps and the clank of a sword come swiftly down the passage. The door was flung open, and ——, his face a pale livid colour, and his eyes blazing with excitement, stood on the threshold. For one moment he stood there motionless, with only his face twitching and working, then, throwing his arms up over his head, he shrieked out, "*Port Arthur ist gefallen!*" and disappeared to carry on the great news. Afterwards Nakamura came in to thank me for what he was pleased to call "my unfailing sympathy." I am sympathetic, and yet to-night I cannot help feeling sad for the vanquished.

COAL-MINES, *January 2nd*, 1905.—Have sent in an application to Marquis Oyama begging permission to visit Port Arthur. I asked the staff officer through whom I made the request, if he would not like to come also, to which he replied by the Japanese proverb, "The housewife cannot leave the house!"

The foreign officers went again to the play. It was held in the same Cossack barrack-room, and the audience must have numbered at least one thousand soldiers. In the middle of the room, just between the pit and stalls, was a table covered with beer bottles, dishes of fried fish, slices of preserved bamboo, pickled beans and hot chestnuts. To this we were led and hospitably pressed to fall too. I sat down and drank beer and ate chestnuts, which reminded me of home, Immense joy was caused to the audience by the appearance of two soldiers dressed as geishas, who came to serve us with saké and beer; but I was sorry for the poor performers on the stage, as they were quite neglected, all eyes being fixed on the foreign officer, to see what he would do. I drank my cup of saké, and then bowed and made my counterfeit Hebe drink a cup herself in true geisha style, whereby I drew loud applause and laughter from all parts of the house. In truth, the foreign officers were more the play than the play itself.

I will not write another account of the stage performance. As usual, there was a minimum of love, wine, plot or problem; but any amount about swords, duels, battles and shooting. The Japanese adore the bright eyes of danger. Courage is the quality they worship. After all, I think I must just jot down the headings of one of the plays acted, as it brings out this point so strongly.

The hero was a very poor young man with a sick wife and a child. His creditors came to worry him, just as they worry poor young men in England, and after a long argument they lost their patience and tore the last blanket off the bed of the poor sick wife. In the midst of the painful scene a postman appeared and handed in the fatal notice which summons a reservist to join his regiment. War had been declared against Russia, and the poor young man must take the field against the enemies of his country. He is thunderstruck. It is the finishing stroke.

When, however, the creditors understand what

has happened, they are pleased, and begin to have pity.

They tear up their bills and receipts, and, not content with this indulgence, they begin in generous emulation to give to their debtor all that they possess. The first takes off his waist-belt and says, "Here; this cost me 7 yen 50 sen—take it!" and so they go on until they are stripped stark naked. There is no alternative but to go home dancing through the crowded streets almost in a state of nature; and, as may be imagined, there is a good deal of fun about this, especially as it is a travesty of something similar in the great historical romance of the 47 Ronins.

The young man, left to himself, reviews the agony of mind through which he has just passed and realises that his affection for his family is so strong that it is calculated to interfere with his whole-hearted performance of his duty as a soldier. He dreads lest his thoughts might wander to his beloved ones when his mind should be entirely concentrated upon how he can best serve the interests of his country. He therefore kills his wife and his child. The audience applaud the act with wild enthusiasm, regarding it as sublime and almost superhuman.

A policeman comes in by chance and discovers the death of the wife by the blood oozing from beneath the blanket. When, however, he fully understands what has happened and for what motive, he is so lost in admiration that he cheerfully resigns his chance of making a name for himself by taking the young man prisoner, and bestows upon him instead his warm congratulations.

COAL-MINES, *January 15th*, 1905.—To-day being the Japanese New Year, I went to a feast with General

JAPANESE FIELD ARTILLERY ON THE MARCH IN WINTER

Kuroki. There were no speeches, but every one was very cheery and kind. The bandsmen, dressed as European women, came in again, and danced a Lancers with others dressed as Chinamen, officers, etc. The costumes were very strange. One little girl had tow hair down her back; her face painted white; a red straw hat and black stockings. Another had a white straw hat with a white feather sticking out of it. I was touched by the kindness of the waiter, who talks a little English. He saw several officers egging these pseudo females on to come and pour me out some wine. So, being afraid I might make a fool of myself, he came, and while pretending to brush away some grains of rice, whispered in my ear, "Do not be deceived—they are only bandsmen dressed up as women."

A deputation of Chinamen came to wait upon Kuroki to-day, and said that in the last fifty years so mild a winter as the present has never been experienced. Putting this together with the phenomenally light rain in the summer which was such a Godsend to the First Army, they think there is magic in it and wish to learn the secret.

The story led on to some general conversation about the Chinese, which interested me greatly. From all I can gather, after a fairly close study of the question on the spot, there is no doubt at all that the northern Chinese peasant will make an excellent soldier. He is hardy, obedient, brave and intelligent. Ample material is also available for the requisite number of non-commissioned officers. But as regards the officer class, the situation is much more obscure. I may safely say that in the meantime, there is very little prospect that China will be able to create a corps of officers. What I have seen myself of Chinese officers and Chinese military students gives me the strong belief that for three or four generations to come it will be impossible for the Middle Kingdom to produce instructors and administrators who will be patriotic enough to resist the temptations of power and to devote their lives to an ideal higher than that of money-making. They are at present so entirely lacking in the true military feeling that they will have to be born again before they will be fit for the position held by military officers.

These are my opinions, but the subject is mysterious and it is of course conceivable that a general change might take place suddenly in the attitude of the nation towards the profession of arms which would awaken enthusiasm dormant for 1000 years, and flower forth into a regenerated corps of officers.

The Japanese are naturally immensely interested in the problem. They would like to put China on her feet, but not on horseback. They listen with amused contempt to the common Western notion that there is some sort of an affinity between a Chinaman and a Japanese. Except the shadowy spiritual link furnished by Confucius, and the more material one of identical ideographs, they consider a Chinaman resembles a Western much more nearly than any inhabitant of Dai Nippon. The Chinaman is as pure a type of individualist as the American of to-day or the Englishman of yesterday. The Japanese is nothing if not an altruist.

COAL-MINES, *January 15th*, 1905.—I rode off in the morning to pay my respects to General Umezawa, an old type Japanese warrior, keen and determined looking, not altogether unlike General Kodama. He told me many interesting things about the Yalu fight and about Liaoyang. He also gave me some news about little Rooski. He says she is well known to have belonged to the Russian general, Count Keller, as staff officers had seen her following him through their telescopes from the top of the Motienling. After the battle of the 31st of July she was found lying in a basket in the house he had been occupying. The Japanese soldiers admired the bravery of Count Keller, and although his body had been sent away to St. Petersburg they intended to hold a funeral ceremony in his honour. Part of the programme was the sacrifice and burial of Rooski, in the ancient Japanese style. However, when they came to lead her out to the execution it was found that she had gnawed her string and escaped. I am not certain whether the general was quite serious in telling me this strange story. Certainly it was told seriously, and certainly when I found Rooski on the 30th of August she had a string round her neck.

## CHAPTER XXXVI

### THE DEVIL'S PLOUGHING

LIAOYANG, *January* 16*th*, 1905.—We have halted here on our way to Port Arthur,* where the Headquarters are sending us on an excursion in a special train. I have much to be thankful for, but this great consideration and indulgence leaves me without words to express my gratitude.

NEAR PORT ARTHUR, *January* 18*th*, 1905.—Arrived at General Nodzu's headquarters, after a cold and weary journey in the train. All the foreign officers with the Second Army are also with us, so we make up an imposing party. The others are accommodated in a long barrack-room made of wood and matting: I am in a tiny room by myself. I can only just turn round in it, but it is as good from my point of view as a palace, for it gives me seclusion and respite to think and write.

NEAR PORT ARTHUR, *January* 19*th*, 1905.—I have been introduced to General Nogi. He is tall, slender and grey, and appears bright, sensible and determined. He shook us warmly by the hand all round and seemed genuinely, and not only politely, glad to see us. He said that most of his staff were busy entraining

* My experiences at Port Arthur would fill a large volume if I treated them at all fully. I will therefore only include a few minor points, more with the object of giving a general idea of my adventures than of attempting to deal seriously with the subject of the siege.—I. H.

troops for Liaoyang, but that he could spare us an officer to take us over his battle-fields. Beyond this nothing passed but compliments, and we soon mounted our steeds. On the way to the forts I made friends with a gay and festive spark, a bright, quick, talkative young officer, who had been summoned from his studies in Paris on the outbreak of the war. It is, indeed, remarkable how the Japanese are able to assimilate the characteristics of the people with whom they consort. But I fear that the joyous effervescence supplied by a Parisian education will soon lose its piquancy and point under the pressure from above and below to which an officer must as a rule be subjected.

I picked up a few odd scraps of opinion and sentiment during my ride. The Japanese think the Russian sailors better men, stronger, more intelligent and more highly trained than their soldiers. The Japanese admit that the Russians fought bravely enough at Port Arthur, and yet there is not a man in the Third Army who does not think it wrong of the garrison to have surrendered. To illustrate the Japanese standpoint I am told that if his Imperial Majesty the Emperor gives a colour to a regiment it is the duty of every single man to die before it is taken. No lower standard of military conduct can find acceptance or even condonation. If a private soldier should see an officer waver in his loyalty so far as to dream of surrender, he would be justified, a hundred times over, in the opinion of his countrymen, if he were to head a mutiny to supersede such a traitor.

It is rather interesting to hear such ideas expressed just at the moment when cables tell us that all Europe is acclaiming the heroism of the Port Arthur garrison,

I stand outside the question altogether, and only say that opinions so conflicting point to the existence of a formidable gulf between the military ethics of East and West.

203 METRE HILL, *January 20th*, 1905.—We left our camp at 1 A.M. Like the young lady of Riga, we were all mounted on tigers. Seriously, I never saw such devils. We had to practise the widest extensions lest we killed one another. In spite of all precautions the horse of one foreign officer reared up, and seizing the attaché of a friendly Power between its fore feet flung him from the saddle. In the confusion which ensued the wild beast bestridden by Vincent kicked the Marquis Saigo on the leg. However, at last we began to move, and then, by degrees, the menagerie became less violent.

I have been noting down these silly trifles to put off, as far as possible, the moment when I must turn to the ghastly charnel-house whither my steps have now led me. So far I have avoided such things because I hate them, and also because I feel that many writers have combined to give the world a false conception of war by piling up its horrors beyond all reasonable measure. But, sitting here, I should go to the other extreme and become a cowardly suppressor of the truth did I try and escape altogether from some analysis of the mountain of death upon which I find myself. (*See* Sketches XXXVI. and XXXVII.)

At a glance it springs to the eyes that this is no ordinary hill. It has been fairly battered out of its natural shape by inhuman agencies, and on its blasted and shot-seared surface there is not so much as one dried blade of grass; nothing to break the harshness of the devil's ploughing to which it has been subjected

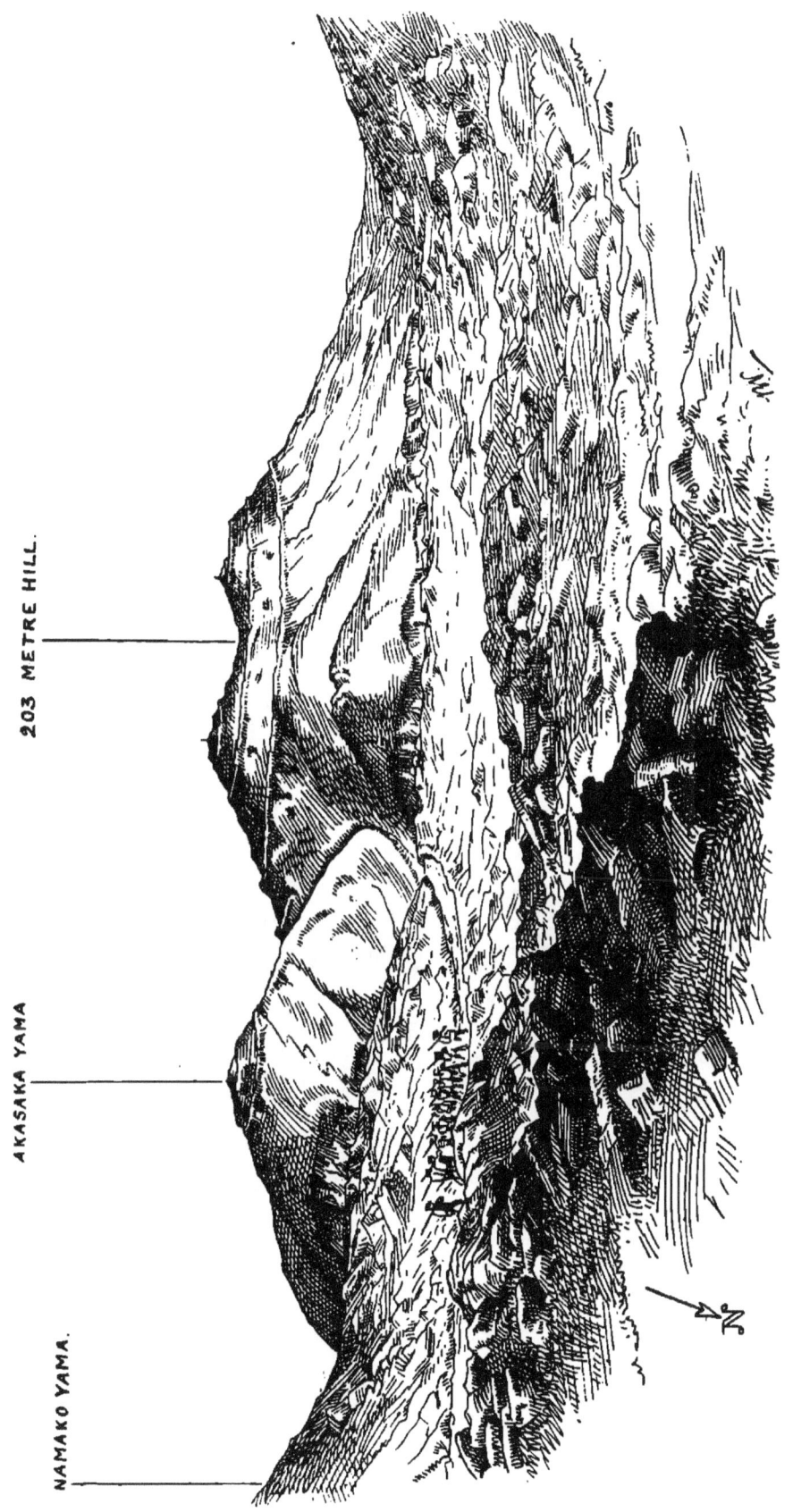

"203 Metre Hill," near Port Arthur

XXXVI

but here and there the faded colour of a woman's gown or petticoat which has been used to make sandbags, or the leprous yellow splotches left by the bursting of the high explosive shells.

The manner of the devil's ploughing is thus: first the hill has been sliced into numberless deep gashes, and then these trenches and their dividing walls have been smashed and pounded and crushed into a shapeless jumble of stones; rock splinters and fragments of shells cemented liberally with human flesh and blood. A man's head sticking up out of the earth, or a leg or an arm or a piece of a man's body lying across my path are sights which custom has enabled me to face without blanching. But here the corpses do not so much appear to be escaping from the ground as to be the ground itself. Everywhere there are bodies, or portions of bodies, flattened out and stamped into the surface of the earth as if they formed part of it, and several times in the ascent I was on the point of placing my foot upon what seemed but to be dust when I recognised by the indistinct outline that it was a human form stretched and twisted and rent to gigantic size by the force of some frightful explosion.

The very walls still standing in places are built of alternate layers of frozen corpses and sandbags. I have written enough; perhaps too much. Sieges are horrible things. A good fight in the open—that is another matter.

Riding back, my French-speaking friend told me that his father had been killed as a lieutenant-colonel in the wars of the Rebellion. He hopes there will be a decisive victory soon.

It is easy to understand that despite the dogged

Japanese courage there must be much anxiety amongst all thinking officers as to the effects of the financial strain of this war. The Japanese have enough, and more than enough territory. If the exhausting conflict lasts too long they will find themselves left, I will not say penniless, but certainly with no superfluous cash in their pockets. How then can they fulfil their destiny and develop Korea, let alone Manchuria? Even as it is, foreign capitalists will, in the first instance, reap the chief benefits of their victories, but if they go on fighting much longer, even the small margin left to them will disappear and they will not be able to draw out of their new possessions anything to compensate them for their efforts. Evidently therefore it must be the Japanese aim to force the Russians into peace as quickly as possible.

HEADQUARTERS, THIRD ARMY, *January* 21*st*, 1905.—Spent the day in going over the captured forts and the trenches, parallels and approaches of the besiegers. The impression left upon my mind is that fortifications are as valuable as ever for vital points. The mistake the Russians made was in beginning with the construction of the inner line of forts instead of first completing the outer ring, including such places as 203 Metre Hill. The Japanese allow that they could never have taken that place had it been crowned by a permanent work. It was very evident from 203 Metre Hill to-day that a harbour or dockyard becomes a mere deathtrap to ships, provided:

(1) That the enemy's guns can get within range for indirect firing.

(2) That the enemy can seize any one point from which a single man can observe and correct their fire.

Against an extended line of guns hidden away behind

View from "Golden Hill" of the Japanese Transports sunk to block the Entrance to the Harbour at Port Arthur

some mountain six or seven miles distant, the armament of a fortress is absolutely useless. The concentrated guns of the fort have not a hundred to one chance of disabling the concealed and dispersed guns of the attack; whereas, given an observation post, the guns of the attack can hit a ship or house every time they fire, and even without an observation they can, by the aid of a map, direct their shells towards the vitals of the harbour or town. In fact, the value of Gibraltar depends upon the neutrality of Spain.

HEADQUARTERS, THIRD ARMY, *January 22nd, 1905, 11 P.M.*—I will turn the day topsy turvy and begin at the end. I have just come from a grand dinner given by Nogi to all foreign officers. I sat on his right hand, and turned the conversation on to the subject of my last entry yesterday. His Excellency said, "The experiences gained during the siege show that a town or harbour cannot be protected by a ring of works concentrated in its immediate vicinity. It can only be saved from destruction by outlying forts twelve kilometres (eight miles) distant from the vitals they are meant to cover. To have forts eight kilometres (five miles) out is, nowadays, no use. As for a fortified harbour or town without any outlying works whatsoever, I would merely call that an expensive shell trap."

One great fault committed by the Russians consisted in not having a sufficiency of howitzers. Another was in their habit of placing their cannon mounted conspicuously on the tops of the hills, where howitzers, by indirect fire, could destroy them without exposing themselves. He made me tell him a great deal about Ladysmith, and he seemed much struck when I said that the only guns we had which ever caused a Boer

Long Tom to run away were two old, black powder 6.3 howitzers dating from the Afghan War.

In this army, as in all others, it was specially interesting to study the differing characteristics of the Divisions. We see the same strong distinction between our own troops, mainly as a rule in consequence of the idiosyncrasies of their commanders. In General Nogi's army it was quite extraordinary how the individualities of his Divisions came out in the nature of their sap. One Division was exceedingly rapid in its work, but left a good deal to chance. Its works were, in fact, horribly unsafe. When any visitor went into the trenches he was always being told to hurry up and pass along quickly, for bullets came hurtling through the thin, scrimped walls, and he found himself committed to an adventure almost as dangerous as an advance across the open. On the other hand, this Division always got through its job in a marvellous short space of time.

Another of his Divisions was fairly safe, but not so rapid.

Yet another Division constructed its trenches so that any one entering them was as safe as he would have been in a Tokio tea-house, but Port Arthur would not have fallen for another year had every one adopted that rate of progress. The prevention of any riot or disturbance in Port Arthur after the capitulation had been a cause of great anxiety. Much trouble had been taken to relieve the Russian guards by Japanese sentries in the due course of relief. This was so managed that before the public had time to grasp what was happening, a Japanese sentry was standing on duty at each of the well-thought-out tactical points fixed in the Russian scheme for the maintenance of internal order.

## The Devil's Ploughing 313

Finally, Nogi told me that his worst night during the whole siege was that of January 2nd, when he could not sleep a wink owing to cessation of the firing.

I have put the foregoing down quickly, so that I may forget as little as possible. Now I must hark back to the morning.

We started on the tigerish steeds at 9 A.M. and rode for Port Arthur. On the way my new friend told me of a former ride with a Russian herald or parliamentaire on January 3rd, when he went in to see General Stoessel. He was the first Japanese who had entered the town since the declaration of war. Naturally he was not quite happy, and feared he might be greeted with some uncomfortable demonstrations. What was his surprise, however, when the Cossacks and groups of soldiers took off their caps, waved them, and called out, "Bravo!" Once he got among the streets he had some difficulty in finding Stoessel's house. At last he was shown the way, and when he asked the sentry if he was at home he said "*Da!*" so he rang the bell. The door was opened by an old man whom he took to be Stoessel's adjutant, instead of which he turned out to be the general himself, who ushered him into a room where Madame Stoessel was sitting. There he delivered his message from his Imperial Majesty the Emperor, saying that, as Stoessel had fought bravely, he might still keep his sword. Stoessel replied in suitable terms, and asked if he might come and call on General Nogi. So next day my friend came in again, bringing presents of chickens and champagne, and arranged an interview for January 5th. On that date the generals met and shook hands.

General Nogi said, "We have been fighting for our countries, and have had to do so as courageously as possible. But now it is peace here, and there is no reason we should not meet for the time being as good friends and soldier comrades." General Stoessel made answer, "Yes; with the cessation of hostilities feelings of anger die, and the mind is well prepared to cherish more friendly feelings."

The generals then discussed the incidents of the fighting, when each was complimentary to the soldiers of the other.

General Stoessel observed that the 11-inch howitzers were the most unpleasant feature of the siege. Messengers of such weight, so imperiously demanding possession, had never before been sent into a fortress.

After a little more talk about the wounded, General Stoessel said, "I have two horses, an Australian and an Arab. They are both beauties, and I want you to accept them as a free, willing gift."

General Nogi replied, "No; I am extremely sorry, but under the orders of the Emperor everything in the fortress has to be handed in without exception or distinction to the Commissioners for captured articles; I promise, however, that I will endeavour to get these horses back from the Commissioners, and if I can succeed I will keep them always in remembrance of a brave adversary."

General Stoessel expressed his deep regret at the sad bereavement the Japanese commander had suffered by losing his two sons during the siege operations.

General Nogi thanked him for his sympathy, but declared that it was cause for self-congratulation and not for sorrow to a Japanese soldier if fate decreed that his family should cease to exist in such a cause and in such a manner. The life of a soldier—his family—all belonged to his country, and if they all went why then they were well gone.

Finally the Russian commander got on his Arab and made him trot up and down to show off its beautiful paces.

Breakfast was then served, after which Stoessel took his leave.

A mile or two before entering the town of Port Arthur we met some carts conveying ladies. I took them to be Russian refugees. My pleasure at seeing the first white women who have gladdened our sight since the far-off days of Fenghuangcheng was tempered by the melancholy thought of their little homes broken up and their husbands or children lost during the terrors of siege. I felt sorry for them, and I suppose I looked it, too, for I was suddenly electrified by one of them singing out in good honest American accents, "Waal, and how are you fellows, any way?" Evidently I had made a mistake.

Going on a little further we met a number of genuine Russian refugees with all their worldly possessions, including their women and children, in Chinese carts. The men all saluted the French attaché, and some of them also saluted the British. Shortly after meeting these pilgrims we rode right into the town and tied up our horses on the wharf.

My impression in passing along the deserted boulevard was melancholy, all the shops being closed and about one house in thirty having been wrecked by shells. On the wharf I met a couple of Sikhs, who were considerably surprised to be accosted in Hindustani. They told me the place had been given up quietly, and that the Japanese *band o bast* * was good.

* Arrangement—organisation—administration.

If, they said, the Japanese had not been adroit in changing sentries with the Russians so neatly and so quickly there would certainly have been pillage. It was their business to know such things, as they were watchmen in the employ of a German firm. The natural good manners of these men had been spoilt. They spoke with a disagreeable mixture of cringing and effrontery. I thought them degenerate fellows, very much changed for the worse since their departure from the Punjaub.

If the town seemed melancholy it was gay compared to the harbour. For in the streets were at least some lingering signs of life. The shops might be closed, but there were Russian Red Cross men riding about with Cossack orderlies and Japanese officers driving about in Russian doikas. But in the harbour there was nothing but the grey water and the scuttled warships; piteous dead things lying on their beam ends or sunken on even keel until the little waves were able to chase one another over the decks. No other inanimate thing gives such an impression of life as a great ship when all is well with her. Hardly anything in this world looks so forlorn, lonesome and desolate as the same ship stranded, ruined and wrecked.

On the wharf was a stack of Cardiff coal. I stood on it a moment just to give myself the nearest sensation possible to " the sweet green fields of Wales." Then we climbed up Golden Hill, where few but Russians had ever climbed before and where few but Japanese will ever climb in future. For this very reason I had better not write about it. The harbour entrance struck me as being extraordinarily narrow. The channel was such that I doubt if, under peace conditions, two ships could safely have passed one another.

View of Port Arthur Harbour and the Russian Warships from "Golden Hill," January 1905

All the more admirable then was the pluck of the sailors who brought their steamers up and sank them right under the very muzzle of the Russian right flank ten-inch gun.

After leaving Golden Hill fort we went to the principal hospital and called on General Balaschieff, Director of the Red Cross. He was a picturesque old gentleman, who spoke French most fluently and volubly. He reminded me exactly of the father of Natascha, I forget his name, in War and Peace. The heat in this hospital was awful; 70°! I suppose the Russians like it so, but the nurses, as well as the patients, looked pathetically ill and pale, especially in contrast with our bronzed and stalwart crowd.

On return to camp at 4.30 P.M. I got an invitation to come and say good-bye to General Nogi, as, although he is going to sit next me at dinner, he thinks I might wish to have some more private conversation before I leave.

The more I see of the Commander of the Third Army the more he impresses me. He is, I feel sure, a man of great nobility of character, endowed with a philosophic heroism which penetrates through the mild dignity of his manners and appearance. He seems utterly simple and unspoiled by success. Although the date of his birth places him amongst the warriors of the old school, yet he has never spared time or labour in his efforts to keep himself abreast of the times. He has read a very large proportion of modern standard military works. If I were a Japanese, I would venerate Nogi. Happy is the army which possesses such a general, and fortunate the nation. Indeed, I would go further and say well constituted must be the army and ably governed the nation which, possessing such a man, puts him exactly in the right place. What is the Power and where does it reside by which, apparently without favour or affection, the very best use is made of available Japanese material? Who are on the Selection Board which fits in each Japanese official just exactly where, without being taxed beyond his powers, he can develop his fullest force?

I do not know, but I feel that we British take these matters of appointments (I am not speaking specially of the Army) far too lightly, because we have a sort of feeling lying at the bottom of our minds that, after all, one Englishman is about as good as another.

This is a frightful fallacy. A man may be selected for an important post in January; in February he may have an attack of illness; and in March, although no one, not even himself, is aware of the fact, he may not be the man he was. Thus, even in an individual, there is scope for a great variation of capacity. Napoleon in good health spells victory; Napoleon with a cold in his head is nothing more than a commonplace commander. But such differences in an individual, important as they may be, are nothing compared to the differences between two different individuals. It is a marvellous thing that out of all the millions of men in this world, it is quite impossible to pick out two of whom it would be safe to say that they would act in precisely the same way under the strain of a similar crisis. Every inhabitant of Great Britain has, somewhere, his precise sphere of action lying ready for him. We consider it almost a miracle when the two are brought together. The biographies of most great men show that they only come into their kingdom, so to say, by the skin of their teeth, and after persistent attempts had been made to force them into some thoroughly uncongenial career. But the eye of the Japanese Government seems to serve it marvellously well in the selection of its instruments.

During my brief interview with the Commander of the Third Army, I asked if he would come and see me in England if I got the command of an army corps. He said that travel was for young men who wanted to learn, for the purpose of placing their experiences at the disposal of their native land. He himself was now too old to pick up new notions which demand fresh and flexible minds. If, therefore, it was fated that he should get through this war alive he meant to settle down quietly to spend his declining years in his own country.

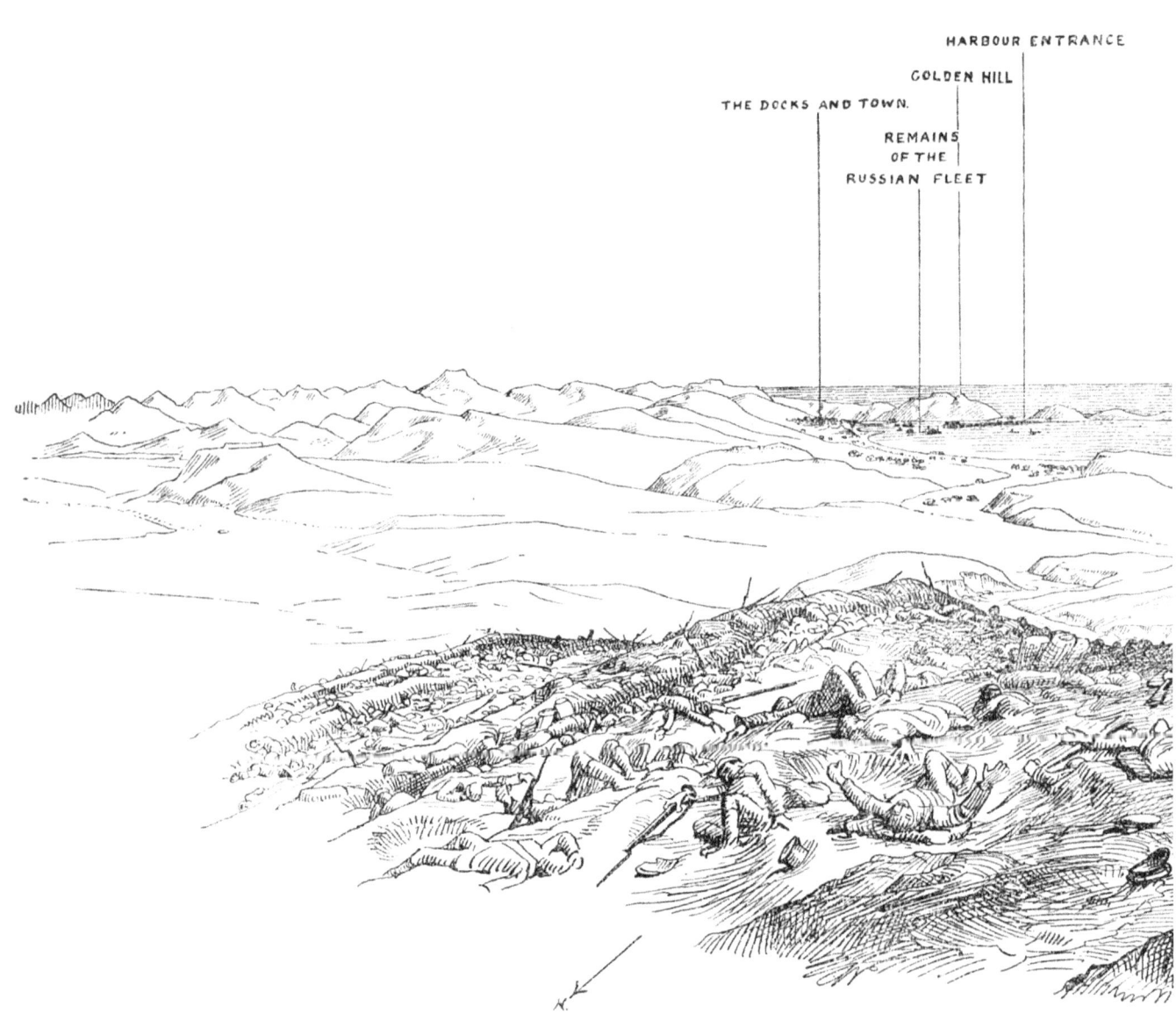

VIEW OF PORT ARTHUR HARBOUR

XXXVII

FROM THE TOP OF "203 METRE HILL"

## CHAPTER XXXVII

### NANSHAN AND TELISSU

KINCHOU, *January 24th*, 1905, 11 P.M.—A fierce blizzard from the north has been blowing for the past twenty-four hours. Last night, after saying good-bye to the Third Army headquarters, I had just time to get into bed with all my clothes on when it began in deadly earnest, whistling through my matting-walled house as if it had been a sieve. I wore a nightcap for the first time in my life, but even that did not keep my feet warm, and I could not sleep.

I rose at 6 A.M., as under the orders issued we were to start at 9, but as a matter of fact we did not get off until 1 P.M. The wing of chicken I got for breakfast was frozen as hard as a brick-bat. I chipped off splinters with my clasp-knife and held them in my mouth until they melted.

After travelling a few miles up the line we halted for an hour, taking in Russian prisoners for Dalny. They were fine-looking men, many of them over six feet. Our third-class carriage tempered to some extent the fury of the blizzard, but in the open trucks it must have been hard to draw breath. One unfortunate man crawled in when Vincent opened the door and seemed on the point of death. He spoke "*A bis'c'l Deutsch.*" We gave him brandy, which seemed to revive him somewhat.

Eventually we arrived at our destination, Kinchou station, at 6.30 P.M. Here we met with a singular adventure which will amuse the Japanese Army very much when it comes to their ears. Hardly had I alighted from the train when fizz! pop!! bang!!! about 500 Roman candles were let off up wind, fiercely discharging their fiery contents upon the ice-laden wings of the blizzard. I stood the unexpected assault bravely, until catherine-wheels and fountains of fire began to sweep the platform like shrapnel, and then, with two or three half-exploded squibs sticking to my coat I fled into a small waiting-room, not, however, before I had observed an amazing crowd of Chinese notables standing closely to windward of the fireworks.

As soon as the fury of the salute had abated I wanted to go out and thank the kind Chinamen for the warm reception they had given us, but the Japanese officers in charge dissuaded me. However, after about five minutes' delay, they brought the chief mandarins into the waiting-room and presented them to me there.

It was so dark that I could hardly see, and I suggested we should either have a lamp or that I should speak to the Chinese on the platform where there was still a little light. But nothing was done; it was not my business to make a fuss, and so the introductions and compliments took place practically in the dark.

When all the Chinese had departed, then, and not till then, I was permitted to start for the house which had been told off for me, rubbing my nose in real agony to try and save it from being bitten off by the atrocious wind. Only on arrival here did a friendly subordinate let the humour of the proceedings overcome his Japanese reticence. He began by asking us if we knew what was inscribed on the banners brought down to the station by the Chinese. Naturally we did not know, and he then told us with a twinkle in his eye that they bore the strange device of "All hail, mighty conqueror, on thy great victory!" Having said so much he could not stop, and bit by bit we got hold of the whole story.

We had been due here at 2 P.M., and General Nogi, who was to have started with his Headquarters Staff for Liaoyang at 1 P.M., was due at 6 o'clock in the evening. Our train was five hours late of starting, which put back the departure of the Commander of the Third Army a proportionate time, and he will not now pass through Kinchou until midnight. But no one had warned the local Chinese mandarins of the change of programme, and they had all come down to give Nogi a grand reception. Before any one could stop them they had opened fire with their Roman candles, and the situation was decidedly awkward for the responsible officers and officials.

But the clever Japanese are equal to any emergency, and when they saw me dart across into the dark waiting-room the brilliant idea struck them of making the Chinese quite happy by letting them imagine they had seen Nogi and of making me even happier in the belief that I had been given a royal salute. So they made me unconsciously personate Nogi in the dark room, and killed their birds with the one cleverly flung stone!

This room is so deadly cold it might be an apartment excavated out of the heart of a glacier.

I hear some one hard by grumbling, "*Wir sind hier eingegraben; es ist schweinlich kalt.*"

Again I shall get between the blankets with all my clothes on, plus a nightcap.

I am writing in pencil, because my ink is frozen quite solid.

KINCHOU, *January 25th*, 1905.—The wind is still in the north, but not nearly so piercing or so strong; thank Heaven!

In the afternoon we were shown over the battlefield of Nanshan by an officer of Kobi who had been badly wounded during the engagement. The Nanshan position consists of a group of bare hills about 300 feet high, blocking the narrowest point of the Liaotung isthmus, which is here pinched in to a width of some three miles from eastern to western sea. (*See* Sketches XXXVIII. and XXXIX.)

The battlefield is as restricted as that of Waterloo, and lies before a spectator on the commanding Russian position in all its minutest detail. Some men are glad of an opportunity of dissociating themselves from public opinion—personally I much prefer to sail with the tide. But occasionally there is no help for it; it becomes absolutely necessary to combat a dangerous delusion.

Nanshan has been called a strong position—the strongest in the world, I think, certain writers have allowed themselves to declare.

In the time of Cæsar, or even Wellington, this might have been so, provided always the defender had command of the sea.

But no Roman general I am sure in the first Punic War, when the Carthaginians were superior on sea, would have elected to fight a battle with both his wings resting on that fickle element, thus giving his enemies a double chance of asserting their special advantage. I say then that Nanshan should never under any conditions have been considered a strong position unless the defenders had command of the sea on both sides, when, with modern ordnance such as it is, no land defence whatsoever would have been required.

But this is not all. Even if the element of sea power be eliminated from the problem, I do not think the writers who have enlarged upon the strength and value of such a position as Nanshan have quite grasped the evolution in tactics caused by the long-range rifle and gun.

The Nanshan hills are, as already stated, at the narrowest waist of the isthmus. Immediately to the north and to the south of the position taken up by the Russians the sea runs back, permitting the land to bulge out in strong curves to the east and to the west (*see* Sketch XXXIX.). Thus an enemy approaching the position from the north can get within 1000 yards of it with a front twice as long as that of the defenders. In the days of Waterloo this would not so much have mattered, except that the artillery of the attack could have brought a converging fire on the hill. But, before the infantry could have made use of their musketry, they must have entered the narrow neck and restricted their front to almost the same extent as that of the defenders. In the year of grace 1904, however, the infantry fire fight becomes hot at 1000 yards, and at this distance, owing to the configuration of land and sea, the Japanese were able to bring a great superiority of rifle-fire, half of it converging, on the hills in the narrow isthmus occupied by the Russians.

In my opinion then the defenders misinterpreted the exceptional geographical advantages offered by the Nanshan Isthmus. Instead of placing themselves so that they must be exposed to a converging fire, they should have used the ground to make certain of

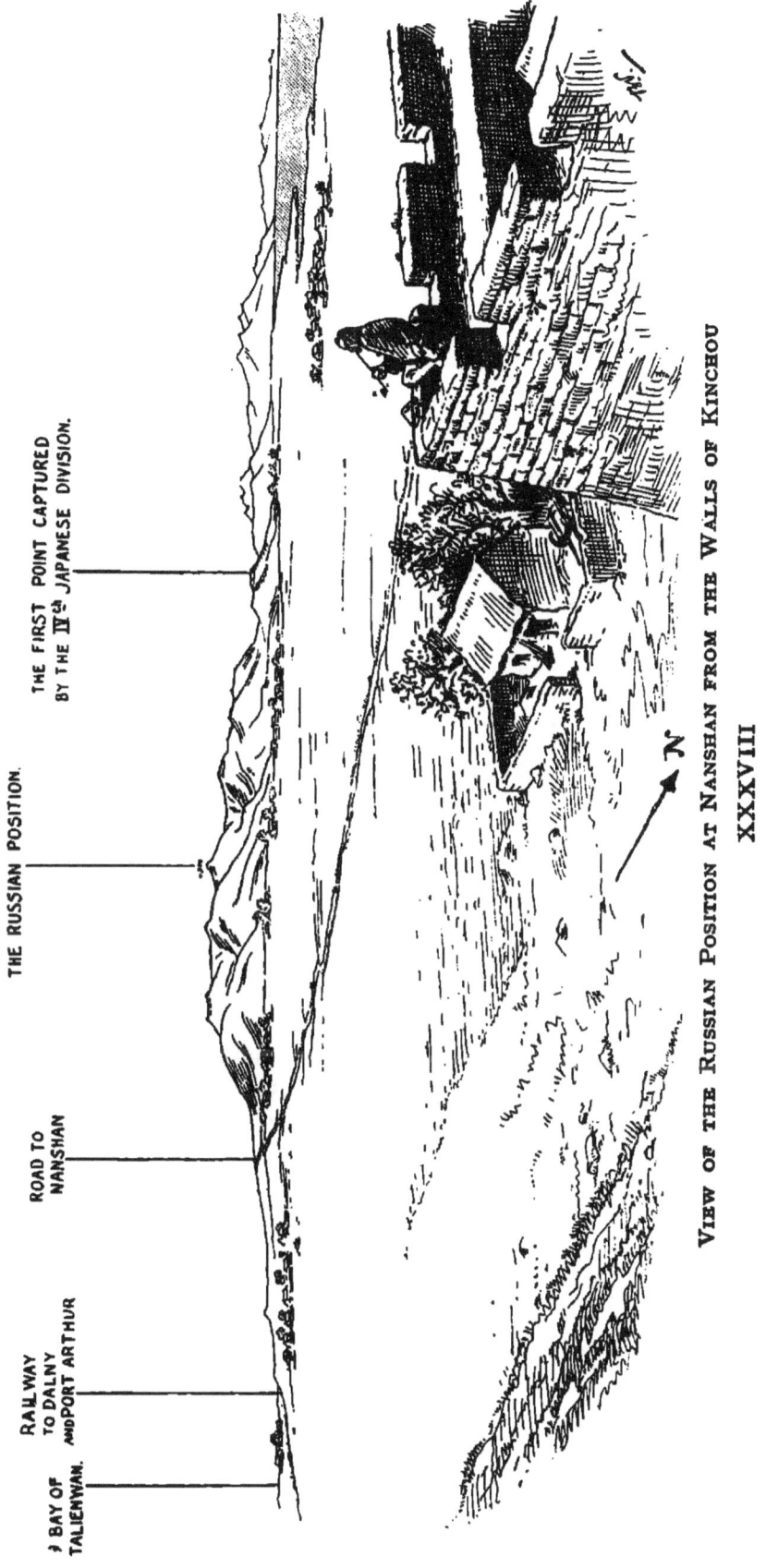

View of the Russian Position at Nanshan from the Walls of Kinchou

XXXVIII

being able to bring a converging fire on the Japanese. The country to the south of the isthmus lends itself admirably to such a scheme. The Russian right wing might have covered Dalny and the *débouché* of Nanshan so as to catch the Japanese with converging fire as they emerged, without exposing themselves to naval attack on the western, or dangerous side of the sea. Their left wing thrown back in echelon on the higher hills in rear would have prevented any attempt of the enemy to turn their left by hugging the western coast line.

In short, Nanshan was an admirable position for the erection of a permanent work which would have been as resistant to fire on the flanks and in rear as to any premature assault in front. A few thousand pounds spent on such a fort would have enabled two or three battalions of infantry and a company or two of garrison gunners to hold the Japanese Army at bay for some days at least, perhaps indeed for weeks. But Nanshan was not a place for a battle of defence, where trenches and gun emplacements of a simple field type could all be easily enfiladed or even taken in reverse by men-of-war from the sea on either side. A mile or two to the south Nature had plainly designated the true position for such a battle of defence ; so at least it seems to me, though the Russians were evidently not of my way of thinking.

I shall not enter into a description of the engagement, except to say that I was surprised to find that the Russians had placed their 15-centimetre howitzers on the top of the hills, although only 300 yards further south there was a deep ravine with steep sides, whence they could have fired with equal effect, and also with perfect safety. Howitzers are meant for indirect fire, and to expose these high angle pieces to the enemy's cannon was a purposeless surrender of one of their chief merits. As well might a chess player handicap himself by refusing to jump his knight over the other pieces, as an artillery commander decide that instead of throwing his shell over a hill from safe concealment behind it, he would take his howitzers into full view of all the enemy's artillery both on sea and land. A howitzer is naturally a modest piece and never would the quality have shown to more advantage than at Nanshan where the Japanese could bring 198 field-guns, as well as the armament of four gunboats, to bear upon the fifty guns of the Russians.

I noticed an important advance on the Yalu defences. The first line of trenches, which followed the curve of the hills about twenty-five feet above their base, was completed with sandbag loopholes. Also there were barbed wire obstacles, which are specially effective against swift-running Japanese. It was owing to the loopholes and the barbed wire that 10,000 Russians resisted the Third Army of 42,000 and the 1st Artillery Brigade until sunset, although their artillery had been completely silenced (owing to the mistake in placing the howitzers) by 9 A.M.

I must now act up to my principles and tear myself away from too serious a consideration of a fascinating example of naval and military combination on the battlefield. Although Nanshan must have had a bad moral effect on the troops who had to fall back, yet it is probable that, in the long run, the victory was dearly bought by the Japanese. They won the position too cheaply at a cost of 4504 killed and wounded, or only about 10 per cent. of their force. They did not quite grasp the inherent weakness of a concentrated force on the Nanshan hills when attacked by modern armaments. Elated at having carried by assault a position which bore some superficial resemblance to a citadel, they began to imagine there were no limits to what their prowess could accomplish, and it was in this spirit that a few weeks later they hurled masses of valorous flesh and blood against the inflexible masonry of permanent fortifications, there to gain the austere glory of dying in thousands—not for victory, for that was impossible, but for the honour of the Army and for the renown of their country and its Emperor.

TELISSU, *January 26th*, 1905.—A day of horror. Started at 7 A.M. in an icy blizzard, but for some unknown cause the train which was to have taken us north at 9 A.M. left us stranded on the station, where we remained kicking our heels to try and keep them warm for six or seven hours. The thermometer was just below zero all the time.

At 5 P.M. a Dubs engine from Glasgow came and carried us to a place named Gebato, where we were preparing some hot coffee at 9 P.M. when suddenly there was a terrific smash; the windows flew into splinters, and all became dark, except a few sparks either from the lamps or perhaps produced in my eyes by the concussion. I got a heavy blow in the ribs from something and a smash on the arm, which was, I thought for a moment, broken. This is my first railway accident. Our good honest Glasgy locomotive had been run into by a pert fussy American shunting engine. The servants were terribly upset. They thought a Russian cannon shot had struck the train. One said, "Are we dead?" The cook exclaimed, "I have lost my eye!" Susaki bawled out, "We must fly!" Matsuda said, "Sit still; a Russian mine has blown the locomotive to pieces, and perhaps there is another under us!"

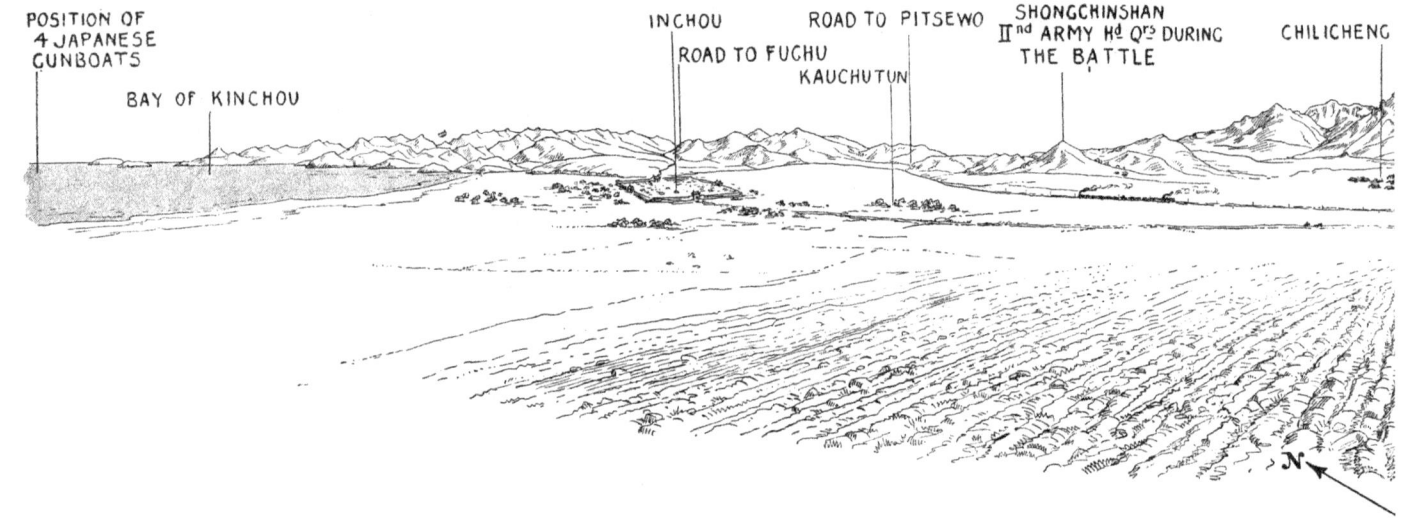

View Looking North from the

XXXIX

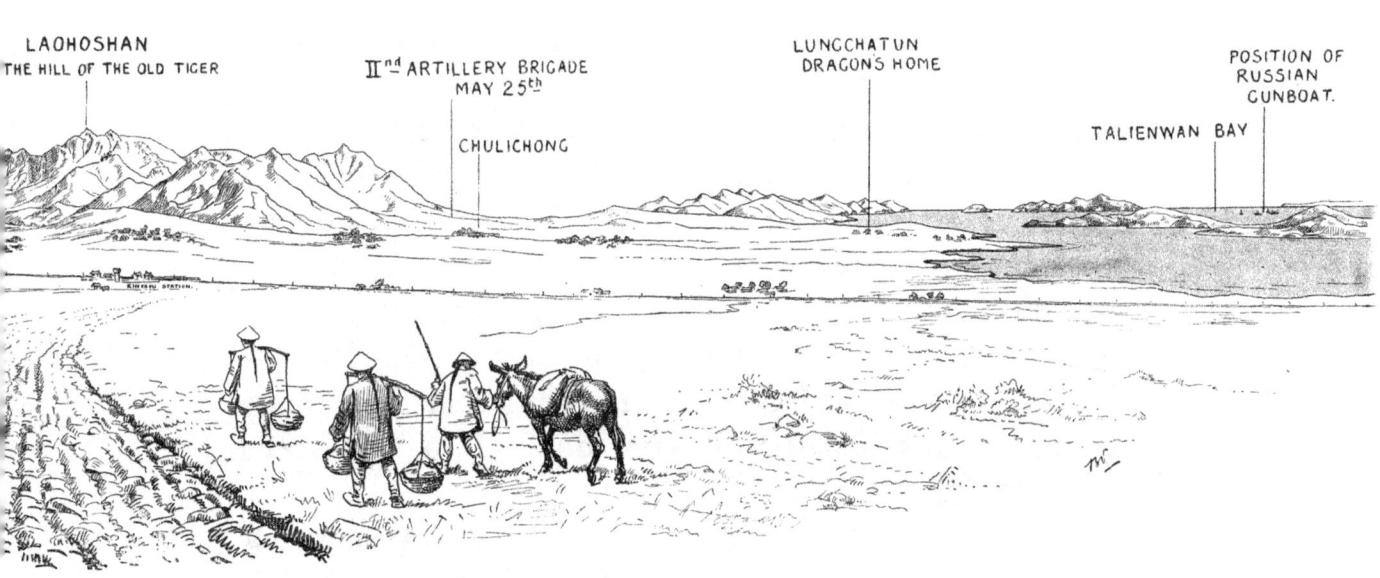

RUSSIAN POSITION AT NANSHAN

However, no one was seriously injured, although most of us have a scratch or two to show as the result of our adventure. Naturally our journey was delayed still further, and we did not get here (Telissu) until 2.30 A.M. I am now in a small Russian house near the station, and its warm stove and the bowl of Japanese soup and rice which I have just gobbled up seem, and therefore are, the acme of luxury.

Socialists, and many good and comfortable people who are not socialists, imagine that the world would be happier if every one was assured of a good dinner every day of his or her life. No greater mistake. Three things make this world worth living in. Food, love and heaven.

Deprive mankind of the natural uncertainty as to where they are to get their next meal and they lose, at one blow, a third of their interest in life. England is such an absurdly safe, luxurious sort of an artificial paradise, and so many of its people go from the cradle to the grave without once having been even twenty-four hours without food or drink, that some folk may think that my platitude is a paradox. If so let them consider further.

Love, they must admit, is the factor which looms most largely in a food-satisfied life. Now, just suppose that the course of love—true or false—always ran perfectly smooth, what then would happen to love as we now understand it? It would disappear, and with it the second third of the interest of life.

One more tie, and one only, would then attach humanity to this terrestrial globe, namely, the uncertainty about heaven. Lest perchance the world was to be the end of all things a man might linger on just to see it through, even if he had neither sustenance nor love to work for and live for. But let him be positively assured, in such a manner as to compel belief, that he was lingering joylessly on the threshold of Paradise, and then who could prevent him from hastening to it by committing the happy despatch?

Often when I have heard a kind-hearted person say, with tears in their voices, of a tramp or a gipsy, "I believe the poor fellow is *really* hungry!" I have thought to myself, "Poor unhappy man or woman, you have now lived the best part of your life without ever once having been half or three-quarters starved. *Ergo*, you know nothing whatever of one of the chief pleasures of life, the pleasure namely of satisfying, not mere appetite, but genuine hunger."

I suppose these thoughts are the result of the railway accident. I must now try to quench such unwholesome mental activity in gentle slumber by the side of this delicious Russian stove.

TELISSU, *January 27th*, 1905.—Slept the sleep of the just till 9.30 A.M. Had some breakfast and went out to see the battlefield. Nakamura recommended me a splendid looking mule. Its owner said it was just about perfect. It seemed very tractable and tame. Quite a nice, confidential beast.

We started. When we had gone a quarter of a mile Rooski came rather close and frightened the mule. Rooski loves to frighten anything, and is very quick to detect when she has made an impression of this sort, especially upon a large thing like a mule. The more the mule drew away from Rooski, the closer Rooski came to the mule. I cursed Rooski frightfully, but she is just like a Boer; when the enemy yields she presses her advantage. I was rapidly losing control over the mule—I lost control—we flew towards the railway embankment, an obstacle like the Punchestown "on and off," only more so. An instinct of the hunting-field made me give the mule its head and it flew right over like a bird. But still we were pursued by the inexorable Rooski now almost beside herself with joy.

We crossed a frozen pond, Lord knows how, but I must say for a mule that, if it takes you into a bad place, it is clever at taking you out again. Twice we circled round the pond and then we went full gallop again for that accursed embankment.

This time we galloped top speed full in the teeth of the blizzard, and I can't much tell what happened. The last thing I can recall (before finding myself up to my neck in a snowdrift) is a sensation of gazing down with mild surprise, as if from a great height, on my own empty saddle, which seemed to be poised for that instant on the very head of the diabolical mule. So occupied was the rest of the party in fighting the roaring, ice-laden wind, that my adventures passed quite unseen by every one. Thus my dignity remains unimpaired although I have a bump on the back of my head to give me good assurance that I have not been dreaming.

Before describing the Russian position and giving my own ideas about it, I feel I must, however briefly, state the conditions leading up to the battle.

After the Fourth Army, consisting then of only the Tenth Division, had landed at Takushan, it was reinforced by a brigade of Guards from our First Army, with whose help it captured Siuyen. The Fourth Army now formed a link between the First Army at Fenghuangcheng and the Second Army at Kinchou, which, until then, had been separated by a mountainous stretch of 160 miles of country. A general advance northwards had become strategically practicable.

Before, however, this converging movement on Liaoyang could actually commence, many difficulties of transport and supply had to be solved. Great, then, was the joy of the Japanese when a cavalry action,* fought on May 30th, some four miles south of Telissu (*see* Map XL.), showed that their problem was about to be simplified by the Russians, who were themselves advancing southwards towards Port Arthur. Stakelberg from the north and Oku from the south each now pressed along the railway, the former hoping to draw off some Japanese from the siege, the latter determined to bring off more than the Russians had bargained for. Oku's force consisted of the Third and Fifth Divisions, with an independent artillery brigade; also of a part of the Fourth Division, moving well to the west by the Fuchou road; total, including the cavalry, 30,000 rifles, 1800 sabres, and 162 guns. The Sixth Division was also expected to effect a landing in time to take part in the battle, but, actually, only one single battalion arrived on the ground before the last shots had been fired. Against this force Stakelberg had some 28,000 men and 90 guns, mostly belonging to his own corps, the 1st Siberians, which did such splendid work in all the succeeding battles.

About noon, on June 14th, the Third Japanese Division, moving east of the railway, came into contact with the two Russian advance-guards sent out respectively from Stakelberg's right and left wings. The right advance-guard was encountered in the valley south of

* The affair was sharply contested, and is memorable as having furnished the only example of a cavalry charge which has taken place in Manchuria. Two sotnias of Cossacks came suddenly upon a Japanese squadron, and as they could not get up enough pace in the short distance to make their lances effective, they used these weapons as quarter-staves, striking the Japanese with them over their heads and across their bridle-arms. The Japanese squadron was defeated, but the general results of the engagement were indecisive.

Tafangshen, and consisted of eleven squadrons, eight guns, and a company of mounted infantry. The left advance-guard was met close by Gabuoho, and consisted of one squadron, six battalions of infantry, and eight guns. The Third Division drove both of these back, but the left advance-guard made a stout resistance and did not retire very far. The artillery on both sides then became heavily engaged.

Now is the time to describe the position (*see* Map XL.). From Telissu we followed the railway down south, both the line itself and the main road beside it, running through a flat valley, very narrow at first but gradually opening out as we proceeded. The country on either side was exceedingly rough and mountainous. Just as much so in fact as the Motienling district, although the altitudes of the principal mountains were not quite so great.

When we reached a point about two miles south of Telissu the road and railway skirted the lower slopes of a long, rounded, grassy spur which came jutting out westwards from the range on the east of our valley. It ran up to a height of about 200 feet, and on it had been the main Russian artillery position which was also the centre of their line. We climbed the spur and found twenty admirable gunpits quarried deeply into the crest line with good solid infantry trenches beneath them.

The trenches were from ten to twenty yards down the south slope of the spur, and they and the gunpits were certainly the best made, and most sensibly placed I have seen. To the west, south-west and south-south-west the field of fire was perfect.

Looking due west the railway and main road ran just at the foot of the spur, then came half a mile of perfectly flat open plain: then the river Fuchou in a double channel about a quarter of a mile across; then another half-mile to the steep hills on the western side of the valley which were held by the Russian right wing. South-west and south-south-west the plain was also perfectly flat, affording no artillery position for the Japanese, unless they chose to advance by night, and dig themselves in before morning. A degree or two to the east of south was a big mountain, 600 feet high and two miles long at the base, from east to west. It was, I reckoned, 2500 yards distant from the gun-pits, and while it almost touched the railway with its western flank, its eastern flank became flattened out, turned northwards and was joined on to the Russian defensive position by a long low neck. The Russians had made no attempt to hold this mountain as an outwork, and the Japanese had not occupied it either. I imagine (for I had time to go over it) that it was too steep to be practicable for artillery.

Looking east, the field of fire was restricted to a distance of about half a mile by the high main ridge running north and south from which Gun-pit Spur,* as I will call the Russian main artillery position, descended. I resolved therefore to cross this main ridge so as to examine very carefully the lie of the ground on and about the Russian left.

After climbing up and down along the Russian line of battle for some two miles, I reached the highest point in the long ridge running north and south and, from an altitude of some 500 feet, I got more of a bird's-eye view than I had from Gun-pit Spur, and, looking southwards, I now recognised three well-marked valleys converged upon the position held by the Russian left wing. The first was the valley of the railway. The second was the valley of the

* Chinese name for locality, Lungwangmiao.

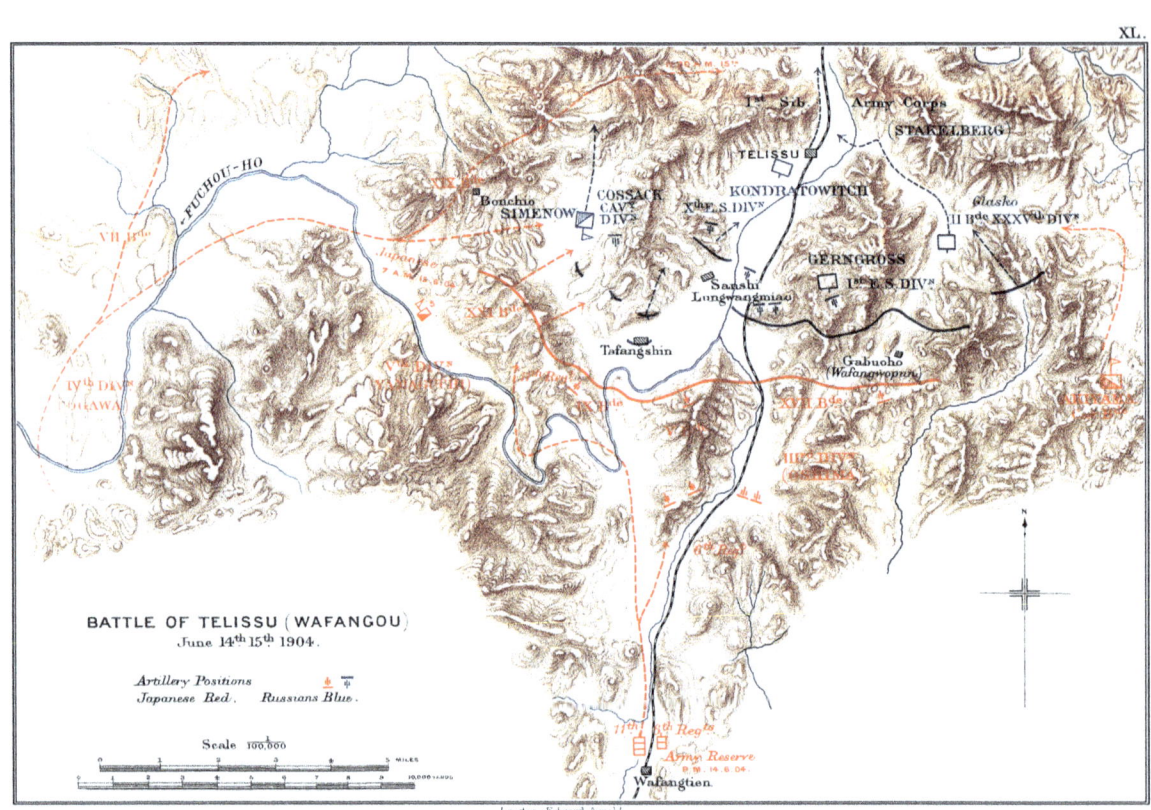

# BATTLE OF TELISSU (WAFANGOU)
## June 14th - 15th 1904.
## Spread 1

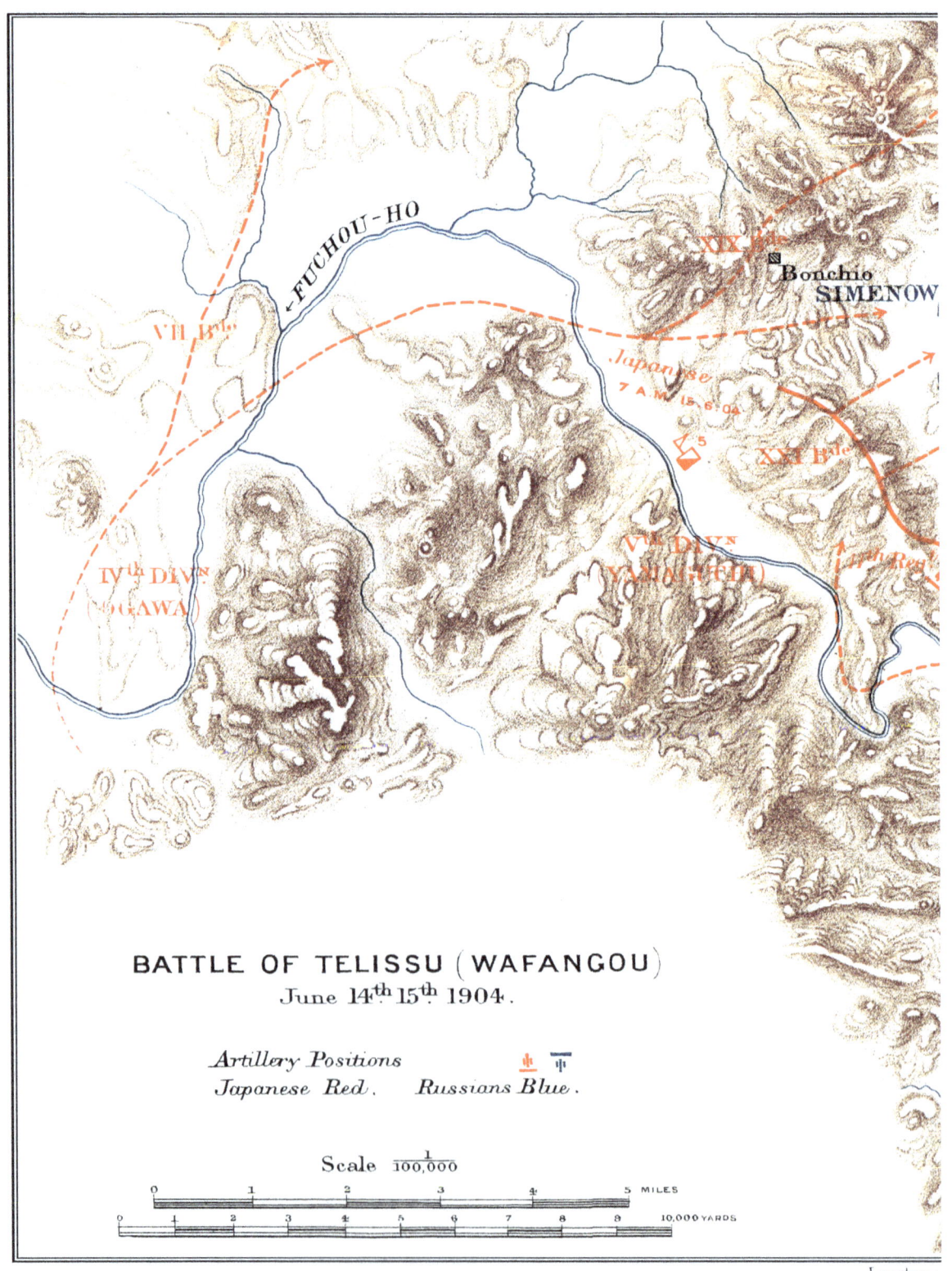

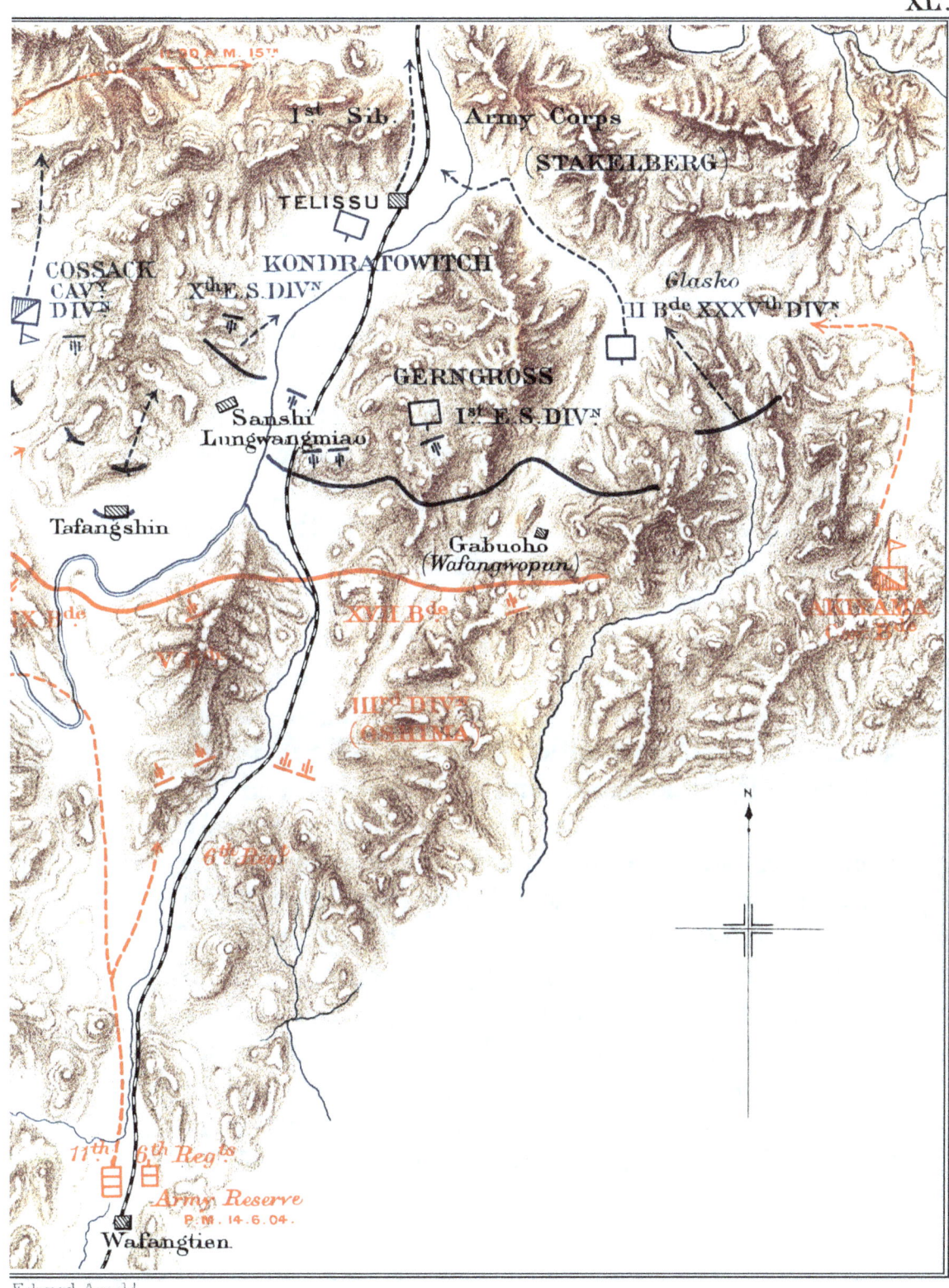

Fuchou river. The third was the valley of Gabuoho.* The Russian guns in the main artillery position commanded the valleys of the railway and river very completely, but the valley of Gabuoho was defiladed by intervening ridges, and special provision had therefore been made to deny that approach to the enemy. This Gabuoho Valley was from 300 yards to 800 yards wide, and four gun-pits on an eminence about 800 yards behind the infantry trenches completely commanded it. The infantry trenches were solidly dug and good, although wanting in head cover or concealment. They were in three tiers, and were very difficult to attack with much prospect of success from the south, as not only was the valley quite open except for the scattered huts of Gabuoho village, but the hillsides down which the Japanese must have come to get to the valley were also quite bare, and afforded no cover at all.

I have now got the position of Stakelberg's centre and left wing well into my head, and it is specially necessary I should commit it to paper, as we have no maps to help us. I will therefore recapitulate. From the central artillery position near the railway to the extreme left, Stakelberg's line of defence extends for about three miles. Taken by itself it is extremely strong. An advance along the railway or an endeavour to turn the left by the Gabuoho Valley (*see* Sketch XLI.) would be most difficult. An attack by the valley of the Fuchou river was also very uninviting, but, if by chance it could succeed, certainly promised to the victors a very special reward. The success of an attack up the railway or Gabuoho Valley would merely press Stakelberg's left wing and guns back upon Telissu. But in case of a successful advance of the Japanese up the Fuchou river valley, the twenty guns

* Chinese, Wafangwopu.

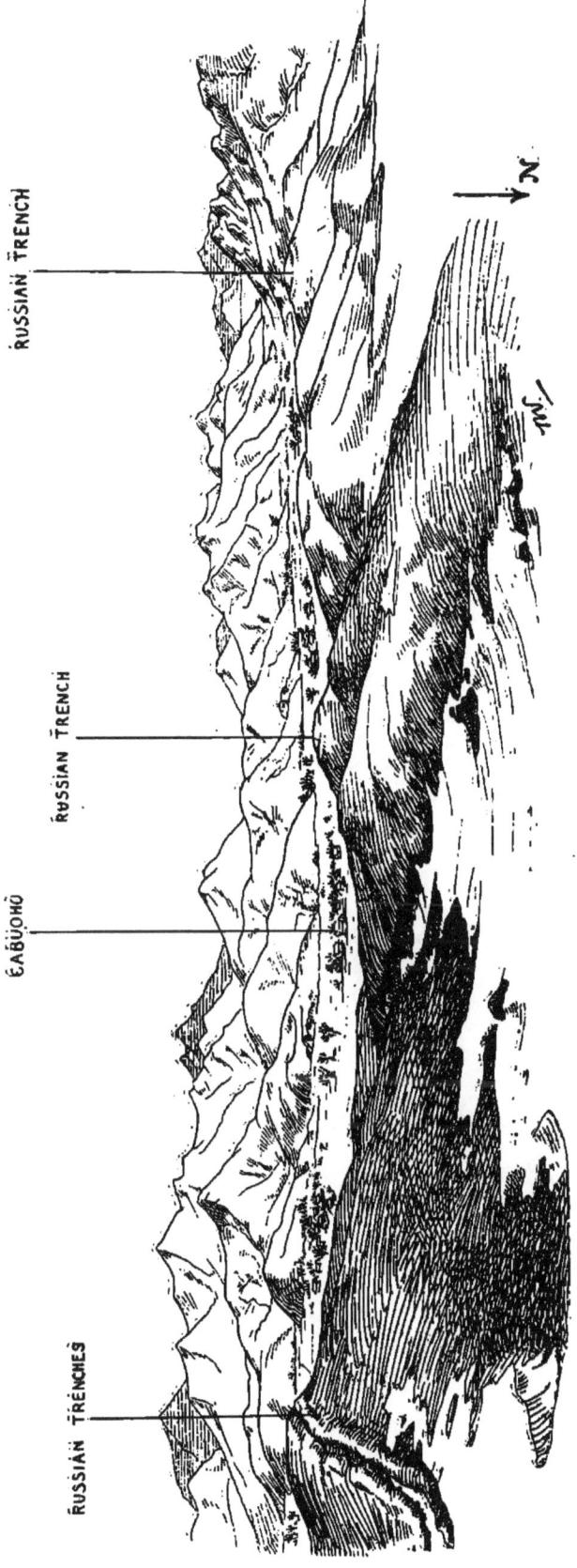

View from the Left of the Russian Position at the Battle of Telissu, June 15, 1904

XLI

of the main artillery position could not retire up the main valley to Telissu from whence they had come. No, the guns must then come down south actually in front of their own infantry trenches and circle round to the rear by the Gabuoho Valley. The lie of the ground then seemed to demand of the Russians that their centre and left wing on the east of the railway should keep a very bright look out as to what was happening on their right, and to the west of the railway generally.

I was labouring under special difficulties to-day, as there was no officer with me who was present on June 15th. But I had a singular guide, who proved himself in some respects well qualified as a battlefield *cicerone*. He was the warrant officer who had been made specially responsible for burying the dead Russians. It had taken him a week to get through the work, and his retentive memory threw a ghastly but extremely vivid light on the vicissitudes of the struggle. I must finish my description of the Russian position before I give some account of the fight. But I cannot do this until to-morrow, when I am to go over the line held by the Russian right wing to the west of the railway.

*January 28th*, 1905.—In the train going north. This morning I went out again with my grim guide, like Dante walking in Hell with his Virgil, and making my way down the western side of the Telissu Valley, climbed the steep hills about a mile and a half northwest of the main Russian artillery position at which I started yesterday. Here I found gun-pits for two batteries on a hill 200 feet high, above the village of Sanshi. The gun-pits were let into the crest like those on the main position on the east side of the valley.

There was an excellent field of fire to the south-west, but only a few hundred yards range lay open to the eastwards, where the view was closed by a higher range of hills. One thousand yards in advance of the guns were the Russian infantry trenches. They were deep and good, but had no head cover.

I rode now to the extreme west, or right, of the Russian line, and climbed the highest point, which was still crowned by an old Chinese fort. A Japanese mountain battery had, I found, occupied this spot during a part of the action. From here the infantry trenches turned from running east and west, and were bent back northwards so as to refuse the Russian right flank. I found I was now standing on the western edge of a wedge of mountainous country. The point of the wedge was about a mile to the south of me, and its width from east to west, where I stood and where the Russian trenches stretched across it, was about one mile and a quarter. The wedge was bounded on the east by the Telissu Valley, and on the west by an offshoot of that valley, which bifurcated from it one mile south of the infantry trenches, and, turning under the southern point of the salient of mountains, ran back in a north-westerly direction. Beneath this southern point lay the village of Tafangshen, which was held at the commencement of the battle by one battalion of infantry, one company of mounted infantry, and eight guns. But seeing that the village was fully a mile to the south of the infantry trenches, the main body of the Russian right wing evidently could not afford much beyond moral and artillery support to the defenders of the village and of the point of the salient. No doubt, however, the artillery on the main position on the eastern side of the railway could bring a powerful enfilade fire on any troops attacking Tafangshen from the south.

Looking north-west from the extreme right of the Russian line, I could see, three miles off, at the foot of a high mountain, a well-defined road passing through a small village called Bonchio. It was over this pass that a brigade of the Fourth Division passed, practically unopposed, to cut into the Russian line of retreat at Telissu. But I am anticipating.

The open gap of one and a half miles between the guns of the Russian right wing and left wing could not be penetrated by an enemy owing to the cross fire which could be brought to bear upon it. Very rightly, therefore, the Russians had not detailed many men to hold it.

I could now grasp the whole of the Russian defensive line very well. To meet an attack from the south it was admirable. Everywhere there was a clear field of fire of one mile. The Russian right and centre possessed this field of fire over a perfectly open plain, which they completely dominated; and although on the extreme Russian left the hills on the east side of the Gabuoho valley closed in until there remained only some 400 yards of flat ground in front of the Russian rifles, still the slopes of these hills were gentle and open, offering no cover to an enemy descending them to attack.

From the point of view of minor tactics there was small fault to find with the position selected by the Russian general. Indeed, it was very clever of him to have succeeded in picking out so defensible a line from the tangle of mountains which often lure the seeker for a good battlefield on and on, from ridge to ridge, each of which is so apt to be commanded by another. But from the standpoint of larger tactics so much can hardly be said. The position was too cramped for the number of troops and guns available. Effective counter-attack was difficult. The true scheme would certainly appear to have been to hold the narrow defile by Telissu with a comparatively weak force whilst employing the bulk of the army to strike at the Japanese left along the Fuchou road. And, undoubtedly, Oku both expected and feared some such attempt.

Having described the position, I am now enabled, by the kindness of the Japanese, to say how, on the morning of the 14th, Stakelberg meant it to be held. The following extracts are from an order found on the body of a Russian staff officer. I have already given the composition of the two advance-guards, which were taken from that document. The left wing was to hold the ground to the east of the railway. It was to be commanded by Major-General Gerngross. The strength was four squadrons, twelve battalions of infantry and thirty-six guns, four of them mountain guns. Six battalions and twenty-eight guns were to be in the first line, and six battalions and eight guns were to be in the second line.

The centre was to hold the open valley between Gunpit Spur and Sanshi west of the railway. It was to be commanded by Major-General Luchkovski. The strength was three companies of infantry and twenty-four guns.

The right was to hold from the railway valley westwards on the high ground. It was to be commanded by Major-General Krause. The strength was $3\frac{1}{4}$ battalions of infantry, eight guns, and half a battalion of Pioneers. The advanced post was to be commanded by Colonel Pachinski, and was to hold Tafangshen. The strength was one battalion of infantry, eight guns, and one company of mounted infantry. The reserve was to be posted at Lijutun, just south-west of Telissu, and was to be commanded by Major-General Glasko. The strength was eight battalions of infantry and sixteen guns.

On the afternoon of the 14th the reserve under Glasko was moved to the left to support Gerngross in making an attack against the Russian right on the morning of June 15th. During the night of the 14th five more battalions of infantry came up by railway, and were held in reserve near Telissu, thus replacing Glasko.

I now come to June 15th, when Oku, with 32,000 men and 162 guns, had resolved to attack Stakelberg's 28,000 Russians and 90 guns before further reinforcements could reach them from the north. Stakelberg, on his side, had also determined to attack the Japanese right.

The plan of the Japanese commander was to attack Stakelberg's left and centre with the Third Division, whilst with the Fifth Division and a mixed brigade detached from the Fourth Division he attempted to turn their right. The Cavalry Brigade of two regiments and six machine guns, aided by a mountain battery from the Fifth Division, was to make a separate wide turning movement round the Russian left and to endeavour to cut their line of retreat.

The dawn was ushered in by a thick mist, which enabled the Third Division to push through the railway gap to fairly close quarters before, at 5.30 A.M., the vapours cleared away and the Russian artillery on Gun-pit Spur opened upon them and drove them back into the defile. Another portion of the same Division moved up the Gabuoho Valley, and, being unsupported by artillery, found themselves overmatched by the Russian fire from their four field-pieces and three tiers of infantry trenches. Seeing that he could hold his enemies in check, Major-General Gerngross, who was commanding in this part of the field, tried frequent counter attacks which met with some success, forcing Oku twice to reinforce his left from his general reserve.

My guide was able to give me exceedingly significant details as to the course of the action in this part of the field. All along the main Russian artillery position in the centre to the trenches on the western side of the Gabuoho Valley, he did not find half a dozen dead Russians. But in the village of Gabuoho itself, and in its immediate vicinity, he had personally superintended the burial of several hundreds. Certainly over three hundred.

I closely questioned him as to whether he had buried any Russians up the eastern or Japanese hill side of the valley, and he said yes, that there were scattered corpses dotted about the slope for a distance of 200 yards up from the valley, but that beyond 200 yards there were none. Most certainly he had found no Russian corpse on the crest line of the hills forming the eastern boundary of the Gabuoho Valley. It seems then that a wrong impression has been given to the world by the accounts which have thus far appeared in the Press concerning the action of the Russian left. From reading these accounts I had imagined that Gerngross had marched some considerable distance, and had attacked and half surprised the Japanese right. Now it seems clear that although he must have counter-attacked with resolution, he did not ever succeed in making much headway. His assaulting lines apparently issued from their trenches, crossed the valley, a distance of 500 yards, and got from 100 to 200 yards up the opposite hill side, when they were brought to a standstill. It is curious to think that the most capable staff officers on either side, or even the generals in local command, could not supply me with information so reliable as that which has descended upon me through the medium of this glorified gravedigger.*

Whilst the Third Division was thus unable to make any impression upon the Russian centre or left, the Fourth Division, with fifty-four guns belonging to the independent Artillery Brigade (in addition to its own guns), moved north-westwards and northwards. Its orders were to hold out a hand to the mixed brigade from the Fourth Division (which at dawn had been still some ten miles to the west of the battlefield), and to attack the village of Tafangshen, just south of the point of the mountainous wedge-shaped salient athwart which the Russian right wing was entrenched This village was captured at 9.20 A.M., after fighting which was not severe. There were hardly any Russian corpses buried there, which looks as if the defenders had trusted mainly to their shrapnel to prevent the occupation of this point.

In my description of the Russian position I have explained, very likely with the cleverness which comes of knowing what happened, that a Japanese success here was just about the most fatal mischance which could possibly have happened to the Russians. Tafangshen, and the high ground immediately to the north of it, was beyond a doubt the Achilles heel of a position otherwise fairly strong. If either flank were turned, all that the Japanese could do would be to press the Russians back into the Telissu Valley, where

* It is said, however, that at St. Privat some of the German burying-parties carried their dead up the hill so that their graves might appear closer to the enemy's position than those of rival regiments.

they could retire at the rate of four miles to every mile that Oku's men could pursue up and down the mountains. But the capture of Tafangshen denied the Telissu Valley as an avenue of retreat to the Russians for as far as shrapnel would range, namely, some three miles.

As might have been expected, directly Tafangshen was captured, Colonel Shiba, one of the very best officers in the whole of the Japanese Army, came hurrying up with the 15th Artillery Regiment and brought a cross fire upon the main Russian artillery position at Gun-pit Spur, thus easing the position on the Third Division. It then became obvious that the Russian guns would have great difficulty in moving. They could not now possibly limber up under Shiba's fire and come slowly down the steep spur into the open valley. They could only retire by coming over the southern brow of Gun-pit Spur and by passing along the front of their own infantry to gain the Gabuoho Valley, where they might possibly, but very improbably, escape by running the gauntlet of the rifle-fire of the Third Division. Why then did not the Russian reserves, half a mile south of Telissu, come up and make at least one good charge against the village of Tafangshen? I cannot say. No counter-attack was made, and the Japanese proceeded to improve their success by capturing the southern point of the mountainous wedge held by the Russian right wing.

A mountain battery now came up on to these hills to help the 15th Artillery Regiment, and by the combined Japanese fire the Russian guns, both in their main position and in the right wing, were silenced at about 11 A.M. At this time also the mixed Brigade of the Fourth Division marching through Bonchio Gap, got into touch with the Fifth Division and threatened to envelop the Russian right and to cut in behind them at a point in the Telissu Valley four miles north of the battlefield. I was assured that when the Mixed Brigade passed through the Bonchio Gap the whole of the Russian Army was still in its trenches. If so, it is marvellous that Stakelberg did not experience a real disaster, instead of a mere defeat. It appears that the Russian cavalry first came into contact with them at the Bonchio gap, but that their advance was not checked until they got within a mile of the Telissu Valley. At this spot my guide had also buried many corpses, but unfortunately I had no time to go and make a personal inspection of the terrain.

Soon after the Russian guns were mastered, the reserves (which had not fired a shot) began to fall back. I cannot, on the spur of the moment, recall another similar example of reserves initiating a retreat. On the north-west frontier of India, the art of retirement has been reduced to an exact science. This sounds sarcastic, but it certainly is not meant so. The hill tribes rarely fight as long as our troops are advancing; but the moment the reconnaissance, or punitive expedition, or whatever it may be, begins to make its way back to camp, it is attacked and pursued by an enemy until then invisible.

In South Africa also, even if the head of the column was pursuing after a victory, the tail of it was almost invariably fighting a rearguard action. I merely quote these experiences to give force to my view that the normal function of a reserve under the conditions obtaining at Telissu would have been (1) to retake Tafangshen; (2) if a retreat were determined upon, to take up a position a rifle-shot north of the Russian line of battle, so as to let all their own troops through preparatory to taking up the duties of rearguard.

By mid-day, the right wing still defending themselves, began definitely, though slowly, to retreat. Strange to say, not a single Russian corpse was found at or near these trenches. It was not until a point nearly half a mile north of the trenches that the grave-digger's work had begun. Possibly the Russians were able to send back their dead until their retreat became more hurried. Possibly the fighting here was not so stiff as it has been represented. But however this may be, it is yet more strange that for some reason, at present inexplicable, Gerngross and the left wing, who were gallantly holding their own, and more than holding their own, were permitted to stand fast, although the retirement of the right wing quite uncovered their western flank. After an hour or two the Japanese cavalry began to make itself felt on the eastern flank of the left wing, and then at last Gerngross issued tardy orders for a withdrawal. There was great difficulty in extricating the infantry, and most of the guns had to be abandoned. My corpse-man told me he buried many Russians along the line of retreat from Gabuoho to Likiatun.

The Japanese now got their guns up on to Gun-pit Spur, in among the captured Russian cannon, and began firing down the Telissu defile. The Mixed Brigade from the Fourth Division was only being held back with difficulty from crowning the western heights a mile north of Telissu. Things looked as bad as bad could be for Stakelberg, when a blinding rainstorm came on, and, blotting everything from view, ended the conflict.

Looked at from the Japanese standpoint, the battle of Telissu was a pretty piece of tactics. But the weakness of Stakelberg on his right wing and the somewhat feeble resistance shown there made the game comparatively easy. If I were to venture on a criticism of General Oku's operations I should say he was strategically in too great a hurry, and that tactically he attempted too much.

I need not labour the point that if he had been able to play with Stakelberg during June 15 until the Mixed Brigade from the Fourth Division had got within striking distance of Telissu, hardly any of the Russians would have escaped. Also, taking the actual attack as it was carried out, the Japanese commander endeavoured to turn both Stakelberg's flanks and to carry the position all along its front, although he had only a small superiority of infantry, and of half as much again in guns.

In my humble opinion, only a superiority of two to one can ordinarily warrant a commander in thus dispensing with all those niceties of warfare which tend to mislead the enemy and to force him to retain troops to meet what is only a feint and not a home thrust. Moreover, Oku's method is costly of life. I know well that British generals stand convicted of the ultimately far more cruel habit of hesitating to spend lives freely. But there is probably a golden mean. Generals should remember that each soldier's life which they carry in their hand is a tiny bit of their country and its power. Then they will probably be guided by Heaven to act aright in the hour of need. The Japanese did not, as a matter of fact, lose much at Telissu; only 1000 or one-tenth of their adversaries' casualties. But it is for this very reason that I choose the present occasion for my remark.

Regarding the problem from the Russian point of view, Tafangshen was so vital a point that it should have been strongly fortified and strengthened by barbed wire, abattis, and loop-holed houses. The whole line of the infantry of the right wing should have been advanced half a mile on to the next ridge to the south to give it closer support. The Reserve, above all, should have been kept handy to meet such a likely eventuality as an attempt by the Japanese to carry this vital point by a *coup de main*. I had not the advantage of being present at the battle, but the cross-fire of shrapnel in front of the village should have rendered it almost impregnable to a day assault, even as it was. Still, it was taken. Well, then, it should have been re-taken, or the battle was lost. What was the Reserve doing?

I hardly know what to say about the Mixed Brigade from the Fourth Division on the Fuchou main road, and its apparently unexpected appearance behind the right rear of the Russians. It is quite possible that the hasty falling back of the Reserve and the consequent loss of the battle may be in some way attributable to the anxiety caused by this menace to Stakelberg's communications. In the ordinary course of military operations, an infantry brigade moving from a highway to participate in an action against a force well equipped with cavalry would have had its movement detected as soon as it arrived within twenty miles of its objective. For the country, though mountainous, was not by any means wooded or close. On the contrary, I have never seen a terrain better adapted for the employment of cavalry either mounted as an observing force or dismounted as a retarding force. There were numberless peaks to give an extensive view of the surrounding country, which was for the most part open and unwooded. There were many ridges where mobile riflemen could have forced regular infantry to deploy for attack, and to come into action with their artillery.

If, of course, the cavalry were bent upon charging with lance and sabre, then the commander must pay the penalty.

I can only say that if Stakelberg had been informed (as he ought to have been) by his cavalry of the spot where the Mixed Brigade camped on the night of the 14th-15th, he should, considering the nature of the country, have been able to make sure that they did not cover the ten miles which separated them from the battlefield before nightfall. Some officers have a theory that owing to the Russians having no divisional cavalry the sympathy between the mounted and dismounted branches is weaker than in other armies, but I confess this idea seems to me a little too fanciful.

I hope I have not been over critical. The highest authority tells us that he is the best general who makes fewest mistakes. All military operations are so dependent for their success upon the aid of fortune, that it is very unjust to attribute blame unless it can be made clear that the accepted axioms of war have, to some extent, been infringed. Unless Kuropatkin can show that he could not spare another Division, and that he had sufficient grounds to justify him in sending a comparatively weak force so far to the south, then he is the chief offender against those recognised axioms. Stakelberg must justify to history his apparent ignorance of the advance of a Japanese Division up the Fuchou road and of the detachment of a brigade from it to turn his right flank. He must show how his cavalry, when they did detect the brigade, failed to delay it with their rifles and horse guns in the succession of confined and rugged passes over which it had to move. He must explain why his right wing fell back independently, leaving Gerngross and his left in the lurch.

Very likely he can do so triumphantly. I merely state a case from information necessarily imperfect.

As regards General Oku, all that can be said against him is that he tried, perhaps, to do too much. Surely, if that is a fault, it is one which is closely akin to the very highest of our virtues.

I have written this in the train, which has been passing through grey, craggy mountains covered with snow wherever the surface is not too precipitous. The red winter sun is setting behind a lofty range on to our left, and in the valley a frozen river winds like a huge serpent with its scales of ice all glittering in the sunset. In the distance I can see a line of Japanese transport passing across the river. The scene is wild and melancholy, but yet strikes me with that sense of familiarity and homeliness which comes of old associations. The reason is, I think, that it reminds me of a picture of adventures in the Arctic regions which used to excite my imagination when I was quite a small child.

## CHAPTER XXXVIII

### FUJI VEILS HER FACE

COAL MINES, *January 29th*, 1905.—We reached our old quarters here at noon, and the salute which welcomed our return was fired by several hundred guns, which are muttering and rumbling continuously from the direction of the far west, whenever the louder but more intermittent cannonade closer to us in the north ceases for a moment to let us hear the ominous undertones of a distant battle. In the midst of the hurly-burly an adjutant from headquarters handed me a cable and asked me to come and breakfast privately with General Kuroki next morning. He said it was too late to go out and see the fighting, as it was virtually decided in favour of the Japanese. Ordinarily I should have struggled against this decision, but I had such a racking headache from the fumes of the charcoal stoves with which we kept life in ourselves during the night in the train that I was only too glad to have so good an excuse for doing nothing.

The cable was to summon me post haste from war's alarms to the safe seclusion of Salisbury Plain.

Well, so be it. I shall miss a great battle, for Nogi's Third Army is hurrying northwards as fast as trains and roads will take it, and the Japanese are bound to try and win the *victoire décisive*\* of which they so

---

\* I use the French phrase because it was always employed by the Japanese, even by the German-speaking officers.

constantly speak before the winter relaxes its iron grip on all the rivers and roads. But, by the time I get back to London I shall have been fifteen months absent, nearly two-thirds of which time I shall have spent actually in the field. I have seen every sort of fight except a cavalry fight, and I have studied and described terrain until I am in danger of knowing Manchuria as intimately as South Africa. In short, enough is as good as a feast; even if it is not so, it is better to try to believe that it is so, for those who wear the King's uniform must accept their destiny wherever it leads them.

COAL-MINES, *January 30th*, 1905.—I have just enjoyed the most agreeable of all the many agreeable visits I have paid to First Army Headquarters. General Kuroki, one staff officer and myself; no one else. The conversation was intimate and unconventional. I gave all my Port Arthur impressions freely, and Kuroki was keenly interested, especially, I think, in hearing that so far no report which has reached us has succeeded in conveying an adequate idea of the stupendous monument to valour raised by victors and vanquished on 203 Metre Hill. I expounded my Nanshan and Telissu theories much as I have entered them in my diary; and whether out of politeness or from conviction my hosts seemed inclined to accept my views. Something, I forget what, turned the conversation on to the feverish restlessness which, at the beginning of the twentieth century, characterises so many great nations. I remarked that the English people, by the dumb, stubborn conservatism which they consistently opposed to the zealous fervour of the Scotch and to the Celtic brilliance of the Irish, kept the ship of State on even keel, and were the true cause of the grandeur

THE BRITISH ATTACHÉ WITH THE 2ND DIVISION 1ST ARMY
CAPTAIN B. VINCENT, R.F.A.

and stability of the British Empire. In the race of nations, it was, I thought, always safe to back the tortoise against the hare.

Kuroki seemed inclined to appreciate this sentiment and said, "Certainly it is dangerous to change old customs hurriedly. Now that we have beaten Russia, I hope my fellow countrymen will see that there cannot be anything so radically wrong with us after all, and that they will be inclined to continue their advance more slowly. My own generation has about run its race. Nothing can change us. But, the coming generation? I would have greater confidence in the future if I were sure that there is a large section of our people who, like the English, have a positive dislike to change, even when it plausibly assumes the guise of improvement."

We spoke of certain officers and of the comparative values of intelligence and force of character. The staff officer incidentally remarked that, being anxious to test the insight, imagination and good taste of his subordinates, he had asked them all separately whether they preferred the cherry-blossom or the plum-blossom. Imagine the Director of Military Education posing such conundrums! And yet, why not? I am sure that in his name questions much less practical are constantly being set to unfortunate candidates. I laughed very much, however, when I heard the answer given by the cautious Major F——. He said he admired both the plum and cherry-blossom in equal degree. His reply hits him off to a T.

It was arranged that I should leave on February 6th, and that a banquet should be given in my honour by Kuroki on the 4th instant. Meanwhile, as good an account as was available of the action of Heikoutai, which ended yesterday, would be dictated to me in the next room.

In taking my leave I said that before very long I hoped the First Army would also be returning home. The war heroes would get a tremendous reception, but it was wise to remember that all the great welcome and attention which would be pressed upon the officers would not last very long—six months at most. Kuroki laughed, and assured me I need not be afraid he would lose his balance. He agreed with me, only he considered I had much overstated the probable period of public enthusiasm. He knew all about that bubble from his own experiences after the China War. Soldiers in all countries were either spoilt or neglected. There was no sense of proportion. Anyway it was all one to him, for he was getting old, and all he wished was to be left perfectly quiet to lead his own life and perform his own duties.

### STORY OF THE BATTLE OF THE 26TH-29TH JANUARY

#### CONDENSED FROM THE ACCOUNT DICTATED TO ME AFTER BREAKFAST ON THE 30TH JANUARY

At midday on January 24th, spies reported that on January 23rd a movement southwards had been noticed at Mukden. Sure enough, on the 25th the enemy began to cross the Hun river opposite the extreme left of the Manchurian Army.

We now know that the Russian forces engaged at Heikoutai amounted to more than four Divisions, namely the Eighth Army Corps, a part of the Fifth Siberian Army Corps, and two Brigades of Sharpshooters. But at first, Marquis Oyama had no idea that he was about to meet an attack from so formidable a force.

On January 26th, news was sent to say that the Russians were approaching Heikoutai on the left bank of the Hunho, forty miles south-west of Mukden. Two other hostile columns were said to be on the move; one coming through Chonan five miles north-east of Heikoutai, and the other a few miles to the south-west of Heikoutai. These three columns were apparently endeavouring to turn our left wing, and in addition several Russian detachments were marching due south and making for the weakly-held gap between our extreme left and the left centre. When our information had so far enlightened us we realised, it is true, that there was something serious in the wind, but we were still sorely puzzled as to whether we had merely to deal with an attempt to gain some local advantage, or whether we were confronted with the preliminaries to a general Russian advance. One thing seemed certain. If Kuropatkin meant serious business he could not confine his attack to one point only. Therefore, as nothing happened elsewhere, we assumed that the manœuvring against our left could not, of itself, possibly develop into a serious attack, and we hurried on our preparations to meet an assault and furious battle along the whole of our line. Still, strange to say, even twelve hours after the enemy had crossed the Hun river we were entirely unable to detect any sign of activity along the front of our main positions.

But theories must yield to facts, and certainly as time went on it seemed beyond argument that the Russians were committing themselves to an important attack against our left. We were driven then to ask ourselves what could be the object of such a movement. From the enemy's point of view nothing could seem less opportune. Several weeks had passed since the fall of Port Arthur, and Russian headquarters must have known that at least a part of Nogi's Third Army had arrived at the front. If Mistchenko's raid had done no other good it must have enabled him to report so much at least to his Commander-in-Chief? In our bewilderment we turned to the explanation that politics must again be at the bottom of the militarily incomprehensible, and we began to think it possible we should after all have to fight an empty, meaningless partial action on our left, instead of a great general action.

Accordingly, the General Reserve, the Eighth Division, was despatched to Heikoutai, and marched there with one Kobi Brigade on the night of 25th-26th January. It comes from the north-west of Japan near the home of our renowned Second Division, and we expect to hear when we get details that they have done just as well or perhaps even better than their comrades. Certainly they made a good start by marching nineteen miles in this awful weather.* The Fifth Division from the Fourth Army was the next to move off, leaving on the morning of the 26th and reaching the

* I heard from another source that the Eighth Division, though they fought bravely, showed some of the qualities of young soldiers as compared with the veteran troops of the First Army. They behaved as if they were at manœuvres; advanced in close regular formations. There was good-natured chaff between the old hands and the newcomers. The Eighth Division wounded were proud of their wounds, and thought themselves great heroes until they were well jeered at by the veterans of the Second Division. They allowed their rice and water to get frozen solid, whilst the wily Second Division took care of their rations by wrapping them up in their "sodenashes" (sleeveless fur waistcoats) and kept them warm and eatable under their coats.

battlefield by the evening of the 27th. Our Second Division followed them closely, and last of all a second Brigade of Kobi marched westwards, making a grand total of four Japanese Divisions of infantry, the Second Brigade of cavalry and an independent Brigade of artillery. Major-General Tatsumi, commanded the Eighth Division, and the Fifth Division was commanded by our old friend Kigoshi, until recently the famous Brigadier in the Twelfth Division. Our Second Division was, of course, under Nishijima.*

So far we have few details of the fight. We know that as the Eighth Division was in the act of attacking westwards, a force of Russians advanced against them from Shujiho, which was four miles to the south of them. Their left wing was forced to face southwards, whilst their centre and right continued to fight with their faces to the west.

This was an awkward situation for an untried Division, but luckily before much harm could be done the veteran Second Division came up and attacked the enemy from the south, forcing them to relax their grip on the Eighth Division.

We know also that the Russian detachments coming down from the north against the weakly-held gap between our extreme left and our left centre attacked the Japanese posts at Chintanpu † and Litajentun. Against the Chintanpu entrenchment, which was held by three companies and two machine guns, the enemy made no less than five determined attacks. Fortunately, they launched their assaults piecemeal, one

* Major-General Baron Nishi had been transferred to the post of Governor of the Liaotung Peninsula.

† Chintanpu is called Shenshanpu by the Chinese and Sandepu by the Russians.

battalion at a time. Their formations were close, and the machine guns worked havoc with them. It is said that 1000 Russians are lying dead in front of Chintanpu. Had they worked on a wide front they must easily have enveloped such a small isolated post, but they chose to run their heads straight against it. Our second Cavalry Brigade was posted at this time near Shohokka, where the Hun and Taitsu rivers meet.* They had a hard time, being opposed by greatly superior forces, but somehow they managed to hold their own. On January 26, one and a half squadrons reconnoitred Heikoutai, but could not make out the Russian forces clearly.

On the morning of the 27th, however, the Russians attacked in force along the line Laokyo-Somaho. Mistchenko also moved south with one cavalry regiment and twelve guns from Ashigu towards Shohokka, and then turned due east, crossing the Hunho opposite Kojiho, which he attacked. There Mistchenko was met by the Eighth Division and by part of the Second Division; and by 6.30 P.M. on the 27th the Russian cavalry was driven back, one party moving due north towards Heikoutai. There was bayonet work in Somaho this day. During the night of the 27-28th, the Eighth Division attacked and took the line Laokyo-Somaho. Meanwhile the Russians had been expelled from Liujoko by the Fifth Division. At Gokashi, two

* A regimental officer said to me, "I can tell you though, it was not only the Second Division who were clever. The Cavalry Brigade were pretty sharp, too, I can tell you. When their eight squadrons were opposed by twenty Russian squadrons, they formed small columns, which advanced, pretending to be the guns of batteries. Each little column dug a little gun-pit, and so the stupid old Russians spent four hours firing shell at what they thought was our splendid horse artillery."

Some of General Nogi's Infantry on their March North from Port Arthur, January 1905

and a half miles south-west of Heikaotai, the Second Division had driven out the enemy after heavy fighting.

But at Heikoutai the Russians fought like heroes. The Eighth Division made some fine attacks upon them on the 28th, but were each time repulsed, mainly by the fire of the Russian machine guns. Had our Division been less reliable than the Eighth, which, as you know, is recruited from the north-east of Japan, perhaps the affair might not have ended quite so well for us.* Curiously, the Kobi Brigade, attached to the Eighth Division, were also from the north-east, so the Russians at Heikoutai were in bad luck. Tatsumi gave orders for a final attack at daylight on the 29th, but during the night Okami's Brigade advanced from Somaho on Heikoutai, on its own initiative, and was repulsed badly. The other Brigade attacked as ordered at 5.30 A.M. and found the Russians in the act of retiring.† You will under-

* A previous footnote throws a sidelight on this statement. I think there is no doubt that the Eighth Division exposed themselves more than was strictly necessary. The 31st Regiment was literally cut to pieces, so I was told, only a few private soldiers remaining.

† From yet another unofficial source I hear that the cavalry suffered much from want of instructions, and that they claim that they might have brought off a big stroke had they any clear idea of the general situation. Thus they were deeply disappointed. I believe that one cause of the lack of orders was that every message to each Brigade and Division had to pass through one telephone station, run by a single half-frozen poor devil of a private soldier.

The cold was intense. Horsemen galloped about the field with the foam and dripping sweat of their horses changing into a crust like snow, and long dangling icicles. The Fifth Division had during the last night but one fairly to choose between frost and fire. They were seventy yards distant from the Russians in Liujoko. When they stamped their feet to keep life in them then the Russians fired. When they remained quiet they lost their toes. Four hundred of them were suffering from Tosho (frost-bite) next morning.

stand that this account is necessarily confused, as we have not yet received our full reports.

Once more, we cannot imagine why Kuropatkin did not time his attack before the arrival of the Third Army from Port Arthur. Nor do we understand why, when he did make it, he did not support it by at least a demonstration all along our front. Had he done so, we could not have spared so many troops to detach to our left, and the attack would have had a much better chance. It is quite true that General Kuroki had promised Marquis Oyama to spare him the Second Division, provided the First Army stuck to its own lines and was not launched at the Russian lines in front of it. Still, had Kuropatkin been lively and active along our position, there might have been some delay in parting with the Second Division, and even so it might have been shorn of a battalion or two, instead of going as it did absolutely complete.

Here ends the slight sketch of the action of Heikoutai given me at Headquarters just as a parting gift to take home with me.

COAL MINES, *February 1st*, 1905.—General Matsunaga came to see me this morning, *en route* to take up his new post as Chief of the Staff to General Nogi and the Third Army. He is a tremendous fellow, built like the Dutch captain of a fishing smack, bluff, burly and broad-chested, with bluff, gruff, hearty manners to correspond.

Matsunaga said he hoped in his new capacity of Chief of Staff of the Third Army, he would soon have the honour of welcoming me to Mukden. I replied that he had thrown off his First Army *esprit de corps* very quickly if he already, before he had left our lines, spoke of the Third Army welcoming the First Army men to Mukden. I said, " On the contrary, by the good help of your old brigade, I shall have the honour of welcoming you and his Excellency General Nogi to Mukden!"

And so we parted; but, alas, I knew I would never see Mukden.

COAL MINES, *February 5th*, 1905.—My days with the Japanese Army are swiftly running to a close. A banquet was given by Kuroki in my honour to-day, and a very large number of officers were present.

Kuroki spoke for six minutes. He said I had been with the army since Korean days, and that he and all his officers had hoped I would remain with them until the very end. Now, however, I had been offered a high command, and their sorrow at losing me was tempered by pleasure that I had gained the approbation of the King of England. The First Army hoped I would remember them and the hardships and battles of the year that was past, and from the First Army he would assure me with all his heart that the British general would not lightly or soon be forgotten.

I felt almost overcome when I rose to reply. I said the King of England, in giving me my appointment, had probably been influenced by knowing I had enjoyed exceptional opportunities of studying my profession with the First Army. For it was first not only in its numeral. It had fought the first battle, first entered Manchuria, first crossed the Taitsuho. Would have been first to cross the Shaho had that been permitted, and I would wager it would be first into Mukden. Thus, although his Excellency and his army were so modest that they did not know it, they were now the most popular military force in the world. If any of them went to London or New York they would be surprised at the warmth of their welcome. The only

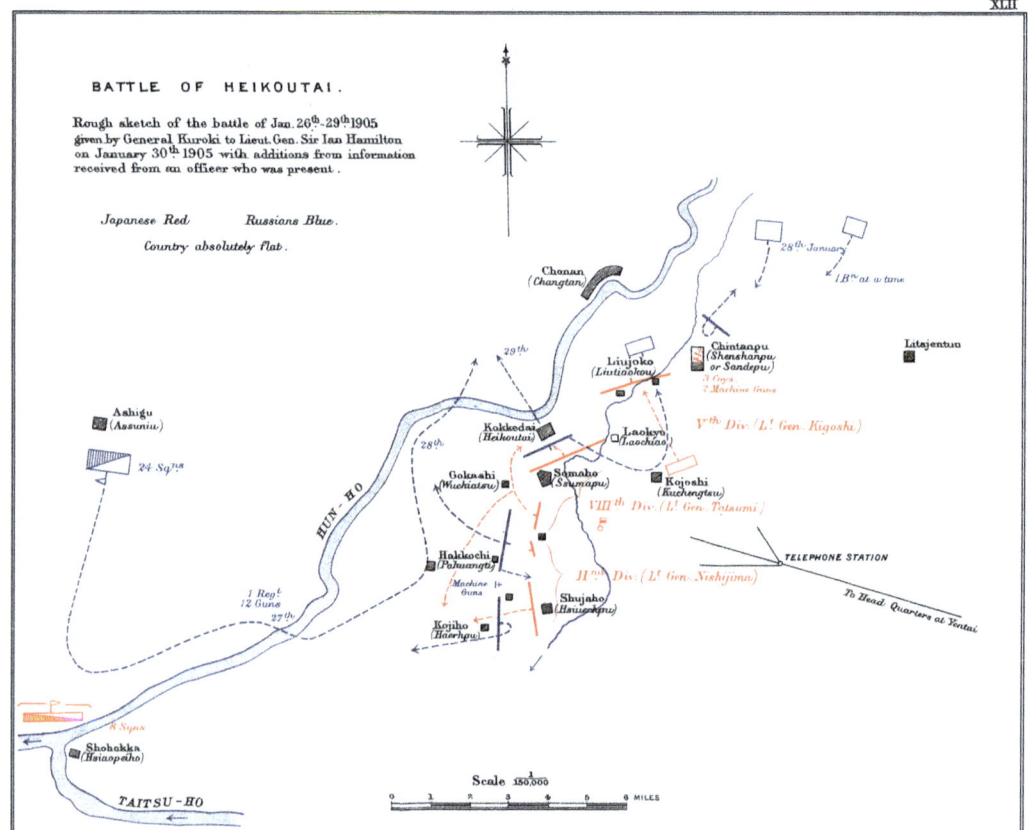

# BATTLE OF HEIKOUTAI
## January 26th - 29th 1905.
### Spread 1

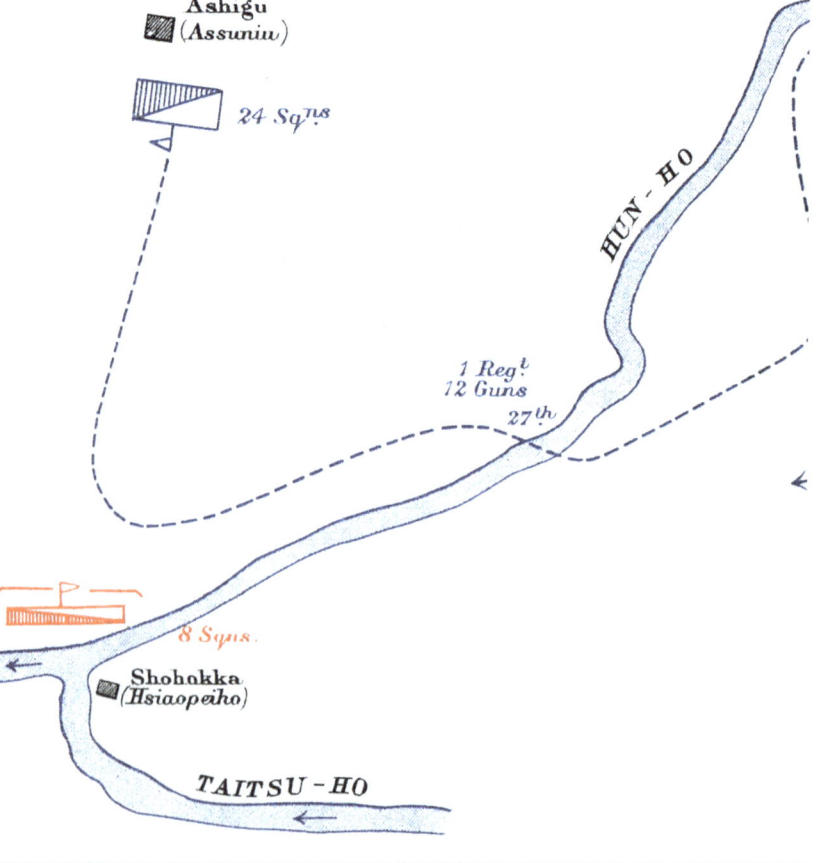

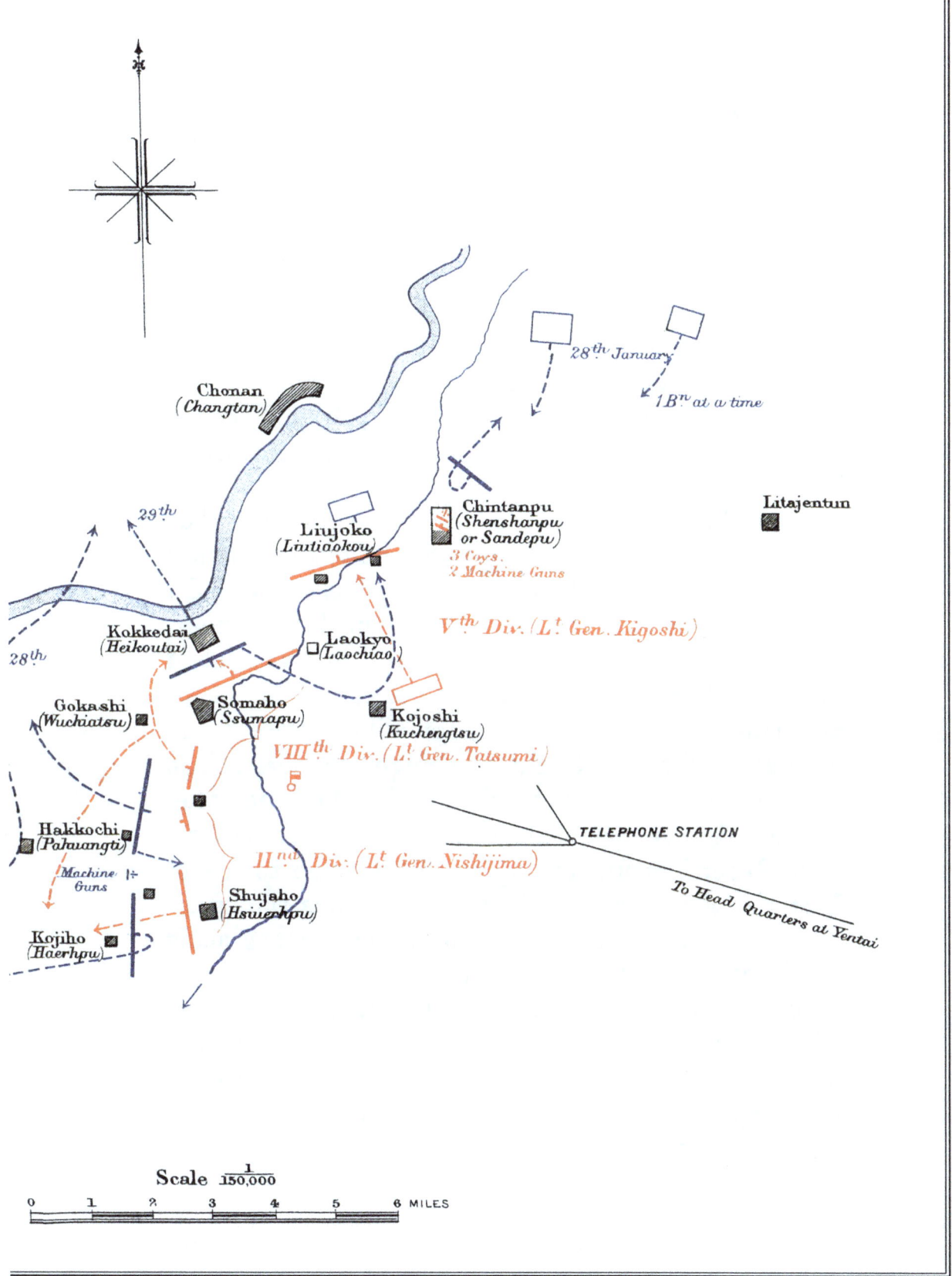

place in the world where they would henceforth be disliked was on Salisbury Plain, for the troops there would so often hear of the virtues of the First Army that they would wish his Excellency General Kuroki had never been born. I wound up, as far as I can remember, by inviting the whole 42,000 to come and stay with me in England for as long as ever they liked.

It was very characteristic of Japanese tact and politeness that, when it came to the turn of the interpreter to translate my remarks, he should have added to the towns of London and New York which I had actually mentioned, the names of Paris, Berlin, Vienna, Rome and Stockholm which I had forgotten myself to include.

After lunch a friend on the Staff told me that Grippenberg was being blamed in Russia for having lost 10,000 men in the last battle at Heikoutai. He said it was mistaken policy to punish a general because he had failed or because he had lost a lot of men. Such action checked initiative, which was of all qualities the most valuable of military assets. A general then began to think it might be more politic to keep his army well together, and to venture little. I agree. I remember that extraordinarily clever young man, General Smuts, saying much the same to me in Pretoria, and explaining to me that it was the crucifixion of their defeated generals by the Carthaginians which lost them the Punic Wars.

After taking leave of the Headquarters, very sadly, I have come back here, where I am to be honoured by another farewell banquet to-night. The cook has been forty-eight hours preparing the dinner, so it ought to be something tremendous.

IN THE TRAIN, *February 6th*, 1905.—The leave-taking is over. It was a painful wrench to tear myself away on the eve of a great battle from so many kind friends; but it is over, and now as is always the case, the future again begins to spread itself alluringly before me.

The dinner last night was superb, and my American *confrère* made a very sympathetic oration, to which I replied as best I might. This morning, at 9.30, with a blizzard blowing and the thermometer five degrees below zero F., I was just starting when Kuroki and the whole of his Headquarters Staff rode in from Hanlasanshi, three miles distant, to drink a last stirrup cup with me before I left. Mugs were filled with champagne, and I confess that after the big dinner the previous night I was for shirking some of mine. Then, to my shame, I saw that Kuroki, who is nearly ten years my senior, had drained his to the last drop. I seized the mug once more and so began the day badly, although in what the Japanese are fond of calling high spirits. Deeply touched at the kindness shown, in my person, to my country by the gallant and glorious First Army of Japan, I set spurs to my horse and rode through the blizzard twelve miles to the headquarters of Marshal the Marquis Oyama.

I lunched with his Excellency and with General Kodama, when I drank more champagne and also some claret, Mouton Rothschild, a special present from his Majesty the Emperor. Oyama and Kodama were in excellent spirits, and were having great chaff and fun. His Excellency said that the American newspapers, who "must manufacture sensations if they cannot get them any other way," had published some news in leaded type about Kodama and himself. It was said that they had quarrelled violently, with the result that the Chief of the General Staff had come off second best, and had been deported from the seat of war to Japan. Both laughed heartily, and seemed hugely amused. I was hoping to hear something more about Heikoutai, but rich as was the feast upon the table of the generals, not even one crumb of news fell from their mouths into my hungry note-book.

After lunch I was greatly concerned to learn that the old Commander-in-Chief was going to mount his horse and ride down to the station with me, a distance of two miles. He rarely goes out riding in such weather, and the blizzard to-day was blowing with special bitterness. However, he would do it, and General Kodama and the rest of the Manchurian Army Headquarters Staff accompanied him. His Excellency rode a handsome, corky little horse, the best-looking Japanese-bred charger I have seen. He told me his horse, that he had ridden all through the war with China ten years ago, was still alive and well in Japan. He had made a promise to it that, if it carried him through the campaign, it should enjoy free quarters for the rest of its life. He said it was treacherous and ungentlemanly to the last degree to promise an animal anything and then to break the plighted word—far worse than to show similar treachery to a man, for a man can speak and claim fulfilment of the promise, an animal cannot. I told his Excellency I had a little Australian horse called Black Monday, who had been ridden by me in the Tirah Campaign of 1896–97, and again in the siege of Ladysmith, and all through the South African War. I told him also about Lord Roberts' famous white Arab charger Volonel, and of how the Queen had given it war medals on its breast-plate. The

Commander-in-Chief was much interested, and I think he would like his own charger also to be decorated.

When we reached the station we had twenty minutes to wait in a cold of which, fortunately for them, few in England have the smallest conception.

At last I was off, and I hope I may never forget the great honour done to the British Army by the Marquis Oyama on this occasion.

YELLOW SEA, *February 9th*, 1905.—I am in a fine ship by Harland and Wolff, of about 6000 tons. We have 1000 prisoners on board, under charge of a Japanese corporal and twelve men. There are no officers amongst the Russians; and the men do not at all know what to make of my uniform.

The Japanese treat them most considerately and kindly. No assumption of superiority or swagger of any sort. The Russians, for their part, are obedient; indeed, they seem astonishingly docile and easily managed, in comparison with Anglo-Saxons. There are 300 sailors amongst the crowd, who strike me as being far and away above the standard of the soldiers in physique, bearing, alertness and intelligence. Some of the prisoners are playing the concertina. Others are dancing. They are excellently and warmly clad, and have lots of flesh on their bones. Very different is their condition from that of our poor fellows after Ladysmith.

YOKOHAMA BAY, *February 13th*, 1905.—We steamed to our moorings at dawn, just as we did eleven months ago. Again the sun rose red in our wake through the misty haze which bounds the far horizon; but Fujiyama, alas! made no answering sign from the depths of the western sky. And as the great mountain concealed its wonders behind the shroud of cold, impenetrable cloud, so, too, my heart remained dead and unresponsive to the charm of the hour and of the place.

Last year my life was about to escape from War Office and other matter-of-fact duties into a mysterious realm of adventure and romance. To-day my course is run; my adventures are achieved, and instinctively I attune my mood to a more prosaic key before exchanging my khaki and my sword for the costume and cane of a commonplace civilisation.

Thus the grey chameleon, captive in some grimy city, cares no more to wear the livery of the forest through whose foliage it once passed like a living emerald.

An officer bearing complimentary messages has come out in a launch to take me ashore. The moment is at hand. But ere the old life quite resumes its sway, let me try in one rapid retrospect to realise the days and nights that are no more:

My peony garden in Fenghuangcheng bathed in the soft moonlight; the Heaven-reaching Pass, reverberating through all its hollows and ridges to the continued roll of musketry; the wall of mist and the writing that appeared thereon; the Swallows'-nest Fort and bloody Rice-cake Hill; the heroic bayonet fight on Okasaki Yama's brow; the rapid march; the manœuvre; the fierce attack; the stubborn defence; the red battle and the crowd of pale corpses. Again I seem to see the advance of the invincible First Army; the dense ranks toiling on, ever onwards, towards the shrieking shell and angry hiss of the rifle bullets. No drums or bugles cheer the march of the phantom army of my thoughts, but ever the rumble and roar of the cannon fills each soldier's heart with exultation as the columns draw nearer and yet nearer to the valley of the shadow of death.

# INDEX

NOTE.—Where the year is not given in a date, 1904 is referrred to.

ABYSSINIA, problem of, i. 6
Afghan War, 1879, parallels, i. 271, ii. 222-3 *note*, 246 *note*
Afghanistan, problem of, i. 6
Africa, South (*see also* South Africa), native question in, i. 6
Aiho river, affluent of the Yalu, Kashtalinsky's entrenchments near, i. 82, ill-concealed, 87; part played by in Yalu fight, 92 *et seq.*, crossing of, by Japanese 12th division, 114-5
Aiyanmen, opposing forces at (June 15-19), i. 182-93, Russian advance on, 199
Aiyanmen-Saimachi-Chaotao Valley, described, in relation to Chaotao engagement, i. 286-7
Alexieff, Admiral, and the Yalu fight, i. 82; flight of, from Port Arthur, 161
America, effects of on the Japanese, ii. 29 *et seq.*
American Civil War, Artillery tactics in, i. 128, civilian strategy in, results of, 180-1; parallels, 322, ii. 117
Amping, i, 308, 309, 318, 319, Russian move towards (Jy. 22), 284; Russian retreat to (Aug. 26), ii. 42, 52-3, 60, 61; Japanese Headquarters at (Aug. 30), 80
Anju, i. 56, 79, fortifications and garrison of, Russian attack on, 35-9

Anshantien, i. 308; Russian evacuation of (Aug. 26), ii. 65
Antung, i. 119, 135, 186, country near, 58; relative positions at (May 12), 62, naval importance of in regard to Yalu battle, 87, 133
Antung—Fenghuangcheng tramway, i. 187
Appointments, importance of selection for, ii. 318
Artillery, Japanese, i. 110, 173; poor horsing of, 188, 234, ii. 128, 241; Japanese comments on (Oct. 12), 224-6, author's remarks, 241-3

Japanese and Russian as employed in various battles, i. 106-10, 121, 130, 256, 269, 275-6, 289, 291-2, 305, 324, 332, 349, ii. 38, 40-1, 52, 94, 182-4, 188-9, 201-2, 226

Russian, remarks on tactics of, i. 121, 126-30
Asada, Major-General, commanding advance guard 1st Japanese army, at the Yalu fight, i. 82, 84 appearance of, 146; at Yoshirei, 323; commanding 1st Brigade Guards Battle of 26 Aug., ii. 44, 54, 56, commanding Guards Division, Oct. 11, '04, ii. 195, 219, Oct. 13, 247
*Askold, Bayan,* and *Cesarewitch* Russian warships, escape of, to Kiaochau, ii. 9

Attack, poor, of Russian soldiers, i. 257, 259, 266, 278
Aug. 31 to Sep. 2. summary of Japanese proceedings, ii. 122 et seq.

BABA, Colonel, commanding 30th Regt. 1st Japanese Army i. 233, at Motienling skirmish (Jy. 4), 230, at the Battle of Motienling (Jy. 18), 267, at Manjuyama, ii. 103, 115
Bajisan, taken by Japanese Guards (Oct. 13), ii. 247
Balaschieff, General, Director of the Red Cross, Port Arthur, ii. 317
Balloons in, warfare, drawbacks to, i. 310 341
Baltic (Russian) fleet, and the Dogger Bank affair, a garbled report, ii. 280-1
Band-playing, during Russian night attack, Chaotao, i. 290
Barstow, Captain, Chinampo, i. 53
Battle of the 26th of August (battle of Liaoyang), Japanese positions before, ii. 34, during 35, 69 and after, 71; official information on, 64 et seq.; author's visit to scene of, and comments, 72 et seq.
Battalions, number of, to a regiment, Japanese and Russian, i. 276
Bayonets, Russian, badness of, ii. 261, 278, unwise use of, i. 235, 238, ii. 231-2, 252-4
Beri-beri in the 1st Japanese Army, i. 302
Boers, Japanese, and Russians (see also S. African War), comparisons between, i. 5, 6, 43, 59, 85, 105, 113, 127, 128, 347, ii. 254
Bonchio Gap, battle of Telissu, ii. 337, 342-3
"Box and Cox" Cave, Coal Mines, ii. 292-3
Bridge-making, Japanese, Yalu battle, i. 99-100

British Artillery tactics, S. African war, i. 129
attachés, difficulties of, with the First Japanese Army, i. 177-9, smoothed by General Fujii, 180-3
Indian and Japanese troops compared i. 8-10, 293, 329-30
N.C.O.s, compared with Russian, i. 302-3
Buddhist ceremony at Feast of the Dead, i. 198-9
Buddhist Sermon, a, ii. 145-7
Bulwana, a parallel, ii. 136
Bunsuirei, Russian forces at, i. 185, their withdrawal from, 221 & note, 222, defences viewed by author, 241-3
Burial of Russian dead by Japanese, i. 264
Burma, road-making in, i. 246
Bushido—and after?, ii. 17 et seq.

CALMNESS, the essential in a Japanese Commander, Kuroki's possession thereof, instances of, i. 313, ii. 42, 43, 205, 208, 257
"Caste" in England, i. 38
Cavalry, a good country for, i. 191
Japanese, equipment of, ii. 278-9; rifle-efficiency of, Motienling battle, i. 273; at Heikoutai, ii. 356 & note; at Liaoyang battle, 153 & note; brilliant success of, at Penchiho, 236, 238-40; at the Shaho fight, 183; at Telissu, 339
Japanese and Russian, dismounted at the battle of Motienling, i. 256; inaction of, Yalu fight, 131
Russian, author's theories borne out by, i. 191
threatening to communications, i. 134 et seq., 319
at Terayama, inaction of, ii. 215-6
Chang Song, Sasaki's feint at, i. 87; base of 12th division (July 15), 252; during Chaotao battle, 292

Chaotao, Russian positions at, i. 224, 230 (Jy. 17 *et seq.*), 286 *et seq.*; engagement at (Jy. 19), 257; Jardine's report on, 281, General Fujii's talk about 282-5, details of, 285 *et seq.*, 318; Inouye's subsequent doings 339-40 *et seq.*; brilliant relief of, by Prince Kanin's cavalry (Oct. 11, 12), ii. 236, 238

Chemulpho, i. 50; Russian naval wrecks at, 47

China, results of anti-militarism in, i. 14

Chinnampo Harbour, i. 47-8, disembarkation in, of Japanese Imperial Guards, 52-5

Chinchaputsu village, in relation to Yoshirei battle, i. 316, 317, 325-7; in relation to the battle of the 26th Aug., ii. 33

Chinchaputsu to Liaoyang viâ Yoshirei, Russian positions designed to block, i. 315 *et seq.*

Chinese, the, as material for soldiers, ii. 303, and officers, 303-4
  coolies, drawbacks to, in war, i. 244, pay of, 245
  fight near mountains, i. 131, 151, ii. 171
  houses in Manchuria,
    the decorations, i. 215
    the "kong" in, and the insects, i. 214
  natives of Manchuria, characteristics of, i. 165-9
  troops at Fenghuangcheng, i. 163-4
  unlikeness of, to Japanese, facial and mental, ii. 289, 304
  view of Japanese and Russian occupations, ii. 158, 160, 168
  view of Russians, ii. 294

Chintanpu, Japanese post, battle of Heikoutai, Russian losses, ii. 356

Chipanling, in relation to battle of Aug. 26, ii. 51, 56

Chiuliencheng, Russian positions at, before, during and after Yalu fight, i. 72, 78, 105, 118, 126; carried by the Japanese, 114

Chiuliencheng — Sheechong line, Russian left, point of Japanese attack, Yalu fight, i. 95

Chongchun river, near Anju, i. 137

Chosenrei, Pass, Matsunaga's attempt to reach (Oct. 12-13), ii. 246-7 & *notes*

Chouyuang, Japanese and Russian troops facing, at, i. 186

Christmas Day in the Japanese Camp, Yentai Coal Mines, Namakura's speech, ii. 296-8, the author's rhyme for, 299

Chukodai village, on the Yalu, i. 92, in relation to the battle, 109, 111

Chulsan, post of, i. 79

Chusan, withdrawal of Russian forces from (June '04), i. 221

Civilisation and military virtue, i. 5, *et seq.* 12

Coal Mines, *see* Yentai Coal Mines

Cocksureness, risks of, i. 227

Colenso, a parallel, i. 279

Colonial troops, dislike of, to spade work, i. 175-6

Commanders, Japanese ideal of, ii. 12 *et seq.*; qualities deemed requisite by the author, 15

Companies, strength of, Russian and Japanese, i. 315

Confucianism and progress, a Japanese dictum on, i. 200

Conscription, in Japan, i. 10, 156, 244, ii. 10, 11

Coolies, *see* Chinese *and* Military *do.*

Conservatism, value of, Kuroki on, ii. 351

Cossack troops, i. 71-2, 136-9, 159
  Crossing by, of Taitsuho, ii. 236, 238
  deficiencies of, i. 59, 166
  failure of, Lentowan, discussed, ii. 136
  Fukushima's views on, i. 33

Countrymen *versus* townsmen as soldiers, i. 5, 6–8, Japanese views, 225–6, ii. 276, endorsed by the author, 277
Courage, Japanese and British, ii. 25–6
Cover, Russian disregard of, i. 271, ii. 157, 201–2, and the need for, 130–1
Crowder, Colonel, U.S.A., i. 46

DAIBOSHI—Joshisan, Russian position at Telissu, i. 194
Daidoko, fight of the 16th Japanese Regt. *en route* to, i. 262–3
Daisan (in Shaho battle), ii. 184, exciting climb up 272–5
Dalny, landing of Oyama and Kodama at (Jy. 15), i. 248
Demidrovitch, Lieutenant, 12th Russian Regiment, i. 85
Demonstrations in force, a note on, i. 279
Disembarkation methods at Chinnampo, i. 53–5
Dogger Bank affair, puzzling news received of, ii. 280–1
Domonshi, hills near, objective of Guards (Oct. 13), ii. 247, 257, the attack, 258
Domonshi—Shotatsuko line, Kuroki's intention to take (Oct. 11, evening), ii. 210
Doornkop, a parallel, ii. 201, 202
Dum-Dum bullets, alleged use of, by Russians, ii. 2
Dundee (S. Africa), British action concerning, and the Russian Yalu parallel, i. 80–1

EDUCATION, Japanese and English compared, i. 12, 15, 17, 18
in the Japanese Army, ii. 9, 10
Edward VII., King, birthday of, Japanese congratulations, &c. on, ii. 286–9
Eighth Division at Heikoutai, ii 354 *& note*, 357 *& note*
Elandslaagte, a parallel, ii. 202
England, attitude of Japanese military men towards, i. 177; how to modify this, 178
in a Japanese allegorical play, i. 157–8

Entrenchments, Japanese and Russian (*see also* Spade work), i. 282, 287, 351, ii. 47, 89, 332, 335
European Russian troops, alleged superiority of, i. 257, 282, 301, an error, corrected, 302–3, how occasioned, 303

FAN, the, in the firing-line, i. 326
Fenghuangcheng, i. 121, 162, Headquarters Japanese First Army, 64, 66 *et seq.* 207, 210; outposts at, 172–3; Japanese position at, after Yalu fight (June 15), 187; Japanese forces at (Jy. 22), 284
Fenshan, life at, Sept. 7 to Oct. 9, ii. 141–170
Firing, bad, of the Russians, i. 112–115, 256, 266, 278, ii. 78, 104, 105 *et seq.*, 110–11, 186
volley, of the same, i. 112, 256, 266, 271, 278, 313
independent, of the Japanese, i. 271–2, 311
First engagements, crucial character of, i. 74
Flags in battle, inspiring effect of, ii. 50, 213 *note*, 233–4, 250
Flexibility, Russian lack of, i. 257, 259
Formations, European and Japanese, relative importance of, ii. 280
Japanese, on various occasions, i. 271, 282, ii. 205–6, 212 *& note*, 227, 229 *note*, 301
Russian, solid or close, i. 271, 277, 278, ii. 184
Formosa, under General Kodama, i. 29, 30
Fortifications, value of, impression as to, left by Port Arthur, ii. 310–11, Nogi's view, 311
Franco-Prussian War, French Artillery tactics in, i. 129; a Manchurian parallel, 133
Fredericksburg, parallel, i. 95, ii. 117
French-trained officers in the Japanese Army, i. 149, ii. 291, 307

"Friends at Court" in Japan, drawbacks of, i. 171
Frontal attack, instances of, i. 256, 314, 318, comment on, 356
Froeschwiller, village of, the key to the position, Battle of Woerth, i. 94
Fuji Yama, i. 1, 3, 4
Fujii, Major-General S., Chief of Staff First Army of Japan, i. 67, 68, 161, 211, 234, 289, 310; smooths British attaché's difficulties, 180-3, 189; cleverness and tact in giving information, 232-3; hospitality of, 314; on the situation on July 5, 231-2; on the military situation after the Yalu fight, 183 *et seq.*, he invites (and receives) criticisms, 188-9; more news on the above, 199; on the position of the Japanese forces (Jy. 15), 247 *et seq.*; on the situation after Motienling and Chaotao, 282 *et seq.*; on the relative quality of European and Siberian-Russian troops, 302; on the strategical considerations before Yoshirei battle, 319, and on that fight, 334-6, 358
Fukuda, Major, head of Operations Section, First Japanese Army, i. 148, 212, 310
Fukushima, Major-General Sir Y., K.C.B., Chief of Second Section General Staff of First Japanese Army, i. 20; his famous ride, 30-1; his attitude to the foreign attachés, etc., 32-3; his views on Indian and Cossack troops, 33-4; his linguistic gifts, 35; the loss of his son, ii. 143
Fusan, i. 50
Fusan—Liaoyang military railway, i. 188

Gabuoho Valley, near Telissu, fighting at, ii. 334 *et seq.*
Gebato, object (assumed) of sharp fighting at, i. 276-7
Gebato - to - Shinkwairei front, covered by Japanese 2nd Division, battle of Motienling, i. 258
Geishas, i. 40-2
Geographical nomenclature, difficulties of, on Korean frontier, i. 89
German militarism, much for Britons to learn from, ii. 97
system of extensions, as employed by the Japanese, i. 141, 143-5, author's criticisms on, 188, Fujii's replies, 189
German-trained medical officers in the Japanese Army, i. 149-5, 304
Military officers in the same, i. 148, 177, 211-2
Gerngross, Major-General, at Telissu, ii. 338-40, 344
Gerschelman, Lieutenant-General commanding Russian forces at Chaotao (Jy. 04), i. 288, 294, retreat of, 295 *et seq.*, criticism on, 299 *et seq.*
Gibraltar, basis of its value, ii. 211
Gochosan, hill, Russian outpost, ii. 93, fighting near, 107
Gokarei, Mountain, Kuroki's standpoint (Aug. 26), ii. 37
Golden Hill, author's visit to, ii. 316
Gravelotte, a desired parallel, i. 309
Guppenberg, General, and the battle of Heikoutai, Russian blame of, i. 359
Gunki Yama affair, gallantry and quick decision of Ota and his men at, ii. 232 & *note*, 236 & *note*
Guns, British and Japanese, outclassed by Russian, ii. 190, 193, 195
Gurkhas, compared with Japanese troops, i. 8-10, 293

Hagino, Colonel, Chief of Intelligence Section, First Japanese Army i. 148, 212, characteristics of, 324; on training of European Rus-

Hagino—*continued*
sian recruits, i. 302 ; his classification of the Russian forces by quality, 303; his lectures on the situation (Oct. 04), ii. 179, 187, 209 ; on the position on Oct. 12, 209

Haicheng region, Russian forces at (June and Jy.), i. 186, 231, 283-4, their departure, 319, arrival of the 4th Japanese Army (Aug. 3), ii. 4

*Haimun*, the "Times" steamer, i. 50-52

Haldane, Colonel, at Liaoyang, ii. 142

Hamaton rearguard fight, i. 63, 73, 88, true account of, 117 *et seq.*, map of, given by Watanabe, 122; a parallel, 260 *et seq.*

Hanchaputsu, i. 317, Japanese attack on (Jy. 31), 322

Hanlasanshi–Domonshi line, author's views of its importance, ii. 266-7

Harbin, i. 231

Harbour or dockyard, when worse than useless to fleet, ii. 310, Nogi's view, 311

Hasegawa, Lieutenant - General, commanding Japanese Imperial Guards, i. 146, 152, 307, at Chinchaputsu, 331, ii. 6 ; promoted as Commander-in-Chief in Korea, 195

*Haya Tori*, Japanese destroyer, i. 52

Heaven-reaching Pass, Battle of the, *see* Motienling Pass, Battle of

Health of the Japanese Armies, to what due, i. 395, ii. 9

Heikoutai, action of (Jan. 26-9), condensed account of, ii. 351-2 *et seq.*: Grippenberg blamed for in Russia, 360

Heyentai, objective of Guards and Headquarters of 1st Japanese Army (Sep. 4), ii. 125

Hikida, Colonel, Intelligence Section, 1st Japanese Army, i. 212

Hiraoka, Major, killed in action Chaotao engagement, regrets of the author, i. 299

Hlangwane Hill, a parallel, i. 104

Hodaichosi, slopes of, i. 115

Honda, Major, and his battalion at Penchiho (Oct. 11), ii. 230-1

Honkeiko, Russians at (Jy. 26), i. 308

Hō-ō-San, or Phœnix Mountain, i. 189 *& note*, excursion to, 205-6, tigers on, 206

Horses, of the Japanese Artillery, inferiority of, i. 188, 234, ii. 128

Hoshuho, objective of Guards (Oct. 14), ii. 244

Houtnek, a parallel, i. 294

Howitzers, at Port Arthur, effect of, ii. 159, 271, 311, 314 ; Russian, at Nanshan, 326, at the Yalu, i. 132

Hsinlitun, Japanese advance to, ii. 95

Hsuehlien, march to, of First Japanese Army, i. 210

Huankufun, intended concentration of 1st Japanese army on, ii. 82, 84, troops at (Aug. 31), 89, 96

Hume, Lieutenant-Colonel, British attaché with 1st Japanese Army, i. 46, 193, attached to the Guards, 205, present at Yoshirei, 326, 328 ; still with the Guards, ii. 68, 158, 195 *note*, 222, 242, 281; rifle-shooting success, ii. 293

Hunho, Russian crossings of (Oct. 4), ii. 175 (Jan. 25, '05), 352

IIDA, Lieutenant - Colonel, Commanding 4th Regt. at Hakashi, Oct. 17, ii. 220 *note* ; at Iida Yama (Oct. 13), 258

Imamoura, Colonel, and the 14th Japanese Regt., remarkable detour march by, Chaotao engagement, i. 293-5, subsequent attack by, 295, and its success, 297 ; comments on, 297-8

Immortality of fame, appeal of, to the Japanese, i. 197
Indian North-West Frontier, rearguard fighting on, ii. 342
Indian troops and their British officers, views on, of Fukushima, i. 33-4
— compared with British, *see* British, Indian, and Japanese
Infantry, *see* Japanese and Russian *do. passim*
Inouye, Major-General, commanding 12th Division, First Japanese Army, i. 73, 147, 152, at Chaotao (Jy. 19), 288, 296, 318, his tactics commented on, 301, 339 *et seq.*; at the battle of Yoshirei, 315; at the Taitsuho crossing, ii. 96
Insect pests in Manchuria, i. 214, 229, 241, 311
Ishido, Sergeant-Major, i. 158
Ishiko, hill north of, i. 88
Ito, Marquis, President of Privy Council, i. 19, 22, 23
Izaki, General, and the Guards, on Oct. 11, 12, and 13, ii. 194, 223, 247

James, Captain, on the *Haimun*, i. 52
Japan, attitude of, during pre-war negotiations, i. 76-7
— Emperor of (Mutsuhito I.), i. 37; his birthday celebrations in Manchuria, ii. 281
— Empress of, her presents to the Army, i. 194; a misapplication thereof, 195-6
Japan, First Army of, i. 73
— ample food and stores of, i. 222
— casualties, a bit of swagger about, ii. 271
— at battle of Aug. 26, ii, 48 *note*
—— Chaotao, i. 290, 299
—— Manjuyama, ii. 109
—— Motienling battle, i. 264, 275
—— Takubokujo, i. 222-3
—— Shaho (Oct. 12), i. 209, ii. 213-4, 224
—— Yalu, i. 115
— cleanliness of, i. 223
— Headquarters Staff of, i. 211

Japan, First Army of—*continued*
— operations of
—— before, during and after Yalu fight, i. 82, 105, 110, 141-5, 183, 184; position of (June 15), 190 *et prævi*, advance of, 203, (June 22), 204-5 (June 26-Jy. 2), 210-29, lines of communication, official information on, 243 *et seq.*; positions of (Jy. 15), 248, (Jy. 26), 308, advance of, from Lienshankuan (Aug. 3), 310 *et seq.*; portion engaged at Yoshirei (Jy. 31), 315 *et seq.*; advance on Taitsuho, how executed (Aug. 28), ii. 66-7, objective of (Aug. 29) 71; position before and during crossing of Taitsuho, 93 *et seq.*; positions and objectives of (Sep. 2), 106; pursuit ordered, 124, positions before, during, and after Shaho 172 *et seq.*; orders to (Oct. 7), 177-8, communications cut (Oct. 10) 181, advancing on the Shaho (Oct. 17), 258-9
— opinion of England held by, i. 177
— sections of, history of work done by
—— Imperial Guards, heavy marching order equipment of, i. 54; at Yoshirei battle, 315 *et seq.*; after Yushuling, ii. 5; in the battle of Aug. 26, 35, 43, 51, 54, 56, 63 and after, 67, 69-70, 71, 74 *et seq.*, 95; sent against mountain, 151 (Sept. 2), 105, 106, 118, orders to (Sept. 4), 124, progress with, 129, positions of (Oct. 9), 172-3, (Oct. 10) 174; work of, at battle of Shaho (Oct. 11), 194-5; orders to (Oct. 11 evening), 210; hill, &c., taken by (Oct. 12,), 219; further progress of 223, orders to and proceedings of (Oct. 13), 244 *et seq.*, 257-8

Japan, First Army of—*continued*
  Second Division, celebration of the Feast of the Dead by (June 19), i. 196; splendid physique of, 201–2, ii. 18, 51; source and character of 277
    work of, at Motienling battle, i. 258; at Yoshirei, 314, 315, *et seq.*; in the battle of Aug. 26, ii. 35, 37–8, 42–4, 46, 52, 56, 58, 62, 63, losses of, 71, and after, 67, 69, 74, 83, 88; at Manjuyama, 104 *et seq.*; occupies Mountain 131 (Sept. 4), 123, orders to (same date), 124, execution of, 129; orders to, and position of (Oct. 7), 177–8, the same (Oct. 13), 244 *et seq.*; at Heikoutai, ii. 354 & *note*, 355 *et seq.*
    6th Company, charactistics shown by, Motienling Battle, i. 266
    16th Regt., work of at Gebato, i. 273; at Shokorei, under artillery fire, 273; at Chaotao, 288 *et seq.*; joint attack by, on Russian right, Chaotao engagement, 295
  Twelfth Division, source and character of, ii. 354 & *note*, 277
    work of, at Aiho crossing; 114–5, at the Yalu battle and Hamaton fight, 150 *et seq.*, 120 *et seq.*; at the Yalu fight, 133; engagement of, at Chaotao (Jy. 19), 257, 281–2, 339; before and during Yoshirei battle, 307, 310, 314, 315; anticipated danger to (about Jy. 31,), 319; Russian Intelligence captured by, ii. 7; in the battle of Aug. 26, 35, 42, 51, 56, 69, and after, 61, 63 *et seq.*, the attack on Manjuyama, 96 *et seq.* and taking of, 102 *et seq.*; positions of, ordered (Aug. 28), 65, and

Japan, First Army of—*continued*
  Twelfth division—*continued*
    gained (Aug. 30), ii. 86–7, they cross the Taitsuho (Aug. 31), 87, 189; orders to (Sept. 4), 124, progress with, 129, fighting near Sandoha, 130; orders to (Oct. 7), 177, position of, 178; near and at Penchiho (Oct. 9–12), 188, 190–1, 231, 236 (Oct. 13), 247
  Twenty-third Brigade, work of, taking of Kosarei ridge, ii. 54–6
  Umezawa Brigade, threatens Penchiho (Aug. 31), ii. 82, 85, 89, and takes it, 90 *note*, 92
Japan, Second Army of, composition of, i. 183, march of on Telissu, *ib.*; in the Liaotung Peninsula (June 1), 220; at Lienshankuan (Jy. 6), 232: at Kaipeng Fujii (Jy. 16), 248, 249, march of to Tashihchiao (Jy. 21), 283; position of on July 24 and after, 303, the battle near Tashihchiao, Fujii on, 305–7; at Haicheng (Aug. 3), ii. 4; news of, (Aug. 27) 66–7; advance of (Aug. 29), 71, (Aug. 31), 95, (Sep. 2) 105; success of at Liaoyang 124, arrival of south of Taitsuho, 125; fighting of (Oct. 11), 199; reverse at Shakako (Oct. 17), 270
Japan, Third Army of (*see also* Nogi), advance of, on Port Arthur (Jy. 26), i. 307, 310; northward advance of (Jan. 29, '05), ii. 354
Japan, Fourth Army of (*see also* Nodzu), composition of, i. 232; advance of against Takubokujo (Jy. 22), 283, attack on that place (Jy. 24–5), 306; objective of, (Aug. 28) ii. 67; advance of (Aug. 29), 71, (Aug. 31), 82;

Japan, Fourth Army of—*continued*
subsequent work of and capture of Hsinlitun, ii. 95, 131 ; progress of (Sept. 2), 105 ; objective of (Oct. 11), 193 ; advance of, and capture of Sankwaise-kisan (Oct. 11), 199, 200, 210–14 *& notes*, subsequent operations, 217, 244 ; news from 250, 251 ; loss by, of Waitosan, 269 and of guns, 269–70, 271 lessons from, 272 ; after Siuyen, 330

Tenth Division, work of at the Takubokujo fight, i. 222

Japanese, the, in 1904, first impressions of, i. 16, later impressions, ii. 21 *et seq.*, place of women, 17, education, 17–18

Army (*see also* Artillery, Commanders, Firing, Signalling, Spade-work, &c.), characteristics of, i. 10–11, 15, 43, 97 audacity, 320, 330, 332, ii. 45, 88, 212, 215 ; efficiency, and its cause, i. 200 ; preliminary care, 97, 134, 175, 349, ii. 129 ; reticence, i. 32, 45, 47, 59, 69, 77–8, 148, 178, exceptions, 202, 228, 265

educational standard of, 9, 10

health of, how maintained, i. 305, ii. 9

pursuit by, remarks on, i. 116, 279, ii. 148–9

regiments, number of battalions in, i. 276 ; strength of companies in, 315

reserves, names for, ii. 43, 44 *& note*, size of, i. 74

secret of its successes, ii. 246 *note*

soldiers of, excellence of, i. 280

calmness of before battle, i. 207, 215

fine material of Infantry, ii. 59

Japanese Army—*continued*
soldiers—*continued*
honesty of, as to live stock, i. 215

speed and initiative of, ii. 198

spirit shown by wounded, i. 281, ii. 62

toughness of, ii. 280

subordinate officers, characteristics of, ii. 16–7

Japanese, civil and military, difficulties of getting in touch with, i. 172, 217, 228

interest in the awakening of China, ii. 303

life and society, pleasant features of, i. 23, 37 *et seq.*

National Anthem, a translation of, ii. 285 *& note*

politeness, ii. 23–4; instances of, 143, 260

pride, ii. 21–2

sailors, sources of the best, ii. 277

suavity, nature of, i. 76

view of Russian sailors, ii. 307

view of surrender of Port Arthur, ii. 307

War Song, author's rhymed version of, i. 169–70, 176

Japanese and British guns outclassed by Russian, ii. 190, 193, 195

military organisation compared, 18

Jardine, Captain, 5th Lancers, British attaché with First Japanese Army, i. 46 ; his knowledge of Japanese, 57, 179 ; departure of, to Aiyanmen, 192–3 ; with 12th Division, 205 ; despatch from on the Chaotao engagement, special value of, 281–2, pith of, 285 *et seq.*, 301 ; news from, on Kosarei and Yentai, ii. 147–8 ; with the cavalry, 211, 279

*Jibouti*, Russian gunboat, arrival of, above Densotai, i. 310

Jokahoshi, i. 260

Jokes, Japanese appreciation of, i. 68, 208

KAIPING, i. 79, 184, details of the position at, 187, anticipated fighting at, 186-7, 243; repulse of the Russians at (Jy. 12), 247; Japanese and Russian forces near, 203, 231, relative value of, Fujii on (Jy. 15), 248

Kakaton, Japanese cavalry from, at Telissu fight, i. 194

Kamiriuka valley, efforts to clear (Oct. 12), ii. 218 *et seq*

Kamimura, Admiral, defeat of the Vladivostock fleet by (Aug. 14), ii. 9

Kanin, Prince, ii. 156, commanding Second Cavalry Brigade, 178-9, brilliant success of near Penchiho (Oct. 11-12), 236, 238-40

*Kanjo*, a, what it is, ii. 263 *note*; a neat pun on, 279

Kankuantun, ii. 90

Kanshio, the Russian stores at, story of, i. 250-1

Kansoten, advance of Second Division Japanese 1st Army to (June 26), i. 218

Kasan, near the Yalu, i. 83, 135

Kaschtalinsky, General, position and entrenchments of, before the Yalu fight, i. 73, 82, defects of, 132; his lost opportunity, 86

Katsura, Major-General Count, Prime Minister, i. 19, 20, 22

Kawasaki, Colonel, 30th Regt., a day with, at Coal Mines, ii. 291-2

Keller, General Count, movements of, discussed (Jy. 22-6), i. 276, 284, 306, 307; at the battle of Yoshirei (Jy. 31), i. 315 *et seq.*, ii. 73; his death, i. 337; foreign opinion of, ii. 163; Japanese admiration of his bravery, 305

Key, the, of a position, defined, i. 94

Kigoshi, Major-General, 23rd Brigade, 12th Division 1st Japanese army, i. 147, 148;

Kigoshi—*continued*
at Chaotao, 289, 292, 297; at Yushuling, 344; at Kosarei, fine feat of (Aug. 26) ii. 42; with the 5th Division at Heikoutai, 355

Kinchou, Marquis Oyama at, i. 25-7; author's comic situation on arriving at, ii. 320-2

Kinkahoshi, i. 230; Russian field battery at, Motienling Battle, 273; in relation to Yoshirei battle, 336; events at, before battle of Aug. 26, ii. 1-34

Kinteito Island, and the Yalu fight in, i. 89, 92, 97, bridge made to, 99, Japanese artillery on, 106-10

Kitashirakawa, Prince, First Japanese army, i. 152

Kitchener, Lord, i. 3, 119, 282

Kobi (Reserve Regiment), battalions of, at Kuantienchen, i. 185; record march of, ii. 44 & *note*; in the battle of Aug. 26, 44-5, 54; Kuroki's use of, 90; at Heikoutai, 354-5, *et seq.*

Kodama, Lieut.-General Baron, Vice-Chief of General Staff of the Army and Governor of Formosa, i. 19-20, 28-30, 35; appointed Chief of Staff to Oyama (June 21), 204, ii. 95, landing of, at Dalny (Jy. 15), i. 248; meeting with, after Liaoyang, ii. 142-3; he goes to Port Arthur (Sept. 19) 156; as a host, 289; an instructive luncheon with, 294-5; last meeting with, 362

Kodama, Major-General T., Commanding Engineer First Japanese Army, i. 149, 151, 212; his garden and its moral lessons, 304

Kohoshi, objective of Imperial Guards, battle of Aug. 26, ii. 51, 52, gained by, 63

Kokahoshi, ii. 59

Kokashi village, Terayama, ii. 201-2

Komura, Baron, Minister of Foreign Affairs, i. 19, 20
Königratz, Von Moltke's concentration at, a parallel, ii. 133 & *note*
Korea, as seen by Captain Vincent, i. 485-7
  Russian operations in, before and after the Yalu fight i. 79, 134 *et seq.*
Korean coolies, utilised by Japan, pay of, i. 245
  houses, dirtiness of, i. 59
  natives first impressions of, i. 47, and characteristics of, 56-7, their live stock, 159-60
Kosarei, Mountain and ridge, in relation to battle of 26 Aug., ii. 39, 41, taken by Japanese, 54-6, 58, 60, 73, 147-8
Kuantienchen, i. 182, good service of the Kobi battalions at, 185
Kujo, Prince M., i. 22
Kungshan Mountain, held by 2nd Division, Japanese army, Aug. 26, ii. 56
Kuni, Prince, A.D.C. to Marshal Kuroki, i. 59, 67 *et passim*, at the Feast of the Dead, i. 196; at a popular play, 57
Kunshintai, 4th Army's cavalry at, Aug. 29, ii. 70
Kurita, Lieutenant-Colonel, head of Transport and Supply Section, First Japanese Army, i. 148, 212, 243, ii. 106; on the Russian cavalry attempt to cut communications in Korea, i. 34 *et seq.*
Kuroda, Captain, Adjutant to General Officer commanding First Japanese Army, i. 212
Kuroki, Marshal Baron, Commanding First Japanese Army, i. 51, 211, *et passim, en famille*, 52, first meetings with, 67, 71; positions of before, during and after Yalu fight, 73,

Kuroki—*continued*
  *et seq.*; his entertainment of the foreign attachés after the Battle of the Yalu, i. 145, 153, the author responds, 153-4, the decorations, 154-6, plays and other amusements, 156-8, the Russian prisoners' dinner, 159; author attached to, during advance of First Japanese Army, 205 *et seq.*; hospitality of, *en route*, 207; success of, at Motienling Battle, to what due, 258; his calmness, 313, and methods with his Staff, ii. 12 *et seq.*, appreciation of his calmness by the Japanese, 43, 205, 208, 251; and the battle of Yoshirei (Jy. 31), i. 315 *et seq.*, 319; at the battle of Aug. 26, ii. 37, 39, 40 *et seq.*; his handling of Reserves, 44-5, 90; check to his left, 83 *et prævi*; on the slopes of Manjuyama, 126-7; during the battle of the Shaho, 187-9; orders of, evening of Oct. 2, 210; congratulations to, on the Emperor's birthday, 281; Japanese New Year's Day feast with, 302 *et seq.*; farewell breakfast with (Jan. 30 '05), 349; farewell banquet given by to the author (Feb. 3, '05), 359-60, a last glass with, 361
Kuropatkin, General (*passim*), and the battle of the Yalu, i. 75, 78 *et seq.*, subsequent positions, of, 203, 220, puzzle provided by, 230-2, 248-50, Fujii's speculations thereon, 283-4, 307, 319; dispositions of, against Japanese (Aug. 12), Yoshirei battle, 340 *et seq.*; date of his resolution to retire, after the battle of 26 Aug., ii. 84 &

Kuropatkin—*continued*
  *notes*; his orders to Stakelberg (Oct. 6), ii. 175; proclamation of, on his retreat, 262; Tanaka's poems on, 286-7 & *notes*
Kuyenthai hills, Russian entrenchments at, ii. 89
Kyokahoshi, advance of Japanese Guards to (June 26), i. 218
Kyoto, Manchuria, *see* Chaotao
Kyurito Island, and the battle of the Yalu, i. 97-9, 110

LADYSMITH, a parallel, ii. 54; use of howitzers at, 311-2
Laing's Nek, a parallel, ii. 136
Lanho, in relation to battle of Aug. 26, ii. 42
Laokyo—Somaho line, taken by 8th Division, Heikoutai fight, ii. 355
Laotai, objective of 2nd Division 1st Japanese Army, (Sept. 4) ii. 125
Lentowan, Japanese crossing of Taitsuho at, ordered, ii. 85-7, executed, 88 *et seq.*
Liao river, bridge-making fête at, ii. 167-8
Liaotung Peninsula, 2nd Japanese Army in (June, 04), i. 220
Liaoyang, Battle of, *see also* Battle of 26 Aug., *and* Yoshirei general impressions on, ii. 132 *et seq.* more and official details, 152 *et seq.*
  Russian movements at and near before the battle, i. 187, 210, 221, 223, 225, 228, 232, 250, 285, 316 *et seq.*; relative position of combatants to, after Yoshirei battle, 362
  forts of captured by 2nd and 4th Japanese Armies, ii. 124
  objective of Stakelberg (Oct. 6-7), ii. 175
  road, character of country near, i. 191, Japanese advance army, 210
    Russian reinforcements *viâ*, battle of Aug. 26, ii. 57

Liaoyang—Mukden road, aim of the Fourth Army (Oct. 11), ii. 193
Lichaputsu, village, Motienling valley, i. 235, 236, 239, 267
Lienshankuan, i. 84, Russian forces at, 185, the burning of their stores at, 222; H.Q. 2nd Division First Japanese Army (July 6), 233, the country near, 233 *et seq.*; in relation to the Motienling Pass battle, 233 *et seq.*, 258, 260, 310 *et seq.*
Linchatai, i. 219, a talk with Fujii at, 220
Lives, risking or sparing by Generals *pros* and *cons* of, ii. 345, 360
Loopholes, in relation to value of cover, i. 130-1
Lotatai, objective of 2nd Division (Sep. 4), ii. 124
Louisbourg, a parallel, i. 247
Loyalty among officers, lessons on, ii. 46, 97
Lydenberg, a parallel, ii. 136

MCCAUL, Miss Ethel, at Fenghuancheng, i. 171-2
MacDonald, Sir Claude, i. 19
Majuba, a resemblance, i. 346
Makau, Russian battery near, Yalu fight, i. 110, 111
Makumenza, Russian forces at, i. 230, repulse 274, fight at, 274-5, position secured by Japanese, 275, 276
Makurayama, Mountain, in relation to Yoshirei battle, i. 340, 342, Japanese attack on, 345 *et seq.*
Manchuria, disposition of Japanese troops in and near (June 15), i. 190
  farming in, i. 65-6, 166
  French, American, and German comparisons of, i. 65
  river valley land of, features of, i. 212-3, 219
  Southern, Japanese estimate of Russian troops in, June 15, i. 186
Manchurian War, lessons of to officers, ii. 497

Manjuyama, Russian Outpost (Sept. 1), ii. 93, 95, Japanese attack on, 96 *et seq.*, and taking of, 102 *et seq.*, position at, next day, 106, Russian assaults on, 113 *et seq.*; after the fighting, 127; some lessons of, 140; more details, 159

Maps, lack of, and badness of, ii. 181–2

March, Captain, U.S.A. Artillery, i. 46

Marui, Major-General, commanding a brigade, in attack on Sankwaisekisan, ii. 213 *note*

Matoriroff, Lieutenant-Colonel, attempt of to cut communications in Korea, i. 135 *et seq.*

Matsuishi, Colonel, Assistant-Chief of Staff, First Japanese Army, i. 148, 191, 211, 243, 305; a send-off, to Tokio (Sept. 15), ii. 150–1

Matsumoto, Colonel, commanding Artillery, First Japanese Army, i. 149, 212

Matsunaga, Major-General, commanding 3rd Brigade 1st Japanese Army, i. 147, ii. 69, 83, at Yoshirei, i. 321, at Manjuyama, ii. 115–6 *& note*; efforts of to reach Sanjoshisan (Oct. 11), 196, successful assault on, 198, further doings (Oct. 12), 218–9 *& note*; attempt of to reach Chosenrei (Oct. 13), 245–6 *& notes*; appointed Chief of Staff to General Nogi, his appearance, 358

Maxwell, Mr., of the "Standard," i. 194–6, ii. 92; and the Japanese war-song, i. 169, 176

Mayapuza, in relation to Yoshirei battle, i. 322

Miage, Captain, Adjutant to Intelligence Section First Japanese Army, i. 212

Military bravery, Japanese admiration for, i. 265

Military—*continued*
conservatism, advantages of, i. 313

coolies, employed by the Japanese, details concerning, i. 243 *et seq.*

Mingshan and Shishan Mountains taken by Stakelberg (Oct. 9), success not followed up, ii. 191, fresh Russian attack on from Penchiho repulsed (Oct. 12), 231

"Minstrel Boy, The," at Fenghuangchen, i. 209

Mistchenko, General, i. 183–5, 191, ii. 354, 356

Mobility, Japanese, i. 266

Modesty, national variants of, ii. 161–2

Mokabo, fighting near (Aug. 30), ii. 75 *et seq.*

*Moral*, part played by at Liaoyang, ii. 139–40

"Most favoured nation," England not in the position of, in Japanese military consideration, i. 178, smooth speech by Fujii concerning, 182

Motienling Pass, i, 223, Russian forces near, 185; Russian withdrawal from, 222

skirmish at, i. 230, an affair of outposts, 230, 252, author's visit to the scene of (Jy. 6), 231 *et seq.*

battle of (Jy. 17), i. 253 *et seq.*, points of note in, 257–8, the progress of the fight in detail, 259 *et seq.*

crossing of, by First Japanese Army (Aug. 3), i. 311–2

importance to the Japanese, during Yoshirei battle, i. 190, 322

Motienling range and valleys, i. 315–6, passes over, 316, Russian positions in regard to, at the battle of Yoshirei, 316 *et seq.*

Mountain guns, insufficiency of, with both contending parties in Manchuria, i. 278, effects of this on the

Mountain guns—*continued*
    Japanese side, 279; used at battle of Aug. 26, ii. 47, 50, 53
Mountain 131, Russian outpost, ii. 92, 93, attack on, 105
Mukden, i. 319, quitted by Russians (Jy. 28), 308, their retreat on (Aug.), ii. 89; Japanese objective (October), 211; Russians falling back on early on Oct. 12, 224
Mutsuhito I., Emperor of Japan, i. 37, his birthday kept by the Army, ii. 281

NAAMAN, the Syrian, his precedent followed by the author, i. 199
Namakura the author's Japanese interpreter, i. 214, ii. 260, as a mimic, 288, his noble efforts on Christmas Day, 296-8, the author's verses on, 299
Nanshan, fight, i. 226; visit to the battlefield of, ii. 323-7
Nanzan, taken by 30th Regt. (Oct. 12), ii. 217 & *note* 217-18
Napoleon I., views of, on use of Reserves, ii. 45; on the importance of the Leader, 139
Napoleon III., and his military attaché at Berlin, 1870., i. 313
Nashimoto, Prince, ii. 156
National life, what it consists in, ii. 33-4
Naval and military fighting, a comparison, ii. 18 *et seq.*
Nenkyaten, burnt by retreating Russians (Jy. 25), i. 306
Newchwang, i. 79, 250, and the missionaries, ii. 104
Nidoboshi, or "cross roads," i. 225
Nishi, Major-General Baron, commanding 2nd Division, First Japanese Army, i. 147, 152, 199, 235; and the advance on Antung, 119-20; at the Feast of the Dead, 196, his oration, 197, the author's association in the ceremonies,

Nishi—*continued*
    198, 199; in the battle of Aug. 26, ii. 43
Nishijima, General, commanding the 2nd Division at Heikoutai, ii. 355
Nodzu, General, commanding 10th Japanese Division Fourth Army, landing of, i. 220; afterwards commanding the Fourth Army, appearance of, ii. 156, a call on, 157
Nogi, General, commander of the 3rd Japanese Army, forces under at Port Arthur (Jy. 5), i. 232, 247, 307, 310; views of, on howitzers, ii. 159; meeting with (Jan. 19, '05), 306, dinner with (Jan. 22), views of on fortifications, &c., 311; attitude on death of his sons, author's impressions of, 317
*Novik*, Russian warship, escape of (Aug. 10), ii. 9, sunk later, 35
Nure, Captain, Chief of Military Police, First Japanese Army, i. 212

OFFICERS and men, combination of ensuring first-class results, a Japanese dictum, i. 200
Oka, Major, killed at Takubokujo, i. 222
Okahoshi, Russian turning movement from, battle of Motienling, i. 260, resulting in a smart fight, 261
Okasaki, General, commanding 15th Brigade 2nd Division, 1st Japanese Army, i. 147, 233, ii. 42; his generosity, i. 281; at Motienling, 267; at Yoshirei, success of, at Penlin, 318, 321, 356 *et seq.*; attack of, on Manjuyama, 96 *et seq*, 118; his assault of Terayama (Oct. 11), ii. 193, 199, 208, comments on the foregoing, 212-6, further success of, at hill near Sankashi, 217; attempts to storm mount

**Okasaki**—*continued*
north of Shotatsuko (Oct. 12–13), 237, 241, 244, 248 *et seq.*, stiff encounter of near Renkwasan (Oct. 13), 254, 263; observance of the Emperor's birthday, 282; departure of, ill (Nov. 22), 290–1, recovery and return, 291 *note*.

**Okasaki Yama (Mountain)** Japanese attempted occupation of (Oct. 5), ii. 175 *& note*, fight for and success of Okasaki (Oct. 12), 217 *& note*, 244, 248–54, importance of, 255–6, 257, author's visit to, after the battle, 260

**Orloff, General,** and his Cossacks concentrated at Yentai, ii. 107, his flight, 110, 115

**Osaka soldiers,** "townies," unmilitary notions of, i. 226

**Osekito Island,** Yalu river, i. 89, 97

**Oku, General,** of the Second Japanese Army, his march to meet troops *en route* for Port Arthur, i. 161; his entry into Haicheng, ii. 114; a visit to, 151, his appearance, 156; with his forces at Telissu, 31, 33, 78, his strategy there, 344–5, 347

**Omdurman,** battle of, a parallel, i. 269

**Omura, Captain,** Adjutant to Operations Section, First Japanese Army, i. 212

**Ota, Lieutenant-Colonel,** gallantry and quick decision of at Taling (Oct. 12), ii. 233

**Outposts, Russian,** carelessness of, ii. 58

**Oyama, Lieutenant - General** (known as Marshal) Marquis, Chief of General Staff of the Army, i. 19, 22, career of, 23–8; appointed to the supreme command in Manchuria, 204, 308–9, landing of, at Dalny (Jy. 15) 248; congratulations of, to the 1st Japanese Army,

**Oyama**—*continued*
on the Battle of Aug. 26, ii. 65; share of, in the success at Liaoyang, 138, author's meeting with, after Liaoyang, 142–3; orders armies to concentrate (Oct. 8), 178; a historic dinner with, and his generals, 156; reserves sent by, to First Army (Oct. 13), 251–2; present from, on the King's birthday, 286; luncheon with, and with Kodama (Nov. 23), 289

**Oyanagi, Colonel** (ranking with), Chief Paymaster, First Japanese Army, i. 212

**PAPANLIN,** in relation to Yoshirei battle, i. 323; and to that of Aug. 26, ii. 51, taken by Japanese, 56

**Patriotism,** Japanese and British, 25, 27, 29, 33; in the military drama, 301–2

**Peace and the Chinese peril,** i. 167 terms of, a discussion on (June), 227

**Penchiho or Honkeiko,** Japanese reconnaissance near, Chaotao fight, i. 292; Russians at, same time, 294; fighting at, Yoshirei battle, 351–2; Russian strength at, and retreat from (Aug. 26), ii. 65, menaced by them (Sept. 19), Umezawa's efforts to protect, 173, 181; affairs at, during Oct. 11, 190, 207; on Oct. 12, 218, 230; Russian attack, 231–2; serious state of things, 236; Kanin's brilliant cavalry success near, and relief of, 237 *et seq.*; the sending of Matsunaga to, discussed, 255; Russian turning movement at, criticised at, 265–7

**Penlin,** taken by Japanese, i. 318, they are driven out, 339 *et seq.*, 344; the Russians again driven off, 353 *et seq.*;

Penlin—*continued*
    topography of the district, i. 343 *et seq.*
Penlin—Lipyui—Huchatsu road, Russian losses along, i. 356 *et seq.*
Personal appearance, different standards of, Japanese and Western, i. 20, 17, 24, 29, 146
    exposure of Russian officers, Motienling battle, bad effects of, 271
Personality, Japanese military indifference to, ii. 15–17 & *see* 139
Physique, differences in, of English, Scotch, and Irish, i. 202
Picquet, Japanese, on Daisan, ignorance of, as to foreign attachés, ii. 272–5
Picquets, Russian, at Makurayama, i. 345–6, 361
Pigeon Bay, success near, ii. 295
Pinamfu, Japanese pursuit to (Jy. 25, 04) i. 306
Pingtaitsu, Umezawa's success at (Sept. 2), ii. 119, his fight at (Sept. 17), 173, and retreat from, 177
Pingyang city, i. 57, 79, 83, curious shape of, 56
    estuary, i. 47, 52
    flats, i. 56
Poetry and warfare, i. 27, ii. 286–7
Pompoms, *moral* destroying qualities of, i. 272
Port Arthur, earlier siege of, Oyama at, i. 25–7, opposing forces converging on, 161, Russian forces at (June 15), 187, Japanese *do.* (June 19), 203, (Jy. 15) 247, progress of her investment, 307, 310, ii. 61, defeat of the Russian fleet at (Aug. 10), 9, further progress of the siege, 20, 159, 168–9, as affected by howitzers, 270–1, the siege continues, 295, fall of, news received at Coal Mines (Jan. 1, '05), 300, Japanese news on, 307

Port Arthur—*continued*
    as seen by the author (Jan. '05), ii. 315–17
Pulienten—Shaoshiatun, base of Japanese Second Army, i. 183

RANGE-FINDING, Russian mode of ii. 94
Rearguard fighting, India, and S. Africa, ii. 342
"Red tape," or etiquette—a lesson, ii. 96–7
Regiments, Russian and Japanese, number of battalions in, i. 276; strength of companies in, 315
Reinforcements, a lesson on, ii. 123
Religion, attitude of the Japanese Generals to, i. 200
Rennenkampf, General, at Saimachi, i. 185, 203, 218, he is wounded, 319, crosses Taitsuho, ii. 181, 236, further movements of, 180, 191, 192, is driven back, 238–40
Renkwasan, action near (Oct. 13), ii. 263
Reserves, bottling-up of, author's view on, i. 301
    Japanese, Kuroki's handling of, ii. 42–3, 54, 90; names of i. 285 *note*, 315 & *note*, ii. 43, 44 & *note*
    Russian (Aug. 29), 71, retreat of, Telissu, 342
Resistance or surrender, ethics of, i. 241, 359
Reticence of Japanese commanders, etc., instances of, i. 32, 45, 47, 59, 69–71, 77–8, 148, 178, 285, "exceptions prove the rule," 202–4, 232–3
Retreat, steadiness of Russian soldiers in, i. 264, 272, 278, 297, 299, ii. 52, 131, 137 *et seq.*
Rice, inadequacy of, as food for Europeans, i. 58, 153, 160, 218, 220
Rihorei, in relation to the Yoshirei battle, i. 326

Rikahoshi, ascending ground beyond, to the Motienling Pass, i. 233
Rikwaho, environs of, i. 57
Roadmaking and repairing, British superiority over Japanese in, i. 246
Roberts, Earl, i. 9, 22, ii. 246 *note*, 294, 362
Rocky Hill, Japanese use of artillery from, Motienling battle, i. 269, effects of, 275-6
Rodoko, advance of 12th Division, First Japanese Army to, i. 218
"Rooski," the terrier, joins the author, ii. 74, 79, 128, 165, 329, her original owner and intended fate, 305
Roshisan, Kuroki's march to (Aug. 28), ii. 63, 64, 66
*Rurik*, Russian warship, sunk near Tshushima (Aug. 14), ii. 9
Ruskin, *cited* on the Benefits of War, i. 14
Russia in Manchuria, opposite views on, of Great Britain and Japan, i. 75-7
Russian action at battle of Motienling, author's comments on, i. 277-8
advance south against Second Japanese Army, i. 183; on Yentai, ii. 107
Army, characteristics of, i. 10, 42-3, ii. 207
size of, i. 74
artillery, Chaotao fight, i. 291-2
tactics, Hamaton fight, 21-30
bayonet charge, Japanese account of, i. 238
bayonets, bending of, ii. 261, 278; *see also* 222 *note*
bravery, conspicuous at Heikoutai, ii. 356, at Penchiho, 231, at Sankwaisekisan, 213-4, at Waitosan, 281, at Yoshirei, i. 359
casualties, at Chaotao, i. 299; Chintanpu, ii. 355; Motienling battle, i. 275, causes of, 275-6; Manyujama, ii. 115 & *note*; battle

Russian casualties—*continued*
of the Shaho, 268 & *note*, 269
cavalry in Korea, attempt of to cut communications, i. 134 *et seq.*; author's theories borne out by, 191
character, attractive traits of, ii. 163
Commissariat, a funny story of, i. 250-1
entrenchments at Chaotao, i. 282, 287, at Penlin, 344, 349
guns, power and activity of as seen at the battle of Oct. 11, ii. 190, 193; captured, Japanese opinion on, 161, 251
gunnery, poor quality of, ii. 227
infantry, at the Yalu fight, i. 130; advance of, near Sanjoshisan (Oct. 11), ii. 189-90
military defects noted
badness of Intelligence Department, and misleading news received, ii. 7, 8, 158, 160
disregard of cover, *see* Cover
disregard of secrecy and swiftness, i. 341-2
indecision, ii. 192
lack of dash, ii. 184-5
of good generalship, i. 359
of initiative, ii. 64, 86-7, 88-9
of mobility and flexibility, ii. 198
picquets at Makurayama, criticism on, i. 345-6, 361
positions before, during and after battle of the Yalu, i. 62, 91, frontal length of, 95, 132, carried by the Japanese, 115, defects and merits, 115, 132; Motienling fight and battle, 230 *et seq.*, 240, 255 *et seq.*, author's criticisms on, 265, after the battle, Fujii on, 283; Japanese crossing of the Taitsuho, ii. 93 *et seq.*, Shaho battle, 171 *et seq.*, 180 *et seq.*

Russian prisoners, author's feeling on seeing, i. 217; other met with, ii. 2, 3, 362
regiment, number of battalions in, i. 276; strength of companies in, 315
retreats (*see also* Retreat), Motienling battle, i. 270, why they lost their advantages, 271; from Chaotao, importance of line of, 287-8, 297-9; after battle of Aug. 26, ii. 42, 52-3, 60, 61, 65, 72, 84 *note*, 137; (Sept. 6), information on, 128-9; (Oct. 13), 245 *et seq.*; general, begun (Oct. 13), 258; Telissu, 342
soldiers,
bad markmanship of, *see* Firing
honesty of, as to live stock i. 215
latent good qualities in, i. 139
*sang froid*, under rifle fire, Motienling battle, i. 272, 279
steadiness in retreat, i. 264, 272, 278, 297, 299
tactical mistakes in battle of the Shaho, author's comment, ii, 261-2
tactics, at Chaotao, i. 282, 289 *et seq.*
threats as to successive European armies, discussed, i, 226-7
troops, European said to be better than Siberian, i. 257, 282, 301, an error, and how it arose, 302-3
wounded, Motienling Pass, i. 234
Russians, a Chinese view of, ii. 81

SAFUTUN, Russian retreat on (Sept. 2), ii. 115
Saigo, Captain, the Marquis, Japanese Imperial Guards, i. 46, 59, ii. 187
Saimachi, i. 184, 294; Rennenkampf's forces at (June 15) 185; march to of Twelfth Division, First

Saimachi—*continued*
Japanese Army, i. 190, 210; Russian advance from, 109; occupation of by Japanese forces, 218, a weak point in the Japanese dispositions (Jy. 5), 237
St. Aubyn, Miss, at Fenghuangcheng, i. 171-2
Saito, Captain, Supplies Section, 1st Japanese Army, i. 212
Sandiasi. hill near, occupied by Second Division, ii. 69
Sandoha, objective of the Twelfth Division, First Japanese Army (Sept. 4), i. 124; fight near, 130 & *note*
Sanjago occupied by Imperial Guards, First Japanese Army, ii. 63
Sanjoshisan, artillery fire on (Oct. 11), ii. 189; Matsunaga's attack on, 196, success of, 198, 218; Japanese battery near (Oct. 12), 244-5
Sanjoshi Yama (hill) taken by Izaki and the Guards (Oct. 12), ii. 223
Sankashi, field hospital at, and its patients, ii. 278-9
Valley, mountains north of held by Russians (Oct.11), 201, their guns on, 206-7; positions in (Oct. 11), 209
Sankwaisekisan hill, Umezawa's fight near (Sept. 4), ii 131, 173; Russian guns on (Oct. 11), 206-7, captured by Nodzu (Oct. 11, night of), 210-14, the hill described, 211
Sanseito, height east of occupied by Japanese (Jy. 24), i. 306
Sanna's Post, a parallel, i. 299
Sasaki, Major-General, 12th Brigade, First Japanese Army, i. 147; at Changsong, 87 at Saimachi, 185; at Chaotao, 291, remarkable march by, 293; success at Penling (Jy. 31), 318, 344, 353 *et seq.*; at battle of Aug. 26, ii. 56

Sassulitch, General, at the Yalu fight, i. 79, 82, 84, 86, 87, defects of his position, 132
Satow, Colonel, Japanese artillery, i. 46, 59, ii. 270, 280
Satsuma, rebellion, i. 24
Seisekirei, a missed opportunity at, i. 338
Seisekisan, fall of, to the Japanese (Jy. 25), i. 306
Sekijo, retreat of Russian left from, Yalu fight, i. 114, Russian guns at, 115, strong resistance at, 118
Sekimonsei range, peak in gained by Matsunaga (Aug. 29), ii. 70
Senkin pass, skirmish at, ii. 238-9
Senkiujo, Matsunaga's dash from, under fire (Oct. 12), ii. 226-9 & *notes*
Seoul, described by Vincent, i. 51
Seoul—Wiju railway, i. 187
Servant question in Japan, i. 36-7
Shaho, objective of 2nd Japanese army (Aug. 28), ii. 66
  Battle of, positions before, during and after, ii. 171, 177
  author's comments on Russian tactics in, 204-7
Shakaho, the 2nd Army at (Oct. 15), ii. 264, reverse of Japanese (Oct. 17), 270
Sheechong, i. 88, 89
Shiba, Colonel, Japanese artillery, i. 48; and his troops, at Chaotao, 292; at Telissu, ii. 340-1
Shibayama, Captain, Adjutant to Genl. Officer Commanding 1st Japanese Army, i. 212
Shibuya, General, Chief of Line of Communications, i. 64
Shi-Ho, river and valley, i. 286-7; Japanese crossing of, during Yoshirei battle, 350; Russian positions on (Jy. 31), 318; Inouye's entrenchments (Jy. 20), 339-40
Shimamura Brigade, defence of, on Manjuyama, ii. 104, 167
Shimamura, General, brings reinforcements into Pen-

Shimamura—*continued*
  chiho (Oct. 9), ii. 191, and regains possession of Shishan, 191-2
Shimonoseki, i. 44
Shinkwairei Mt. (*see also* Gebato), Russian repulse on, i. 274
Shinto ceremony at Feast of the Dead, i. 196-8
Shintoism, as a military faith, i. 199
Shisan, i. 339, Russian position and guns on, 340, 342, 354 Japanese mountain guns on, excellence of arrangements, 349-50, Russian withdrawal from (Jy. 31), 352-3
Shishan, ridge, &c., taken by Stakelberg (Oct. 9) and by Shimamura (Oct. 10), ii. 191-2
Shohokka, Japanese cavalry at (Jan. 25 '05), ii. 356
Shokonsai, the, or Feast of the Dead at Fenghuangcheng (June 19), i. 196 *et seq.*
Shokorei Mountains, affair of the 7th Japanese Company on, i. 262; Russian left on, Motienling battle, 269, 270
Shotatsuko, fighting at (Oct. 11), ii. 199
Shiusenpu—Kotagai (S. of Taitsuho) line, objective of First Japanese Army (Aug. 29), ii. 71
Siberian troops, good qualities of, i. 303, *see also* European; at Yoshirei battle, 315, good marksmanship and courage of, a Japanese tribute, 328
Signalling, visual, in the Japanese army lack of arrangements for, i. 173-4, 196 & *note*, 241, 323, author's criticisms, on, 188, Fujii's reply, 189; a case in point, 121
Siuyen, i. 184, Japanese Guards at, 190
Smokeless powder, Russian and Japanese, bright flash

Smokeless powder—*continued*
emitted by, i. 314, 350, haze from, 278, 314
Smuts, General, his view on expenditure of life in warfare, endorsed by the author, ii. 359
Socialistic error, ii. 328
Sodaiko Eikaseki outworks, carried by Japanese 3rd Army (Jy. 29), i. 310
Sokako, Japanese march to, i. 224; position of, 228–9
Soldiers, peasants *versus* city-bred men as, i. 5, 6, 8, Japanese views, 223–6, 276, endorsed by author, 277
South African War, lessons from, and parallels to, i. 5, 6, 8, 80–1, 91, 110, 127–9, 157, 175, 181, 199, 210, 211, 215, 233, 266, 279, 294, 299, 310, 313, 329, 346, 354, 359; ii. 11, 27, 34, 58, 97, 136, 167, 182, 188, 195, 201, 202, 235 *note*, 254, 311, 343
Spade work (*see also* Entrenchments), British and Russian neglect of, i. 175, Japanese attention to, 175–6, 226
Speed of Japanese infantry in attack at the double, i. 142–5, instances of, ii. 202, 205
Spion Kop, a parallel, ii. 235 *note*
Staff-officers, Japanese ideal of, ii. 12 *et seq.*
Stakelberg, General, ii. 180, foreign opinion of, 163; at Telissu, 331 *et seq.*
Stöffel, Colonel Baron, French military attaché, Berlin, 1870, i. 313
Stoessel, General, the first Japanese meeting with, after the siege, his meeting with Nogi, ii. 313–5
Strategy at Liaoyang, ii. 136 *et seq.*
Sugiura, Dr., ii. 9
Suitechansa, artillery duel near, Yoshirei battle, i. 324 *et seq.*
Sukaton, Japanese troops from, at Telissu fight, i. 194

Sumeda, Captain, gallantry of and of his men at Sankwaisekisan, ii. 214 *note*
Sumino, Sergeant-Major, ii. 2
*Suminoye Maru*, military transport-ship, i. 44, 44
Suribachiyama Hill, Yalu fight, i. 111 & *note*, 114, 117, after the battle, 119; Russian guns, north of, 126; author's ice-breaking pun on, 151
Hill (No. 2), *see* Okasaki-yama
Swallow's Nest Hill, ii. 89, 81, scene from, at crossing of Taitsuho, 92 *et seq.*
Swat valley, road-making in, i. 246

Tachibana, Major, commanding Japanese outposts, Chaotao engagement, i. 289, his casualties, 290
Tactics at Liaoyang, ii. 136
Tafangshen, in relation to the Telissu battle, ii. 341–2
Taheirei, Russian first line of works on, carried (Jy. 24), i. 306
Taitsuho, the, in the line of march Japanese First Army (Jy. 15), i. 249; Kuroki's march on (Aug. 28 *et seq.*), ii. 67, and crossings of, 85 *note*, 87 *note*, 88 *et seq.*
Taiyo, ii. 171–2; the tactical position on (Oct. 9), 172 *et seq.*
Takubokujo, advance against, of Fourth Japanese Army (Jy. 22), i. 283; Russian position near, after evacuation (Jy. 24–5), 307; Fourth Japanese Army at (Aug. 3), ii. 4
Takushan, landing of Nodzu's division at (May), i. 220; Japanese Division landed at (about June 19), 203; landing of Fourth Army at, ii. 331
Talana Hill, a parallel, i. 126
Talienwan, mines at, i. 187
Taling Pass, ii. 175; Umezawa's position near (about Oct. 10), 180, 190–1; fighting at, Ota's gallantry, and its lessons (Oct. 12), 233–4

# INDEX

Tanaka, Captain, and the King's birthday, ii. 280; his three poems on Kuropatkin and their translation, 286–7 & *notes*

Taneguchi, Major-General, Chief Medical Officer, First Japanese Army, i. 149, 151, 212

Tangei, General, Chinese Eastern Flying Column, visits exchanged with, i. 163, 169, his troops, 163-4, his geographical studies and their result, 164

Tang Ho, in relation to battle of Aug. 26, ii. 37 *et seq*.; Russians driven back across, 63

Taniyama, Colonel, commanding 16th Japanese Regiment at the Battle of Motienling, i. 259 *et seq*.; remarkable march of, 289; at Chaotao, 295–7

Tapinrei, Russian position on, penetrated (Jy. 24), i. 306

Tashihchiao, march to, of 2nd Japanese Army, (Jy. 21), i. 283, battle near, (Jy. 24) Fujii's news of, i. 305–7; town of, burnt by the retreating Russians (Jy. 25), 306

Tatsumi, Major-General, commanding Eighth Division, Heikoutai, ii. 354

Taygunzi, Japanese occupation of during the Chaotao fight, i. 298

Telissu, Russian position south of, i. 185, battle at, 186; Japanese victory at, 193–4, 222; conditions leading up to, ii. 330 *et seq*.; journey to, 327, and visit to the battlefield, 329, 332 *et. seq.*

Temperance in the Japanese army, ii. 283

Temples, old and new, on the Motienling Pass, in connection with the battle, i. 234 *et seq.*, 254, 267, 270, 273, 312

Tenlanyuan — Tsaofantun, line forming 4th Army's objective (Aug. 28), ii. 67

Teraoutsi, Lieutenant-General, War Minister, i. 19, 21, ii. 156–7

Terayama, ii. 189, Okasaki's fine assault on, 193, 199, 206; Japanese entrenchments on (Oct. 12), 209; author's visit to, after the battle, 259

Tiensiutien, Russian detachments at, i. 225; entire reserve called up from (Aug. 26), ii. 44, 54; strategical importance of, i. 256, 307–8, 317

Tiger Hill, Yalu battle, i. 91 *et seq.*; manœuvre against, in, 100, Russian evacuation of, and re-occupation, 104, 110

Tips, Japanese soldiers' disdain of, ii. 7, 26–7

Tirah campaign, lesson of, as to value of valley *versus* hill, i. 278

Togo, Admiral, defeat by, of the Russian fleet at Port Arthur (Aug. 10), ii. 9

Tokayen—Amping line, Russian menace from, i. 284, 319, Russian retreat to, after Yoshirei battle, i. 362

Tokio, arrrival of the author at, i. 1, departure from, for the front, 44; farewell to soldiers at, 15, 44

Tolstoi, *cited* on effects of action of isolated individuals against masses of troops endorsing author's own view, i. 355; on the way to check aggression, ii. 53

*Tori No Umi*, Japanese gunboat, i. 52

Toryako, Japanese troops from, at Telissu fight, i. 194

Towan, Russian forces at, i. 224, 230; Russian stand at, after Motienling skirmish, i. 239; Japanese frontal attack on, success of, i. 318

Towan salient battery, value of to the Russians, i. 317, 332
Towan tower, taken by the Japanese, i. 336-7
Towan to Liaoyang *via* Yoshirei, Russian positions designed to block, i. 316 *et seq.*
Tshusmina, Russian naval defeat at (Aug. 14), ii. 9
Tsuyenpu, Russian prisoners from, i. 217, 219
Tumenling Pass, ii. 180, Russian troops menacing (Oct. 11), 190; heavy fighting at (Oct. 11-12), 235; Russian artillery attack at (Oct. 13), 247
Turcheffsky, General, and his troops at the battle of Yoshirei (July 31), i. 315, 339 *et seq.*, ii. 73
Turkestan, Russian troops from, high quality of, i. 303
Turning march of the Japanese on Chaotao, a brilliant feat, i. 282
Twamitsu, Major, Chief Adjutant, First Japanese Army, i. 212
Tweefontein, a parallel, i. 360
203 Metre Hill, after the siege, ii. 308-9; valour shown at, 350
"Two-o'-clock-in-the-morning courage," i. 360

UMEZAWA, General, and his Brigade at Yoshirei, i. 318; at Penchiho (Aug. 31), ii. 82, 85, 89; they take it, 90 *note*, 92; advance of, 106, 119; fight of Sept. 4, 131; his position (Sept. 17), 173 *et seq.*; his clever retreat, 177, and after, 180; position of, on Oct. 8-10, 180-1; on Oct. 11, 190-1; on Oct. 12 (at Penchiho), 231; on Oct. 13, 247; an interview with, 304-5

VALLEYS, waste of life to deploy men in, i. 278

Vincent, Captain, British Attaché, First Japanese Army, i. 46, ii. 91-2; his experiences in Korea, 48-57; his knowledge of Japanese, 57, 179; his ornithological tastes, 163; his love for the Chinese, 165; his deportment to Aiya men (June 19), 191-2, 193; he is attached to Second Division, 205, 218, 289; is present at Lienshankuan (Jy. 6), 233; at Motienling battle, 256, a talk with him after that fight, 280; at the battle of Yoshirei, 313
Vladivostock fleet, defeat of (Aug. 14), ii. 9

WAGGON HILL, a parallel, i. 329
Waitosan, taking and re-taking of (Oct. 17), ii. 269, (Oct. 27) 280
War, British idea of, not borne out by facts, in Manchuria, i. 215-6
  British stinginess concerning, i. 266
  "horrors" of, i. 235
  Ruskin, cited on, i. 14
  some advantages derived from, i. 168
War Office, the, a good word for, i. 193
War-correspondents, difficulties of, during the Manchurian war, i. 68-71 *et passim*
Wasoko, objective of 2nd Division (Oct. 3), ii. 244
Watanabe, Major-General, i. 64, 146; Camp Commandant at Head-quarters, First Japanese Army, 149, 212; information afforded by, on the battle of the Yalu, 73; at Hamaton fight, 123-6; map of this fight furnished by, 122; at Yoshirei battle, 324; commanding 2nd Brigade Guards, battle of Aug. 26, ii. 54, 56; the Guards, hill taken by (Oct. 11), 194;

# INDEX

Watanabe—*continued*
    successful attack of, on Hill 238 and Hakashi village (Oct. 12), ii. 219-23 *notes*; objective of (Oct. 13), 247

Watanabe, Sergeant-Major, a martinet, i. 280; compliment by, on the King's birthday, ii. 288

Waterloo, a parallel. ii. 231-2

Waziri Expedition, a parallel, i. 347

Wei-hai-wei, i. 211

Weining, crossing of the Taitsuho at, by Rennenkampf and his Cossacks (Oct. 8), ii. 236, 238

Weizugo, Russian resistance at (Aug. 29), ii. 70

Welcome Farm (South Africa), a parallel, i. 346

White, Field-Marshal, Sir George, i. 81

Wiju, view from, i. 60; Japanese strategy and minor tactics at, 60-1; dirt of the town, 61, Japanese advance to, 182 *et seq.*, and concentration near, 86

Woerth, battle of, "key" of, i. 94

Women of Japan, characteristics of, i. 17

Women, when most appreciated, a personal view, i. 247

YALU, battle of the, preliminaries, course, i. 73 *et seq.*, and result of, 132-4; Japanese plan of the fight, 88; use of big guns at, 45
    soldier's model of, 155

Yalu river, first sight of, i. 80

Yalu and Yoshirei, battles of, Japanese view of the relative importance of, i. 320

Yalu—Aiho plain, features of, i. 89-90

Yamagata, Marquis, President of the Imperial Council of Defence, i. 19, 22

Yamamoto, Baron, Naval Minister i. 19, 20

Yamorinza Valley, Russian retreat upon, i. 275, and position relative to (Jy. 16), 307; in relation to the battle of Yoshirei, 316 *et seq.*, 330, 331-2; Russian positions barring, 323, 324 *et seq.*

Yasumura, Colonel, commanding Himeji Regiment, Sankwaisekisan fight, ii. 213

Yentai Coal Mines, ii. 93; Russian menace from 96, 98-9, 104; fight of, 107; news of, from Jardine, 147-8; line of Japanese Army from, to railway, 172-3; 8th Division at, ii. 271; in tense cold, and rifle meeting at (Dec.), 293; Christmas Day in camp at, 269-9; battle near (Jan. 29, 05), 348

Yokohama Bay (Feb. 13, 05) "and there an end," ii. 362

Yongampho, Japanese cavalry reconnaissance at, i. 82

Yoshi, Lieutenant, derring-do of, at Motienling skirmish, i. 234-7

Yoshirei, Russians at, i. 225-230, 239; withdrawal of Russians from (July 26), 307; battle of (July 31), 314, details of, 315 *et seq.*; four categories of the fighting, 318; author's comments, 337-8; results of, and relative positions of combatants, 362

Yushuling—Penling on the Shi-Ho, Turcheffsky's position on (Jy. 31), i. 318, the attack on, 344 *et seq.*

Yoshirei—Yushuling line, error of Russians on fighting from (Jy. 31), ii. 73

ZENSHOTATSUKO, knoll, carried and held by Matsunaga (Oct. 12), ii. 228

www.ingramcontent.com/pod-product-compliance
Lightning Source LLC
Chambersburg PA
CBHW080752300426
44114CB00020B/2707